D0083667

READING RESEARCHERS IN SEARCH OF COMMON GROUND

"What sets this book apart is its wonderful demonstration of the dynamic nature of the reading field. Resisting the rhetoric that our understandings of reading and reading education are complete and realized in current research, policies, and programs, Flippo's experts articulate the possibilities of the different ways in which we define and pursue our consensus around many concepts. As well as identifying common ground, this book helps us to define our differences, to identify their origins, and to learn how we can live and work together. Read it. It's powerful!"

Patrick Shannon, Penn State University, USA;
Author of *The Main Danger: Reading Toward Democracy*

"This volume's power comes from Rona Flippo's approach to the convergence of knowledge and experience in reading education by leading theorists, researchers, and practitioners. Rona Flippo does not dismiss the national reports based upon syntheses of research; her work's credibility surpasses them. The earnest discussion of reading development by each contributor puts reading practices on trial in a more critical and constructive way than a SIMPLE mass of disembodied research findings. Readers interested in American education will learn a great deal that will contribute to a better road map for improving the teaching of reading."

Robert J. Tierney, University of Sydney, Australia

"This book provides a valuable set of thoughtful perspectives on the complexities of reading and language arts instruction. Readers will explore a history of contrasting views from experienced, top thinkers in the field. Importantly, shared goals clearly emerge. From these varied perspectives readers can develop their own rich theoretical and philosophical understanding."

Alan E. Farstrup, Executive Director of the
International Reading Association (1992–2009)

In *Reading Researchers in Search of Common Ground, Second Edition*, Rona F. Flippo revisits her groundbreaking Expert Study, in which she set out to find common ground among experts in the much-fragmented field of reading research.

The original edition, published in 2001, has become a classic in the field. The Expert Study's findings and discussions related to it remain provocative, viable, and highly relevant. Taking a fresh look at it, and its current implications for literacy education and common ground in light of the newest thinking and research of today, the Second Edition includes four new chapters from leaders in the field who discuss the study from their unique vantage points (literacy trends, emergent writing development, a comprehensive literacy curriculum, and a comparative analysis of the study's findings and recommendations).

Rona F. Flippo is Professor of Education, Department of Curriculum and Instruction, College of Education and Human Development at the University of Massachusetts Boston.

READING RESEARCHERS IN SEARCH OF COMMON GROUND

The Expert Study Revisited

Second Edition

Edited by Rona F. Flippo

Routledge
Taylor & Francis Group

NEW YORK AND LONDON

Second edition published 2012
by Routledge
711 Third Avenue, New York, NY 10017

Simultaneously published in the UK
by Routledge
2 Park Square, Milton Park, Abingdon, Oxon OX14 4RN

Routledge is an imprint of the Taylor & Francis Group, an informa business

© 2012 Taylor & Francis

First edition published by International Reading Association 2001

Library of Congress Cataloging in Publication Data
Reading researchers in search of common ground : the expert study
revisited / edited by Rona F. Flippo. – 2nd ed.
   p. cm.
   1. Reading (Elementary) 2. Children–Books and reading. I. Flippo,
Rona F.
   LB1573.R2799 2011
   372.4–dc22
   2011001103

ISBN: 978-0-415-80112-6 (hbk)
ISBN: 978-0-415-80111-9 (pbk)
ISBN: 978-0-203-83608-8 (ebk)

Typeset in Bembo
by Wearset Ltd, Boldon, Tyne and Wear

Printed and bound in the United States of America on acid-free paper by
Sheridan Books, Inc.

For Tyler, Tara, Todd, Elena, and Zoe, and for my Mom and Dad

CONTENTS

FOREWORD

When Rona Flippo asked me to write the Foreword to this new volume, I gladly accepted the invitation to endorse this important book. I did it for three reasons. One, when I read Rona Flippo's study in her 1999 book, *What Do the Experts Say? Helping Children Learn to Read*, written for classroom teachers, I strongly agreed with the public school reviewer, Isabel Barrow, who said, "*What do the Experts Say?* finally provides educators with ideas and perspectives on reading instruction upon which the experts agree!" Second, the teachers I taught in a masters-level seminar which addressed the question "What is literacy?" repeatedly shared with me that Rona Flippo's book on her study was by far the one that gave them a much needed "wake-up call." It caught the teachers' attention when Timothy Rasinski, one of the researchers who wrote a review of Flippo's book, referred to the book in those very terms:

> The power message in this book should act as a wake-up call for those of us most closely connected with school reading instruction—reading teachers, reading teacher educators, and reading education researchers—to focus on our core and common beliefs so that our voices and our expertise, in advocacy for learners, will be heard beyond our own venues and into those places where decisions that affect the future of reading education will be made.

More importantly, Flippo's study gave teachers the courage and knowledge-base to challenge the phonics *or* whole language controversy, and come to some agreements in their own schools as to how they should teach the children sitting in front of them in their own classrooms. The new edition of the original *Reading Researchers in Search of Common Ground* (Flippo, 2001) promises to do all of this again, plus update and provide reflections from the experts and other leading scholars on the last decade of literacy research. And third, writing the Foreword became quite personal, as I began to reflect on the fact that the phonics vs whole language debate is in many ways similar to the debate concerning Standard English and African American Vernacular.

As an African American scholar, I have had many conversations with African American teachers and parents about the phonics vs whole language debate. I found that they felt that whole language learning fails to provide many positive outcomes for a large number of African American children. Many African Americans are very familiar with the educational and political battle between proponents of a phonics emphasis in reading versus a whole language emphasis. Proponents of phonics point to the declining reading test scores that they view as a result of whole language instruction, and point to scientific studies that indicate phonics instruction produces better reading scores than other methods (National Institute of Child Health and Human Development, 2000). Whole language advocates point to the limitations of measures to explain those declining reading scores, and turn to qualitative studies of students successfully engaged in classrooms to support their position. P. David Pearson (2004) and Kenneth Goodman (1998) provide excellent discussions regarding the "Reading Wars."

Two critical books in the Reading Wars debate are *Broken Promises: Reading Instruction in Twentieth-Century America* (1989), and *The Struggle to Continue: Progressive Reading Instruction in the United States* (1990), both by Patrick Shannon. In his work, Shannon discusses the ways that educational reform changed reading into a technological rather than historical and cultural practice. Rejecting the notion of reading as a cultural practice that depends greatly on the interaction of students and teachers, programs were developed that diminished the value of human understanding, social interaction, and human intentionality. Underestimating the influence of these variables, schools have produced a decreased number of students engaging in meaningful interaction. As a result, students are becoming autonomous, self-motivated critical readers. Lisa Delpit, a prominent African American scholar and author of a widely cited article, "The Silenced Dialogue: Power and Pedagogy in Educating Other People's Children" (1988), and book, *Other People's Children: Cultural Conflict in the Classroom* (1995), criticizes the lack of a display of power and authority in process-oriented classrooms: "The teacher has denied them access to herself as the source of knowledge necessary to learn the forms [of language] they need to succeed" (1988, p. 288). Delpit believes that African Americans should not be taught from an only process-oriented perspective; they also should be explicitly taught literacy skills and patterns. I agree with Delpit's belief that African American children often learn more effectively with some explicit instruction. The implicit teaching and communication that occur in classrooms are often the source of inadequate student learning (McMillon, 2001; McMillon & Edwards, 2000). Delpit further asserts that in addition to academic knowledge, rules or codes of power should be explicitly taught to African American students.

While I agree with Delpit's assertion, I have softened my stance over the past few years. After thinking more about whole language vs phonics, I suggest the following: To say that whole language is better than phonics or vice versa is wrong. The different strengths that each method offers suggest that a mixed approach or what some might call a "balanced approach" for each child will probably be most beneficial. These approaches are not mutually exclusive.

In the second edition of *Reading Researchers in Search of Common Ground: The Expert Study Revisited*, Rona Flippo invited all of the original experts, as well as other leading scholars/authors, to revisit the original Expert Study findings and to participate in a new study. Her new research focuses on answering questions regarding the most important research from the past 10 years, along with the impact, effect, and implications they each see for literacy education in classrooms now and in the future. What I found most interesting about the second edition was that Flippo again avoided the trap of focusing on the inevitable question, "...what approach to teaching reading works best?" Flippo admits that if cornered by someone who insists on asking this question, her response is typically, "For whom? For what? Why? When? And Where?" I wholeheartedly agree with Flippo when she says, "Of course, this never satisfies the questioner, but without the answers to all of these questions, how could anyone suggest the 'how'?"

In this highly readable and informative volume, Flippo and the chapter authors continue to *not* attempt to tell the reader "how," but instead help the reader better understand the need for many questions that are often raised by teachers, researchers, newspaper reporters, and politicians. This book is extraordinary in its depth and breadth and coverage of various and diverse philosophies and orientations. It is a refreshing look at how highly respected reading experts could agree on contexts and practices for teaching reading, and the new areas of common ground revealed by this new study. This book is a very important contribution to the field, and will be a useful resource for preservice and experienced teachers, as well as researchers and policy-makers. Thank you, Rona, for another groundbreaking study, and the will to challenge our thinking about the contexts and practices for teaching reading.

Patricia A. Edwards
Michigan State University
President, International Reading Association, 2010–2011
Past President, Literacy Research Association
(formerly the National Reading Conference)

References

Delpit, L. (1988). The silenced dialogue: Power and pedagogy in educating other people's children. *Harvard Education Review, 58*, 280–298.

Delpit, L. (1995). *Other people's children: Cultural conflict in the classroom.* New York, NY: New Press.

Flippo, R.F. (1999). *What do the experts say? Helping children learn to read.* Portsmouth, NH: Heinemann.

Flippo, R.F. (Ed.). (2001). *Reading researchers in search of common ground.* Newark, DE: International Reading Association.

Goodman, K. (1998). *In defense of good teaching: What teachers need to know about the "reading wars."* York, ME: Stenhouse.

McMillon, G.M.T. (2001). *A tale of two settings: African American students' literacy experiences at church and at school.* Unpublished doctoral dissertation, Michigan State University, East Lansing.

McMillon, G.T., & Edwards, P.A. (2000). Why does Joshua "hate" school, but "love" Sunday school? *Language Arts, 78*(2), 111–120.

National Institute of Child Health and Human Development (2000). *Report of the National Reading Panel. Teaching children to read: An evidence-based assessment of the scientific research literature on reading and its implication for reading instruction: Reports of the subgroups.* Washington, DC: National Institute of Child Health and Human Development.

Pearson, P.D. (2004). The reading wars: The politics of reading research and policy—1988 through 2003. *Educational Policy, 18*(1), 216–252.

Shannon, P. (1989). *Broken promises: Reading instruction in twentieth-century America.* New York, NY: Bergin & Garvey.

Shannon, P. (1990). *The struggle to continue: Progressive reading instruction in the United States.* Portsmouth, NH: Heinemann.

PREFACE

Some studies are particularly important to revisit, and the "Expert Study" is one of them. This study has been called a classic study in the field of reading, and it is time to revisit it in light of the newest research and thinking of today. Based on comments from others, we will likely find that the learnings of the Expert Study and the discussions related to it, in all quarters, are still provocative, viable, and highly interesting. In fact, in many universities the first edition of this book has been used by various professors to discuss paradigms, promote discussions, and give their graduate students in reading/literacy an opportunity to respond to the Expert Study findings (engaging students to present their own rationales and cite other research for agreement or non-agreement discussions).

The first edition of *Reading Researchers in Search of Common Ground* was published in 2001 by the International Reading Association (IRA), and chosen as an IRA Book Club selection. The edition consisted of 19 chapters discussing the Expert Study, which I had researched over a 10-year period. This study, which others have called *groundbreaking*, investigated what 11 eminent literacy scholars with diverse philosophies could agree to regarding contexts and practices for teaching reading. The first edition presented each of the experts' individual views, perspectives, and reactions to the findings of the study, as well as the reactions and thoughts of other well-known leading scholars in the field of literacy based on their own research and specialty areas.

Now, 10 years after the first edition, this new second edition, *Reading Researchers in Search of Common Ground: The Expert Study Revisited*, published by Taylor and Francis/Routledge, comes back to the original study, its findings, and the discussions by the experts as well as the other scholars involved. However, in this edition several new chapters and authors have been added, along with a follow-up study in which authors have participated as they reflected, and prepared their chapters for this new book. All authors—the original experts, as well as the other leading researchers—have participated in this new study answering questions regarding the most important research from the past 10 years, and the impact, effect, and implications they each see for literacy education in classrooms now and in the future.

Readers of this new edition will have an opportunity to review the original Expert Study and the wonderful expert and leading scholar chapters from the first edition, and also read new chapters discussing the Expert Study. Additionally, readers will learn what the experts and other literacy scholars *now* see as the most important research coming out of the past decade: the research they see as having a positive impact on classroom instruction in literacy, as well as the research they see as having a negative impact.

In preparation for this new edition, when I asked the chapter authors to reflect on the most important literacy research from the past 10-year period, more than one responded by saying, "What if I don't think any of it was good?" I realized then that it was important to provide opportunities for both positive and negative responses. The experts and the other invited researchers, in all their diversity, did not disappoint me at all. In fact, readers of this new edition will see first-hand what the experts and other leading researchers each believe to be positive results of the research, and what they each believe to be negative results of the research. Plus, as I reviewed their individual responses, I saw some new areas of common ground. Not only did they continue to validate the original Expert Study findings, but in this new edition they have also shown some additional agreements regarding the results and implications of the research and policies from the past decade. I reveal and discuss these in the final chapter (Chapter 22) of this volume.

This entire work of revised and new chapters (22 in all) presents an interesting *read* for scholars in the field, teachers, school leaders, graduate students in education, researchers, and policy-makers and shapers. Chapter authors in this new edition include experts, icons, and other leading researchers in the fields of literacy (reading and writing) as well as testing and evaluation. Most of these authors have been past presidents of the International Reading Association (IRA), the National Reading Conference (NRC), the College Reading Association (CRA), and the National Council of Teachers of English (NCTE); editors of the most prestigious journals in the field of literacy; elected to the Reading Hall of Fame; or served other prestigious organizations in key capacities.

When people outside the reading field ask me about the research related to the Expert Study discussed throughout this volume, they often pose what to them seems an inevitable question: "But what approach to teaching reading works *best?*" Typically, my response will be, "For whom? For what? Why? When? And where?" This, of course, never satisfies the questioner, but without the answers to all these other questions, dealing with the "how" makes little sense.

In this volume, no one will attempt to tell you "how." Instead, many notable scholars of literacy and educational research with diverse perspectives and expertise will try to help you better understand the need for these many questions, and more. They will reflect on their own research and understandings, the findings from the Expert Study, and the politics and policies that have driven their research in the past decade and longer.

The Expert Study arose out of my interest in discovering what a group of eminent, highly respected reading experts, representative of various and diverse philosophies and orientations, could agree to regarding contexts and practices for teaching reading. I asked them each to respond with their ideas, and to review each other's responses. The original study took place over a 10-year period—neither the experts involved nor I had any idea that it would take so long, but once we got started, it became clear that it was not as simple as one might think. In Chapter 1, I share the findings of the original study as well as provide the details on how it was conducted.

In addition to the evidence of common ground, from the original study (reprinted in Chapter 1), you will see more threads of it in the remainder of Part I, "The Study, Findings, And Experts' Points of View: Revisited." As you will note, the format of the chapters in Part I is as diverse as the experts themselves and, often, their points of view. Many have been written by the actual experts who took part in the study, while several were written by other well-known scholars acting as biographers or voices for some of the experts. These scholars—Linda Fielding for Richard Anderson, Diane DeFord for Jerome Harste, and Robert Rude for Wayne Otto—were former doctoral students, and have remained close associates of these experts. Richard Robinson, both a scholar of the history of reading and an admirer of George Spache, does an excellent job of conveying George's views, based on his work and well-known publications. Additionally, Rand Spiro, one of the original experts, added two of his doctoral students to his revised chapter (Paul Morsink and Benjamin Forsyth, who contribute to his most current research). Although each author was given an identical set of specifications as to what to include in his or her chapter, true to their diversity, they approached the task by different paths. Even though the formats, writing styles, and content of these chapters, not to mention the authors, are diverse, readers of this volume are asked to keep in mind that the experts again agreed to the findings of the Expert Study, as shared in Chapter 1. In fact, one of them (see comments of Rand Spiro in Chapter 12) indicated "but more so."

In Part I, their respective points of view will enlighten you, and you will probably be amazed they were able to reach agreements, sharing some common ground, even if it took 10 years to evolve. Their responses to the new questions posed for this edition are included in their chapters, providing insight into more common ground areas.

Next, in Parts II and III, yet more evidence of this common ground appears in the discussions prepared by additional distinguished literacy researchers. In Part II, "What We Know about Literacy: Revisited," I asked literacy scholars with particular expertise in the areas of multicultural education and students of diverse backgrounds (Kathryn Au), motivation and reading (Jacquelynn Malloy and Linda Gambrell), emergent writing development and second language learners (David Yaden and Joan Tardibuono), parent and family collaboration (Timothy Rasinski), and literacy instruction and curriculum (Nancy Padak and Timothy Rasinski) to review the literature and research in these areas, to discuss the extent to which these might support the findings from the Expert Study, and to look at the relevant research from the past 10 years.

In Part III, "Toward a Common Ground: Revisited," other researchers with specialized experiences and vantage points from which to view the Expert Study were invited to review the findings reported in Chapter 1 and share their insights. Richard Vacca, former IRA president, and Maryann Mraz, his coauthor and colleague, discuss the media, the policies, and Vacca's experiences with these as president of IRA, offering suggestions regarding use of the Expert Study findings, and discussing the research from the past 10 years. Jay Campbell, Executive Director of the National Assessment of Educational Progress (NAEP) who worked with NAEP in 1994 when the "Reading War" controversies began, discusses the past NAEP data and the findings of the Expert Study, and reviews the NAEP data over the past 10 years. Jack Cassidy and Corinne Valadez share the most recent literacy trends and issues, discuss the relationship to the Expert Study findings, and also reflect on the past 10 years of research. Cindy Jones, D. Ray Reutzel, and John Smith focus on the research related to struggling readers, and provide a comparative analysis of the findings of the Expert Study and the major research reports that were subsequently published.

Chapter 22 brings together and shares the threads of new common ground as I see them. Although some of the experts involved in my study may still be somewhat in denial of common ground, or the benefit of it, and one of them has actually explained why (see remarks by Scott Paris in Chapter 9), I really do see common ground throughout this volume, and in the final chapter I point it out and provide a summary (Table 22.1) of the responses to the new questions answered by all the chapter authors. These questions are:

1. What are the most important things that you believe literacy research has shown over the past 10 years? (Positive and/or Negative)
2. How do you think this should inform the contexts and practices of reading instruction in the classroom?

Although there are differences and diverse responses, there is also evidence of common ground in the responses. I reflect on these, as revealed in the summary, and delineate the new areas of common ground in Table 22.2.

It is my hope that readers of this volume will reflect on the common ground revealed, and, just as important, think about how it can be used as a stimulus to grand conversations and grand actions. We need to find ways to get more involved in the politics and policies that have been shaping literacy education in all of our schools. If we can agree in some areas, perhaps we can influence others to understand that literacy assessment and instruction are not simple: contrived solutions and mandates don't work with all children in all contexts. More high-stakes testing, more requirements, and more standards are not the answer. In fact, they have become more of the problem. We do need *more*, but instead what we need is *more* thought and *much more* flexibility in our classrooms in order to reach and make a difference for the *many* students who are most in need. What they are currently learning is to dread and fear school, rather than developing what should be everyone's goals, *a love of reading, a love of writing, and a love of learning.*

Rona F. Flippo

ACKNOWLEDGMENTS

A project of the magnitude of this volume certainly involved a major amount of my time and energy, but it could not have been completed without the help and encouragement of many others. During the course of writing and preparing this second edition, my mother, Molly Fleig, almost 99 years old, passed away. While I miss her, I'm grateful that I was fortunate enough to have my mother for so many years. Mom also left behind my son (her grandson, Todd Graham), my daughter (her granddaughter, Tara Flippo), and my husband (her son-in-law, Tyler Fox)—all of whom she loved and adored. Each was there for me and Mom at the end. I especially want to acknowledge my husband, Tyler Fox, for his love, constant help, support and patience throughout this very difficult time for our family, and my daughter and son for their help, presence, and support.

My husband, Tyler, warrants additional recognition for the many hours he spends with me discussing and analyzing the "politics" and policies outside as well as inside the field of literacy education. Also, my daughter, Tara Flippo, whose unwavering love, support, and interest in my work have always sustained me. Additionally, special recognition must go to my graduate students at University of Massachusetts Boston, Laurel Woodward, Amy Rhee, Elizabeth Paulsen, and Jordan Weymer, each of whom made valuable contributions to various stages of this volume, working with me "behind the scenes" throughout this endeavor.

John Smith, Professor, University of Texas–Arlington, is thanked for his wise counsel and help in formulating the two research questions used in this new edition; likewise, P. David Pearson, Professor, University of California, Berkeley; Scott Paris, Professor, Nanyang Technological University, and Head of the Centre for Research in Pedagogy and Practice at the National Institute of Education, Singapore; and Richard Robinson, Professor, University of Missouri–Columbia, are also thanked for their insight and assistance with further tweaks to the questions.

Naomi Silverman, Senior Education Editor, Taylor and Francis/Routledge, is thanked for her wisdom, help, and support of this second edition. Ron Elbert, my typist, deserves acknowledgement for his work and advice during the final manuscript preparation. Last but not least, I also thank Patricia Edwards, Professor of Education at Michigan State University, and President of the International Reading Association (2010–2011), for writing the Foreword to this volume. In spite of her very demanding schedule with IRA, Pat agreed to carve out the time to write her excellent Foreword. She has used the Expert Study results for many years with her graduate students at MSU as a basis for discussing the issues, politics, and paradigms in the field of reading education.

Finally, I applaud and am grateful to *all* of the many experts who contributed to this volume—both those involved in my original study and the other experts, also distinguished researchers in the field of literacy and education, each of whom contributed expertise, time, thoughtful reflections, and chapters. Thank you all for your insightful and wonderful contributions.

I want to take a moment here also to pay my respects to Ed Fry, one of the 11 Experts of the original Expert Study, who passed away while this new edition was still in progress; I feel fortunate to have worked with him and to have received his responses to the new study, the past 10 years of literacy research in retrospect, before he died.

Also to George Spache, one of the experts of the original study, who passed away before the first edition was published; though fortunately he was able to take part in the entire Expert Study, providing his input to all the points of final agreement.

Permissions

"Points of Agreement: A Display of Professional Unity in Our Field" in Chapter 1 was previously published in *The Reading Teacher*, Flippo, Rona F. (1998), *52* (1), 30–40. © 1998, by the International Reading Association. Reprinted with permission of the publisher.

Parts from the article by Flippo, R.F. (2004). "The 'Expert Study' Revisited: An Introduction" were adapted from the *Reading & Writing Quarterly: Overcoming Learning Difficulties, 20*(1), 1–9. © Taylor and Francis Ltd. Adapted with permission of the publisher and used in Chapter 1.

"The Emergent Writing Development of Urban Latino Preschoolers: Developmental Perspectives and Instructional Environments for Second-Language Learners" by Yaden, D.B., Jr., & Tardibuono, J. M. (2004). *Reading & Writing Quarterly: Overcoming Learning Difficulties, 20* (1), 29–61. © Taylor and Francis Ltd. Reprinted with permission of the publisher and used in Chapter 15.

"Beyond Consensus – Beyond Balance: Toward a Comprehensive Literacy Curriculum" by Rasinski, T., & Padak, N. (2004). *Reading & Writing Quarterly: Overcoming Learning Difficulties*, *20*(1), 91–102. © Taylor & Francis Ltd. Adapted with permission of the publisher and used in Chapter 17.

Parts from the article by Cassidy, J., & Cassidy, D. (2004). "Literacy Trends and Issues Today: An Ongoing Study" were adapted from the *Reading & Writing Quarterly: Overcoming Learning Difficulties*, *20*(1), 11–28. © Taylor & Francis Ltd. Adapted with permission of the publisher and used in Chapter 20.

"Accelerating Struggling Readers' Progress: A Comparative Analysis of Expert Opinion and Current Research Recommendations" by Reutzel, D.R., & Smith, J. A. (2004). *Reading & Writing Quarterly: Overcoming Learning Difficulties*, *20*(1), 63–89. © Taylor & Francis Ltd. Adapted with permission of the publisher and used in Chapter 21.

PART I

The Study, Findings, and Experts' Points of View

Revisited

1

ABOUT THE "EXPERT STUDY"

Report and Original Findings

Rona F. Flippo

This first chapter revisits the findings of the Expert Study. Although the *idea* that very diverse experts in the field of reading and literacy education could agree on *anything* was a novelty in 1998 when the full data from the study were published (Flippo, 1998a), it seems that it still remains novel today as we continue to view inaccuracies in the literature and the decision-makers ignore our findings, often disparaging various methods and approaches that reading experts and teachers use successfully with certain children and in certain situations. However, given the history of the field, it is not really surprising that the polarizing, imminent sense of crisis and media inaccuracies I reported in *Phi Delta Kappan* (see Flippo, 1997) are still going on. As I later showed (Flippo, 1999a), reading researchers and reading educators had managed to become embroiled in a full-blown political war. As we pointed out in the first edition of this book (Flippo, 2001a), the field of reading has throughout its history been involved in various political struggles. Perhaps, as Ogle (2001) indicated, although many reading educators had not wanted to be involved in politics, more and more the political nature of the decisions made about schools has influenced how we do our jobs, and Vacca (2001) indicated we must *all* become more politically aware. Meanwhile, more often than not, others outside the field of reading have been deciding what is good reading instruction and what is not (e.g., see "Leaving No Child Behind," 2001), and making their version of it "the law."

Considering the climate, then, it would be useful to situate the first publishing of the Expert Study data and other conflicts historically. After all, the Expert Study, which is addressed in this book, developed, evolved, and reported within the milieu of this history.

The Expert Study in Historical Context

As noted reading historian Richard Robinson (2001) emphasized, reading educa-tion has a long history of engaging itself in a seemingly never-ending pursuit of the best teaching methods. He indicated that "at almost any point in this history, there have been both philosophical and pedagogical [struggles] between various positions on what constitutes effective reading instruction" (p. 1). Robinson, Baker, and Clegg (1998) concluded that these continuing struggles point to an ever-present "pendulum of change" in the field of reading education, character-ized by methods and approaches extending from one extreme to the other.

Robinson (2001) further proposed that two recurring themes have dominated these pendulum swings. One, the belief that one approach to reading instruction is better than another, he explained was proved wrong by arguably the most extensive evaluation made of various approaches to the teaching of reading, the First-Grade Studies (Bond & Dykstra, 1967). These studies, funded by the US Office of Education, compared 27 different classroom reading programs and approaches, and the findings did not support any particular approach as being best. The other recurring theme, Robinson noted, "has been the belief that there are few, if any, commonalities between the understandings of those representing various philosophies and approaches in the field of reading; however, [he stated] the Expert Study ... has proved that belief wrong, too" (p. 1).

Richard Vacca (2001) categorized the US public's preoccupation with a national "reading crisis" as another recurring theme in the history of reading education. He reminded us of Flesch's 1955 bestselling book, *Why Johnny Can't Read—And What You Can Do About It*. This book, which stayed on *The New York Times* best-seller list for 37 weeks, convinced the general public at that time that there was a reading crisis going on around them; authored by a man who Vacca indicates was not considered a reading professional or an expert in the field, it isolated the problem as the "method" used to teach reading. Flesch boiled all approaches down to two methods, "look-say" and "phonics," with the phonics method clearly superior in Flesch's view. Vacca maintained that the more recent "media-driven" Reading Wars have continued to cloud the pub-lic's perceptions, citing examples such as the media's misinterpretation, derived from the popular press, of the National Assessment of Educational Progress (NAEP) data and his own experiences with the media during his 42nd presi-dency of the International Reading Association (IRA) (Vacca, 2001, pp. 169–173).

Vacca (2001) nevertheless went on to identify what he believed were the two rallying points that had emerged for reading professionals in the midst of all this. The first he cited was the findings of the Expert Study, which he asserted

> make clear that the field of reading is not as fractious as it has been reported in the media. [These] findings serve to identify a set of core literacy practices

that would tend to make learning to read difficult for students, and a set of core literacy practices that would tend to facilitate learning to read.

p. 173

The second rallying point he identified is an emphasis on balance that had emerged from the portrayal of the Reading Wars in the media. While he believed the search for balance is clearly critical, Vacca also cautioned that we should all be careful of what we accept as "balanced instruction." A narrowly construed concept of balanced instruction adopted in several states has proven, when carefully examined, to be in reality an extension of the "back to basics" movement, and *not balanced instruction* (p. 174).

Why Revisit It Now?

About the same time that the Expert Study findings were published, other more prominent reports, which had been initiated and funded by the federal government through their agencies and the US Department of Education (DOE), provided their own version of consensus: the National Research Council report, edited by Snow, Burns, and Griffin (1998), followed closely by the National Institute of Child Health and Human Development, National Reading Panel report (2000). Published when they were, these large and federally endorsed reports in effect displaced the evidence gleaned by the Expert Study findings. Instead, the newest "scientific evidence" which served as the basis for critical national and state legislative decisions seems rather to have been drawn entirely from the two cited government-funded reports.

In this new edition of *Reading Researchers in Search of Common Ground: The Expert Study Revisited*, reading researchers have been invited to revisit the Expert Study and its follow-up discussions. It is the hope of all of us involved in this process that the Expert Study findings will be reconsidered and, as intended, used to (1) dispel the notion that diverse reading researchers agree on very little; (2) remind decision-makers and thereby inform the media that, in light of these findings, "some" of the new policies regarding education are inappropriate and even harmful to many students; and (3) remind all of us that the wisdom of the Expert Study is that there is no one best way or method to teach reading to all children. "It all depends" (Spiro, 2001) on the context, child, and situation (Flippo, 2001b); and indeed, there is a danger in not seeing that (Pearson, 2001; Vacca, 2001).

Finally, I want to make it clear that this revisiting of the Expert Study is *not* an attempt to discredit or diminish in any way the two cited national reports or the others that have followed them. I believe in the wisdom and knowledge of the experts with whom I worked over the years, and I know "there is no one way": our findings *aren't* better than theirs, just as the contexts and practices the experts reached agreement on are not any more valid than theirs. However, things are always more complex than they seem. Let us not accept the notion that we must simplify reading instruction, using *only* the government-approved version of how to teach all children. Instead, if there are multiple versions of appropriate reading instruction—as the experts of the original Expert Study suggested there should be—let us model that idea so that those responsible for teaching reading will be better prepared to actually craft their instruction to teach students in all their complexity, diversity, and challenges.

Call me an optimist, but I have always believed that most people, whoever they are, share something in common—some common denominator that makes them human, that allows them to reason, to share, to discuss, and then to reason some more—to search for their common understandings, beliefs, and goals. That is probably why I was so interested in beginning, in 1986, what has come to be known as the "Expert Study."

I believed *then*, and I still believe *now*, that, despite their many and obvious differences and orientations, reading experts with very diverse philosophies and experiences do share some common ground. I set out to find it, and I believe I did.

The remainder of this first chapter reviews the background, rationale, procedures, and findings of the original Expert Study. With the permission of the International Reading Association, my article "Points of agreement: A display of professional unity in our field" (Flippo, 1998b) has been reprinted in its entirety (including the Expert Study agreement data) in this chapter to provide necessary details and information. In the chapters that follow, contributors to this new volume reflect again on the clustered summary agreements displayed in *The Reading Teacher* article (here in Chapter 1). The experts involved in this study are themselves each briefly described, and they each present their personal definitions and philosophy statements regarding education and literacy development as well in the reproduced article.

I do want to emphasize that these agreements, both the lists of contexts and practices that "would make learning to read difficult" and those that "would facilitate learning to read," are the very carefully agreed-upon wording of the experts—all 11 of them who took part in my original study. These are not my words or ideas: the ownership of these agreements rests with the experts you will hear from in the remaining chapters of Part I of this volume. Also, it should be understood that these agreements are not ordered in any way (e.g., from most important to least important), and neither do they represent all that is important to reading development.

Finally, it is essential to understand that these agreements are not about approaches or methods of teaching reading. They were not about that originally, and they *still* are not about that today. The experts clearly did not endorse any particular approach. They instead developed and agreed on certain contexts and practices that they collectively believed would tend to facilitate reading, and others that they believed would tend to make reading more difficult for *most* children. However, they would all quickly point out that teachers' decisions need to be both child- and situation-specific. *There are no absolutes.* And I believe that there never will be.

For those readers who are interested in perusing some of the other publications I have authored pertaining to this study, and also more about the politics I saw surrounding the so-called "Reading Wars," see Flippo (1997, 1998a, 1999a). For the complete, original listings of the expert agreements—as well as a look at what classroom teachers, experts in their own right, think about these findings, and how the findings relate to actual classroom situations—refer additionally to Flippo (1999b).

References

Bond, G.L., & Dykstra, R. (1967). Interpreting the first-grade reading studies. In R.G. Stauffer (Ed.), *The first grade reading studies: Findings of individual investigations* (pp. 1–9). Newark, DE: International Reading Association.

Flesch, R. (1955). *Why Johnny can't read—and what you can do about it.* New York, NY: Harper & Brothers.

Flippo, R.F. (1997). Sensationalism, politics, and literacy: What's going on? *Phi Delta Kappan*, 79(4), 301–304.

Flippo, R.F. (1998a). Finding common ground: A review of the Expert Study. In E.G. Sturtevant, J. Dugan, P. Linder, & W.M. Linek (Eds.), *Literacy and community: Twentieth yearbook of the College Reading Association* (pp. 31–38). Carrollton, GA: College Reading Association.

Flippo, R.F. (1998b). Points of agreement: A display of professional unity in our field. *The Reading Teacher*, 52(1), 30–40.

Flippo, R.F. (1999a). Redefining the Reading Wars: The war against reading researchers. *Educational Leadership*, 57(2), 38–41.

Flippo, R.F. (1999b). *What do the experts say? Helping children learn to read.* Portsmouth, NH: Heinemann.

Flippo, R.F. (Ed.) (2001a). *Reading researchers in search of common ground.* Newark, DE: International Reading Association.

Flippo, R.F. (2001b). The "real" common ground: Pulling the threads together. In R.F. Flippo (Ed.), *Reading researchers in search of common ground* (pp. 178–184). Newark, DE: International Reading Association.

Leaving No Child Behind (2001). *Community Update*, US Department of Education. Washington, DC, November–December, 4–7.

National Institute of Child Health and Human Development (2000). Report of the National Reading Panel: Teaching children to read. An evidence-based assessment of the scientific research literature on reading and its implications for reading instruction. Washington, DC: US Department of Health and Human Services/ National Institute of Child Health and Human Services and US Department of Education.

Ogle, D.M. (2001, October/November). It's political! *Reading Today*, 19(2), 8.

Pearson, P.D. (2001). Life in the radical middle: A personal apology for a balanced view of reading. In R.F. Flippo (Ed.), *Reading researchers in search of common ground* (pp. 78–83). Newark, DE: International Reading Association.

Robinson, R.D. (2001). The study, findings, and experts' points of view. In R.F. Flippo (Ed.), *Reading researchers in search of common ground* (pp. 1–4). Newark, DE: International Reading Association.

Robinson, R.D., Baker, E., & Clegg, L. (1998). Literacy and the pendulum of change: Lessons for the 21st century. *Peabody Journal of Education, 73*, 15–30.

Snow, C.E., Burns, M.S., & Griffin, P. (Eds.) (1998). *Preventing reading difficulties in young children.* Washington, DC: National Research Council, National Academy Press.

Spiro, R.J. (2001). Principled pluralism for adaptive flexibility in teaching and learning to read. In R.F. Flippo (Ed.), *Reading researchers in search of common ground* (pp. 92–97). Newark, DE: International Reading Association.

Vacca, R. (2001). A focus on the media, policy-driven literacy practices, and the work of reading professionals. In R.F. Flippo (Ed.), *Reading researchers in search of common ground* (pp. 167–177). Newark, DE: International Reading Association.

Reprinted from *The Reading Teacher, 52,* 30–40, September 1998.

POINTS OF AGREEMENT: A DISPLAY OF PROFESSIONAL UNITY IN OUR FIELD

Rona F. Flippo

A headline from a recent article in *Parents Magazine* (Levine, 1996) graphically illustrates a growing misperception that poses a serious dilemma for the literacy education community: "Parents report on America's reading crisis: Why the whole language approach to teaching has failed millions of children" (p. 63). How does this affect our field? Looking a little further, we read:

> Concerns are being echoed nationwide by thousands of parents, who have been fighting for more skills instruction in schools. Parents have pressed at least 15 state legislatures to pass pro-phonics legislation. And many parents have had to hire private tutors to teach the reading skills their schools ignored.
>
> *p. 64*

A spirit of divisiveness about reading instruction now exists that is causing a tangle of problems for communities, schools, teachers, and children and their families. This divisiveness has led to misunderstandings of the issues, discrediting of teachers and schools, misinformation being disseminated to parents and families, searches for simplistic solutions, and, not least, to the media and politicians "stepping in" to exploit these concerns. (See Flippo, 1997, for some examples of what has been going on.)

The media, politicians, and general public believe that the field of literacy is so divided that we do not agree on anything. Therefore, they take it upon themselves to seek solutions and make decisions without regard to the informed opinion of the literacy education community.

But are we as a field really that divided? The study reported in this article explored the idea that, as a field, even within a continuum of very divergent beliefs and philosophies, there must be some things that most of us really do agree on. Public misperceptions of intractable divisions within the field of literacy education need not persist. We do have many common agreements about contexts for learning and instruction in classrooms, as this study shows.

The Study

In 1973 Frank Smith, a leader in the psycholinguistic movement, published a list of practices that he felt would impede children's reading development. Smith's list of statements has been cited fairly often in the literature, and it seemed to furnish an adequate starting point on which to stimulate interest and discussion, to identify what might be the areas of agreement among acknowledged experts in an often contentious field. Beginning in 1986 I contacted leading experts in the field of reading to arrange a meeting of the minds on Smith's statements. The question was how to conduct the discussion, and I decided to use the Delphi technique.

Linstone and Turoff (1975) define the Delphi "as a method for structuring a group communication process so that the process is effective in allowing a group of individuals, as a whole, to deal with a complex problem" (p. 3). The problem in my study was "What can you agree to regarding contexts and practices for teaching reading?" Linstone and Turoff suggest there are no hard and fast rules for conducting a Delphi technique study—which endows it with a flexibility that actually enhances the problem-solving process. The Delphi technique thus provided an opportunity for structured communication, by which expert panel members could provide feedback, revise judgments, and contribute to the development of agreed-upon practices—all with complete anonymity.

Through the use of this technique, the selected group of reading experts responded to Smith's 1973 list individually, each expert agreeing or disagreeing with each of the statements. The items on the Smith list that they all agreed would make learning to read difficult I have indicated with an asterisk (see Figure 1.1). Then, over a period of 10 years (which was unplanned but necessary to effectively complete the procedure), they each generated their own items that they believed would make learning to read difficult for children and a separate listing of items they believed would facilitate learning to read. During this time, each of the participants anonymously reviewed items generated by the others to thus produce lists of items most of them agreed with.

Each time we communicated, I reminded the experts to accept, modify, or reject any of the suggested items. All changed items were added to the suggested list to be scrutinized by the others. None of the participants directly communicated any of the items to any of the other participants—they did so only to me as the researcher, during follow-up interviews, when clarification seemed necessary. If at any time more than two experts disagreed with the idea or wording of an item, it was dropped from the lists. This procedure continued for the duration of the study.

I wanted the 11 participating experts selected to represent the broad and diverse range of research, beliefs, and philosophies regarding reading instruction. I did not choose participants at random. When I planned the study, I generated listings of the names of leading representatives of each of the three most prevalent philosophies (*traditional, whole language,* and *interactive*). I sought experts who had achieved wide recognition from their peers for their publications and leadership in the field of reading and literacy, and whose contributions teachers, administrators, and politicians would respect. P. David Pearson, who edited the first *Handbook of Reading Research* (1984), which surveyed the entire field, reviewed the list of those who had accepted the invitation and confirmed that, in his opinion, the list was balanced and representative of all the major philosophies.

FIGURE 1.1 TWELVE EASY WAYS TO MAKE LEARNING TO READ DIFFICULT

1. Aim for early mastery of the rules of reading.
2. Ensure that phonic skills are learned and used.
*3. Teach letters and words one at a time, making sure that each new letter or word is learned before moving on.
*4. Make word-perfect reading the prime objective.
5. Discourage guessing; be sure the children read carefully.
6. Encourage the avoidance of errors.
7. Provide immediate feedback.
*8. Detect and correct inappropriate eye movements.
9. Identify and give special attention to problem readers as soon as possible.
10. Make sure children understand the importance of reading and the seriousness of falling behind.
11. Take the opportunity during reading instruction to improve spelling and written expression, and also insist on the best possible spoken English.
12. If the method you are using is unsatisfactory, try another. Always be alert for new materials and techniques.

Note: We had total agreement on each of Smith's (1973) items noted with an asterisk (*).

Figure 1.2 presents a listing of these experts and what they are each generally most known for in reading and literacy. Of the 11 experts, four have been featured in *The Reading Teacher* (three in its Distinguished Educator Series), and eight have been elected to the Reading Hall of Fame. All have published seminal works or designed widely accepted theories, models, strategies, and assessments/tests affecting the field of reading education.

About halfway through the study, I again asked Pearson to confirm my list, to determine whether he still felt it struck a representative balance among the current major perspectives. Finally, at the conclusion of the study, I called on an outside panel of six reading educators, all familiar with the past research and publications of the 11 experts, especially their best known works, to each independently evaluate the list's representativeness in regard to the three main (and notably divergent) philosophies in contemporary literacy education.

FIGURE 1.2 EXPERT PARTICIPANTS: WHO ARE THEY? WHY ARE THEY IMPORTANT?

Richard Anderson
Coauthor of the national report *Becoming a Nation of Readers* (Anderson, Hiebert, Scott, & Wilkinson, 1985), and elected to the Reading Hall of Fame in 1991.

Brian Cambourne
Australian author of the Conditions for Learning model (see Cambourne, 1988), featured in *The Reading Teacher* Distinguished Educator Series (November 1995), and elected to the Reading Hall of Fame in 1998.

Edward Fry
Author of the Fry Readability Graph (see Fry, 1977), and elected to the Reading Hall of Fame in 1993.

Yetta Goodman
Author of the Reading Miscue Inventory (see Goodman, Watson, & Burke, 1987), known as the original "kidwatcher," featured in *The Reading Teacher* Distinguished Educator Series (May 1996), and elected to the Reading Hall of Fame in 1994.

Jane Hansen
One of the conceivers of the Author's Chair concept (Graves & Hansen, 1983) and featured in *The Reading Teacher* Distinguished Educator Series (November 1996).

Jerry Harste
Author of whole language books (e.g., Short & Harste, 1996), featured in *The Reading Teacher* (Monson & Monson, 1994), and elected to the Reading Hall of Fame in 1997.

Wayne Otto
Author of "The Wisconsin Design" (Otto, 1977)—a plan that was used throughout the US for managing classroom reading instruction with a focus on specific skill development. Authored the "Views and Reviews" column in the *Journal of Reading* for over 10 years and was elected to the Reading Hall of Fame in 1992.

Scott Paris

Author of many publications on authentic/portfolio assessment and the development of reading strategies (e.g., Paris & Ayres, 1994; Turner & Paris, 1995).

P. David Pearson

Editor of the *Handbook of Reading Research* (1984), codirector of the original "Standards Project for English Language Arts" (1992–1994), and elected to the Reading Hall of Fame in 1990.

George Spache

Author of the *Diagnostic Reading Scales* (1981)—a widely used reading test originally published in 1963, past President of IRA (1958–1959), and elected to the Reading Hall of Fame in 1974.

Rand Spiro

Author and editor of many research books and articles on reading comprehension, text processing, and schema theory (e.g., Spiro, 1980; Spiro, Coulson, Feltovich, & Anderson, 1994).

Although these experts would not want to be "labeled" in any simplistic way, the works that they are each most known for often put them into one of the three main camps or positions: the *traditional* perspective, also known as the "text-based," "specific skills," or "bottom-up" perspective of how text is processed by readers; the *whole language* perspective, also known as the "reader-based," "holistic," or "top-down" perspective of how readers process text; and the interactive perspective, also known as the "integrated" perspective of text processing, which employs both text-based and reader-based processing.

All too often in recent years, the misleading and false issue of "phonics or whole language" has been raised by media, politicians, and special interest groups. (In this debate the "phonics" side is usually attributed to those who represent a *traditional* position.) This type of public debate and posturing renders it all the more vital that this study should represent all sides, not forgetting the middle, on its panel of experts. Although the debates about reading instruction go much deeper and broader than discussions about how readers process text, these text-processing designations (*traditional, interactive,* and *whole language*) have come to represent a range of ideas in the field of reading that for most of us express the much larger viewpoints. Thus I sought to ensure that all of these "camps" would be represented.

The Findings

The experts, as it turned out, unanimously agreed on a whole range of contexts and practices that would make learning to read difficult for children and many other practices that would facilitate learning to read. In order to organize the items into a more usable and readable form, I reviewed and sorted the items into natural categories. Figures 1.3 and 1.4 present clustered summary lists of these points of agreement.

The agreements from each of the original lists are sorted into five clusters: "Combining Reading with Other Language Processes," "Contexts, Environment, and Purposes for Reading," "Developing (or Shaping) Students' Perceptions and Expectations," "Materials," and "Reading Instruction." Some items clearly fit into more than one cluster. When this was the case, I included the items in as many clusters as I conceptualized them to fit. My choice of cluster categories and my arranging of the agreements into these categories are unique to my conceptualizations and purposes. Others, of course, might choose other descriptors or categories for their purposes.

In order to make this information more useful to classroom teachers and other practitioners, I also eliminated or collapsed many of the more redundant points of agreement from the original lists and edited them for clarity. The original list of contexts and practices the experts totally agreed would "Make Learning to Read Difficult" shrank from 33 to 29, and the number of non-redundant contexts and practices they unanimously agreed would "Facilitate Learning to Read" fell from 15 to 12 when combined or eliminated. The experts subsequently reviewed and approved these edits and cluster categories.

The items listed under these categories are not all equally significant or equally central to reading. Many are clearly more important than others. Additionally, these items are not inclusive of or representative of every aspect or dimension of reading. However, these are the summary items on which the experts agreed, and they are important because they are the beginning of an opportunity for public pronouncements of some agreements in our field regarding contexts and practices for reading instruction in the classroom.

This is not to say, of course, that the experts agree on everything. We all know they do not, nor would agreement even be desirable, since without differences and discourse in the field there would not be growth. Differences extend our understandings. But where there is some agreement, it is important that such agreements be shared with all concerned.

Figures 1.3 and 1.4 show contexts and practices on which the participating experts unanimously agreed; however, there were several other items they felt it was important to qualify and share with teachers and other classroom decision-makers. These items on which there was near total agreement among the experts on contexts and practices that "would make learning to read difficult" included *Encourage perfection; Use workbooks each day; Stress the "classics" of literature; Avoid wasting instructional time encouraging students to use linguistic and cognitive strategies as they read; and Always ask a lot of comprehension questions after children read*. On contexts and practices that "would facilitate learning to read," likewise, nearly all the experts agreed on the following items: *Make reading fun and authentic; Encourage learning about strategies; Encourage learning to paraphrase and summarize; Allow learners to use techniques that help them become consciously aware of what*

FIGURE 1.3 CLUSTERED SUMMARY AGREEMENTS: CONTEXTS AND PRACTICES THAT "WOULD MAKE LEARNING TO READ DIFFICULT"

Combining Reading with Other Language Processes

- Teach reading as something separate from writing, talking, and listening.
- Require children to write book reviews of every book they read.

Contexts, Environment, and Purposes for Reading

- Make sure kids do it correctly or not at all.
- Avoid reading for your own enjoyment or personal purposes in front of the students.
- Encourage competitive reading.
- Expect pupils to be able to spell all the words they can read.
- Focus on the single best answer.
- Make a practice of not reading aloud very often to children.
- Select all the stories that children read.
- Stop reading aloud to children as soon as they get through the primer level.
- Reading correctly or pronouncing words "exactly right" should be a prime objective of your classroom reading program.

Developing (or Shaping) Students' Perceptions and Expectations

- If students are weak in reading, let them know that reading is a difficult and complex process and that you do not expect them to be able to do the more difficult reading work.
- Avoid reading for your own enjoyment or personal purposes in front of the students.
- Expect pupils to be able to spell all the words they can read.
- Focus on the single best answer.
- Make sure children understand the seriousness of falling behind.
- Remove the freedom to make decisions about reading from the learner.

Materials

- Follow your basal's teaching procedures as detailed without making any modifications.
- Use workbooks with every reading lesson.
- If a child is not "getting it," assign a few more skill sheets to remedy the problem.
- Select all the stories children read.

- Have kids read short, snappy texts rather than whole stories.
- Drill children on isolated letters and sounds using flashcards, chalk or magnetic boards, computers, or worksheets.
- Never give children books in which some of the words are unknown (i.e., words that you haven't previously taught or exposed them to in some way).

Reading Instruction

- Teach the children in your classroom letters and words one at a time, making sure each new letter or word is learned before moving on to the next letter or word.
- Detect and correct all inappropriate or incorrect eye movements you observe as you watch children in your classroom during silent reading.
- Emphasize only phonics instruction.
- Make sure kids do "it" correctly or not at all.
- Teach reading as something separate from writing, talking, and listening.
- Follow your basal reading program's teaching procedures as detailed without making any modifications.
- Use workbooks with every reading lesson.
- Focus on kids learning the skills rather than on interpretation and comprehension.
- If a child is not "getting it," assign a few more skill sheets to remedy the problem.
- Focus on the single best answer.
- Group readers according to ability.
- Have the children do oral reading exclusively.
- In small groups, have children orally read a story, allowing one sentence or paragraph at a time for each child, and going around the group in either a clockwise or counter-clockwise rotation.
- Drill children on isolated letters and sounds using flashcards, chalk or magnetic boards, computers, or worksheets.
- Test children with paper and pencil tests whenever they complete a new story in their basal, and each time you have finished teaching a new skill.
- Be sure that you provide lots of training on all the reading skills prior to letting children read a story silently. Even if there isn't much time left for actual reading, you have to focus first on skill training.
- Reading correctly or pronouncing words "exactly right" should be a prime objective of your classroom reading program.

Note: We had total agreement on all of the items listed. Items on which we had near total agreement are considered separately elsewhere in this article. ("Near" total agreement means that only one, or possibly two, expert(s) found fault with the item, or qualified the item.)

FIGURE 1.4 CLUSTERED SUMMARY AGREEMENTS: CONTEXTS AND PRACTICES THAT "WOULD FACILITATE LEARNING TO READ"

Combining Reading with Other Language Processes

- Use every opportunity to bring reading/writing/talking/listening together so that each feeds off and feeds into the other.
- Instead of deliberately separating reading from writing, plan instruction and individual activities so that, most of the time, students engage in purposeful reading and writing.
- Encourage children to talk about and share the different kinds of reading they do in a variety of ways with many others.

Contexts, Environment, and Purposes for Reading

- Focus on using reading as a tool for learning.
- Make reading functional.
- Give your students lots of time and opportunity to read real books (both narrative and expository) as well as time and opportunity to write creatively and for purposeful school assignments (e.g., to do research on a topic, to pursue an interest).
- Create environments, contexts in which the children become convinced that reading does further the purposes of their lives.
- Encourage children to talk about and share the different kinds of reading they do in a variety of ways with many others.
- Use silent reading whenever possible, if appropriate to the purpose.

Developing (or Shaping) Students' Perceptions and Expectations

- Develop positive self-perceptions and expectations.
- Create environments, contexts in which the children become convinced that reading does further the purposes of their lives.

Materials

- Use a broad spectrum of sources for student reading materials.
- Include a variety of printed material and literature in your classroom so that students are exposed to the different functions of numerous types of printed materials (e.g., newspapers, magazines, journals, textbooks, research books, trade books, library books, menus, directions).
- Give your students lots of time and opportunity to read real books (both narrative and expository) as well as to write creatively and for purposeful school assignments (e.g., to do research on a topic, to pursue an interest).

Reading Instruction

- Provide multiple, repeated demonstrations of how reading is done or used.
- Instead of deliberately separating reading from writing, plan instruction and individual activities so that, most of the time, students engage in purposeful reading and writing.
- Use silent reading whenever possible, if appropriate to the purpose.

Note: We had total agreement on all of the items listed. Items on which we had near total agreement are considered separately elsewhere in this article. ("Near" total agreement means that only one, or possibly two, expert(s) found fault with the item, or qualified the item.)

---

they do as readers: through metacognitive probing, help learners think about how they arrived at an answer, or how what they read influenced their personal understanding; and Provide feedback that includes clues about meaning, as well as letter sound information.

Two of the most interesting aspects of doing this study were reading the notations the experts made concerning suggested items, and the follow-up discussions I had with the expert participants throughout the study concerning their remarks, edits, or qualifiers for some of the items they added, eliminated, or rewrote. Brian Cambourne mostly agrees, for instance, that to *use workbooks each day* without explicit reasons given to and understood by children would make learning to read difficult for them. On the other hand, he also wants it noted that using practice materials, such as workbooks, does not have to be considered poor practice if children understand the reasons they are doing this work and if their responses to questions in the practice materials are genuinely valued (personal communication, May 2, 1995). Then again, while mostly agreeing that if teachers *make reading fun and authentic* they would facilitate learning to read, Cambourne also wants it noted that "learning isn't always *fun*" (personal communication, May 2, 1995).

Rand Spiro, while mostly agreeing that if you *always ask a lot of comprehension questions after children read*, it would make learning to read difficult, also indicated that he believes "it's usually a good idea to have kids discuss what they've read in some way—and I don't know how this would not involve 'comprehension' questions (at least indirectly)" (personal communication, September 27, 1995). As one more example of the qualifiers that the experts wanted noted about certain items, Rand Spiro mostly agreed that we should *allow learners to use techniques that help them become consciously aware of what they do as readers: through metacognitive probing, help learners think about how they arrived at an answer, or how what they read influenced their personal understanding.* Spiro wanted this practice qualified, however, because he indicated that "at higher levels of reading expertise, increasing conscious awareness can cause disintegration of reading processes." So, he says, "My response on this one is 'Yes, but decreasingly so as reading expertise increases'" (personal communication, September 27, 1995). (For listings and discussions of the qualifying statements, see Flippo, 1996.)

An example should suffice to give the reader some sense of the dynamics involved in the study. Referring to *Encourage perfection*, Brian Cambourne crossed it out and indicated, "When an individual seeks his/her own perfection, that is fine. But it must be an internal drive as opposed to perfection imposed by the teacher" (personal communication, May 2, 1995). Wayne Otto, also objecting to this item, remarked, "encourage covers *a lot*" (personal communication, November 23, 1993). When questioned again, in a later interview, he stated, "I disagree because it is legitimate to encourage perfection, but I also see that this could lead to abuse" (personal communication, November 17, 1995).

Discussion

Toward the end of the study, I asked each of the experts to share his or her own individual definition or philosophy statement regarding literacy. These are displayed in Figure 1.5.

From these statements it becomes clear how, in the decade this study spanned, we have all continued to read, reflect, and learn. I see these learnings, growth, and changes as highly desirable for all of us, experts, researchers, and teachers alike. "Constructivism" and related research that influence our present-day thinking about learning, such as the influences of social processes and cognitive learnings, and the effects of students' interests and motivations on their comprehension, have affected the experts as well. Interestingly, some of the participating experts generally thought to have opposing perspectives have come to describe their views using terms like "social constructivist" and "sociocognitive." In fact, considering the definitions or philosophy statements furnished by most of the experts, it is difficult to detect that they are generally considered to represent several entirely different perspectives.

The data generated by this study do show us that as a field we have learned and grown, and as a result, because of all we know, we tend to shy away from absolutes. No matter whether we call ourselves, or others call us, *whole language* persons, *traditionalists*, or *interactivists*, or we fall into any other camp, we have learned enough to know that certain practices, environments, and conditions usually tend to nurture the development of reading; on the other hand, we have learned enough to know that other practices, environments, and conditions usually tend to make learning to read difficult. (It is important to note that a key word in this discussion is *usually*. The experts' agreements regarding these practices ought always to be considered in the context of actual situations with specific students.)

We see, too, that the experts agreed to many more practices and contexts that would make learning to read difficult for children (especially in the area I have categorized as "Reading Instruction") than they did for those that would facilitate learning to read. This is important because, as we have seen already (Levine, 1996), many of these very practices that the experts believe hinder progress in reading are the ones now being promoted by legislators and others.

FIGURE 1.5 EXPERT PARTICIPANTS: PERSONAL DEFINITIONS/PHILOSOPHY STATEMENTS REGARDING EDUCATION AND LITERACY DEVELOPMENT

Richard Anderson

(November 15, 1995)   My current perspective is sociocognitive. The language of student–student and teacher–student interactions provides a social context within which meanings of written texts are constructed. This context, in turn, influences the nature of individual students' attending, thinking, talking, writing, and learning. Discussions of written texts create socially constructed "extended texts." Access to this extended text is governed by students' participation in the lesson. As teachers and students interact to construct the academic content of the lesson, students simultaneously receive information about norms for participation.

Brian Cambourne

(May 2, 1995)   "Effective reading" to me means having sufficient control over language and the processes and skills, and understandings and knowledge of written language to be able to interact with written texts, comprehend what the author(s) of the text intended, and be able to interrogate these texts and "unpack" the agendas of those who wrote them. The major purpose of reading is to provide a mechanism for internalizing the linguistic patterns of various forms of discourse so that learners have a cultural resource that will enable them to get access to power in their culture and bring about social change. It ("effective reading") should be available to as wide a spectrum of the community as possible—therefore it should be taught using a pedagogy which makes it accessible to all, not one which privileges a powerful elite.

Edward Fry

(December 5, 1994)   All any teacher can do is move a student ahead a notch or two. He or she should try to move all children from brightest to dullest ahead. Teachers should have great latitude in selecting methods and no major method should be totally forbidden. Personally I would use a variety of methods such as (a) match student ability to book difficulty (readability), (b) give lots of reading practice in both narrative and expository text, (c) teach vocabulary—high frequency words and roots, (d) teach phonics, (e) teach comprehension, (f) develop writing ability, and (g) give students success, praise, and love.

Yetta Goodman

(December 15, 1994)   Social constructivist learning theory and sociopsycholinguistic transactional reading theory.

Jane Hansen

(November 26, 1993)   I believe the larger the picture provided by and of a reader, the better. We know who a reader is when we know her viewpoint on herself over the years at home and school, her sense of herself in relation to others in school and at home, and the others' sense of her.

Jerry Harste

(November 30, 1995)   My paradigm is whole literacy—for me, instructionally, that means building curriculum from kids. I define literacy as a much broader concept than just reading and writing. It's the ability to mediate the world through sign systems—including those from music, math, drama, movement, and art. To be literate is to be able to flexibly orchestrate various sign systems to create text that is successful to the context.

Wayne Otto

(November 23, 1993)   Social constructivist—but with a skeptic's stance much of the time.

Scott Paris

(November 24, 1993)   A developmental approach emphasizing the collaborative construction and assessment of meaning for authentic purposes that are cognitively engaging, intrinsically motivating, and metacognitively stimulating.

P. David Pearson

(March 13, 1995)   Children need to work in classroom communities in which they regularly read and write for, to, and with one another.

George Spache

(February 2, 1994)   I believe reading instruction should provide a progression of reading experiences that promote vocabulary growth in critical but enjoyable selections of gradually increasing difficulty. The pupil should be taught and encouraged to use word analysis techniques such as common word elements and the context to aid his comprehension. In primary grades, phonics can be an aid to some pupils. But it is not a basic mode of instruction because many pupils cannot make the auditory discriminations it demands and the knowledge of phonics has no relationship to comprehension. Heavy emphasis upon letter sounds produces readers who are slow and too analytical with consequent poor comprehension.

Rand Spiro

(September 27, 1995)   I believe in the importance of employing multiple approaches, each coordinated with the others. Each paradigm for teaching reading and each theory of reading has strengths and weaknesses—the trick is to harness the strengths of each to counteract the weaknesses of the others. A byproduct of this kind of "principled eclecticism" is that readers will become more flexible in adapting their own approaches to the needs of different reading situations. (The above beliefs are consistent with the overarching paradigm of "cognitive flexibility theory.")

While, clearly, these diverse experts have generally very different ideas about "how" reading should be taught, they certainly all see many contexts and practices that would not be wise to impose or force on children.

Not only do their ideas diverge on how to teach reading, but different experts espousing different philosophies can also attribute different meanings to words like *reading* and *comprehension*. This happens, of course, because the experts belong to different communities of discourse. A mutually acceptable scaffolding was therefore needed to allow them each to meaningfully compare items generated by the other participants with their own ideas (and vice versa), and this consideration is what accounts for the qualifying words, and in some cases, the extreme wording of the practices and contexts generated. It also explains the occasionally unwieldy or cumbersome character of the language used to describe them. (Yet as extreme as they might appear in the context of this study, we have already begun to see evidence, as the opening quotation indicates, of legislation in many states aimed at installing these very practices.)

We can say with certainty that quick fixes and simplistic solutions are just that. Rather than pursue such solutions, the experts and I instead would prefer to focus on where we as a field can agree and how we use this information to combat inappropriate and potentially damaging policy decisions. However, the participating experts are equally concerned that teachers and readers of these data understand there are no absolutes when one deals with learning and children—even the best of practices can sometimes be overdone, and even what appears on the surface to be a poor practice is sometimes not unreasonable under certain circumstances. Each of the agreed upon practices, then, should be interpreted within specific contexts with specific situations, students, and their needs in mind. As Pearson (1996) has emphasized, teachers must be able to understand literacy and learning well enough to adapt teaching and learning environments, materials, and methods to particular situations and students.

Conclusions

Teachers should consider these points of agreement when they discuss, plan, shape, and deliver their reading instruction, as well as when they meet or communicate with parents and families and with their supervisors or administrators. Once again, these lists are not meant to be "do" and "don't do" lists. Instead they represent the ideas of experts who are representative of a continuum of beliefs and philosophies. These experts did not participate in this study to impose restrictions on teachers. Professional teachers should be allowed to make their own decisions and plan classroom instruction and learning opportunities based on their situations and the needs, interests, motivations, and strategies of the children with whom they work—not based on any particular list, restrictions, or absolutes.

Second, we are not nearly as divided as some would like the public to believe. There are points of agreement, even among people with the most diverse of philosophies. I believe we need very publicly (a) to share the results of this study with the media, policy-makers, parents, communities, and the general public, and (b) to emphasize that no one has endorsed any particular method or approach. Rather, experts have simply pointed out a number of contexts and practices for reading instruction on which they agree. These are relevant to most methods and approaches. Decisions about reading instruction are multifaceted, on the other hand, and only the classroom teacher who works with a child every day is in a position to know what is appropriate instruction for that particular child and when. We as a field want policy to reflect beliefs, ideas, and learnings based on the extensive research and practice in our field (exemplified in the very diverse work of these experts), not simplistic solutions that the media and politicians create and then legislate, and with which most of us disagree.

As a postscript, I think it is important that practicing teachers be given an equal voice concerning beliefs, ideas, and learnings based on their classroom research and practice. I have already begun the process of collecting teachers' responses to the experts' lists (see the call for responses in Flippo, 1999).

References

Anderson, R.C., Hiebert, E.H., Scott, J.A., & Wilkinson, I.G. (1985). *Becoming a nation of readers*. Champaign, IL: Center for the Study of Reading.

Cambourne, B. (1988). *The whole story*. Auckland, New Zealand: Ashton Scholastic.

Cambourne, B. (1995). Toward an educationally relevant theory of literacy learning. *The Reading Teacher, 49*, 182–190.

Flippo, R.F. (1996). *"Seeds of Consensus": The beginnings of professional unity*. Paper presented at the Annual Meeting of the National Reading Conference, Charleston, South Carolina.

Flippo, R.F. (1997). Sensationalism, politics, and literacy: What's going on? *Phi Delta Kappan, 79*(4), 301–304.

Flippo, R.F. (1999). *What do the experts say? Helping children learn to read*. Portsmouth, NH: Heinemann.

Fry, E.B. (1977). Fry's readability graph: Clarifications, validity, and extensions to level 17. *Journal of Reading, 21*, 242–252.

Goodman, Y.M. (1996). Revaluing readers while readers revalue themselves: Retrospective Miscue Analysis. *The Reading Teacher, 49*, 600–609.

Goodman, Y.M., Watson, D.J., & Burke, C.L. (1987). *Reading miscue inventory: Alternative procedures*. Katonah, NY: Richard C. Owen.

Graves, D., & Hansen, J. (1983). The author's chair. *Language Arts, 60*, 176–183.

Hansen, J. (1996). Evaluation: The center of writing instruction. *The Reading Teacher, 50*, 188–195.

Levine, A. (1996). Parents report on America's reading crisis: Why the whole language approach to teaching has failed millions of children. *Parents Magazine, 71*(10), 63–68.

Linstone, H.A., & Turoff, M. (Eds.). (1975). *The Delphi method: Techniques and applications*. Reading, MA: Addison-Wesley.

Monson, R.J., & Monson, M.P. (1994). Literacy as inquiry: An interview with Jerome C. Harste. *The Reading Teacher, 47*, 518–521.

Otto, W. (1977). The Wisconsin design: A reading program for individually guided education. In H.J. Klausmeier, R.A. Rossmiller, & M. Saily (Eds.), *Individually guided elementary education: Concepts and practices* (pp. 137–149). New York, NY: Academic Press.

Paris, S.G., & Ayres, L.J. (1994). *Becoming reflective students and teachers with portfolios and authentic assessment*. Washington, DC: American Psychological Association.

Pearson, P.D. (1996). Six ideas in search of a champion: What policy-makers should know about the teaching and learning of literacy in our schools. *Journal of Literacy Research, 28*(2), 302–309.

Pearson, P.D., Barr, R., Kamil, M.L., & Mosenthal, P. (Eds.). (1984). *Handbook of reading research*. New York, NY: Longman.

Short, K.G., & Harste, J.C. (with Burke, C.). (1996). *Creating classrooms for authors and inquirers* (2nd ed.). Portsmouth, NH: Heinemann.

Smith, F. (1973). Twelve easy ways to make learning to read difficult. In F. Smith (Ed.), *Psycholinguistics and reading* (pp. 183–196). New York, NY: Holt, Rinehart, and Winston.

Spache, G.D. (1981). *Diagnostic Reading Scales: Revised edition*. Monterey, CA: CTB/McGraw-Hill.

Spiro, R.J. (1980). Constructive processes in prose comprehension and recall. In R.J. Spiro, B.C. Bruce, & W.F. Brewer (Eds.), *Theoretical issues in reading comprehension: Perspectives from cognitive psychology, linguistics, artificial intelligence, and education* (pp. 245–278). Hillsdale, NJ: Erlbaum.

Spiro, R.J., Coulson, R.L., Feltovich, P.J., & Anderson, D.K. (1994). Cognitive flexibility theory: Advanced knowledge acquisition in ill-structured domains. In R.B. Ruddell, M.R. Ruddell, & H. Singer (Eds.), *Theoretical models and processes of reading* (4th ed., pp. 602–615). Newark, DE: International Reading Association.

Turner, J.C., & Paris, S.G. (1995). How literacy tasks influence children's motivation for literacy. *The Reading Teacher, 48*, 662–673.

2

POINT OF VIEW:
RICHARD C. ANDERSON

Linda G. Fielding

Not long after I arrived at University of Illinois at Urbana-Champaign as a new doctoral student, I enrolled in a course taught by Richard (Dick) Anderson. By that time in 1982, the Center for the Study of Reading, funded by the Office of Educational Research and Improvement and directed by Dick, had been in operation for about six years. Much research had been conducted there about human learning and cognition, basic processes in reading and comprehension, the state of US textbooks and reading instruction, acquisition of vocabulary, and many other areas. The Center was turning its attention more and more to research that might have very direct implications for classroom instruction. It was toward that goal that Dick hired me, with my 10 years' experience as a middle school reading and language arts teacher, as his research assistant that fall. I write this commentary from my vantage point as a participant in some of his research and many discussions with him about reading research, a beneficiary of his counsel as codirector of my dissertation, and an avid reader of the research he continues to conduct.

A Brief Intellectual Biography

A 1960 graduate of Harvard, Dick had taught at Rutgers; had coauthored an influential educational psychology textbook (Anderson & Faust, 1973) and published research about programmed learning, human learning, and cognition; and even had written an influential article about achievement tests (Anderson, 1972) by the time he began discussions with colleagues at the University of Illinois that led to their successful bid for the Center for the Study of Reading in 1976. In the early years of the Center, Dick was involved in ground-breaking research about schema theory that led to new understandings about the role of background knowledge in reading comprehension (Anderson, 1984). Research with William Nagy and other colleagues about how people learn word meanings suggested that learning words in context through wide reading must make a substantial contribution over what is possible through direct instruction in word meanings alone (Nagy, Anderson, & Herman, 1987). This vocabulary research as well as his studies of the role of interest in learning (Anderson, Shirey, Wilson, & Fielding, 1987) contributed to his decision to study the role of independent reading of trade books in children's reading achievement. From this research, he concluded that wide independent reading makes substantial contributions to children's present reading achievement and their growth as readers over time (Anderson, Wilson, & Fielding, 1988). With other colleagues he also began to study the reading group as a staple of US classroom reading instruction, and found that a meaning focus during reading lessons was superior in every way to a focus on accuracy of word reading (Anderson, Wilkinson, & Mason, 1991).

Arguably, his most widely-read work is the research synthesis *Becoming a Nation of Readers* (Anderson, Hiebert, Scott, & Wilkinson, 1985), which he co-wrote as chair of the National Academy of Education-established Commission on Reading. Its purpose was to "summarize the knowledge acquired from research and to draw implications for reading instruction" (p. 3). Five descriptors that answer the question "What is reading?" framed the conclusions—namely, that skilled reading is a constructive, fluent, strategic, and motivated process, and a lifelong pursuit. Critics argued that among other things, the report did not include enough research from non-experimental paradigms, go far enough in its recommendations, recommend practices consistent with its description of what reading is, address special issues in the education of minorities, or adequately address reading's social dimensions (Davidson, 1988). However, Dick's current investigations of collaborative reasoning during text reading (Anderson, Chinn, Waggoner, & Nguyen, 1998) underscore the social and collaborative dimensions of reading, and undoubtedly are fundamental to his current characterization of his theoretical orientation as "sociocognitive" (Flippo, 1998; refer to Chapter 1 in this book).

So far, I have focused on a chronology of Dick's research and research syntheses. To adequately explain his agreement with the contexts and practices that would facilitate learning to read or make it difficult, I must also comment on other aspects of his intellectual history.

First, his own belief in the social construction of meaning is evident in the talk that has always surrounded my research experiences with Dick. The oral history of the Center has it that noisy, vigorous, and usually good-natured arguments about reading processes laid the foundation for the proposal that originally brought the Center to Illinois. (Incidentally, an anonymous source goodhumoredly reported that these discussions easily seeped through office walls, sometimes interfering with the thinking of those not involved.) Friday afternoon research presentations accompanied by ample time for discussion, almost always with Dick in attendance, were a regular occurrence before, during, and after my years at the Center. And regular meetings of Dick's various research teams depended on garnering opinions and suggestions from everyone involved.

Dick has also participated actively in developing and confirming his understandings in other ways. For instance, he always has been committed to learning from experienced teachers about ways to make his classroom-based research more authentic, and his suggestions for classroom practice more grounded in reality. The Center-produced videotape series *Teaching Reading: Strategies From Successful Classrooms* (1990) is one example of this commitment; his hiring of me and a number of other former teachers as research assistants is another. Dick's direct involvement with *Reading Recovery* (Clay, 1993) is yet another example of his own alternative ways of learning. When *Reading Recovery* began gaining recognition and respect in the United States, Dick was instrumental in bringing it to Illinois. Noteworthy is the fact that he participated in one of the first training groups by tutoring three first-grade youngsters. Dick learned methods of teaching about phonics and word identification in the context of text reading, in connection with what the reader already knows, and as strategies rather than isolated items of knowledge—practices that are more contextualized and reader-specific than the general approaches suggested in *Becoming a Nation of Readers* (Anderson et al., 1985). A final example of Dick's active learning: When Dick became interested in the role of wide reading in learning to read, and realized that he had not read any children's literature in some years, he asked me to select several good examples for him. I remember he was particularly impressed with the depth of plot and theme and richness of language in Katherine Paterson's *Bridge to Terabithia* (1977). These examples suggest that although much of Dick's belief system is built on his own research and syntheses of others' research, he also engages in hands-on practical and intellectual exchanges with others who influence his thinking.

Agreement with the Contexts and Practices

Part of my role in writing this contribution is to point out and speculate about the agreed upon contexts and practices from the Expert Study that Dick feels most strongly about. I address these in the order that the contexts and practices as described in the Flippo (1998) article reprinted in the first chapter of this book.

Combining Wide Reading with Other Language Processes

My guess is that Dick is in very strong agreement with all of the practices included in the Expert Study category "Combining Reading with Other Language Processes." His own most recent research about collaborative story discussions (Anderson et al., 1998) is based on the notion that talking and listening to others' talk are central to meaning construction. In addition, *Becoming a Nation of Readers* suggests writing as an important practice in its own right as well as a vital alternative to a steady diet of workbook pages.

Contexts, Environment, and Purposes for Reading

Both Dick's own research about the role of interest in learning (Anderson et al., 1987) and the characterization of reading as "a lifelong pursuit" in *Becoming a Nation of Readers* (Anderson et al., 1985, p. 18) support his agreement with the Expert Study statements that reading should focus on functional purposes and students' interests. His own research about children's independent reading (Anderson et al., 1988) was instrumental in providing empirical support for the practice of allotting time and opportunity for reading real books and other materials. On the other hand, it is not surprising that Dick agrees with the suggestion to "use silent reading whenever possible" because it is qualified with, "if appropriate to the purpose" (Flippo, 1998; refer to Chapter 1 in this book). *Becoming a Nation of Readers* suggests that "frequent opportunities to read aloud make sense for the beginning reader" (Anderson et al., 1985, p. 51) and that oral reading also makes sense in some contexts beyond the beginning stages. In a more recent re-analysis of data about the value of silent reading, Dick and colleagues also suggested that the value of silent over oral reading may not be as strong as previously thought (Wilkinson, Anderson & Wardrop, 1988). However, it is important to note that these caveats about silent versus oral reading assume meaning-focused, as opposed to accuracy-focused, oral reading. His own reading group research indicates that meaning-focused prediction questions produce better recall, recall of more important information, and more accurate reading than questions and prompts focused on accuracy of word pronunciation (Anderson et al., 1991).

Materials

My guess is that Dick is in very strong agreement with the suggestions in the Expert Study category "Materials." As stated, his own research supports the wide reading of trade books and other authentic reading materials. In addition, research about commercially published reading materials conducted at the Center and summarized in *Becoming a Nation of Readers* directly cautions against many features of materials that would make learning to read difficult, such as using workbooks with every reading lesson, following all suggested teaching procedures to the letter, and assigning more skill sheets to children who do not understand a skill. From his research about the role of interest in earning (Anderson et al., 1987) and the value of trade book reading (Anderson et al., 1988), I am sure he agrees strongly that if the teacher made all reading choices for children, or limited their reading to selections in which they had been taught all of the words, learning to read would be difficult. Dick has served as senior advisor for one of the many 1990s basal reader series that also support these ideas.

Reading Instruction

I have already commented on my guess that Dick agrees strongly with the suggestions in the "Reading Instruction" category of the Expert Study clustered summary agreements, based on his own research about vocabulary learning and independent reading. Another suggestion in this category, to "provide multiple, repeated demonstrations of how reading is done or used" (Flippo, 1998; refer to Chapter 1 in this book), is made directly in *Becoming a Nation of Readers*, and is based to a great extent on research conducted by colleagues and former graduate students at the Center. Furthermore, it is described as one of the teacher's roles in his recent investigations of collaborative reasoning during story discussions (Anderson et al., 1998), and is illustrated through suggestions to teachers in the basal series for which Dick was senior advisor.

Conclusion

Was I surprised to find Dick in full agreement with the Expert Study lists of contexts and practices that would facilitate learning to read or make it difficult? Not at all. As this chapter illustrates, Dick conducted research in many of these areas himself, and through *Becoming a Nation of Readers* and other reviews he analyzed and synthesized others' research in all of the areas. Furthermore, in the areas in which he has done his own research, there often is a progression from research about basic processes to research about classroom practices. But Dick participates actively in developing his beliefs and understandings in ways other than research and synthesis—through intellectual exchange with other researchers and teachers, and various kinds of hands-on practice. Nearly 50 years of active involvement in and critical thinking about the field of reading research would lead almost inevitably to these agreements.

However, I am sure Dick would never want these points of agreement to halt the inquiry process or make us complacent about our consensus. In fact, I expect he would say that we still have much to learn about the finer points of contexts and practices that facilitate learning to read—and that it is in these finer points that the success or failure of a particular practice often lies. In fact, much of his recent research, such as his line of inquiry into small-group reading lessons and collaborative story reasoning, is focused on these finer points. The evolution of Dick's own research over time illustrates his ongoing thinking about what we need to know next to further the improvement of reading instruction. Although he clearly agrees with the listed contexts and practices that evolved from the Expert Study and that are supported by his own and others' research, I am confident that Dick wants us to continue to search for gaps where our knowledge needs to be deepened and extended, and that he will do the same.

The Past 10 Years: In Retrospect

1. *What are the most important things that you believe literacy research has shown over the past 10 years? (Positive and/or Negative)*

The most important positive finding of the last decade is the persuasive evidence about the importance of stimulating classroom talk. The most important negative finding is evidence about the dumbing down of instruction because of high stakes testing of low-level skills.

2. *How do you think this should inform the contexts and practices of reading instruction in the classroom?*

My recent research on children's language provides support for my response regarding the importance of language-rich discussions and stimulation of classroom talk. Specifically, I have been researching how a peer-led open-format discussion approach, which I call *Collaborative Reasoning* (CR), impacts the development of oral and written language. My findings show that CR discussions have accelerated ELL (English-Language Learner) students' oral and written English development as well as their listening and reading comprehension. Additionally, these discussions enhanced students' motivation, engagement, and attitudes toward English learning. I have done these studies with Spanish-speaking, Chinese, and Korean ELL students.

In CR, students learn to use the discourse of reasoned argumentation to discuss stories and texts they have read. CR features open participation in which students speak freely without raising hands and waiting to be given permission to speak by the teacher. Students are encouraged to manage all aspects of discussion as independently as possible. CR is a highly interactive approach to discussion that may promote language development because children must learn to take and yield the floor, speak clearly and listen carefully, express reasons and cite evidence to justify positions, issue challenges, and respond to the challenges of others. In comparison to typical forms of classroom discussion, students' rate of talk almost doubles during CR, and talk more frequently involves cognitive processes known to be productive for learning (Chinn, Anderson, & Waggoner, 2001). Also, children's ability to produce coherent stories probably is improved because CR leads to deeper reading of the set of stories, enabling students to obtain a better understanding of narrative structure. Finally, the results of these studies offer evidence that engaging English-language learners in language-rich discussions accelerates receptive and expressive language development, and I believe that these findings should inform the contexts and practices of reading, writing, and other literacy instruction in classrooms with ELL youngsters. Additionally, I believe that the impressive results I've seen should be considered when instruction is planned for classroom instruction in general with all populations of students.

As for the negative finding and how it should inform the contexts and practices of reading instruction in the classroom, this is a complicated question. The fact is that, like it or not, we are living in an era where we are driven by high stakes standardized tests. Moreover, we are holding teachers responsible for their children's learning using some Mickey Mouse, simplistic measures; however, children's literacy development and literacy learning are not simple. Rather, they are complex and not easy to measure even if we used the finest instruments and assessments available. Frankly, I believe that almost no one in the field of literacy would disagree with this. In fact, we'd have to look pretty hard to find those that would.

Not surprisingly, according to the report of the National Literacy Panel on Language—Minority Children and Youth, the major impediment for ELLs' reading comprehension is their limited oral English proficiency (August & Shanahan, 2006). Unfortunately, rather than the rich discussions that CR students in the aforementioned studies have been engaged with, more typically literacy instruction for ELLs is dominated by individual seatwork and teacher-directed whole class instruction as teachers prepare them for the mandated tests. Or, alternatively, teachers provide fast-paced low-level question–answer routines that limit students' opportunities to talk, formulate their own questions, and express extended ideas. In these situations, language is treated as a "formal" subject (e.g., phonics, vocabulary, grammar), with little opportunity for interactive language that is comprehensible, interesting, and relevant. Unlike this typical traditional classroom discussion, which emphasizes low-level mastery of the information in the reading, the dumbing-down of information read, and a focus on mastery of information to pass yet another high-stakes test, CR is intended to stimulate critical reading and thinking and to be personally engaging (Clark, Anderson, Kuo, Kim, Archodidou, & Nguyen-Jahiel, 2003).

In summary, Collaborative Reasoning appears to help bridge a serious gap in the education of ELLs, providing them opportunities otherwise limited in today's schools to use English for extended meaningful communication. Readers may want to refer to some of this cited work, including Dong, Anderson, Kim, and Li (2008), and Zhang and Anderson (2010), to see the research behind my basic understandings.

References

Anderson, R.C. (1972). How to construct achievement tests to assess comprehension. *Review of Educational Research, 42*, 145–170.

Anderson, R.C. (1984). Role of the reader's schema in comprehension, learning, and memory. In R.C. Anderson, J. Osborn, & R.J. Tierney (Eds.), *Learning to read in American schools: Basal readers and content texts* (pp. 24–25). Hillsdale, NJ: Erlbaum.

Anderson, R.C., & Faust, G.W. (1973). *Educational psychology: The science of instruction and learning.* New York, NY: Dodd, Mead.

Anderson, R.C., Hiebert, E.H., Scott, J.A., & Wilkinson, I.A.G. (1985). *Becoming a Nation of Readers.* Washington, DC: National Institute of Education.

Anderson, R.C., Shirey, L., Wilson, P.T., & Fielding, L.G. (1987). Interestingness of children's reading material. In R. Snow & M. Farr (Eds.), *Aptitude, learning and instruction* (pp. 287–299). Hillsdale, NJ: Erlbaum.

Anderson, R.C., Wilson, P.T., & Fielding, L.G. (1988). Growth in reading and how children spend their time outside of school. *Reading Research Quarterly, 23,* 285–303.

Anderson, R.C., Wilkinson, I.A.G., & Mason, J. (1991). A microanalysis of the small-group guided reading lesson: Effects of an emphasis on global story meaning. *Reading Research Quarterly, 26,* 417–441.

Anderson, R.C., Chinn, C., Waggoner, M., & Nguyen, K. (1998). Intellectually stimulating story discussions. In J. Osborn & F. Lehr (Eds.), *Literacy for all: Issues in teaching and learning* (pp. 170–196). New York, NY: Guilford Press.

August, D., & Shanahan, T. (2006). Developing literacy in second-language learners: Report of the National Literacy Panel on Language-Minority Children and Youth. Mahwah, NJ: Lawrence Erlbaum Associates.

Center for the Study of Reading. (1990). *Teaching reading: Strategies from successful classrooms.* Urbana, IL: Author.

Chinn, C.A., Anderson, R. C., & Waggoner, M. (2001). Patterns of discourse in two kinds of literature discussions. *Reading Research Quarterly, 36* (4), 378–411.

Clark, A.-M., Anderson, R.C., Kuo, L.-J., Kim, I.-H., Archodidou, A., & Nguyen-Jahiel, K. (2003). Collaborative reasoning: Expanding ways for children to talk and think in school. *Educational Psychology Review, 15*(2), 181–198.

Clay, M. (1993). *Reading recovery.* Portsmouth, NH: Heinemann.

Davidson, J. (Ed.). (1988). *Counterpoint and beyond: A response to becoming a nation of readers.* Urbana, IL: National Council of Teachers of English.

Dong, T., Anderson, R.C., Kim, I.-H., & Li, Y. (2008). Collaborative reasoning in China and Korea. *Reading Research Quarterly, 43* (4), 400–424.

Flippo, R.F. (1998). Points of agreement: A display of professional unity in our field. *The Reading Teacher, 52,* 30–40.

Nagy, W. E., Anderson, R.C., & Herman, P.A. (1987). Learning word meanings from context during normal reading. *American Educational Research Journal, 24,* 237–270.

Paterson, K. (1977). *Bridge to Terabithia.* New York, NY: Avon.

Wilkinson, I.A.G., Anderson, R.C., & Wardrop, J. (1988). Silent reading reconsidered: Reinterpreting reading instruction and its effects. *American Educational Research Journal, 25,* 127–144.

Zhang, J., & Anderson, R.C. (2010, May), *Language-rich discussions for English language learners.* Paper presented at the Annual Meeting of the American Educational Research Association, Denver, CO.

3

POINT OF VIEW: ON BEING AN "EXPERT" WITH A POINT OF VIEW

Brian Cambourne

More than two decades ago, Rona Flippo sent me a list of statements about reading that Frank Smith made notorious in the early 1970s (Smith, 1973). In the letter that accompanied this list, she informed me that I was among a small group of "world reading experts" whom she had selected to comment on Frank's list. I was vain enough to succumb to such flattery. For the next 10 years, she regularly asked me to reflect on my comments and those of fellow "experts." As a result, the "Expert Study" came to be, and here I am again, a so-called expert revisiting the opinions I expressed to statements made by myself and statements made by the other experts about ways of facilitating learning to read or making it difficult.

Revisiting My Responses

It is obvious that when I first responded to Smith's list and then those generated by myself and the other experts, I had some strong views about learning and language. It is also obvious that I was predisposed toward what could be described as a "holistic" or "constructivist" perspective with respect to learning and teaching. The origins of these views are not difficult to identify. I am conscious of rejecting the fragmented, mechanistic theories of learning and language with which I had been imbued during my 1950s teacher-preparation course. That is probably why I agreed in the Expert Study that integrating the four modes of language, "so that each feeds off and feeds into the other," would facilitate learning to read; that is probably why I claimed that "multiple repeated demonstrations of how reading and writing is done or used" rather than "deliberately separating reading and writing" or "teaching letters and words one at a time" would facilitate learning to read for children (Flippo, 1998; also refer to Chapter 1 in this book).

There were other reasons that help explain why I responded the way I did. As a young teacher, I continually noticed that there seemed to be a significant number of non-mainstream students in the classes I taught who were capable of the most complex kind of learning outside of the classroom setting, but who failed to learn even the most simple concepts of reading, writing, spelling, math, and so forth that I tried to teach them. I knew from my conversations and interactions with these children that they did not experience the same problems when it came to understanding and mastering the skills, tactics, and knowledge of complex sports like cricket; carrying out tasks such as sight-reading complex music and singing it in tune; running a successful afterschool lawn-mowing business; reading and understanding the racing guide; calculating odds and probabilities associated with card games; or speaking and translating across two or three languages. These experiences led me to explore models of learning that were different from the mechanistic models to which I had been exposed during my teacher training.

At the same time, I was being influenced by the work of others. Frank Smith's work helped me think of the brain as an "organ of learning." This simple analogy led me to explore the hypothesis that the human brain had evolved primarily as a survival mechanism—that is, it had learned to learn in ways that ensured that certain skills and understandings necessary for species survival would be learned successfully and easily. As well, after years of applying Chomsky-an linguistic principles to the reading process, I was introduced to Michael Halliday's functional systemic-linguistic theory (1985). His work helped me understand the functional (i.e., "survival") purposes that language served both in individuals' lives and the cultures in which they lived. It seemed to me that learning to use and understand the language of the culture into which one was born was a universal example of this kind of complex "survival" learning. I therefore decided to try to understand the nature of this kind of learning by systematically observing toddlers in experimenter-free settings (using recording devices and unobtrusively taking field notes) as they used, listened to, and responded to language with caregivers, siblings, relatives, neighbors, friends, and teachers, both in home and in school settings.

As a consequence of this research and the literature I had reviewed on language acquisition, I concluded that because certain conditions always seemed to be present in the environment in which language was being used and learned, these conditions could be considered "necessary" conditions for such learning to occur.

No wonder I responded the way I did. I was firmly convinced that if I could just work out ways of turning the conditions of learning that underpinned everyday cultural learning into classroom practice, the complexity of learning to read would be significantly reduced. In fact, I spent a considerable amount of my research time in those days trying to work out what these conditions were. Eventually I identified these:

- Immersion
- Demonstration
- Engagement
- Expectations
- Responsibility
- Employment
- Approximations
- Response.

I firmly believed that if teachers could implement these conditions appropriately, they would begin to make the acquisition of literacy as barrier-free and uncomplicated as possible. Given the beliefs I had about such things at the time, it would have been hypocritical of me to respond any other way.

Although I would not change in any significant way how I would respond to the items included in the lists reprinted in this volume, with the benefit of hindsight I would add this caveat: prolonged and persistent observation in classrooms has helped me realize that teaching literacy is a lot more complex than I ever imagined when I first responded to Smith's list. Part of these observations included the opportunity to ask many teachers variations of these three questions:

1. What is effective literacy?
2. How is it best learned?
3. After it is learned, how should effective literacy be used?

Their responses have helped me understand the following:

- What happens in classrooms in the name of teaching literacy is far more complex than the listing of a set of contexts and practices for facilitating reading, or the careful application of some preferred "teaching method," or indeed the use of a carefully designed set of resources.
- Rather, what one observes in classrooms is embedded in and enclosed by the formal theoretical knowledge and understandings that teachers carry around inside their heads. In the main, this comprises knowledge and understandings about learners, the learning process, language, and the role that language plays in learning.
- This formal theoretical knowledge is in turn embedded in and enclosed by another, less formal, kind of knowledge and understandings, which comprises a teacher's ideology. By ideology, I mean beliefs and values about the purpose and nature of literacy, schooling, and society.

Figure 3.1 depicts classrooms as a series of "enclosed–enclosing" systems, each of which is related, either through being embedded within, or embedding,

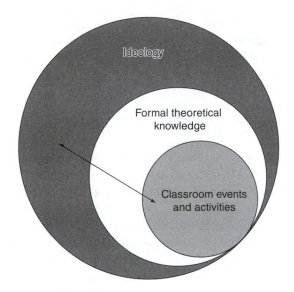

FIGURE 3.1 The relationships between classrooms, knowledge, and ideology

the others. The system comprising the events and activities that occur in classrooms is embedded within a system of formal theoretical knowledge. This in turn grows out of an informal kind of non-conscious system of tacit knowledge (ideology), which comprises the set of beliefs and values about literacy, schooling, education, and the world in general. While the "knowledge" component is relatively easy to get at through interview and debriefing sessions, the "ideological" component is less amenable to conscious awareness, is harder to get at, and is resistant to being made explicit.

"Unpacking" Each System

The Ideological Layer

Although I cannot identify the origins of teachers' values and beliefs, our data indicate that many of our teachers' ideologies were very similar (Cambourne, 1988; Cambourne & Turbill, 1994). They tended to talk about "effective" literacy in terms of *"high degrees of control of language."* By *control*, they meant giving their students access to a wide enough range of linguistic choices that made it possible for them to shape, use, and interpret a broad range of discourses, especially those that were involved in academic learning. The data also indicate that they tended to agree that language and knowing, thinking, understanding, and learning are so closely related that control of one (language) led to control of the others (knowing, thinking, understanding, and learning). As a teacher commented during a debriefing interview,

I believe that we [teachers] should be helping kids get control of as many forms of language as possible because that's one way of giving our less privileged kids access to power. [Not] power in the sense of dominion over, but power in the sense of being able to negotiate and gain access to the good things of life and to succeed in education.

The Formal Theoretical Knowledge Layer

The formal theoretical knowledge that effective teachers made explicit during the debriefing and sharing sessions we had seemed to be made up from three overlapping domains, namely "Learning and How It Works," "Language and How It Works," and "The Role of Language in Learning."

With respect to the first of these domains, "Learning and How It Works," as a group, teachers held two strong beliefs about learning: (1) learning should be as uncomplicated and barrier-free as possible (related to the conviction that unnecessarily complicated learning tended to exclude the less privileged members of our society); and (2) learning should be "durable"—what is learned and mastered should continue to be "known" and used long after formal schooling has finished.

The learning theory that best fitted in with these beliefs was "natural" learning (Cambourne, 1988). Sometimes this was referred to as "child-centered learning," "acquisition learning" (Holdaway, 1974), "whole learning" (Cordeiro, 1992), and "comprehensible input" (Krashen & Terrell, 1983). It is similar to the learning theory that is used to explain how children learn to talk, with an extra dimension—an emphasis on helping learners get "inside" texts and reflect on how they need to be shaped to achieve different communicative and cognitive purposes with different audiences.

With respect to the second of these domains, "Language and How It Works," as a group, teachers drew on the theory of language that was essentially "functional linguistics" as developed by Michael Halliday (1978, 1985). This theory of language describes language in functional terms, and, among other things, supports the notion that control over language is facilitated by a conscious understanding of how linguistic choices can be made to shape text so that specific purposes can be achieved with specific audiences. Halliday-an linguists promote this slogan, which was at the core of much of the planning and teaching that occurred in the classrooms in which these teachers taught: "We learn language, we learn through language and we learn about language simultaneously as we use it."

With respect to the third of these domains, "The Role of Language in Learning," these teachers believed that language was the major medium of thinking, learning, knowing, understanding, and problem solving. In this respect they were definitely Whorfian in essence (see Whorf, 1956). They were also cognizant of the "linguistic data pool," a visual metaphor created by Burke (Harste, Burke, & Woodward, 1979; see Figure 3.2 for my rendition of what a

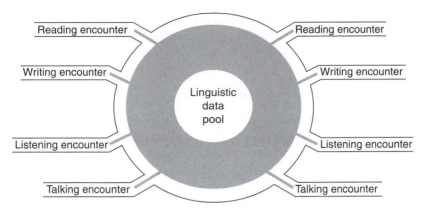

FIGURE 3.2 Linguistic data pool

linguistic data pool might look like). All claimed it helped them understand the relationships between reading, writing, listening, talking, linguistic choice, and the construction of texts for different purposes and different audiences.

End Point

So what is the result of my involvement with Rona's study? Unfortunately, it sounds like a bland truism: *Effective literacy classrooms are very complex settings.* Given the constraints of this chapter, it is difficult to capture this complexity fully. All I have done is provide some elementary insights into its nature. What is important is that this complexity has to be orchestrated. The more time I spend engaged in research and thinking about literacy, the more I am convinced that those classroom settings we call effective are much too complex to be orchestrated and maintained by teachers who are armed only with a set of teaching strategies, activities, or even contexts and practices for facilitating learning to read. At 9:00 a.m. on any school morning when that setting known as Mrs Brown's first- (or fifth-)grade language session comes to life with its physical properties, its human inhabitants and their ways of operating, no such set of teaching practices alone will be of much use in informing Mrs Brown about how to organize and orchestrate the complexity of the setting she is about to guide. Rather, the range of contexts, practices, teaching strategies, and options she employs will need to be underpinned by formal theoretical knowledge about learning, about language, and about the role that language plays in learning. Furthermore this formal theoretical knowledge will need to be accompanied by a conscious awareness of her values and beliefs (i.e., her ideology) pertaining to the nature of literacy and the purposes and functions it should serve in our culture. Once these things are in place in the ways described here, she will be creative enough to design her own contextually relevant instruction, and flexible enough to cope with the unpredictability that occurs in the sessions she designs and initiates. Then, and only then, will she be able to truly facilitate learning to read.

The Past 10 Years: In Retrospect

1.   *What are the most important things that you believe literacy research has shown over the past 10 years? (Positive and/or Negative)*

For me, only one thing of importance has emerged from the past 10 years of literacy research. It is this (emphasis intended):

> Despite more than one hundred years of research and theory building, our field is ***still riven*** by theoretical squabbles.

A close look at the history of literacy education (which began as "reading education in the late 19th century") shows that there are few points in this history when the field has not been in a state of theoretical conflict. Rarely has there been a time when literacy researchers and/or theory builders were not embroiled in a theoretical squabble of some kind. Unfortunately, the past decade has continued this tradition.

While the presence of such internecine conflict within a theoretical domain might be attributed to a robust and democratic research regime within that domain, it could also be a symptom of a much deeper, less obvious malaise within. My involvement with reading education over the past 50 years has convinced me that it's the latter—i.e., it's a symptom of a deeply entrenched, long-standing malaise.

For as long as I can remember, the field has been characterized by intense, often strident, theoretical squabbles and disagreements. Historically these squabbles began as a series of competing *"Method A versus Method B"* arguments which were hotly defended and/or attacked by advocates and adversaries within the professional bodies representing reading research, theory building, and pedagogy. While the focus of these squabbles may have centered on reading, in later years these same squabbles have spilled over to writing, spelling, grammar, and other accouterments of what we today refer to as "literacy."

This is especially true of the 50 years I've been involved in literacy education. I began teaching in the mid 1950s. As a new graduate of the 2-year pre-service teacher training program I'd completed, I was aware that in the 1950s the dominant debate in reading education typically involved a choice between two pedagogies, one based on a *"look-and-say" (or "whole word") "visual-recognition-of-word-shapes"* principle, the other based on a *"transform-the-visual-signs-to-speech-sounds"* principle *("phonics")*.

After the publication of Chall's classic volume, *Learning To Read: The Great Debate* (Chall, 1967), the focus shifted a little to "*code-based*" versus "*meaning-based*," again with conflicting pedagogies based on an either/or choice between two theoretical options. One option was based on transforming the visual display to sounds, and then rapidly blending these sounds together to make words (i.e., *breaking the alphabetic code*). The other was based on accessing meaning directly from the visual display without first accessing sound (i.e., "*meaning-based*").

By the 1970s and 1980s, this code-based vs meaning-based debate had morphed into "*whole language* versus *direct instruction*," which in turn generated a series of variant strains of the same dichotomy. For example, during this period "*literature-based* versus *skills-based*" emerged, accompanied by others such as "*implicit* versus *explicit teaching*," "*holistic* versus *fragmented teaching*," and "*objectivist* versus *constructivist pedagogy*."

From the late 1990s to the present time, these dichotomies seem to have coalesced into something much more sinister and complex. They are no longer perceived as "debates;" rather, they seem to have assumed the stature of "wars." Thus we now have the so-called "*The Reading (or Literacy) Wars*." Instead of "*debating*" the pros and cons of a simple bi-polar dichotomy, the profession seems to be engaged in an all-out "*take-no-prisoners*" war. One consequence of these "Reading Wars" is the demand that only pedagogies which are "evidence-based" or "scientifically derived" should be applied in literacy classrooms.

However, invoking "science" and "evidence-based research" as a way to reduce the theoretical confusion surrounding literacy education doesn't seem to have helped much. It turns out there are quite distinct views of "good science" and "good evidence" held within the education research community, and all that seems to have happened is a new round of argument and debate about "whose science" and "whose evidence should be considered" has begun (Larau & Walters, 2010). As a consequence, today's teachers of reading are heirs to a long tradition of (often acrimonious) debate about pedagogical methods which are presented either as bi-polar opposites, or as positions along a bi-polar continuum of some kind. *It's as if the field of reading (by extension "literacy") has, for a long time, suffered from something analogous to serious bi-polar disorder.*

The failure of the massive intellectual investment of so many researchers and theory-builders for so many years to develop consensus would not sit well with William of Occam (a 12th century English Franciscan friar and scholastic philosopher known for Occam's razor). Nor would it be acceptable to Charles Darwin, or indeed many modern theory builders in fields as diverse as physics, biology, astronomy, cosmology, evolution, ecology, and other scientific domains. Scientists from other disciplines would suggest that there must be something inherently wrong with the approaches taken by the theory builders who have attempted to develop these theories of literacy learning.

Surely, they would argue, after more than 100 years of experimental research and theory building, the field should have moved beyond the theoretical squabbling and sniping that still characterizes it? In other theoretical domains new theories evolve, and converge toward a single set of derivative, explanatory principles. Theories which lack either internal and/or external validity are eliminated from serious consideration.

Why hasn't this happened in our field? Shouldn't there have been a convergence toward a more universal, narrower range of complementary theories of literacy learning? After more than a century of research, shouldn't theories derived from similar, converging assumptions about literacy and literacy learning start to emerge? These questions suggest something has hampered literacy education's evolution as a legitimate knowledge domain subject to scientific experimentation.

I think it's got something to do with the profession's failure to agree on operational definitions for two key concepts in our field as well as make these known to external critiques and policy-makers.

> Effective literate behavior
> Effective literacy learning

Effective operational definitions are essential because they ensure that everyone in the field has the same understanding about how the phenomenon being studied is actually manifested in the world (i.e., what it "looks like" when it occurs). For example:

> Is "effective reading behavior" the ability to match and errorlessly reproduce (i.e., pronounce) every *word* on the page, or is it the ability to match the *meanings* which the author of the text intended, perhaps using different words (e.g., "dad" for "father")?

Does effective literacy learning proceed best from part to whole (as behaviorist-oriented theories of learning would attest), or from whole to part (as holistic-oriented theories of learning would attest)?

Without agreement of how key concepts like these should be operationally defined, researchers and theory builders use terms like "effective reading" and "effective learning" to mean different things. Thus, a researcher who operationally defined effective reading as accurate word-matching would measure quite different things and collect quite different data from those who operationally defined "effective reading" as matching meanings. Similarly, those who operationally defined "effective literacy learning" as mastery of a predetermined sequence of larger and larger units of written language would conduct research involving different clusters of dependent and independent variables from those who had a more constructivist view of "effective literacy learning." Stated simply, without agreement on operational definitions of such key concepts, researchers and theory builders tend to use the same general conceptual terms (and their cognates) to describe and measure quite distinctly different things.

These are concepts the reading education profession should have operationalized long ago. For some reason, we seem to have avoided addressing them. As a consequence, the research and theory building into reading education which has been published over the last decade reflects the research of the previous five, six, seven, or even more decades.

Until the profession resolves and agrees upon operational definitions of such key concepts we will continue to be perceived as an internally dysfunctional, epistemologically immature, and scientifically naïve rabble. Little wonder politicians want to take control of the field away from those who call themselves "literacy educators."

2. *How do you think this should inform the contexts and practices of reading instruction in the classroom?*

The response I've made to Question 1 suggests teachers need to be metacognitively aware of the necessity of being able to operationalize key concepts such as "effective reading" and "effective learning." This in turn presupposes that those who are admitted to the teaching profession will have achieved levels of education and critical thought that enable them to address such concepts for themselves. It also presupposes that pre-service teacher education institutions and those who offer in-service professional development courses are also aware of the consequences of not operationally defining key concepts. All providers of professional learning, and the authorities that accredit them, will need to ensure that significant opportunities for teachers to develop their own critical awareness of how concepts could/should be defined are built into all professional learning programs.

References

Cambourne, B.L. (1988). *The whole story: Natural learning and the acquisition of literacy.* Auckland, New Zealand: Ashton Scholastic.

Cambourne, B.L., & Turbill, J.B. (Eds.). (1994). *Responsive evaluation: Making valid judgements about students' literacy.* Melbourne, Australia: Eleanor Curtain.

Chall, J.S. (1967). *Learning to Read: The Great Debate.* New York, NY: McGraw Hill.

Cordeiro, P. (1992). *Whole learning: Whole language and content in the upper elementary grades.* Katonah, NY: Richard C. Owen.

Flippo, R.F. (1998). Points of agreement: A display of professional unity in our field. *The Reading Teacher, 52,* 30–40.

Halliday, M.A.K. (1978). *Language as a social semiotic: The social interpretation of language and meaning.* London: Edward Arnold.

Halliday, M.A.K. (1985). *An introduction to functional grammar*. London: Edward Arnold.

Harste, J.C., Burke, C.L., & Woodward, V.A. (1979). *Children's initial encounters with print*. National Institute of Education grant proposal.

Holdaway, R.D. (1974). *The foundations of literacy*. Auckland, New Zealand: Ashton Scholastic.

Krashen, S.D., & Terrell, T.D. (1983). *The natural approach: Language acquisition in the classroom*. Oxford, UK: Pergamon.

Larau, A., & Walters, P.B. (2010). What counts as credible research? *Teachers College Record* (retrieved from www.tcrecord.org).

Smith, F. (1973). Twelve easy ways to make learning to read difficult. In F. Smith (Ed.), *Psycholinguistics and reading* (pp. 183–196). New York, NY: Holt, Rinehart & Winston.

Whorf, B.L. (1956). *Language, thought, and reality*. Cambridge, MA: MIT Press.

4

POINT OF VIEW: MY POINT OF VIEW

Edward Fry

I have been asked to focus on my beliefs and position regarding reading instruction in this point-of-view piece. Specifically, I have been asked to focus on my background and my most well-known works, publications, and studies so that readers will know where I am coming from. Rona Flippo believes that it is important for readers of this book to realize that the experts who took part in her study represent different backgrounds, philosophies, and points of view. In the sections that follow, I share some of my professional works and views with you.

Testing

I like testing. I know that, recently, some of my colleagues do not think much of formal testing, or informal testing either. However, most of my career I have been in charge of a university-based reading clinic where parents send their children for reading improvement. Since more children applied than there were spaces, some sort of screening was necessary. Either we admitted students on a first-come, first-served basis, or by a table of random numbers, or by some type of screening process. I opted for a screening process.

Before becoming a university instructor, I spent a year as a teacher of mentally retarded elementary children with IQs ranging from 50 to 75. 1 was well aware that a child with an IQ of 50 could not learn to read at the same level as a child with normal intellectual ability. To even try to get that child up to grade level frustrated the child, the teacher, and his or her parents with false expectations. In the clinics, therefore, we rejected these below-normal students because the remedial reading instruction we offered was not quite the same as the special education they needed, and we did not wish to create false hope on the part of the parent.

Another curious thing happened with reading clinic applicants. Every semester we saw applicants who were quite normal in every respect. For example, a perfectly normal third grader, reading at third-grade level, would be thrust forward by a parent who wanted the normal student to be a super student. We rejected these students because it is the mission of the regular classroom teacher to improve the reading of these students, not the mission of expensive remedial education (Fry, 1959).

So screening tests were a great help in selecting students of normal learning ability (a non-verbal IQ test) who were underachieving in reading skills (an oral and silent reading test). I am well aware that tests are sometimes inaccurate, but I am also aware of the great waste of time, money, and teaching effort on students who do not need expensive remedial education.

Now testing is not just for reading clinics. I am continually amazed by classroom teachers who just start teaching with no notion of their students' present abilities. They select textbooks, supplemental reading materials, and lessons with some sort of vague hitting toward the middle. These same teachers have been exposed to educational psychology courses in which the normal distribution curve is carefully explained, but somehow it does not sink in that a normal fourth grade can have children reading from first-grade to seventh-grade ability. In only 1 or 2 hours, teachers could administer an oral reading paragraph test to every student in their classroom and see that indeed the normal distribution curve, amazingly, applies to even their class. Some students read well and others poorly. I believe that they can be assessed by formal or informal tests, and that instruction and material selection can be made much more efficiently.

Readability

"Testing" is a term usually applied to assessing the student. "Readability" is an assessment applied to the reading material. For example, is this book at the third-grade level or the eighth-grade level?

The purpose of readability is to help the teacher place a student with a book or material at the proper level. This is sometimes referred to as "matching."

There have been over a thousand research articles on the efficacy of using readability formulas. Basically, they show that proper matching increases comprehension, increases inclination to continue reading for pleasure, and facilitates written information communication. Proofs include improved scores on comprehension tests, decreases in oral reading errors, increases in amounts of non-assigned reading, and subjective reader self-reports.

I believe that if every teacher would match the proper reading material to the students' ability, there would be much less need for remedial reading. A serious problem in most secondary schools is the dropout rate (about 25% nationally, and worse in low socioeconomic status areas). Many of the dropout students are continually given reading materials on the wrong readability level by their well-meaning but non-thinking teachers and administrators. Giving students the wrong material continually tells them that they are failures, so they quit. What good schools need to do is to continually give students successful experiences. I believe that readability formulas can help to do this.

As many readers of this expert piece know, I developed a simple readability graph (formula) based on two inputs: (1) semantics as evidenced by word length, and (2) syntactics as evidenced by sentence length. It is amazing that these two simple inputs have stood up so well in research (Klare, 1984). What many readers might not know is that my readability graph was originally developed in Africa while I was on a Fulbright scholarship. It seems to me that African students are just like US students—they need reading materials at the proper level. And African teachers are just like US teachers—they need simple, reliable methods of judging the readability of a text (Fry, 1977).

The important point is that we need to give students lots of reading practice, most of which should be on reading material that each can successfully read. Yes, some material can be "challenging" (a euphemism for difficult material), but most of the material for pleasure or instruction should be at a reasonable level for that student.

Frequency

Another thing I learned well in directing reading clinics is that teaching time is very limited. Therefore, it is extremely important that the teacher focuses on exactly what the student needs. An important case in point is vocabulary. What words should be taught first? If you like research, the answer is surprisingly simple. I developed a frequency list, called Instant Words, based on the Carroll, Davies, and Richman study (1971), and this list clearly showed that the 100 most common words make up 50% of all written material, the first 300 words make up 65%, and the first 1000 words make up over 90%. Yes, you read correctly—just 100 words comprise half of all the words in *The New York Times*, half the words in an encyclopedia, and half of all the words in any children's book, such as *The Wind in the Willows* (Grahame, 1968).

Beginning readers need to recognize these words instantly. If they have to fool around and try to sound out the, or of, they are not apt to have much interest or brain power left to pay attention to comprehension, fluent oral reading, or enjoying what they read. The same is true of writing. It is practically impossible to write a sentence without using one or more of the first 100 Instant Words.

For those who would like just a bit of technical information on how the list of Instant Words was developed, here it is: The Carroll et al. (1971) list, also called the American Heritage list, was a count of 5 million running words (some 87,000 different word forms). The problem was that early computers were not too smart, and they gave a different count to any change on word form. Hence, a different count (based on total appearances) was given for run, runs, Run, and running. For the Instant Words, the weights for each of the different word forms were added to the base word "run," and this of course gave run a far different rank. So the Instant Words, while based on the Carroll et al. 5-million-wordcount data, have a totally different rank order (Fry, 1957, 1994).

The Instant Words have appeared in numerous college reading methods texts, handed around on interminable photocopied sheets, published on flash-cards, and apparently used by thousands of classroom and remedial teachers. I take some particular pleasure in knowing that they have been a help in adult prison literacy programs, as well.

I have tried to apply the same sort of frequency thinking to phonics, but not quite so successfully. While there was a massive phonics (phoneme–grapheme correspondence) study done at Stanford (Hanna, Hanna, Hodges, & Rudorf, 1966), the data do not lend themselves to a simple count as with individual words. For openers, phonics is usually taught in some kind of grouping, such as short vowels, Final E Rule, regular consonants, and so on. But then as you get more technical (as the Hanna et al. study did), the position or environment of the grapheme in the word can change the phoneme. A simple example is the vowel O in the words go and got, or the consonant C in city and cat. I tried to make a sort of teacher's compromise between the raw research data and the fre-quency count of Hanna et al. and an earlier study (Moore, 1951), which resulted in a study I did called "A Frequency Approach to Phonics" (Fry, 1964a). This information has resulted in some phonics charts (as a suggested curriculum) that have appeared in charts, flashcards, and other materials, and in chapters on phonics in some books, such as my little remedial reading handbook *How to Teach Reading* (Fry, 1995).

Failure

Not everything in the reading field is a success. If you have not failed to teach some children how to read, you have not taught very many children. Oh, I know that most journal articles, convention speeches, and teachers' room talk is about success with this method or that student, but I would like to state that if we are careful observers, we all have failures.

One of my greatest failures was with something called the Diacritical Marking System (Fry, 1964b). In the late 1960s and early 1970s, US teachers were being bombarded with the supposed success in England of something called the Initial Teaching Alphabet (ITA), in which the traditional alphabet was revised to make it more phonetically regular and traditional spelling was modified to make spelling more phonetically regular. About the same time, the US Office of Education came up with some grant money to fund the First-Grade Studies to try out different reading teaching methods. Some 27 dif-ferent researchers, mostly at different universities, each compared two or three different methods of teaching reading in first grade (a few studies, like mine, were carried on into second and third grades). We all used the same reading tests and did the same statistical analysis—a major research first. I elected to try out ITA and my own version of a similar idea called the Diacritical Marking System (DMS). DMS did not have a different alphabet, but used the regular alphabet and regular spelling; hence the word form was not changed, but diacritical marks were added to every word in all the first-grade basal readers. For example, long vowels had a bar over the letter and silent letters had a slash mark through them. To make a long story short, there was not much difference between the reading test scores of those pupils taught with DMS, ITA, or regular old basal readers. Differences between the three methods did not show up at the end of Grade 2 or Grade 3, or between boys and girls, or between bright or slower pupils (Fry, 1966). Hence, due to this study and others, you do not hear too much about ITA or DMS any more, though we'd better not forget it because, as sure as the sun rises, somebody is going to have a new alphabet reform to aid beginning readers. Benjamin Franklin had one, and so did the National Education Association in 1910.

My Agreements

Overall, I agree with all of the items on the Expert Study agreement lists (Flippo, 1998) reprinted in Chapter 1 of this book. However, I would emphasize some of the items more than others, and if I were to individually create my own lists again, I would probably add things as well. In other words, yes, these are contexts and practices that would make learning to read difficult, and others that would facilitate learning to read, but it is also a matter of emphasis. The items are not all equal to me; I believe that some are more important than others. However, Rona Flippo has done a good job of emphasizing this in her 1998 article and in the first chapter of this book. (As experts in this research project, we were asked only to provide and then later to approve positive and negative contexts and practices for teaching reading. If we had also been asked to rank them, we probably would have never gotten closure to this study.)

The great controversy in the most recent years has been between the so-called new whole language or literature approach, and the so-designated old-fashioned basic skills approach. The First-Grade Studies (Bond & Dykstra, 1967) taught me that there is not any best method of teaching reading. We had something quite similar to the whole language idea back then, only it was called the language experience approach, and we had some pretty drastic phonics methods too. Some reading experts saw a slight difference favoring phonics, but in my view there was not a great deal of difference between any of the methods. However, the indisputable fact is that in using any method there was a great deal of difference between the teachers. Would you believe that teaching ability may also follow the normal distribution curve?

There is nothing wrong with trying out new methods of teaching reading, only it might best be done in a limited-controlled comparison research study—not with something like the whole state of California. If I were a principal or a superintendent or a curriculum director, I would like to think that I would allow each teacher to select his or her own methods of teaching reading, because the method is not as important as that vague and wonderful thing called "teaching ability." Despite the method label put on the district curriculum manual or the basal series, most teachers are somewhat eclectic, and this is probably for the best.

Most reading specialists inside the whole language movement consider me as being outside that movement, and I can agree with that too. But what I would like to think of as my position is that there is nothing wrong with most of the methods and ideas included in whole language instruction. It is fine to have children read good literature and write creative stories, but not to the exclusion of teaching some basic skills like vocabulary, phonics, spelling, and comprehension.

Maybe Rona Flippo is right. Maybe it is important to know how different the experts are who agreed to the contexts and practices listed in this book. Maybe those agreements can be the beginning of some common ground.

The Past 10 Years: In Retrospect

1. *What are the most important things that you believe literacy research has shown over the past 10 years? (Positive and/or Negative)*

Looking at the research, here is what I have seen:

> Essentially, over the past 50 years, the National Assessment of Educational Progress (NAEP) has been showing no significant change in results. No matter what we've been doing, we've been getting the same results. For example, phonics isn't better than anything else. If we look back to the first-grade studies, we found it made no difference what method was used. It was the teacher that made the difference in the first-grade studies, not the method. The same has been true in the past 10 years.

2. *How do you think this should inform the contexts and practices of reading instruction in the classroom?*

It is obvious to me, and it should be to others, that because of this, we know that there are many ways to teach reading successfully. A good teacher can make most of the various methods work well with most students. A bad teacher can't make any of it work. Rather than the continual focus and arguments regarding methods and approaches, focus instead on hiring good teachers, and then allow them to teach reading using the practices that fit best in the particular contexts. Let the teachers make the decisions regarding how they will teach reading!

References

Bond, G.L., & Dykstra, R. (1967). The cooperative research program in first-grade reading instruction. *Reading Research Quarterly*, *2*, 135–142.

Carroll, J.B., Davies, P., & Richman, B. (1971). *The American Heritage word frequency book*. Boston, MA: Houghton Mifflin.

Flippo, R.F. (1998). Points of agreement: A display of professional unity in our field. *The Reading Teacher*, *52*, 30–40.

Fry, E.B. (1957). Developing a word list for remedial reading. *Elementary English*, *34*, 456–458.

Fry, E.B. (1959). A reading clinic reports its methods and results. *Journal of Educational Research*, *52*, 311–313.

Fry, E.B. (1964a). A frequency approach to phonics. *Elementary English*, *41*, 759–765, 816.

Fry, E.B. (1964b). A diacritical marking system to aid beginning reading instruction. *Elementary English*, *41*, 526–529, 537.

Fry, E.B. (1966). First grade reading instruction using the diacritical marking system, the initial teaching alphabet, and a basal reading system. *The Reading Teacher*, *19*, 666–669.

Fry, E.B. (1977). Fry's readability graph: Clarifications, validity, and extensions to level 17. *Journal of Reading*, *21*, 242–252.

Fry, E.B. (1994). *1000 instant words*. Laguna Beach, CA: Laguna Beach Educational Books.

Fry, E.B. (1995). *How to teach reading: For teachers, parents, and tutors*. Laguna Beach, CA: Laguna Beach Educational Books.

Grahame, K. (1968). *The wind in the willows*. New York, NY: Golden Press.

Hanna, P.R., Hanna, J.S., Hodges, R.E., & Rudorf, E.H. Jrn (1966). *Phoneme–grapheme correspondences as cues to spelling improvement*. Washington, DC: US Department of Health, Education and Welfare.

Klare, G.R. (1984). Readability. In P.D. Pearson, R. Barr, M.L. Kamil, & P. Mosenthal (Eds.), *Handbook of Reading Research* (pp. 681–744). New York, NY: Longman.

Moore, J.T. (1951). *Phonetic elements appearing in a 3000 word spelling vocabulary*. Unpublished doctoral dissertation, Stanford University, Palo Alto, California.

5

POINT OF VIEW: ALWAYS A TEACHER—FROM TEACHER TO TEACHER EDUCATOR TO RESEARCHER

Yetta M. Goodman

There is a Jewish folktale about a teacher in a small *stetl* (village) in Eastern Europe talking to one of the prominent citizens. The teacher says, "If I were Rothschild [the epitome of a wealthy man to poor Jews], I'd be richer than Rothschild." "How is that possible?" responds the citizen. "Because," responds the teacher, "of course, I'd do a little teaching on the side."

This vignette establishes the significant role of the teacher in my Jewish culture: teaching is so enriching that no matter in what other work they engage, teachers are enriched as a result of their teaching. Once a teacher, *always a teacher*.

I present the knowledge and beliefs about the learning and teaching of reading (I now prefer to use the term literacy) that I developed during my over 50 years of professional history within the context of the parable. I make clear through my history the support I have for the clustered summary agreements presented in Rona Flippo's Expert Study (2001). My professional history also embeds my responses to the questions Dr Flippo asked chapter authors to consider as we updated our chapters. I include the most important things that I believe literacy research has shown over the past 10 years, and I suggest pathways to inform the contexts and practices of reading instruction in the classroom. I answer the questions directly at the end of the chapter.

My views about the reading process, learning to read and reading instruction are supported by my years as a reading researcher, but they have been equally informed by my teaching in elementary and secondary classrooms, and my years of working with highly successful teachers, often as researchers, in their classrooms. The understandings I have about research and pedagogy that facilitate learning literacy were well in place before I became a reading researcher. My history as a teacher informed my work as a teacher educator, and stimulated the questions I continue to explore as a literacy researcher. In these capacities—classroom teacher, teacher educator, and researcher—I always identify myself first as a teacher. In Yiddish, my native tongue, the words for *to teach* and *to learn (leren)* are homonyms. As a retired Regents Professor at the University of Arizona, in the College of Education, Department of Language Reading and Culture, my professional journey to understanding the importance of literacy research and how it should inform the classroom began as a middle school teacher in a self-contained classroom in southern California.

Classroom Teacher

In 1952, as a beginning teacher, I was comfortable calling myself a progressive educator, based on my learning about John Dewey's philosophy and progressive educational pedagogy. I believed, based on my understandings of Jean Piaget, that children constructed their own knowledge. These foundational beliefs were central to my teacher education program influenced by Hilda Taba and Helen Heffernan, California educators, where I came to understand the power of integrating language arts with social studies; the need for careful planning for a curriculum in which students were involved as active learners; and the important role of a professional teacher who understood how to support students' intellectual development informed by their interests and needs. I used a range of methods and materials in order to encourage my students to discover their own capabilities. I helped them explore significant concepts by connecting what they were learning and wanted to learn with what they already knew, and to expand on that learning in their search for meaning making.

My sixth- to eighth-grade students in public school classrooms over the years studied their communities, and found many ways to provide evidence of what we were learning to parents, peers, and other school personnel through many different kinds of presentations. One of my principals led a school-wide study of sex education (yes, in the 1950s), in which we studied ourselves, our bodies, and our relationships, that resulted in discussions among students and parents. We took field trips to help us understand the environment and the world of work, and wrote booklets about what we learned. We mapped our families' migration patterns to California. Students kept samples of their written work and lists of their readings for purposes of self evaluation. They selected their readings from a range of genres, including pamphlets, magazines, and first-hand documents of varying difficulty levels, often working collaboratively with their peers. Although most of my students read and wrote independently, I took dictation from a few who needed support to get their ideas onto paper, and what they wrote, they could read and share with others. Students wrote letters, articles, stories, and musicals for authentic purposes. They kept personal dictionaries, and gave each other spelling tests based on the words they selected from their work. We read basal stories selectively, and I set aside time for students to read by themselves or quietly with peers.

I set this stage with my own teaching to make clear that although my specific research questions came later, my questions were stimulated by my teaching. I taught struggling readers and writers. I noted how hard these students worked at reading carefully, by attending to each word, reading slowly, sounding out. I observed how meticulously they wrote because they wanted to be neat and were afraid to use words they couldn't spell. I was successful with such students in our rich literate environment in which they were valued members making their own contributions to a learning community. They developed their literacy abilities as I provided them with opportunities to use reading and writing to expand on what was important to them. Such classrooms remain vibrant and alive to these days (Lewison, Leland, & Harste, 2008).

Teacher Educator

Although my roles as teacher educator and researcher emerged about the same time, I was comfortable as teacher educator long before I comfortably defined myself as a researcher. The research questions I began to explore as a teacher were highlighted throughout my work as teacher educator. For years, I participated in on-site experiences for preservice teachers as they apprenticed themselves to experienced teachers. I visited the classes of my graduate students, and of inservice teachers I met in long-range professional development settings in school districts. Observing teachers at the chalk face provided opportunities for me to consider the kinds of literacy contexts and practices that do and do not facilitate learning to read. I had continuous opportunity to carefully observe what transactions between students and teachers were most successful. I studied such transactions carefully.

I observed students in ability reading groups; doing worksheets; copying words, sentences, and morning messages from the board; and playing games with flashcards. I saw teachers correcting the exact same miscues differentially for children in lower and higher reading groups, and from different ethnic groups. I observed teachers within seconds of any hesitation by the reader giving the student "the word," telling him or her to "sound it out" or "look more closely." I saw readers look up at their teacher after every word they read to verify that they were right, and I saw them change their correct answers because their teacher questioned them. I was in some classrooms where activities changed every 12 minutes to sustain students' attention, in others where children were not given material to read until they could speak the "correct" dialect or language, and others in which children were unable to write texts until their handwriting was neat and spellings were accurate. I concluded that the *practices* of transmission model teaching control both learning and teaching; the *contexts* of such practices make learning to read and write difficult (Smith, 1973).

But perhaps more importantly, I also observed many teachers who organize classrooms in which students discover themselves as learners, define themselves as literate members of society as they use literacy practices to learn about their world and to pose and solve their own problems. My understandings about progressive education, of establishing a democratic society in classrooms and organizing relevant learning opportunities for students to construct their own meanings, continue to be confirmed by teachers who support what they are doing with knowledge and understanding. Such teachers, many of whom identify themselves as whole language or constructivist teachers, organize their reading and writing instruction in ways that reflect the belief that learning to read is integral to reading to learn, and learning to write is a result of writing to learn. They view reading and writing as tools to inquire about the significant aspects of their world. They know that reading is always focused on meaning making in the same way that writing is (K. Goodman, 1996).

As a teacher educator with preservice and inservice teachers, I incorporated my views of constructivism and progressive educational philosophy. With like-minded colleagues, we developed whole language principles that value and help teachers to value their own abilities and to discover answers to their own questions (Whitmore & Goodman, 1996). I continue to engage teachers in becoming introspective about their own reading and writing practices in order to have realistic expectations about their students' literacies. Teachers develop a research stance as they participate in miscue analysis with their students, analyze their written compositions, and reflect about their own interactions in discussions with their students focused on literacy learning and experiences. They document students' language knowledge and language use. The responses of teachers to their own thoughtful analyses of their students led me to popularize the term *kidwatching* (Goodman, 1978). Kidwatching teachers observe their students using a variety of evaluative tools to diagnose strengths and to understand weaknesses (Owocki & Goodman, 2002). They take careful field notes about their students' literacy events as they observe kids during a science experiment, as they record a reader's miscues during an individual conference, or as they list the resources used by a group at the writing center. They use the knowledge and insights about their students to inform their instructional practices and curricular decisions. My understandings about kidwatching have been informed by knowledgeable teachers who use analytic observations of their students to organize dynamic contexts that facilitate success in learning to read and to write. Theory and research cannot be directly applied to classroom settings through mandated and scripted lessons for teachers. *Theoretical constructs and research insights are transformed, based on teachers' understandings and knowledge, into classroom practice.* For these teachers, there is no separation between educational theory, research, and practice. They come to their own understandings of "the contexts and practices that facilitate learning to read" (Flippo, 2001). As teachers define themselves as researchers and become comfortable with that role, they empower themselves.

Researcher

My research has been richly informed by my teaching with children and adolescents, and my work with teachers in teacher education and professional development. Since 1965, I have worked with Kenneth Goodman and colleagues in the development of miscue analysis (its procedures and research design) in order to discover how readers transact with written text (Paulson, Flurkey & Goodman, 2007). In miscue analysis, readers read orally from a whole story or article. The reader is not given assistance, and is asked to retell it after the reading. Miscues are analyzed to determine the degree to which they enhance or disrupt the reader's construction of meaning. From the analysis, we gather insights about the knowledge readers have about the language cueing systems, and the ways in which they use a range of reading strategies (K. Goodman, 1996). We examine how the context and language use in the written text affect their reading. The retelling is used to corroborate what we understand from the miscue analysis. I have miscued over a thousand readers of all ages, with different reading abilities, and from different language and dialect communities. I have analyzed tens of thousands of miscues. I have worked with hundreds of teachers as they gain knowledge about individual readers through miscue analysis and use their knowledge to organize instruction to benefit their students.

During collaborations with miscue researchers, we realized the power of what we were learning about the reading process, and the impact of this knowledge on reading instruction. Since most of us had been classroom teachers, we often discussed what we would have done differently if we had known as teachers what we were now learning as reading researchers. We were eager to share our learning with other teachers. We presented at professional conferences, organized workshops for school districts, developed syllabi for university courses, wrote articles and books to inform teachers and researchers about our findings, and provided suggestions for classroom applications (Allen & Watson, 1976; Whitmore & Goodman, 1996). We developed materials to guide teachers in using miscue analysis, to help researchers follow miscue analysis research design, and to provide strategy lessons for research purposes and to support developing readers (Goodman, Watson, & Burke, 1996; 2005). The strategy lessons and reading instruction based on miscue research in these works are compatible with the Clustered Summary Agreements (Chapter 1, this volume).

Through discussions with teachers about the ways in which they use miscue analysis in classroom and clinical settings, I extended my research focus and began to explore retrospective miscue analysis (RMA). In RMA, readers listen to their own taped readings and, with the support of a teacher or a researcher, evaluate the influence of miscues on their comprehension. They become consciously aware and begin to articulate their knowledge of language, the reading process, and their use of reading strategies. Through RMA, we create environments in which students revalue themselves as literate members of society. RMA research highlights the importance of students' expectations about themselves as learners, and documents that when readers are involved in talking about their reading, they develop greater confidence as readers and at the same time become better readers (Y. Goodman, 1996).

Most recently, with former students and colleagues we have developed ways of using eye movement research in combination with miscue analysis (EMMA). This research corroborates the meaning-seeking reading process we explore through miscue analysis and RMA. We have information regarding how the eye accesses information, and know that the reader uses much more than the print on a written page to comprehend (Paulson & Freeman, 2003).

Early in miscue analysis research, I began to wonder how young children come to know the functions that reading and writing serve in their lives, and how they come to comprehend literacy as an object to know and understand. With graduate students and colleagues, I documented that children from a range of backgrounds and literacy experiences know a great deal about literacy before they come to school.

My inquiry and understandings about early literacy development led to my roots of literacy metaphor, suggesting that for reading instruction to be effective, teachers need to know about the history of the literacy experiences and knowledge that each child has before they come to school (Goodman, 1986). I have worked with other researchers interested in constructivist views of literacy learning to expand knowledge and insights about young children's literacy development for researchers and teachers. Literacy is a major cultural phenomenon that must be understood within the context of society, and not treated as simply reading and writing skills taught only in school. Each young reader and writer constructs their own literacy knowledge as a member of the social community in which they live (Goodman & Martens, 2007).

With graduate students and colleagues, I studied the writing development of Tohono O'odham Indian third and fourth graders (Goodman & Wilde, 1992). It was evident, through our careful documentation of their writing experiences, that reading served many purposes for them. They used stories, non-fiction texts, dictionaries, and signs in their environment as resources for their writing. They often remembered a word or phrase from a particular book, searched for it in the classroom library, and shared their finds with their classmates. We became aware of the importance of talk, illustration, and other print media in the community, on the walls in the school, and in classrooms on the writing development of the students. We documented students' interest in each other's writing, and the impact of the classroom social community on writing development. The impact of the social aspects of teaching and learning indicate the importance of contexts rich in literacy opportunities for facilitating learning to read and write, and for understanding language as an object of study by children (Y. Goodman, 2003).

Through my reading and writing research and the research of others (Goodman & Martens, 2007), I have concluded that children invent knowledge about literacy within the constraints of literacy conventions in society. Readers and writers are dynamically involved in their own learning about the reading and writing processes and the strategies they use. They learn about the various subsystems of language and how they work in reading and writing as a result of being readers and writers, not as a result of didactic teaching of discrete skills and not as a prerequisite. The latter kind of teaching for too many children results in learning that negatively affects their literacy development. These conclusions highlight the important differences between contexts and practices that make learning to read difficult and those that facilitate learning to read (Smith, 1973). Research provides a range of rich settings and interactions with children and teachers that help me deepen my theoretical understandings about the teaching and learning of reading, and at the same time allows me to continue wondering about literacy processes.

The Past 10 Years: In Retrospect

Rona Flippo asked the authors to respond to two questions as we updated our chapters.

1. *What are the most important things that you believe literacy research has shown over the past 10 years? (Positive and/or Negative)*
2. *How do you think this should inform the contexts and practices of reading instruction in the classroom?*

I believe the answers to these questions are embedded in my history as I've recounted. As a beginning teacher, I applied to my classroom curriculum the research and theory that best fit what *I believed*. Professional teachers cannot successfully apply to classroom settings what they do not understand unless it is turned into technological scripts. What happens in classrooms is not affected by what researchers do in any direct way. Researchers provide one component of a highly complex, integrative system—knowledge that needs to be understood by the teachers and believed in by those who work in the classrooms. As "experts, reading researchers," as we are identified in this book, we must come to understand the limitations of research alone, and work respectfully with teacher researchers/practitioners in this complex enterprise of coming to understand the teaching and learning of literacy in schools.

The past 10 years have been especially useful and painful in the understanding that research alone does not drive the enterprise of schooling and education. We need to understand the growing influences that legislation and politics have on what happens in classrooms. It seems that research knowledge and reading researchers are even locked out of the movement to improve test scores and establish a mandated curriculum in reading. Classroom reading instruction is not only influenced by what communities believe, but also impacted by power relationships in the political and business communities even as it disregards the conclusions of more than a century of reading research.

I am disheartened that the literacy research reported in this book seems to have less influence on classroom practice than it had over 10 years ago. Frank Smith's "Twelve Easy Ways to Make Learning to Reading Difficult" (1973) is visible in many classrooms legitimatized by federal, state and local mandates. The common ground that Rona Flippo (2001) hoped for has not turned into the dominant theme of reading instruction at the present time. It obviously takes more than research to influence classroom practice. Research on the politics and social cultural issues that surround literacy teaching and learning has illuminated the problems teachers face in trying to put into practice the results of research that work for them. Unfortunately, professional organizations are reluctant to get involved in critiquing and protesting dysfunctional reading practices, even though the common ground exists.

Research in classrooms has shown ways in which integrated practices have been successful in the teaching of reading and writing, and is documented by authors in this volume. Research in early literacy highlights the constructivist nature of literacy learning. And perhaps most importantly, research strongly supports the importance of knowledgeable and experienced teachers in children's learning literacy.

Somehow, we must work harder than ever before, collaboratively and through professional organizations, to support the research that makes clear that knowledgeable teachers in collaboration with their students are most successful in developing readers and writers. We must speak more strongly as experts to highlight our common ground, and ask why such grounds are not part of the conversation about reading and writing instruction in the schools. Teacher educators and researchers must continue to work collaboratively with teachers to involve them in their own research to understand the ways in which the results of research impact literacy instruction.

As I come to the end of this piece, I focus back to my students and myself as teacher. As my early years as a teacher resulted in my research questions, my theoretical and research knowledge provides insights into my students in a way I did not understand at that time. I understand that Arthur was frustrated every time I asked him to read because he did not believe that he was a reader or a writer. I understand that when William wrote about making himself "dzam" and "pina buder samwhiches," he was reflecting his knowledge of the graphophonic cueing system. When Tanya read only horse stories, she was building concepts and language that stayed with her throughout her life. I have greater insight into why each of them succeeded in learning to read and write. Arthur was the first student in his family to graduate from high school; William became valedictorian of his graduating class; Tanya became a successful biologist at a research lab. My work has always focused on ways to document that ethnically, racially, linguistically, and culturally diverse youngsters who are not part of the mainstream are capable learners, and what they know must be valued. I believe that they benefit most from contexts and practices that facilitate learning to read and write. My concerns about valuing learners not only tie to the children I taught but also to my own childhood experiences as a supposedly unsuccessful learner, often chided for my inadequate performance because of my "Yiddish-speaking home and working-class parents." My understanding about what facilitates or makes learning to read difficult is informed by both my personal history and my professional one.

My teaching informs my research questions as significantly as my research informs my teaching. I no longer believe that university research is where significant ideas have their origin, and that research results can be directly applied to classrooms. I understand the complexity of classroom teaching, and the central role of the teacher in her daily decision-making. The Expert Study agreements (see Chapter 1) on what facilitates learning to read will have minimal impact on schools without professional elementary and secondary teachers who understand what they do in classrooms, and why. As teachers research their own questions and use their knowledge and understandings in their classrooms with a passion for teaching and a commitment to learners, dynamic transformations take place.

If we work together with greater understanding about the roles we each play—teachers, teacher educators and researchers—we come to know that long-lasting change can only take place in classrooms that value and support the work of the teacher. In this way, my concept of always a teacher comes full circle.

References

Allen, P., & Watson, D. (Eds.). (1976). *Findings of research in miscue analysis: Classroom implications.* Urbana, IL: ERIC and National Council of Teachers of English.

Flippo, R.F. (2001). Points of agreement: A display of professional unity in our field. In R.F. Flippo (Ed.), *Reading researchers in search of common ground* (pp. 7–21). Newark, DE: International Reading Association.

Goodman, K. (1996). *Ken Goodman on reading.* Portsmouth, NH: Heinemann.

Goodman, Y. (1978). Kidwatching: An alternative to testing. *National Elementary School Principal, 57,* 41–45.

Goodman, Y. (1986). Children coming to know literacy. In W. Teale & E. Sulzby (Eds.), *Emergent literacy: Writing and reading* (11th ed., pp. 1–14). Norwood, NJ: Ablex.

Goodman, Y. (1996). Revaluing readers while readers revalue themselves: Retrospective miscue analysis. *The Reading Teacher, 49* (8), 600–609.

Goodman, Y. (2003). *Valuing language study: Inquiry into language for elementary and middle schools.* Urbana, IL: National Council of Teachers of English.

Goodman, Y., & Martens, P. (Eds.). (2007). *Critical issues in early literacy: Research and pedagogy.* New York, NY: Lawrence Erlbaum Associates.

Goodman, Y., & Wilde, S. (1992). *Literacy events in a community of young writers*. New York, NY: Teachers College Press.

Goodman, Y., Watson, D., & Burke, C. (1996). *Reading strategies: Focus on comprehension* (2nd ed.). Katonah, NY: Richard C. Owen.

Goodman, Y., Watson D., & Burke, C. (2005). *Reading miscue inventory: From evaluation to Instruction*. Katonah, NY: Richard C. Owen Publishers.

Lewison, M., Leland, C., & Harste, J. (2008). *Creating critical classrooms: K-8 reading and writing with an edge*. New York, NY: Lawrence Erlbaum Associates.

Owocki, G., & Goodman Y. (2002). *Kidwatching: Documenting children's literacy development*. Portsmouth, NH: Heinemann.

Paulson, E., & Freeman, A. (2003). Insight from the eyes: The science of effective reading instruction. Portsmouth, NH: Heinemann.

Paulson, E., Flurkey, A., & Goodman K. (Eds.). (2007). *Scientific realism in reading research*. New York, NY: Routledge.

Smith, F. (1973). Twelve easy ways to make learning to read difficult. In F. Smith (Ed.), *Psycholinguistics and reading* (pp. 183–196). New York, NY: Holt, Rinehart, and Winston.

Whitmore, K.F., & Goodman, Y.M. (1996). *Whole language voices in teacher education*. York, ME: Stenhouse.

Whitmore, K.F., Martens, P., Goodman, Y.M., & Owocki, G. (2004). Critical lessons from the transactional perspective on early literacy research. *Journal of early childhood literacy, 4* (3), 291–325.

6

POINT OF VIEW: WHEN A RESEARCHER STUDIES WRITERS IN THEIR CLASSROOMS

Jane Hansen

When I wonder about what has prompted the evolution of my beliefs, I think of my years as a pre-service teacher, teacher, teacher educator, and researcher.

At Drake University in the mid-1960s, we students taught for half days for an entire year in two classrooms, one each semester. My second-semester placement was with silver-haired Mrs Wilson, who used no worksheets in her second-grade classroom. The children made things from colored paper, paints, crayons, scissors, and paste. They did not always sit at their desks, and they did not always work in the classroom—sometimes a few of them worked on the floor in the coat closet. I remember nothing from my theory classes to support the comfort I felt there, but maybe it was not simply because I appreciated the children's paintings more than I would have appreciated worksheets. Maybe it was Mrs Wilson's quiet way of letting her students know that she valued them as creators—of sometimes messy creations. As my University of Virginia (UVa) students and I value their mobiles, daybooks, and drafts.

Professor Marvins, a gray-haired, bespectacled, well-suited man, invited us to experiment in his children's literature class. We actually walked to a real classroom as part of that course, saw him shed his suitcoat, sit on a small chair, and come to life as he lived the books he read to the children. Then, each of us took a turn, and I read *Caps for Sale* to second graders. Later, as an elementary teacher, I always read to my students, and, as a professor, I continue.

Finally, I remember Dr Weaver. Articulate, bone-thin, face lined with experience, and hair dyed to match her black dresses, she repeated over and over, in several sessions of our reading methods class:

> Don't ever use the phrase *ability groups*. You must not presume to know what a child's ability is; you see every child as a person with ability.

However, unfortunately, some of your children will not achieve as much as others. Because of this difference, we form *achievement groups*.

As an elementary teacher, I lived her words. I took care to see each child as someone with ability, and looked closely at the children I placed in achievement groups.

As a professor, however, I found I could not live her words; I could not divide my students into achievement groups. Well, I could have, but my soul would not let me. I stopped advocating achievement groups the day I realized I could not treat adults that way; I just could not bring myself to divide the pre-service and inservice teachers in my classes into achievement groups. To find another way to teach was not easy, but I had to figure this out.

At that time, I was learning about writing instruction, and it informed my use of groups (and a lot of other things!). As a relatively new professor at the University of New Hampshire, I accepted an invitation from Donald Graves to conduct research on reading–writing instruction. He had just completed a huge study on the teaching of writing (Graves, 1983/2003), I was a professor of reading, and he wondered if we could combine fields. We researched in Ellen Blackburn Karelitz's first-grade classroom in Somersworth, a blue-collar community, where I spent two mornings a week, for 2 years (Hansen, 1987/2001), studying the children as readers and writers.

Every child, on the first day of school, said they could write, and they all did—many of them drew pictures, which they called writing. They conveyed what they wanted to say in the form of drawing, and they soon learned to produce print. Eight of them could not write their names, and they learned to do so in the important context of: I must put my name at the top of my writing.

Each day, when they sat around tables to write, they started by reading/ talking about their writing from the previous day. Then they added to it or wrote something new, and as they wrote they talked among themselves as if writing and talking were one seamless process. Ellen always sat at a table, and nudged each child forward—in the presence of the others at the table, who sometimes paid attention to the conferences she held with their classmates. The children sat in mixed fashion; those who could not write their names did not sit off at one table by themselves. All of these young writers received information of all kinds from each other. They asked their classmates about everything, from "How do you spell *bicycle*?" to "What time do you have to go to bed?" to "Show me how to make my name."

This procedure continued all year, and the children interacted around their published books, as well. On the second day of school, Mark read his first book to the class. Ellen had published it the previous evening from the news he wrote on the first day, when he wrote three thoughts about a fire in their town. Ellen placed one sentence per page when she typed his book in a large font; Mark created an illustration for each page and practiced reading his book. His own printing had been sparse; he recorded the sound–symbol correspondences he heard and identified. When Ellen typed his text in conventional spelling, many of the words looked unfamiliar to this young reader, but within minutes he could read his own language. Mark proudly sat on the little chair Ellen sat on when she read to the class, his 27 classmates clustered on the carpet, necks upturned, eyes on him, as Mark amazed them with his book. Then they all talked about the fire!

Later that day, Ellen read to the class from the same chair, as she did more than once a day. She read a book about fire engines, and the children compared what the author of that book wrote to what Mark had written. Ellen started a network of pieces of writing (Blackburn, 1985), some written by classroom authors and others by professionals. The children knew they were part of an august group, as now happens within the current trend to use mentor texts (Ray, 1999; Dorfman & Cappelli, 2007, 2009).

Also on that day, Mandy sat on the same chair, and read a book from the classroom library to the class. This book was about giants, and the class talked about these mythical creatures. Mandy's classmates wanted to know how she could read this book, and that conversation began a year-long one about what readers—and writers—do. Every day for the rest of the year, at least two children read to the class each day. They read their own drafts, each other's, and their own published books, or the writing of professionals, from the chair soon to be known as *The Author's Chair* (Graves & Hansen, 1983; Karelitz, 1993).

Every day, the children spent time learning to read—as they spent time learning to write. They decided what to write about and in what form; they decided what to read. Each day when it was time for reading, each child either chose to stay with a book(s) from the previous day(s) or select a new one(s). The children chose books available at the listening center, easy books Ellen had read to the class several times, books written by classmates who could help others learn to read them, or children's literature their classmates could read. They chose book(s) they wanted to *learn* to read—as different from choosing a book to read—and worked on their choices.

The children scattered all over the room—alone, at the listening center, with a friend, in self-made clusters around the classroom. They sought help from those who could read; they wanted to learn, and they sought assistance. Often, they also devoted some of their reading time to enjoying, looking at, and rereading various books—frequently, their own published books. There was one thing they did not do: they did not put themselves in achievement-level groups.

Ellen moved among the readers, leaned in closely as each little voice read, listened as they told each other and her about what they were reading and what they were doing as readers, and conferred with these wanna-be readers as they read, reread, and practiced the one book they were "workin' on."

I was struck by how excited the children were about learning to read and write, and about how much sense reading made to them. In contrast to my students when I was a reading resource teacher, Ellen's children expected print to make sense. When they did not know words, they did not substitute them with others that did not make sense and continue as if nothing were amiss. They knew, because they created print, that writers do not put random words on paper. These children wrote their own compositions—their news—every day. They had things to tell, assumed all writers did, and came to the pages of books to find out what those authors had to say.

In order to keep these young children's strong voices vibrant, Ellen knew she could not place some of them in low achievement groups; this might make them feel less worthy than others. If they started to question their status, their voices might become hesitant. This could affect them as writers, as learners, as readers, as persons. Given that only 2 of the 28 children in this class, on the first day of school, could read books from the classroom library, the majority needed lots of help—which they received from their classmates and her. And they all became readers, in large part, because they first-of-all were writers.

Ellen, similar to other teachers (Shagoury, 2009), spent her time outside the school day thinking about how to ensure the overall classroom context would continue to keep all the children immersed in reading, writing, and learning. She did not spend her time creating worksheets or thinking of project ideas for the children, and they did not spend time working on projects or worksheets. This was a classroom of readers and writers—children who enjoyed their collective immersion in both.

I then became a member of a research team to study reading–writing in an entire school (Hansen, 1987/2001). We studied the readers and writers in various classrooms—all of which were similar to Ellen's; the children enjoyed their collective immersion in reading and writing. Their teachers' beliefs were quite similar throughout the building, and, importantly, the manifestation of those beliefs varied. These classrooms were different and similar. As a research team, we started to wonder about the magnetism that brought the children together as engaged/intentional learners in this school. What was it?

Noting the evaluative comments we had recorded in our field notes, we created another research team, and studied students as evaluators, in a different school. For 3 years we documented evaluation as the central task of the children while they intentionally became better writers and readers. They responded to each other as learners—and their teachers did likewise. Response and evaluation melded as the support system within which the children revisited their past, studied their present, and planned their future days as readers and writers. These learners knew what they could do, what they had learned, of options for their growth, and could make decisions about what to do next. Their self-evaluations kept them intentionally engaged.

Looking for a broader setting in which to further study self-evaluation, and with a new research team, I spent 6 years trekking down the highway to Manchester, one of New Hampshire's largest cities. Here, we studied students who evaluated themselves as readers and writers in the context of portfolios (Hansen, 1998).

We moved beyond elementary schools, into a collection of five schools— three elementary, one junior high, and one senior high—that constituted a feeder pattern, the one in the center of the city with a more diverse population than we had seen in our work near the university. For three of the years, I collected my own data in a high school, US history classroom, attending the lowest of four levels and a college prep class twice a week. I was totally fascinated by these students—and those of the entire team.

Our research, however, while fascinating, was frustrating—at first. Too idealistic, we expected the students to create portfolios that answered the question: *Who am I as a reader and writer?* Well, some of the high school students had devoted years to perfecting a persona—one of someone who does not do school. Because they did not do school, their answer to the question was: *I am not*. Thus, their portfolios were—intentionally—blank. Indeed, as reflections of the students as readers and writers, their portrayal of themselves was truthful.

Some sixth-grade girls came to our rescue—inadvertently. They did not read and write in school, either, but they did at home. So, on their own, they put cards from out-of-state grandmothers in their portfolios. And the possibilities this brought spread. To our twice-monthly research team meetings of the five classroom teachers and five university doctoral students and professors, each brought a sample of a student's work, and a one-page analysis/reflection/research update on the significance of that sample. So, with the news of the sixth-grade girls, other teachers' suggestions to their classes brought evidence of reading and writing outside of school into school—and that started to influence the students' work as readers and writers in school. Some students started to create cards for family members who remained in the countries they had fled as refugees.

A few students, however, maintained blank portfolios. They insisted they never read or wrote. So, we asked a different question, "*Who are you?*" This made little difference. We heard these exact words, "I am nobody." Tough words. The intentional blankness of those students became the focus of our attention.

Then a kindergarten child, unknowingly, opened some of those portfolios. Because she didn't understand her teacher's invitation to bring reading and writing from home, she simply brought something from home—for her portfolio. The necklace her father gave her before he went to prison. Well, her teacher could not tell her no, you can't put that in your portfolio. So, students at all levels started to bring artifacts. One teen brought the yo-yo he and his little brother played with; his little brother had a childhood, something this teen did not remember from when he grew up in a South American country. He wrote about it. Writing and reading started to creep into the portfolios as the students' acknowledgement of their existence started to emerge. When you let yourself become, you can write.

They became engaged and, via their self-evaluations, intentionally moved forward. They became ethnographers of their lives, and began to place varied, and sometimes valuable, artifacts in their portfolios. We saw naturalization certificates, soccer schedules, and photos of beautifully painted eggs. These students, who had seen themselves as insignificant, began to value themselves, their families, their cultures. As they shared these items in their classrooms, they began to value one another. In these radically re-formed classroom environments, they began to see themselves as readers and writers.

Over the 6-year period of this project, almost all of the students became readers and writers. A few of the high school students in one-semester classes did not move. A semester is not long enough to overcome nobody.

Then, I moved to become a professor at the University of Virginia, where I have focused on a Writing Across the Curriculum research project that is now 9 years old. The team of university- and teacher-researchers varies each year, and we all study writers of various ages in different schools (Hansen, 2005, 2008, 2009a; Lawrence, 2006; Kissel, Hansen, Tower & Lawrence, 2011) as they use writing to learn—their content, how to read and write, about each other, and about themselves.

My journey has led me to various beliefs: Engagement/Intention, Response/ Evaluation, and Writing Across the Curriculum. In a way, one belief holds them all together: writing is the most important thing in the world!

The Past 10 Years: In Retrospect

As I write about my three beliefs, I will keep in mind these questions:

1 *What are the most important things that you believe literacy research and practice has shown over the past 10 years? (Positive and/or Negative)*
2. *How do you think this should inform the contexts and practices of reading instruction in classrooms?*

I place Engagement/Intention as my first belief. It is the first belief I actually remember noticing, feeling—and it shook me, bothered me, upset me. It happened during one of those early days when I was a researcher in Ellen's classroom, and those little children, many of whom could not write their names, were ultra-engaged in their writing! This worried me. My history was in reading, and these children—I had to admit—preferred writing. So, I zeroed in on just what brought these young writers in. I wondered why they were so determined to figure out this writing thing. Then, I was going to translate that into good reading instruction.

Instead, I started to see reading–writing as a unitary endeavor, within which engaged learners intentionally become better at these arts—or this art. Today, a glimpse of titles of books, articles, and educators' titles seems to show that not only have reading/writing merged; they are now referred to as *literacy*. The *Journal of Reading Behavior* is now the *Journal of Literacy Research*. A close look, however, shows literacy, in many cases, is only reading. Literacy specialists are often reading specialists who know little about writing (McKinney & Giorgis, 2009), and children often see literacy as reading (Martens, 1996).

The gap between reading and writing has widened during the last decade, as other manifestations of a belief in engagement/intention have emerged (Wilson, 2007; Scott, 2008). In those classrooms, students are intentionally engaged in getting high test scores to prove their ability in the areas tested by standardized tests. Students are intentionally engaged in the pursuit of high test scores on reading tests. With scores on high-stakes tests of *reading* seen as the operational definition of *literacy* within assessment, it is curious that *literacy*, rather than *reading*, is often the term used in research and practice.

In some states, my own included, if schools received Reading First grants, they were *prohibited* from providing writing instruction within the required 90-minute *literacy* block. We know that decision was based on a review that analyzed mostly quantitative research. What I'm not sure of is whether the persons who decided to focus on quantitative research knew enough about writing to know that it is, in essence, subjective—that the value of a piece of writing is usually not quantifiable. I don't know if they chose to focus on quantitative research because they wanted to delete writing. All I know is they did.

Writing, therefore, was in danger of becoming unimportant; it was not one of the five pillars. Writing, however, is starting to resurge. Actually, it never became less important—it simply took a back seat as far as instruction went. Not enough policy-makers understood: whenever readers read, they are reading writing. Readers study writing—seriously, carefully, and with intention (Newkirk & Miller, 2009).

Maybe, as trends in research move toward online literacy and students' engagement as creators of online communications becomes understood in terms of reading *and* writing, engagement in writing will provide policy-makers with an insider's view of reading (Leu, 2002; Hull & Katz, 2006). Maybe researchers who study students as online writers/readers will find they intend to become increasingly proficient. Maybe such research will bring authentic writing–reading—with engagement/intention—back into legitimacy.

I place Response/Evaluation as my second belief. Response/evaluation creates and maintains—or destroys—the students' engagement and intention. I have come to believe that when evaluation works, it energizes the learner. To a great extent, my belief in the importance of response/evaluation flourished when we studied self-evaluation via portfolios in the urban K-12 schools in Manchester, NH. When those students forced us to find them, our response to their plea led us to value who they were—and they could find value in themselves. Self-evaluation became the act of finding value in self. These students led us to the core of our work. They led us to the place where we could start to teach reading/writing—and that response on our part led them to the place where they could intentionally engage in the literacy experiences of school.

They evaluated what they read—everything they read. They quoted well-penned passages from texts, all texts: those they composed, those of professionals, and those of their classmates. Similarly, they questioned texts, all texts. These learners and their teachers approached all writers with awe and intrigue. Their response fostered the students' intentions as readers/writers.

Today, whereas there are notable exceptions to what I am going to say, the national story—and the local story where I live—is of not successfully responding to who students are, of not finding value in many students, especially African American and Hispanic students. There is a significant disparity between their test scores and those of their white classmates. Plus, diverse students are often segregated off into classes/groups/situations with lower achievement-level students. Vibrant voices, owners of fascinating tales and ways with words, are intentionally kept from others who also have fascinating tales and ways with words.

Similarly, reading instruction trumps the classification of likeness—rather than seeing the value of diverse groups of readers working together to learn from, teach, and work with each other, many of the teaching materials script the explanations and interactions between teachers and students.

To reinforce a belief in the value of standardization, some schools, in addition to the ever-present standardized reading program, have now adopted canned writing programs. It is alarming. It is scary.

We must, in some way, keep—or return to—evaluation in the context of classrooms in which the students know they are valued, classrooms where response/evaluation energizes them (Fu & Lamme, 2002; Gee, 2004). I sometimes think I live in a time warp. How many decades ago was it we learned of the value of diversity? Of mixtures of students learning together, from each other, teaching each other, sharing their strengths—and they all do have strengths. Instead, the standardized tests beget standardized curricula, even though diverse students fill our classrooms with the hopeful voices of writers, and we must be *very* careful to not let standardized curricula blur their words.

Again, I'm not convinced that the disregard for difference has been intentionally fostered by research. I do know, however, that our educational system is in jeopardy, and standards are seen as the way up. I worry that response/ evaluation as processes—in which students intentionally become engaged as readers/writers—are not prominent on the horizon.

I place Writing Across the Curriculum as my third belief. Writing Across the Curriculum can strengthen the impact of response/evaluation. The response students receive to their work across the day can energize them as learners—beyond their language arts, literacy, English, reading, writing classes (Behrman, 2003; Luke, 2003). Continued research to impact the role of evaluation across the curriculum is needed.

When I arrived at the University of Virginia, I started to focus on writing. I was to create a course on writing instruction for elementary pre- and in-service teachers; there had never been one here. Also, I was to teach Content Area Reading, and I learned, to my surprise, that it was viewed as a course for secondary teachers. Knowing that many young children love to read content, I decided to merge my teaching of writing and reading. Thus was born what has now become a 9-year research project on Writing and Reading Across the Curriculum (WRAC).

As planned, we started with young children in pre-kindergarten through Grade 2, and over the years we have included all grade levels, and all content areas. Along the way we have substantiated much of what I already knew, and now know in new contexts. Portfolios have fallen by the wayside, but a focus on who the students are remains: we no longer need the crutch of the portfolio. We do need, however, the documentation of the students' work—and their perceptions of it and themselves as learners.

Much of what I have learned has been through the inclusion of teachers as researchers on my research team. Whereas the teachers in my last project in New Hampshire had attended our research meetings twice a month, the structure of the research project—I hate to admit this—privileged the university researchers. At UVa I set out to change that, with difficulty. When I first requested IRB permission, I was denied—because of the inclusion of teacher researchers. I met with the head of the IRB unit and convinced him that teachers can be researchers (Juarez, 1999; Gaughan, 2001)—in fact, it is a stance toward teaching that many professionals advocate. Teachers as researchers became recognized at UVa.

Because all teachers' voices are equal on my team, we know our data are credible. I always believed my data were; I collected data carefully in repeated classroom visits, but now, with teachers at every team meeting, bringing their own data from their own students, I feel more confident. These teacher researchers do not have university researchers in their classrooms. They bring their own students' work to our weekly team meetings, and they write their own research analyses/updates.

We document the engagement of young students in content area topics; not all students begin their engagement in writing via personal narratives (Hansen, 2009b). We document the evaluation students engage in as they intentionally learn about mathematics, social studies, and other content. Importantly, WRAC is seen by the wider community as worthwhile (Moss, 2005; Read, 2005). To officially move writing beyond the domain of English not only gives it the meaningful placement it holds in the world beyond school, but also may provide a way to keep writing in school alive.

I internalized the above beliefs by being a researcher twice a week, for more than two decades, in elementary, middle, and high schools, in classrooms where the teacher teaches everything, to classrooms where the teacher teaches only language arts, math, science, or US history. I have collected my data in rural, white, suburban, poor, urban, and multi-ethnic/cultural classrooms. Never in a large city, however. In all of the above situations the teachers—and they have taught any number of years, and have been the recipients of zero awards, many awards, and even a national award-winner—have been searchers. They are engaged, intentional, know their students as people, value their students' total selves, and are searching for ways to create environments in which their students are engaged, intentional, know each other as people, and value their total selves.

References

Behrman, E. (2003). Reconciling content literacy with adolescent literacy: Expanding literacy opportunities in a community-focused biology class. *Reading Research and Instruction, 43*(1), 1–30.

Blackburn, E. (1985). Stories never end. In J. Hansen, T. Newkirk, & D. Graves (Eds.), *Breaking ground: Teachers relate reading and writing in the elementary school* (pp. 3–13). Portsmouth, NH: Heinemann.

Dorfman, L., & Cappelli, R. (2007). *Mentor texts: Teaching writing through children's literature, K-6.* Portland, ME: Stenhouse.

Dorfman, L., & Cappelli, R. (2009). *Nonfiction mentor texts: Teaching informational writing through children's literature, K-8.* York, ME: Stenhouse.

Fu, D., & Lamme, L. (2002). Assessment through conversation. *Language Arts, 79*(3), 241–250.

Gaughan, J. (2001). *Reinventing English: Teaching in the contact zone.* Portsmouth, NH: Heinemann.

Gee, J. P. (2004). *Situated language and learning: A critique of traditional schooling.* New York, NY: Routledge.

Graves, D. (1983/2003). *Writing: Teachers and children at work.* Portsmouth, NH: Heinemann.

Graves, D., & Hansen, J. (1983). The author's chair. *Language Arts, 60*, 176–183.

Hansen, J. (1987/2001). *When writers read.* Portsmouth, NH: Heinemann.

Hansen, J. (1998). *When learners evaluate.* Portsmouth, NH: Heinemann.

Hansen, J. (2005). Young children's versions of the curriculum: How do you turn a square into a grown-up? *Language Arts, 82*(5), 269–247.

Hansen, J. (2008). The way they act around a bunch of people: Seventh-grade writers learn about themselves in the midst of others. *Voices from the Middle, 16*(1), 9–14.

Hansen, J. (2009a). Young writers use mentor texts. In B. Cullinan & D. Wooten (Eds.), *Children's literature in the reading program: An invitation to read* (3rd ed., pp. 88–98). Newark, DE: International Reading Association.

Hansen, J. (2009b). Multiple literacies in the content classroom: High school students' connections to US history. *Journal of Adolescent and Adult Literacy, 52*(7), 597–606.

Hull, G.A., & Katz, M.-L. (2006). Crafting an agentive self: Case studies of digital storytelling. *Research in the Teaching of English, 41*(1), 43–81.

Juarez, D.A. (1999). A question of fairness: Using writing and literature to expand ethnic identity and understand marginality. In S.W. Freedman, E.R. Simons, J.S. Kalnin, A. Casareno, & the M-CLASS teams, *Inside city schools: Investigating literacy in multicultural classrooms* (pp. 111–125). NY: Teachers College Press and Urbana, IL: National Council of Teachers of English.

Karelitz, E.B. (1993). *The author's chair and beyond.* Portsmouth, NH: Heinemann.

Kissel, B., Hansen, J., Tower, H., & Lawrence, J.K. (2011). The influential interactions of pre-kindergarten writers. *Journal of Early Childhood Literacy,* in press.

Lawrence, J.K. (2006). Revoicing: How one teacher's language creates active learners in a constructivist classroom. *The Constructivist, 17*(1) (www.odu.edu/educ/act/journal/vol. 17no1/).

Leu, D. (2002). Internet workshop: Making time for literacy. *The Reading Teacher, 55,* 466–472.

Luke, C. (2003). Pedagogy, connectivity, multimodality, and interdisciplinarity. *Reading Research Quarterly, 38*(3), 397–403.

Martens, P. (1996). I already know how to read: A child's view of literacy. Portsmouth, NH: Heinemann.

McKinney, M., & Giorgis, C. (2009). Narrating and performing identity: Literacy specialists' writing identities. *Journal of Literacy Research, 41,* 104–149.

Moss, B. (2005). Making a case and a place for effective content area literacy instruction in the elementary grades. *The Reading Teacher, 59*(1), 46–55.

Newkirk, T., & Miller, L. (Eds.). (2009). *The essential Don Murray: Lessons from America's greatest writing teacher.* Portsmouth, NH: Heinemann.

Ray, K.W. (1999). *Wondrous words: Writers and writing in the elementary classroom.* Urbana, IL: National Council of Teachers of English.

Read, S. (2005). First and second graders writing informational text. *The Reading Teacher, 59*(1), 36–44.

Scott, T. (2008). Happy to comply: Writing assessment, fast-capitalism, and the cultural logic of control. *Review of Education, Pedagogy & Cultural Studies, 30*(2), 140–161.

Shagoury, R.E. (2009). *Raising writers: Understanding and nurturing young children's writing development.* Boston, MA: Pearson.

Wilson, M. (2007). Why I won't be using rubrics to respond to students' writing. *English Journal, 96* (4), 62–66.

7

POINT OF VIEW: JEROME C. HARSTE

Diane DeFord

I first met Jerome Harste when I went to Indiana University in 1974 to complete a master's degree. The fact that I stayed on to complete a doctoral degree was due, in large measure, to this man. As a reading professional, he is dedicated to two goals that are critical to learning: inquiry through invitations, and collaboration. What he works to create for himself as a learner he also strives to create for all learners. All of us who studied at Indiana University experienced the call to come to the seminar room to listen to a new idea, to think, to create, and to revise as part of a thought collective (Fleck [1935], 1979).

What I took away from these experiences was the sense that it was not important whether the idea was "good" or not, but that in that thinking together, we learned more. Jerry has put this basic theory into practice across years and across institutions as his students moved on to work at other universities. However, as a collective, his students and colleagues keep the thread of the collaborative thought intact across space and time.

I was asked to provide a theoretical sketch of Jerry's life work. I still feel I am a student of his teaching, even after 30 years of working as a reading educator in higher education. What drew me to him were his academic curiosity and the respect he shows for the learning of teachers and children. I present his point of view as evidenced in his scholarly writing, organizing it within the framework of categories from the Expert Study (Flippo, 1998; refer to Chapter 1 in this book): (1) Combining Reading with Other Language Processes; (2) Contexts, Environment, and Purposes for Reading (3) Developing (or Shaping) Students' Perceptions and Expectations; (4) Materials; and (5) Reading Instruction.

Combining Reading With Other Language Processes

Reading is but one mode of language. In some curriculum models, it is separated from the other modes (speaking, listening, and writing) when "reading instruction" occurs. From Jerry's perspective, this makes learning to read difficult. Rather, reading should be purposefully embedded within settings that encourage speaking, listening, and writing as well. Within his theory of learning, children construct knowledge of the reading process for themselves. He sees the expression of reading, writing, speaking, and listening as *authorship*, and the children as *authors*. As they engage in reading, writing, speaking, or listening, they originate or give existence to their ideas and the meanings they create. This is the way children learn. In fact, this is the way we all learn.

By juxtaposing all of the modes of language within a literacy curriculum, common features become apparent to and supportive of the learner. Harste, Short, and Burke (1988) argue "This is so because reading and writing, like all forms of communication, involve authoring. They are processes in which we originate, negotiate, and revise ideas" (p. 5). In this view, learners seek to make sense of and use information from their current hypotheses, interests, needs, and purposes to make meaning or form ideas. The curriculum framework that grows out of this perspective is termed the *authoring cycle* by Jerry and his colleagues. The authoring cycle is actually a metaphor for the learning cycle that occurs when children engage in complex literacy events.

An expanded notion of the authoring cycle as a curricular framework was published in the volume *Creating Classrooms for Authors and Inquirers* (Short, Harste, & Burke, 1996). The new vision infuses their beliefs about learning, language, and social relationships through an inquiry curriculum. The focus on inquiry connects theory and practice as a curricular framework for making decisions about learning *with* learners rather than *for* learners.

Harste combines reading with other language processes to accomplish similar goals articulated by the other experts within this volume. When reading and writing are purposely embedded within a curriculum model that highlights authoring and inquiry, learners make meaning and connections through any communication systems available within the setting (language, drama, art, math, and music). Communication is expanded, as is the learner's potential, when the language arts curriculum focuses on the social and psychological strategies of successful learners as they employ the language arts as both tools and toys for learning. This stance facilitates learning to read as well as learning of the other communication systems.

Contexts, Environments, and Purposes for Reading

One thread that is visible across Harste's scholarly writing is his belief that a low-risk environment facilitates learning. The learning setting must provide unlimited time to engage in rich literacy activities that provide demonstrations of reading and writing as ways of exploring and expanding the learner's personal world. In his words, this is a "self-maintaining environment" (Harste et al., 1988, p. 117). Another critical ingredient in his supportive context is social interaction. These natural language contexts provide ample opportunities for learning, to engage in and see others engaged in purposeful literacy activities, and to engage in collaborative inquiry.

This perspective offers a conception of curriculum as made up of literacy events, with literacy events made up of demonstrations and engagements. By engaging in literacy events and observing demonstrations by other literacy learners, readers and writers will become strategic, or able to vary the content of their strategies and the contexts of their use as needed (Harste, 1986). Some of the contexts that will provide these opportunities for learners include writing and reading to others, producing newspapers, writing and sharing poetry, reading and sharing literature, and reading and writing for a variety of purposes (e.g., journals, stories, information, and lists). When children learn in settings that acknowledge the social and functional nature of language, they learn what it is important to attend to and why (Harste et al., 1988).

As Short et al. state (1996), "Curriculum as inquiry is a philosophy, a way to view education holistically" (p. 51). This view of curriculum embraces teachers and students as authors and inquirers studying real issues (e.g., access, equity, and justice), looking for alternate answers and interpretations through multiple literacies (through the use of language, mathematics, art, music, movement, and other sign systems) to explore and expand our world.

Developing (or Shaping) Students' Perceptions and Expectations

Within the authoring cycle, children learn through engagement and demonstration. As a group of children discuss and reflect on what worked and what did not work, they "come to value the strategies of successful language use and learning" (Harste et al., 1988, p. 119). As they come to value language, learning, and the strategies that make them successful in literacy activities, they become conscious rather than intuitive in their actions. Harste et al. (1988) state that "with this consciousness comes choice, and with choice comes empowerment" (p. 110). It is this process that shapes children's perceptions and expectations.

Children who have come to own reading and writing in these powerful ways interact with and are actively involved in their world as literate beings. They come to see and appreciate their world in new ways. Jerry recounts a story told by Heidi Mills (Harste et al., 1988, p. 121) about a preschooler from her classroom on a field trip to the post office. The young child told Heidi, "I can hardly wait to get back to school to write about this in my journal!"

Writing is a way of recounting, remembering, and recasting experience to share with others. It provides a different way for the learner to live through the experience at the time the experience is occurring, as well as at different times. As readers and writers shift perspective from participant to spectator, from monitor to critic, from speaker to listener, and from reader to writer or artist, they come to understand the multiple roles they can take as a member of a literate society. This shapes their perceptions and expectations (of self and others) and expands their communication potential.

In his most recent writing, in *Creating Critical Classrooms: Reading and Writing with an Edge* (Lewison, Lealand, & Harste, 2008), Jerry and his colleagues go beyond shaping perceptions and expectations by adopting a more critical stance. In his most important work to date, Lewison et al. (2008) promote an instructional model of critical literacy that is based in critical pedagogy and theories of social justice to create personally responsible citizens. They see critical literacy instruction as "a transaction among the personal and cultural resources we use, the critical social practices we enact, and the critical stance that we and our students take on in classrooms and in the world" (p. 5).

This critical literacy curriculum described by Lewison et al. (2008) has four dimensions of critical social practice that are used as tools in planning curricular engagements:

> Disrupting the commonplace;
> Interrogating multiple viewpoints;
> Focusing on sociopolitical issues; and
> Taking action and promoting social justice.
>
> *p. 7*

These dimensions of this critical literacy curriculum grew out of a synthesis by Lewison, Flint, and Van Sluys (2002) of the professional literature and research conducted on critical literacy across the past three decades. In my view, this is the most important literacy research that has been conducted in the past 10 years and beyond. As Lewison et al. (2002) argue:

> By making a decision to use critical social practices, teachers create spaces that have the potential for students to disrupt what is considered to be normal by asking new questions, seeing everyday issues through new lenses, demystifying naturalized views of the world, and visualizing how things might be different.
>
> *p. 7*

This was a perspective first articulated by Giroux (1994). Through the use of critical literacy practices, Lewison et al. (2002) believe students learn how social and cultural forces shape the choices they make, and they engage in inquiry to confront the real-world issues that impact their lives; constructing knowledge, not consuming it, taking responsibility to inquire, and acting to promote social justice. Through this critical stance, Harste and his colleagues impact as well as inform the contexts and practices of reading instruction in today's and tomorrow's classrooms about reading and writing *on the edge*.

Materials

I visited the Center for Inquiry several years ago, the school that Jerry and his colleagues developed that is based on these theoretical perspectives. As I observed children at work, it was clear that life experiences were the cornerstone upon which the curriculum is negotiated. The materials of instruction were predominantly those that supported learning in general, and literacy development specifically. Reading, writing, speaking, listening, drama, music, and art were the multimodal experiences in which children were engaged. Consequently, there was a variety of text materials that met the range of life experiences children encountered in the real world—a range of literature (fiction and non-fiction, poetry, magazines, newspapers, lists, labels, descriptions, reports, and journals). The classrooms were rich in art supplies, props for drama and movement, and artifacts from the world.

As Harste et al. (1988) write in *Creating Classrooms for Authors*:

> There is in this sense no "pure" act of reading or writing—writers talk, read, write, listen, draw, and gesture, all in the name of writing; readers discuss ideas they find problematic, listen, sketch, underline, and do a number of other things, all in the name of reading.
>
> *p. 53*

The range of experiential, cultural, and linguistic resources that students bring is the center of the curriculum that can touch their lives and passions, as well as meet their needs. The methods used in the critical classroom are negotiated between what the kids want to learn, and the teachers' goals. In one vignette from *Creating Critical Classrooms* (Lewison et al., 2008), the stories of two young girls in a multi-age, multicultural, and multilingual classroom (Grades 4–6) illustrate how open choice engagements touch the "life-space" and passions of learners, and position them to use their strengths to learn collaboratively about and through literacy.

Sara arrived in the United States from Algeria. She spoke Berber, Arabic, and French, but not English. Her new classroom, Room 4, was also very different from the classrooms she had been in back in Algeria. With so much being so new, Sara spent a lot of time at first observing what the other kids were doing. After a mini-lesson on how to write in their writer's notebooks, the teacher wrote a message to Sara's father, who could read English:

> A notebook is a tool for thinking … a place to keep ideas. Today we talked about 'firsts' but again the topic is not mandated. Please encourage Sara to write at home each night and in class when we have notebooks out.
>
> *p. 26*

The teachers describe how Sara wrote in Arabic in her notebook, and how the children she sat with became interested in Arabic script. Using globes, they wrote about places they had been and drew maps to go along with their texts. As Sara and the children shared their experiences together using a variety of medium and sign systems, she began to use more English—but composing in Arabic was always her first step into writing. Her father helped her with the English translations at home. So Sara was able to learn using a variety of previous and current experiences, and relate to new experiences through her strengths. Eventually, she was writing in both Arabic and English.

The writer's notebook and open invitations allowed Sara to form connections between home and school, with her classmates and teachers, with the language strengths she brought to the classroom, and to communicate with others while simultaneously learning about reading, writing, speaking, and listening in a new language.

These same teachers shared another vignette that illustrates how books can relate to the life-space of learners. Rachael, an African American girl, the oldest of seven children, came to Room 4 as a new student. She lamented previous academic struggles "catching up on stuff" (p. 26). Rachael used the writer's notebook to write about her family and childhood stories. She also formed connections with books like Alice Hoffman's (1991) *Amazing Grace*, Jacqueline Woodson's (2001) *The Other Side*, and *The Circuit: Stories from the Life of a Migrant Child* (Jiménez, 1998). When they read *Just Juice* (Hesse, 1998), Rachael saw commonalities between herself and the main character:

> She [Juice] took care of her brothers and sisters a lot and helped out her mom. She told things about her mom, like whenever a guest comes over she brings out the sugar cubes and things and she describes her sisters and how they are, like she knows them. She helped her mom when she was going through birth.
>
> *p. 27*

Rachael connected strongly with these books because she knows a lot about bearing and raising children and caring for other people. In this classroom, she became a respected resource as the class began to study "Birth and Pregnancy" within one of the classroom learning centers. Rachael worked for weeks on a PowerPoint presentation that described how she was just like Grace in *Amazing Grace*—she could do anything if she put her mind to it. Her classmates also recognized Rachael because she could read *The Other Side* in a way that sounded like poetry. They asked her to read it aloud again and again. Later in the year, Rachael described her school experience as being better than in previous years. She talked about her ability to get things done even though everything wasn't necessarily easy, and that she was interested in what she was learning. She was now an active agent (she has taken on *agency)* in her own learning.

Creating Critical Classrooms: Reading and Writing with an Edge (Lewison et al., 2008) describes the work of dedicated teachers who construct a curriculum around the big ideas that matter to children. The work they describe, from morning meetings, debates on social artifacts, museum exhibits, posters that interrogate the commonplace, research projects conducted to understand sociopolitical issues like hunger in the world and in their own town, or discussions of risky books, all demonstrate how to touch the life-space of students and create exemplary literacy practices intended to liberate the minds of the children they teach. Because no text is neutral (oral, written, visual, theatrical, or artistic, etc.), taking a critical stance is an obligation as well as a right.

Reading Instruction

Across the different books and articles written by Harste and his colleagues, one central theme is clearly articulated—language, communication, learning, and inquiry must be part of the social fiber of the life of teachers and children. The teachers are reflective and intentional—seeking to reflect on their own work and world, and guiding children to do the same. The lessons that are embedded in the critical classroom must address students' learning needs, but also fulfill a primary goal—for students to take on agency, or the ability to act independently and make their own choices.

In his earlier writing, this theme is enacted through a dynamic literacy curriculum wherein the teacher's goal is to introduce, support, and guide students to incorporate the range of strategies and options available to them to process written language. While this goal is met throughout the school day as learners engage with and observe literacy activities, it also happens through an intentional frame of strategy lessons. "Strategy lessons help make students consciously aware of their strategies; this awareness makes choice possible and allows learners to be strategic" (Harste et al., 1988, p. 102).

Through the vehicle of strategy lessons, learners explore how language operates. Children learn about new forms of language, about different genres, new techniques, and new ways to use language within and across written language events. From a natural language setting (the reading of a book rich in description, for example), students might have an opportunity to discuss how description paints a picture that is vivid for the reader. Connections are then made to their own writing, and to other books they have read. Finally, they have an opportunity to return to their own writing and reading to apply what they have learned about the purpose or function of description in text. They learn how to use description to clarify their own meaning or get closer to the author's meaning. Most importantly, no strategy lesson has only one aspect of language in operation—rather, many language lessons could be demonstrated and explored, but, for the teacher's purposes, one aspect is highlighted. "Strategies are not given as formulas or rules to be applied, but rather as options that can be used to construct meaning" (Harste et al., 1988, p. 101).

The teacher selects different strategy lessons across the year, focusing in each instance on the strategies used by successful readers. A student may also notice a strategy that has been helpful. The goal is to discuss and demonstrate what happens within the reading and writing process in psychological as well as socio-logical terms. Self-correction and monitoring, and talking with peers and brain-storming, are examples of these psychological and sociological strategies. The teacher observes patterns within reading and writing to determine what types of strategy lessons are needed. Some of these might have the following foci:

> What do I do when I come to something I do not know when I am reading?
> How are different genres organized?
> How do I use what I know when reading new material?
> What did what I just read mean? How might I paraphrase this?
> What do I do when I am stuck and do not know what to write next?

The goal of these complex interactions within the ongoing life of the classroom is that strategies from the instructional setting are taken on and used by the students as part of the authoring cycle, and also as a way to learn in general, in and out of school. Scibior (1986) studied the authoring cycle within the classroom setting and found that even though the teachers saw each of the steps of the authoring cycle as distinct, the children began to use this as a learning cycle or a general process framework that guided their learning.

In his most recent writing, the theme of language, communication, learning, and inquiry as part of the social fiber of the life of teachers and children is enacted in a critical literacy curriculum. Harste and colleagues (Lewison et al., 2008) make a compelling case for personal responsibility and social action—for teachers and children to be actors in the world rather than spectators. They believe learners have a responsibility to inquire, interrogate, and position themselves in the world with a critical stance. They demonstrate that teachers can encourage student investigations, taking a "problem-posing" rather than a "problem-solving" stance to curriculum: Are boys better at sports or math than girls? What does this author want you to believe? Is this what *you* believe? In this way, students play a major role in decisions about the curriculum; engage in planning, gathering resources, and assessing their own learning. Teachers become partners with students in meaningful inquiry.

The import of these ideas to the educational community is a message of social action and social justice. As participants in a critical literacy community, each of us is a part of the social contract of learners and actors in the world. We engage in grand conversations, share and explore the meanings that we create, and greet opportunities to explore as well as critique what we read and write. In this way, we ask questions about our world, learn, take responsibility, and seek to make a difference. "Critical literacy begins with awareness, ends in social action, and, in between, supports us envisioning a different world" (Lewison et al., 2008, p. 127). This is Jerry Harste's view of literacy teaching and learning to create a more just and equitable world.

References

Fleck, L. (1979). *Genesis and development of scientific fact.* Chicago, IL: University of Chicago Press [originally published 1935].

Flippo, R.F. (1998). Points of agreement: A display of professional unity in our field. *The Reading Teacher, 52,* 30–40.

Giroux, H.A. (1994). *Disturbing pleasures: Learning popular culture.* London, UK: Routledge.

Harste, J.C. (1986). *What it means to be strategic: Good readers as informants.* Paper presented at the National Reading Conference, Austin Texas.

Harste, J.C., Short, K.G., & Burke, C.L. (1988). *Creating classrooms for authors: The reading–writing connection.* Portsmouth, NH: Heinemann.

Hesse, K. (1998). *Just Juice.* New York, NY: Scholastic.

Hoffman, A. (1991). *Amazing Grace.* New York, NY: Dial.

Jiménez, F. (1998). *The circuit: Stories from the life of a migrant child.* Albuquerque, NM: University of New Mexico Press.

Lewison, M., Flint, A.S., & Van Sluys, K. (2002). Taking on critical literacy: The journey of newcomers and novices. *Language Arts, 79* (5), 382–392.

Lewison, M., Lealand, C., & Harste, J.C. (2008). *Creating critical classrooms: K-8 reading and writing with an edge.* New York, NY: Lawrence Erlbaum Associates.

Scibior, O.S. (1986). *Reconsidering spelling development: A socio-psycholinguistic perspective.* Unpublished doctoral dissertation, Indiana University, Bloomington.

Short, K.G., Harste, J.C., & Burke, C. (1996). *Creating classrooms for authors and inquirers.* Portsmouth, NY: Heinemann.

Woodson, J. (2001). *The other side.* New York, NY: Putnam Juvenile.

8

POINT OF VIEW: WAYNE R. OTTO

Robert T. Rude

The year was 1970. We were in the midst of the Vietnam War and the accompanying protests by college and university students across the United States. The streets passing through the University of Wisconsin-Madison campus were littered with bricks that students, standing on the roofs of high-rise dormitories, had thrown on the patrolling National Guardsmen below them. Innocent students, myself included, were tear-gassed by police brought on campus to control the unrest and protests. Universities—indeed, the country—were being ripped apart at the seams. It was the age of Robert McNamara, Secretary of Defense, and his systems approach to solving the problems of the world. Quantifying educational outcomes in terms of behavioral objectives was a part of many school curricula. It was in this context that the Wisconsin Prototypic Reading System, later known as the *Wisconsin Design for Reading Skill Development* (1970), was born.

The *Design*, as it became known, was developed at the Wisconsin Research and Development Center for Cognitive Learning, one of a handful of educational research centers around the United States. Under funding from the US Department of Education, the *Design* was spearheaded by principal investigator Wayne Otto and a staff of full-time employees and graduate students at the University of Wisconsin-Madison. The ultimate goal of these research and development centers was to infuse the developed programs into US schools.

Wayne's *Design* was truly a grassroots phenomenon. Over the years, administrators, reading specialists, and teachers in several schools and school districts in the Madison, Wisconsin, area had worked with the Research and Development Center staff in an attempt to develop a consensually agreed upon list of reading skills that students should know before they graduated from elementary school. The list eventually consisted of six elements: Word Attack, Comprehension,

Study Skills, Self-Directed Reading, Creative Reading, and Critical Reading. One of the major accomplishments of the *Design* team was to develop and field test a series of criterion-referenced reading tests that teachers could use to measure student skill acquisition. The plan was to design tests for the Word Attack element first, then the Study Skills, followed by the Comprehension element. Finally, the latter three sections of the program—Self-Directed, Creative, and Critical Reading—would be fine-tuned, although there was never an intent to develop criterion-referenced tests for these facets of reading. They were always considered candidates for the more open-ended objectives of the affective domain.

The former three components were developed in roughly that sequence. They lent themselves to being evaluated more readily with formal paper-and-pencil tests than did the latter three areas. The Word Attack element, for example, consisted of 45 skills, 39 of which were measured with paper-and-pencil tests. The latter three components did not lend themselves to criterion-referenced measures as readily, and were therefore left more to teachers' interpretation of how to assess and implement the respective skills. The time, resources, and money needed to conceptualize, pilot test, revise, field test, and finally market each of the *Design* components was considerable.

In the early and mid-1970s, teachers relied heavily on basal readers and workbooks. Few integrated literature with reading as we know it today. A small percentage of teachers dabbled with the individualized reading of trade books, but for the most part instruction was driven by published basal reading systems. In the context of this regimented instructional milieu, the *Design* was cutting-edge. Students in the *Design* were administered the criterion-referenced "mastery tests" in groups, the tests were machine or hand scored, and instructional groups were formed based on skill needs. The *Design* allowed teachers to use virtually any basal reader or trade books, and yet keep a systemized accounting of the reading skills that each child knew. An additional component of the program was a McBee keysorting system (this was long before personal computers and database management systems were found in schools) that could be used for determining skill needs. Finally, there was a file folder system—a compendium of teaching ideas and related materials, one folder for each skill—that enabled teachers to quickly determine what type of instruction (or materials) could be used during ad hoc skill group sessions. Thus the *Design* was a management system that could be overlaid onto any reading program or plan, thereby providing teachers with a means of knowing what each student knew at any point in time. Teachers could be accountable.

Wayne's *Design* attempted to provide teachers with what they intuitively knew would work with children-focused reading instruction. This is not unlike the principle that guides today's Reading Recovery teachers when they observe children "Roaming the Known." Reading Recovery teachers, however, work with individuals, not groups, and they attempt to build on students' strengths, whereas the *Design* was predicated on finding children's weaknesses and then eliminating these skill deficits. The *Design* was based on a deficit (medical) model similar to that used at reading clinics throughout the country: find out what is wrong with the student (patient) and then remediate the problem (disease).

Critics of the *Design* argued that you should not teach reading skills in isolation. It was never the intent of the program, however, that these skills would be taught in a contextual void. The intent was to provide teachers with a system that would free children—as soon as possible—from the drudgery of decoding, and get them into reading meaningful text. Nevertheless, some teachers, perhaps those looking for simple solutions to complex problems, began to instruct students almost exclusively with worksheets and dittos that took reading from its meaningful contextual setting and put it into an isolated skill-and-drill routine. In its worst manifestation, some teachers stopped teaching "reading" altogether and only taught "skills." Children were left on their own to discover the joy of literature. For the most part, however, the *Design* was used as a system to piggyback on top of the existing basal reading programs, thereby ensuring that students did not miss essential skills.

One of the many positive outcomes of the *Design*'s commercial publication by National Computer Systems was that teachers and administrators were introduced to a legitimate alternative to basal reader instructional programs. Wayne and the other developers did not see the *Design* as a replacement for these programs, but simply as a supplement for those teachers wishing to move beyond the current state of reading instruction at the time. The *Design* was a springboard enabling teachers to be responsible, professional decision-makers regarding their students. No longer were they limited solely to the scope-and-sequence charts and plans found in commercial basal readers. In that sense, the *Design* was a breakthrough. Furthermore, teachers in the same school or same district who used the *Design* began to communicate with each other about their students' progress, as well as how they went about their day-to-day reading instruction. This collaboration also had a positive effect on teachers throughout the country.

In the early to mid-1970s and in the 1980s, however, alternative views of reading began to develop. *The Reading Miscue Inventory* was developed by Yetta Goodman and Carolyn Burke (1972). Teachers began exploring how reading skills could be viewed from a psycholinguistic perspective. Slowly, the importance of a reader's background knowledge and its role in understanding text began to be understood. Qualitative differences in miscues were studied. The psycholinguistic movement helped teachers view reading from a variety of perspectives, the most important one being that the reader's behavior was influenced by a variety of cue sources. Goodman and Burke's investigations were followed by the work of Richard Anderson and his associates (1985) at the Center for the Study of Reading at the University of Illinois. Anderson and his colleagues focused much of their landmark work on the area of reading comprehension. Also in the early to mid-1970s, Frank Smith's views on reading education began to popularize the need for putting both reading and writing in meaningful contexts (1973). Smith espoused the close interrelationship between reading and writing. The later works of Donald Graves (1983), Jane Hansen (1987), Lucy Calkins (1986), and Nancie Atwell (1987) have helped us integrate the reading–writing connection.

More recently, Pat Cunningham and Richard Allington (1999), as well as others, have taken reading instruction to a new level of practicality by focusing on classroom practices that work. Integrating the language arts on a day-by-day level has been explored. Reading Recovery teaching strategies popularized by Marie Clay (1991) have proven effective for beginning readers. The training of Reading Recovery teachers has taught us much about the positive collaborative effects of working together as professionals, and the importance of careful observation of student reading behavior. Thus, in the 40-plus years since Wayne and his colleagues conceptualized the *Design*, the field of reading instruction has continued to evolve and mature. Likewise, we as professionals have refined our views of the reading process. Today, we understand much better what it takes to become a mature reader. With that brief historical context, some specific comments regarding the *Design* and what we know about reading instruction today are in order.

Combining Reading with Other Language Processes

It is unfortunate that the *Design* was seen only as a stand-alone skills emphasis program. The skill development aspect was merely a means to an end, and not an end in itself. Wayne and his colleagues expected that teachers would integrate the *Design* with the other language arts skills in their instructional program. The *Design* was never touted as a complete reading system—only as a means of monitoring a student's skill development. Today, of course, we recognize more fully the interrelatedness of reading, writing, listening, and speaking. Language is language. Yet there are still students who benefit from focused skill instruction. Interestingly, the reading skills identified within the *Design* are still found in virtually every reading program on the market.

Contexts, Environment, and Purposes for Reading

Today, astute teachers accept the fact that we—students and adults alike—learn primarily in two ways: through our experiences, and by having good models. We also understand that background experiences play a heavy role in understanding what we read. There is consensus that good teachers of reading model appropriate reading behavior for their students. A 10-minute read-aloud each day sends a powerful message to students. It helps teachers say, "I value reading.

As a model, I'm showing you how good readers read." Eventually, all readers will be asked to read silently, however. Therefore, it is important that students be given ample time for silent reading in their classrooms. The *Design* was intended to see that children had the requisite skills to allow them to pursue this independent silent reading, whether it be expository or narrative text. Again, the *Design* was only a monitoring system for skills—not the entire reading system. More than ever before, it is important that today's teachers understand the skill profiles of their students. With today's emphasis on state and national standards, students must be "skill proficient."

Developing (or Shaping) Students' Perceptions and Expectations

If the *Design* was guilty of one shortcoming, it was identifying students' weaknesses rather than their strengths. In the *Design*, students were tested with criterion-referenced tests and grouped together for instruction if they failed to meet a specified criterion level—usually 80% on one of the criterion-referenced paper-and-pencil tests. (Teachers also had the option of making subjective decisions about a student's skill development.) Even in today's more enlightened environment, good teachers use small ad hoc groups to fine-tune students' reading skills and strategies. Their groups are formed after systematically observing the reading and writing behavior of students. The means may be different, but the goal is the same—to develop fluent, independent readers. When students feel good about themselves as readers, they are more apt to choose reading as a leisure activity. A student with a solid skill base is more apt to be a competent reader than is someone with a patchwork skill background. Good teachers, even back in the 1970s and 1980s, knew the importance of a solid skill development base.

Materials

During the development of the *Design*, there was a purposeful decision made not to include instructional material as part of the complete system. Instead, a Teacher's Resource File of teaching ideas and a listing of commercially available instruction materials was keyed to each of the skills in the program. Basal reader workbook pages, skill sheets, games, and kits were all coded to skills included in each of the six elements of the *Design*. Some teachers developed elaborate organizational schemes enabling them to retrieve instructional worksheets, tapes, or games at a moment's notice. Other teachers teamed together and pooled their instructional material in school media centers. These materials were shared by all. The hope was that children, after receiving instruction with these materials, would master the skills and then be turned free to read materials of their choice.

It is interesting to look back at the basal readers of the day. In the 1970s, basals differed only minimally from the old Scott Foresman Dick-and-Jane series. The characters may have changed, but the physical layout of the materials and the stories were basically unchanged from 20 years earlier. More recently, there has been a drastic shift in story content and physical appearance. Basals developed into abridged stories of award-winning Caldecott and Newbery Award books. Famous authors abound. Teachers use the stories in basals to turn student interest to the original works by these famous authors. It is not at all unusual to see and hear first graders talk about Eric Carle, Bill Martin Jr, or Tomie dePaola. Intermediate-grade children discuss Judy Blume, Katherine Paterson, Jerry Spinelli, and Gary Paulsen as if they were familiar neighbors. Does anyone know who penned the infamous Dick and Jane stories? Finally, book reports have been replaced by Book Blurbs, response journals, and Blogs.

Reading Instruction

While we have made tremendous progress in materials development, there are days when I visit school classrooms wondering if we have made any progress in reading instruction. Some classroom teachers continue placing every child in the same book, leaving many readers struggling at their frustration reading level. Some teachers continue to use round-robin oral reading as their primary teaching vehicle. When I ask my undergraduate students what they remember most about their elementary school reading instruction, one topic always surfaces— the dreaded practice of round-robin oral reading. It is invariably hated by all. Yet it still exists. But times are changing. More and more teachers are using silent reading. More and more teachers are systematically observing children engaged in reading and writing activities. More and more teachers are using buddy reading. More and more teachers are using instructional strategies that actually teach children to become better readers. More and more teachers are using effective comprehension strategies. Given what we know today about reading comprehension instruction, the Teacher's Resource File of the *Design* would no doubt be very different from its 1970s incarnation.

Sophisticated teachers of today also understand the qualitative differences among reading miscues. They understand the interrelatedness of the phonological, semantic, and syntactic cueing systems. Young readers are taught that phonics without meaningful contextual reading does not make sense. Young readers are taught metacognitive strategies to help them monitor their reading. If things do not make sense, they are urged to use "fix-up" strategies. Young readers are taught to be writers. Meaning drives all. Without meaning, there cannot be reading. Furthermore, because we understand that background knowledge is such an important component in reading comprehension, we, as teachers, are more willing to accept alternative responses to our comprehension questions. Again, we have learned and grown.

A Personal Concluding Remark

I became a classroom teacher in 1965. When I walked into my first classroom, I had never seen a basal reader. As an undergraduate, my reading methods course was taught by a junior high school English teacher. We spent the semester studying poetry, not learning about teaching reading. Once I entered my first classroom, I learned to follow the teacher's guide religiously, and had my students do round-robin reading and workbook exercises. I knew that it was wrong, but I needed a "life preserver" to keep from drowning in ignorance. Today, more than 45 years later, I teach undergraduate and graduate college students. I am a different person than I was back then. Today, my students know and understand things I never expected myself to know. They use portfolios. We read quality children's literature. We write in our journals. We have book discussions. We have hands-on experiences with culturally diverse students at our field sites. We use technology unheard of in the 1960s. We even dabble in poetry.

Frequently, I am reminded of a story an old-time reading sage once shared. He was giving a keynote address to a group of teachers. When he had finished, one of the participants raised her hand to ask a question. When called on, she read an excerpt from a professional publication to the keynoter.

"So, what do you think of that quote?" she asked the speaker.

The speaker responded, "I think that's the most absurd thing I've ever heard."

"Do you know who wrote that?" the teacher asked.

"No," responded the keynoter.

"YOU DID!" she shrieked.

The keynoter gathered his thoughts, looked the woman in the eye, and replied, "Well, madam … I've changed."

We have all changed. I have changed. Wayne Otto has changed. And you, the reader, have changed. Without change, there cannot be growth. May we all change—and continue to do so during our professional life—so our students become the benefactors of our wisdom and change.

The Past 10 Years: In Retrospect

1.   *What are the most important things that you believe literacy research has shown over the past 10 years? (Positive and/or Negative)*

I will have been retired for 16 years as of June 2011, so although I have been reading lots of books and articles, I have not been reading much of anything that has to do specifically with the teaching/learning of reading. I did, however, "keep up" with the reading research for the previous 30 or so years, and I never thought that the research was having much impact on how reading was being taught in actual classrooms. I suspect that things have not changed very much in the past 10 years.

I don't think that reading/literacy research, per se, will address the real problem. The real problem is the mess that has resulted from letting self-serving politicians and profit-seeking hucksters take control of the context of school and the content of schooling. Diane Ravitch states the case much better than I can in her recent book, *The Death and Life of the Great American School System* (2010a), and sums it up nicely in her *Wall Street Journal* piece (Ravitch, 2010b):

> On our present course, we are disrupting communities, dumbing down our schools, giving students false reports of their progress, and creating a private sector that will undermine public education without improving it. Most significantly, we are not producing a generation of students who are more knowledgable, and better prepared for the responsibilities of citizenship.
>
> *para. 17*

2.   *How do you think this should inform the contexts and practices of reading instruction in the classroom?*

I firmly believe that to teach reading—and to learn to read—what's needed is (a) a teacher who is a skilled and avid reader, and (b) someone who wants to learn to read and is able to do so. (Kids who are physically or emotionally challenged need to have those problems addressed before someone tries to bang phonics—or some other ill-conceived bag of tricks—into their heads. And even then the learner must have—or be mightily encouraged to develop—a will to read.)

References

Anderson, R., Hiebert, E.H., Scott, J.A., & Wilkinson, I.A.G. (1985). *Becoming a nation of readers*. Washington, DC: The National Institute of Education.

Atwell, N. (1987). *In the middle: Writing, reading, and learning with adolescents*. Portsmouth, NH: Heinemann.

Calkins, L. (1986). *The art of teaching writing*. Portsmouth, NH: Heinemann.

Clay, M. (1991). *Becoming literate: The construction of inner control*. Portsmouth, NH: Heinemann.

Cunningham, P.M., & Allington, R.L. (1999). *Classrooms that work: They can all read and write* (2nd ed.). New York, NY: Longman.

Goodman, Y., & Burke, C.L. (1972). *Reading miscue inventory: Procedures for diagnosis and evaluation*. New York, NY: Macmillan.

Graves, D. (1983). *Writing: Teachers and children at work*. Portsmouth, NH: Heinemann.

Hansen, J. (1987). *When writers read*. Portsmouth, NH: Heinemann.

Ravitch, D. (2010a). *The death and life of the great American school system*. New York, NY: Basic Books.

Ravitch, D. (2010b). Why I changed my mind about school reform. *The Wall Street Journal*, March 9. Retrieved from http://online.wsj.com/article/SB100014240527487 04869304575109443305343962.html.

Smith, F. (1973). *Psycholinguistics and reading*. New York, NY: Holt, Rinehart and Winston.

Wisconsin Research and Development Center for Cognitive Learning (1970). *Wisconsin Design for Reading Skill Development*. Minneapolis, MN: National Computer Systems.

9

POINT OF VIEW: GLOBAL PERSPECTIVES ON TEACHING CHILDREN TO READ ENGLISH

Scott G. Paris

The opportunity to write a chapter in the second edition of this book is a rare privilege, because the editor has invited authors to offer scholarly but unabashed personal views of historical trends in the field of reading. Perhaps the chapters will lead to more common ground, shared insights, and shared concerns about how research in the past 10 years has affected reading and, more broadly, literacy assessment and instruction, but I am skeptical because academics have no incentives or traditions to seek consensus. Indeed, academic reputations and tenure are built on new discoveries and perspectives that may be provocative and debatable. It seems ironic to me, therefore, that consensus about the pedagogy of reading in English has emerged during the past 10 years from an unlikely source: national governments. Governments who pay for education are more interested in finding best practices and solutions in teaching and assessing reading than academics who are not accountable for educational achievement of schools and nations. I think that economic and political forces around the world to enhance national literacy levels have stimulated government initiatives to identify effective ways to teach children to read, to train teachers, and to assess academic success. Comparisons of international test results also motivate national reforms in education. The politics of pedagogy, I think, is the global engine driving educators to identify best practices and to use evidence-based instruction, assessment, and materials to teach children to read in English.

As I reflect on the past 10 years of research on reading, the most salient feature is the growing political use of research for the control of pedagogy in English-speaking countries such as the USA, the UK, Australia, New Zealand, and Singapore. National commissions and reports in these countries in the past 10 years have had dramatic impact on national policies and classroom practices, and they reach similar conclusions. I will review some of these reports and ensuing pedagogical strategies to highlight the global movement toward common solutions. My focus in this review is on similar approaches to assessing and teaching English reading to young children around the world, because there has been a global impetus in the search for common solutions that must be acknowledged. After describing these similarities, I will point out some risks in homogeneous pedagogy, and describe why similar goals among national policies for reading do not need to lead to single-minded methods for teaching reading.

Significant Reports in the USA

Periodic research reviews and syntheses in the USA have had enormous influence in directing research, practice, and policy-making. For example, *Beginning to Read: Thinking and Learning About Print* (1990), by Marilyn Adams, was one of the first compilations of the research on the importance of "bottom-up" processes, including phonemic awareness, phonological and orthographic skills, and fluent decoding skills. It was published during a period in American reading education when there were genuine arguments about whether priority in early reading instruction should be given to bottom-up or top-down processes, when teachers were confronted with a variety of approaches from Australia, New Zealand, and the UK, and when American publishers were trying to offer teachers newer, better, and different basal reading series. The clash between approaches was characterized as the "Reading Wars," but it might be more apt to describe it as a "free market" enterprise. The "Reading Wars" were ideological in many ways, with whole language and phonics instruction characterized as polar opposites, but throughout the 1990s the debate became more informed by scientifically-based reading research.

Two seminal events culminated in the end of the Reading Wars and marketplace competition. First, in 1998, Snow, Burns and Griffin published *Preventing Reading Difficulties in Young Children*, a report commissioned by the National Academy of Education, and then, in 2000, the National Reading Panel (NRP), commissioned by the Institute of Education Sciences, issued its report that identified (among other things) five essential skills of reading. These reviews were comprehensive and scholarly; they received international respect for their methods and conclusions; and they had enormous impact on policy-makers. The effects trickled down quickly to state departments, local districts, and educational publishers, who in turn revised instructional materials, assessments, and professional development training to be aligned with the NRP Report. Criticisms based on the select NRP membership, the exclusion of many research studies in the meta-analyses, and the stringent criteria used to evaluate studies were overwhelmed by the scientific credibility of the report and the emerging consensus on how best to teach reading.

The NRP Report provided the scientific basis for the No Child Left Behind Act of 2001 (NCLB), a sweeping reform of reading and mathematics education in the USA that imposed specific benchmarks of success (i.e., adequate yearly progress, AYP) and consequences for schools who did not meet AYP. States were required to establish achievement tests to be given annually to students in Grades 3–8 to measure AYP, and thus assessments drove the reform and, by implication, what and how reading was taught. Despite the good intentions, the government did not provide the resources to support such large-scale changes in reading assessment and instruction, and the unattainable goals of 100% of students meeting AYP doomed most schools to failure. Political rhetoric and ambitions were not translated into effective pedagogical practices, so states were forced to "game the system"—for example, by retaining students in grade and by creating easier state-wide tests so more schools could demonstrate AYP. In retrospect, it is remarkable how quickly research was distilled to a few core principles that provided benchmarks for success with corresponding policies and penalties.

The Reading First part of NCLB was the specific legislation that provided more than 5 billion dollars to K-3 classrooms to support reading education, and it was controversial because it specified that programs and materials must be based on "scientifically-based reading research." It was barely acknowledged that this type of evidence is derived almost entirely from a psychological, cognitive, and quantitative orientation to reading research, so the search for evidence was biased from the start. Of course, the evidence was provided by the NRP and clearly favored a primary emphasis on skills related to decoding and automatic word recognition, so schools were forced to choose instructional programs that emphasized phonics, decoding, fluency, and basic skills if they wanted federal funds. Even after political scandals and compromises within the Reading First bureaucracy, it remained the main source of funding for reading education in the USA.

In 2008, the National Early Literacy Panel released a report entitled *Developing Early Literacy* (NELP, 2008) in which they investigated the scientific evidence for factors, programs, and conditions, from birth to age 5 years, that had significant impact on the development of early literacy. Like the NRP, the panel used rigorous criteria for including studies in the meta-analyses, and culled about 300 studies from over 7000 to use as primary evidence. The panel concluded that six variables have consistent and large impact on literacy development, and are significant predictors of literacy skills at preschool and kindergarten. These are alphabet knowledge, phonological awareness, rapid automatic naming (RAN) of digits or letters, writing letters or one's name, and phonological memory; the meta-analysis also showed that code-focused instructional programs had the largest effects on early literacy development. Thus, the national reports over the past 10–20 years have revealed consistent scientific evidence for the importance of code-based skills to promote early literacy and to prevent reading difficulties. Although academics have more varied opinions of the research and the conclusions, policy-makers regard the evidence as solid, and that it provides common solutions for reading pedagogy.

From my perspective, the reports have had long-lasting and far-reaching consequences. There have been many benefits of the research syntheses, but let me point out two persistent problems. One is the emphasis on prevention of reading failure rather than a focus on nurturing learning and motivation to read. Reports in the 1990s were aimed at preventing reading failure and helping struggling readers. The focus on prevention is a perspective from special education and early childhood education, not the field of reading psychology or literacy education, and it has connected assessment to instruction with overarching goals of prevention and remediation of early difficulties. The clearest evidence of the connection and popularity of the remedial approach is the popularity of early reading assessments that give priority to basic skills such as letter knowledge, phonemic awareness, and fluency measures or fast decoding. Many states (e.g., Texas, Michigan, Illinois) created their own assessments of early reading skills that gave priority to the skills in the NRP. The *Dynamic Indicators of Basic Early Literacy Skills* (DIBELS, Good & Kaminski, 2002) quickly became a popular assessment tool to screen and monitor children who are learning to read. It was then connected to a model of remedial instruction known as Response to Intervention (RTI), in which students who scored poorly on DIBELS (or similar assessments) were given instruction on those same skills. The methods were derived from special education, and follow a traditional behavioral format of diagnostic testing followed by progressively intense instruction on low-performing skills. My main concern about the DIBELS–RTI connection is the narrowness of the reading assessments that focus on fluent decoding, with little attention to comprehension, vocabulary, new media literacies, strategic and purposeful reading, and motivated uses of reading for learning. Reading words quickly, the benchmark of success with DIBELS, is simply not an adequate goal for young readers.

A second consequence of the reports is growing consensus about the kinds of research that count and the kinds that do not. The repeated use of the phrases "scientifically-based research evidence" in the NRP reinforced the importance of experimental methods, quantitative measures, and large-scale randomized field trials as the "gold standard" of research. Although rigorous methods are desirable, they are not always possible, and dismissing all other research evidence ignores valuable insights, especially qualitative insights about idiosyncratic schools and students. The drive to find common solutions cannot exclude studies of students with special needs, students with inadequate opportunities to learn, and unusual contexts of learning just because independent variables cannot be controlled. Relegating such differences to "error variance" by randomization does not provide information about teaching special children in special circumstances. I am concerned that nationally commissioned reports over-simplify pedagogy in order to identify uniform policies for teaching reading, and we know that there is no quick fix or single method for teaching all children to read.

Reading Pedagogy in the UK

In the past 10 years, English-speaking countries around the world have emulated the USA's model of national reports as the basis for reforming reading education, and, indeed, primary education more broadly. The Rose Report (Rose, 2006) provides a good summary of trends in literacy education in England, as well as significant recommendations for how to teach beginning reading. The National Curriculum in England from 1989 to 1998 provided guidelines for teaching reading, but apparently was not successful in raising literacy levels of students. Thus, the National Literacy Strategy (NLS) was implemented in 1998 (later revised as the Primary National Strategy), with a stronger focus on teaching decoding skills to children early and explicitly. The teaching methods relied heavily on systematic phonics instruction that matches graphemes with phonemes in regular lessons. The Rose (2006) review of research included many of the same studies as the NRP in the USA, but also a wider collection of reading research in the UK. Not surprisingly, the conclusions were similar.

Having considered a wide range of evidence, the review concluded that the case for systematic phonic work is overwhelming and much strengthened by a synthetic approach, the key features of which are to teach beginning readers:

- grapheme/phoneme (letter/sound) correspondences (the alphabetic principle) in a clearly defined, incremental sequence,
- to apply the highly important skill of blending (synthesizing) phonemes in order, all through a word, to read it,
- to apply the skills of segmenting words into their constituent phonemes to spell,
- that blending and segmenting are reversible processes (Rose, 2006, p. 20).

Rose (2006) reviewed evidence that shows systematic phonics instruction can be supported by assessments that are detailed and specific so the results can be connected to instruction, a model similar to the DIBELS–RTI alignment. Instruction on systematic phonics can also be supported by decodable books, ICT software, and a variety of commercial materials, but Rose (2006) cautions that each must provide comprehensive, explicit, and sequential instruction on phonics. Formal instruction can begin with pre-reading activities from about ages 3–5 years, a period labeled the Early Years Foundation Stage in the PLS, but the onset and pace of systematic instruction must be gauged for individual children. Moreover, early reading activities with teachers and parents should include play as well as instruction, and should provide social interactions that bolster children's confidence and enjoyment with emerging literacy. The English perspective is broader and more social than the American reports.

Rose (2006) described three waves of intervention for struggling readers. Wave 1 includes all children in daily, high quality instruction. Wave 2 includes specific interventions to bring students up to grade-level expectations. Wave 3 includes personalized action plans similar to Individual Education Plans (IEPs) in special education in the USA. American educators will recognize these progressively more intense forms of remedial instruction as similar to tiers 1, 2, and 3 in RTI models of reading instruction. The Rose Report includes additional suggestions for enhancing reading instruction by providing better training for initial teacher training, in-service teacher training, paraprofessionals, and managers and administrators, but "better training" is described as greater understanding of the importance of phonics and decoding skills and how to teach them effectively to beginning readers. The common ground for pedagogy is clear and consistent within the Rose Report, backed by reviews of research, reviews of successful schools, and commentaries by experts in the UK. The scientific basis and the policy outcomes of the Rose Report parallel the impact of the NRP in the USA.

An ambitious national report, the *Cambridge Primary Review*, was released in late 2009 under the authorship of Robin Alexander and a committee of academics. It was the first comprehensive review of education in 40 years in the UK, and boldly points the way to future directions in all aspects of primary education and children's development. The *Review* provides 75 recommendations based on research and discussion that include, among other things, raising the age of school entry to 6 years, reforming teacher education, eliminating the Primary National Strategy, decoupling assessment for accountability from assessment for learning, revising the primary curriculum, reforming funding, and increasing local school autonomy. The recommendations for pedagogy are consistent with previous reports, but the *Review* makes clear that teachers, not policy-makers, need to be in control of instruction. The four summary points about "a pedagogy of evidence and principle" are worth quoting:

> Work towards a pedagogy of repertoire rather than recipe, and of principle rather than prescription.
>
> Ensure that teaching and learning are properly informed by research.
>
> Uphold the principle that it is not for government, government agencies, or local authorities to tell teachers how to teach.
>
> Avoid pedagogical fads and fashions and act instead on those aspects learning and teaching, notably spoken language, where research evidence converges.
>
> *p. 8 in the summary report "Introducing the Cambridge Primary Review," 2009*

The *Cambridge Primary Review* (2009) traces the history of politics, policies, and pedagogy in the UK from 1944 until 2009, and the historical parallels with American political insinuations into classroom pedagogy are remarkable. For example, government intrusion in UK pedagogy increased substantially after 1988 through mandated national curricula and assessments, just as in the USA. The *Review* notes that:

> In contrast to the pre-1988 era, when government intervention in class-room life was minimal, policies are now imposed on teachers at a rate which has made their assimilation and implementation nearly impossible. By one count, between 1996 and 2004 government and national agencies issued 459 documents just on literacy teaching. That's more than one every week for eight years.
>
> *p. 11*

The problems in primary education and reading instruction in the UK and USA are similar in terms of government influence, disparate experiences of children, and diverse training of teachers. The *Cambridge Primary Review* (2009) provides a circumspect view of the key issues; it de-polarizes the arguments; and it re-focuses attention on the needs and rights of children who are facing an unpredictable future. Instead of policy prescriptions, the review admonishes policy-makers to pay attention to the research, to the local community contexts, to a broader curricular agenda, and to the development of teacher competence required to meet the needs of an increasingly diverse population of students.

Global Perspectives

Other countries in which English is the primary language of instruction have experienced similar cycles of reviews and reforms in primary education and reading pedagogy. Singapore, for example, has had numerous new programs initiated by the Ministry of Education, including *Thinking School, Learning Nation* (Goh, 1997), *Teach Less Learn More* (2005), *Curriculum 2015* (2008a, 2008b), and the *Primary Education Review and Implementation* (PERI, 2009). All of these initiatives were designed to broaden Singaporean education from reproductive, fact-based, and test-driven curricula to more innovative and inventive thinking with greater student resilience and autonomous learning. The C2015 and PERI documents have developmental aims for students that are similar to those of the *Cambridge Primary Review*. The PERI seeks to foster in every student "a confident person, a self-directed learner, a concerned citizen, and an active contributor" (p. 3). The pedagogical recommendations are also similar. The PERI suggests that knowledge (i.e., facts) should be balanced with skills and values through broader application of "active learning" in all areas of the curriculum. It suggested moving away from summative examinations and using formative and "bite-sized" assessment on a daily basis to support assessment for learning. This includes more holistic assessments to inspire confidence and motivation in students, and more detailed feedback to students and parents. Like other national reports, PERI recommends investing in a high quality workforce by providing better training and professional development for teachers (PERI Committee, 2009).

New Zealand has reformed literacy education, too, with government documents that describe effective teaching practices for literacy education. A recent document entitled *Literacy Learning Progressions* (2009) provides detailed benchmarks for what students should be able to do with reading and writing in the curriculum at the end of each year of primary education. It is intended to be a tool for professional development so teachers can share similar expectations and aspirations for their students. It is not a pedagogical recipe; it is an effort to establish common ground among teachers for what students should be able to do within the curriculum.

Australian educators have also provided government documents and guidance about early years education and literacy benchmarks for students. Each state and territory designs its own curriculum, pedagogy, and teacher training, with some, such as New South Wales and Queensland, providing emphasis on early years programs for literacy in comprehensive models of innovative pedagogies. However, the lack of comparability of standards and tests among states motivated the creation of the National Assessment Program in Literacy and Numeracy (NAPLAN) in 2008. NAPLAN assesses students in Grades 3, 5, 7, and 9 every year in four core domains; Reading, Writing, Language Conventions (i.e., spelling, grammar, and punctuation), and Numeracy. Standardized scores are reported according to 10 bands of increasing proficiency, and the results are compared among states, territories, and schools. Although some may applaud the uniform benchmarks, critics point out that the summative tests are traditional, and inconsistent with new curricula and productive pedagogies. Australian educators have always emphasized professional development more than standardized tests to provide common understandings among teachers, so the challenge will be to use NAPLAN to support rather than penalize teachers.

Conclusions

There is an unsettling pattern to the international politics of reading pedagogy. It began in the 1980s with increased national and international testing that revealed surprisingly low levels of proficiency. Accusations were leveled at disjointed curricula, low expectations for students, lack of rigor in teaching methods, inadequate materials, and poorly trained teachers. National reviews pointed out that teachers were ignoring the scientific evidence about the importance of teaching basic decoding skills such as the alphabetic principle, phonological awareness, and phonics, so they became more prominent in prescribed practices.

A new wave of instruction aimed at building decoding skills and reading fluency was accompanied by new assessments of early reading. In the USA, federal funding for schools was linked to AYP and reading achievement, and in many countries summative assessments were publicized in league tables that compared and ranked schools, states, and nations. The response in many cases was to design national curricula, uniform pedagogical tactics, and careful monitoring through regular testing. The *Cambridge Primary Review* suggests that government control of literacy education was implemented by stealth in the 1990s, and it aims to redress that trend by empowering local schools to design pedagogies and curricula that serve the students in their communities.

The value of searching for best practices in reading education is to identify effective practices for teaching children to read English, but the liabilities are significant. One danger is that certain kinds of research, mostly psychological and quantitative, are privileged over other types of research. A second danger is that uniform pedagogies and assessments set minimal standards for all students. A third liability is that teachers lose control over classroom instruction, and cannot adjust their teaching methods and materials to the needs and abilities of their students. The *Cambridge Primary Review* warns of the dangers of mandated pedagogy that unduly narrows the curriculum, and it describes how literacy teaching must be embedded in broader contexts of children's educational needs.

Scientific research is pluralistic, multi-disciplinary, exploratory, and often inconclusive, so the search for common ground is motivated by political as much as research or pedagogical goals. Although national policy-makers have the responsibility and authority to design and prescribe national curricula, assessments, and pedagogical methods, this power must be exercised with caution in order to accommodate the needs of diverse students and the talents of individual teachers. The politics of pedagogy should not lead to hegemony or orthodoxy in the search for best practices and the most effective teaching methods.

References

Adams, M.J. (1990). *Beginning to read: Thinking and learning about print*. Cambridge, MA: MIT Press.

Cambridge Primary Review (2009). Cambridge, UK: University of Cambridge, Faculty of Education.

Goh, C.T. (1997). Shaping our future: Thinking Schools, Learning Nation. Speech at the Opening of the 7th International Conference on Thinking on Monday, 2 June 1997. Available: http://www1.moe.edu.sg/speeches/1997/020697.htm

Good, R.H., & Kaminski, R.A. (Eds.). (2002). *Dynamic indicators of basic early literacy skills* (6th ed.). Eugene, OR: Institute for the Development of Educational Achievement.

Ministry of Education New Zealand (2009). *Literacy learning progressions: Meeting the reading and writing demands of the curriculum*. New Zealand: Ministry of Education.

Ministry of Education Singapore (2005). *Nurturing every child: Flexibility & diversity in Singapore schools* (retrieved March 15, 2011, from http://www3.moe.edu.sg/corporate/edu_info_booklet/pdf/edu-booklet english.pdf).

Ministry of Education Singapore (2008a). Speech by Dr Ng Eng Hen, Minister for Education and Second Minister for Defence, at the MOE Work Plan Seminar 2008, on Thursday, September 25, 2008 at 9.30 am at the Ngee Ann Polytechnic Convention Centre (retrieved December 29, 2009, from http://www.moe.gov.sg/media/speeches/2008/09/25/speech-by-dr-ng-eng-henat-the-moe-work-plan-seminar-2008.php

Ministry of Education Singapore (2008b). Recent developments in Singapore's education system: Gearing up for 2015. International Education Leaders' Dialogue: Third Conference (retrieved March 15, 2011, from http://www.eduweb.vic.gov.au/edulibrary/public/commrel/events/ield/singaprecasestudy.pdf

Ministry of Education Singapore (2009). Report of the Primary Education Review and Implementation Committee (retrieved June 3, 2009, from http://www.moe.gov.sg/initiatives/peri/files/peri-report.pdf).

National Early Literacy Panel (2008). *Developing early literacy: Report of the National Early Literacy Panel.* Jessup, MD: National Institute for Literacy.

National Reading Panel (NRP) (2000). *Teaching children to read: An evidence-based assessment of the scientific research literature on reading and its implications for reading instruction: Reports of the subgroups.* Bethesda, MD: NICHD.

No Child Left Behind Act of 2001 (2001). Public Law No. 107–110, paragraph 115 Stat. 1425.

Primary Education Review and Implementation Committee (2009). *Report of the Primary Education Review and Implementation Committee.* Singapore: Ministry of Education.

Rose, J. (2006). *Independent review of the teaching of early reading: Final report.* London, UK: Department for Education and Skills.

Snow, C.E., Burns, S., & Griffin, P. (1998). *Preventing reading difficulties in young children.* Washington, DC: National Academy Press.

10

POINT OF VIEW: LIFE IN THE RADICAL MIDDLE

P. David Pearson

Most days, I think I have adjusted to my role as a member of the radical middle in the debates and discussions of reading theory and practice (Pearson, 1996). I am pretty sure that I am somewhere in the middle, because colleagues in neither the whole language nor the new phonics crowd seem to accept my position. In the 1980s, when whole language ideas about literacy instruction were on the rise, I was often constructed by others as a cognitive behaviorist, a skills monger masquerading as a champion of comprehension and schema theory. More recently, with the political ascendancy of what I call the new phonics—a term I use to characterize what I see as a combined emphasis on phonemic awareness, explicit synthetic phonics instruction, and decodable text—I have been reconstructed by some as a "whole language advocate," a characterization that will no doubt bring a smirk to the lips of respectable whole language folks and a bewildered expression to the countenance of close colleagues and students. Not that there is anything wrong with either position—but neither really fits. I am also pretty sure that I am radical about being there, in the middle. In fact, as the debates go on, ad infinitum, and as the research evidence in favor of centrist positions on curricular and instructional issues piles up, I get more radical every day. Instead, I am someone who has great respect for a middle ground, and I believe that most of my well known work and most of the roles I have played in the field belie this preference. As the most convincing evidence of this middle ground, 1 would point to my editorial role. First as a coeditor of *Reading Research Quarterly*, then as first editor of the original *Handbook of Reading Research*, and later as coeditor of Volumes II and III of the *Handbook*, I have tried to promote paradigmatic tolerance and respect—not always with resounding success, but always with conviction. Even in my less savory role as a basal author (just short, in the eyes of some, of being a demon), my goal was to make sure that reading research was given as much play as market research, and that literature and integrated curriculum were as prominent as skills and strategies.

Sometimes, however, I find myself resenting the implication, more often left unsaid than proudly asserted, that those who occupy the middle of intellectual controversies are just too wishy-washy to stand for something of substance. If I am completely honest, I usually realize that I am the one who attributes—to those who live at the extremes—the accusation that middle grounders are without conviction. And that realization causes me to wonder how deep my convictions really are. This was just such a mood of self-doubt that swept over me when I sat down to write this personal essay about my views of reading theory and practice. Not surprisingly, then, I chose to construct this piece as an apology, an attempt to provide readers (including myself) with as thorough an account as I could muster of why I live in the radical middle.

Let me begin by explaining what I think it means to say I am a member of the radical middle, and then provide the apology. These are the premises, the basic tenets, the fundamental beliefs about reading that prompt me to accept that label.

1. *I subscribe to an interactive model of the reading process.* That model's fundamental principle is that the relationships among reader, text, and context are constantly shifting. Sometimes we reach out to the text, grabbing whatever meaning we can before the text has a chance to fully assert its own. Sometimes we sit back and let the text, and its meaning, come to us. We call the first top-down, inside-out, or hypothesis-driven reading because the reader dominates. We call the second bottom-up, outside-in, or text-driven reading because the text dominates. Sometimes particular purposes, such as updating knowledge when we read the newspaper or trying to get an author's argument straight, determine the stance we take. In my interactive view, whatever we are and whatever we do as readers changes day by day, hour by hour, and moment by moment.

2. *I accept the research suggesting that the most skilled readers are those who have both well-honed automatic word identification processes and rich stores of knowledge that they use to construct, monitor, and refine the models of meaning they construct as they read.* This view is consistent with the fact that I believe both the miscue research of Goodman and colleagues (see, for example, Goodman, 1967), which suggests that good readers are more likely to make meaning preserving miscues, and the eye-movement research reviewed by Adams (1990), which suggests that instead of sampling text to confirm hypotheses, good readers attend to each and every part of each and every word. When readers are in an automatic processing mode, they just move along, recoding everything in sight to a phonological code that can be processed in working memory. But when the going gets tough (as it often does when miscues are more frequent), good readers shift to a conscious-control mode and use every conceivable resource, including context and meaning, to

make sense of things. Thus, good readers are both more skillful at using context, and less reliant on it for basic word identification tasks.

3. *I believe that reading occurs as a fundamentally individual process, with eyes on print, consumed by the goal of creating a satisfactory model of meaning that fits both the facts of the text and the facts that a reader brings to the reading.* But reading is also fundamentally a social process, readily influenced by a wide range of social and cultural factors. In the most obvious social sense, we change our minds about what a text means when we discuss it with others. At a more subtle level, we engage in a conversation with an unknown author when we read his or her text. Even more distant, the same cultural forces, some of them handed down over several generations within a community or a culture, that shape our values and our behavior also shape our reading.

4. *I subscribe to the view that reading is the whole point of reading instruction* (and, by the way, that writing is the whole point of writing instruction). Thus, a curriculum that postpones real reading for more than an instant does kids a disservice by raising in their minds the possibility that reading may not be the point of reading instruction.

5. *I believe that skills are essential features of both reading and reading instruction.* It would be nice—wonderful, in fact—if all kids acquired the skills and strategies they need to be successful independent readers and writers without explicit instruction or any other form of arduous effort on the part of teachers. However both research (see Pearson, 1996; McIntyre & Pressley, 1996) and the experience of teachers suggest that students benefit from the modeling, scaffolding, and guidance that teachers can provide.

6. *I believe skills and skill instruction should always be regarded as means to an end rather than ends unto themselves.* The point of any skill instruction—be it phonics, vocabulary, or comprehension—is that students can understand, appreciate, and critique what they read; in fact, the ultimate test of the efficacy of any skill instruction is not whether students can perform the skill as it was taught, but whether it improves their critical understanding. In a sense, the job of phonics is not completed until a reader finds joy, inspiration, or fault with a text.

7. *I believe that reading and writing are synergistic processes—what we learn in doing the one benefits the other.* And this synergy can be seen in all aspects of the processes, from the level of phoneme–grapheme relations (e.g., invented spelling activities benefiting reading phonics) to genre-like features of text (e.g., reading stories to get ideas for how to structure one's own).

Given these fundamental tenets, my position in the radical middle should be at least a little more transparent; equally transparent should be some of the internal contradictions I live with: top-down and bottom-up, text and reader, individual and social, reading and writing, and equal respect for both authentic activity and explicit skills instruction. But I have told you only what I think it means to occupy the position I do, not why I embrace these beliefs. Here is the why.

Sometimes I think that I have a personal attraction to contradiction and dialectic tension. I sometimes say to myself, "Maybe you just enjoy theoretical inconsistency and internal contradictions; perhaps they are your concession to post-modernism." But reading theory and practice are not the only intellectual arenas in which I find myself attracted to embracing what others see as binary opposites. In educational research more generally, I find the debate about qualitative versus quantitative research about as compelling as the new phonics versus whole language debate. I cannot imagine why any field of inquiry would want to limit itself to a single set of tools and practices. Even though I find both debates interesting and professionally useful, I fear the ultimate outcome of both, if they continue unbridled by saner heads, will be victory for one side or another. That, in my view, would be a disastrous outcome, either for reading pedagogy or for educational research. A more flattering way to express this same position is to say that I have always aspired to the Greek ideal of moderation in all things, or to the oriental notion that every idea entails its opposite. Neither statement would be untrue, but either would fail to capture the enchantment I experience in embracing contradiction.

A second reason for living in the radical middle is the research base supporting it. I read the research implicating authentic reading and writing, and find it compelling. I read the research supporting explicit skill instruction, and find it equally compelling. What occurs to me, then, is that there must be a higher-order level of analysis in which both of these lines of inquiry can be reconciled. That would be a level in which authentic activity and ambitious instruction were viewed as complements rather than alternatives to one another. The radical middle, with its (or rather my) fascination with apparent contradiction, allows me to work comfortably at that level. It is, most likely, exactly this disposition that allowed me, as a member of the panel on which the Expert Study (Flippo, 1998; refer to Chapter 1 in this book) was based, to find so much to agree with in the statements that emerged in each iteration of the agreement process.

Third on my list is the wisdom of practice as I have come to understand it by interacting with scores of classroom teachers. As the new phonics–whole language debate has played itself out in the last few years, I have found the reaction of classroom teachers particularly insightful. The debate rages in the public press and in academic venues; by contrast, my impression from talking to teachers about the debate is that they find it fairly unproductive. They tend toward an enlightened eclecticism when it comes to matters of practice. So they see no contradiction in embracing an authentic writing activity in the same breath as a new approach to teaching conventional grammar. Thus, even though the consensus statements in Chapter 1 represent a display of "eclecticism" from experts who represent very different views of reading contexts and practices, classroom teachers who embrace this eclectic stance probably find many, if not most, of them reasonable and helpful. I would probably side with them.

Those who aspire to theoretical consistency find this sort of eclecticism disturbing because they see it as a disconnection between theory and practice. But I find this negative connotation for eclectic positions surprising, given the traditional denotation of the word. The dictionary definition of eclectic is "selecting or choosing from among various sources." An eclectic stance implies agency (making a selection) and an implicit set of criteria (to make the selection) on the part of the agent. It is exactly this intentionality that I have observed in teachers' eclecticism. My hunch is student engagement (will this appeal to my students?) and perceived helpfulness (will it help them better do their job as readers?) are the two criteria teachers use in deciding whether to incorporate a new practice into their teaching repertoire. It is only fair to confess that I have always taken a decidedly eclectic stance toward my own teaching, both as an elementary classroom teacher and as a college instructor.

Fourth is the modest view of evidence that I hold for the positions we advocate in education. Although I think we have learned a great deal in the past 30 years about the nature and development of the reading process, and even more about instructional practices that promote individual growth in reading (for an account of what I think we have learned, see my review of the Snow, Burns, and Griffin (1998) report sponsored by the National Research Council (Pearson, 1999)), I think we can do better. I think there is still room for more evidence and better methods of inquiry. Whatever the reasons, I cannot rid myself of nagging doubts about the strength and quality of our current evidence. And any time one's confidence is shaky, then dispositions of tolerance (for ideas, practices, and research methods) and inquiry (we should try it out and see what happens) make sense to me.

Fifth, the radical middle provides a nice home for the particular approach to curricular balance that I have been moving toward. The metaphor of the fulcrum of the scales of justice has never particularly appealed to me because it suggests that we are carving out a political balance—balancing off one element from the new phonics with one from whole language, anon, anon. But there is another, more powerful, metaphor in the "balance of nature." In this ecological approach (see Pearson & Raphael, 1999), balance is not a matter of evening the score; instead, it is a matter of assembling an array of skills, strategies, processes, and practices that are sufficiently rich and synergistic to guarantee a full and rich curriculum for all students (one that, incidentally, would honor tenets 4 through 7 in my list of tenets).

So there you have it—my apology for being a member of the radical middle. As I said, it is sometimes a difficult position to maintain. There are those who wonder whether those of us who occupy this middle ground have any standards at all. And there are many ideological bulldozers lurking nearby, ready to forcibly remove us from our newly gained intellectual ground. But it is a satisfying ground to hold. And it offers, unfortunately, all too clear a view of the constant, regular, and periodic swing of the curricular pendulum.

The Past 10 Years: In Retrospect

1. *What are the most important things that you believe literacy research has shown over the past 10 years? (Positive and/or Negative)*

Two things that literacy research has shown over the past 10 years:

*   Integrated curriculum, using reading and writing and language, to support inquiry in the disciplines, promotes both disciplinary learning and literacy acquisition. (Positive)

Summarizing a whole range of research endeavors, Pearson, Moje, and Greenleaf (2010) marshall compelling evidence that reading and writing (and with a somewhat smaller evidence base, oral discourse) promote both the acquisition of knowledge and inquiry in science while also improving literacy learning.

*   Strategy instruction, especially in the ways in which it has been put into practice in modern curriculum (e.g., basals and kits), stands in need of reform. (Negative)

Strategy instruction may not be as effective as conventional discussions that, in one way or another, focus on knowledge acquisition (McKeown, Beck, & Blake, 2009; Wilkinson & Son, 2011). And strategy instruction may breed an excessive reliance on abstract, content-free, metacognitive introspection about strategy use (Pearson & Fielding, 1991).

2. *How do you think this should inform the contexts and practices of reading instruction in the classroom?*

This combination of findings (see above) suggests three modifications to the way in which we teach reading.

We need to keep our eye on the prize of knowledge acquisition (I'd add insights and understandings about the human condition as a big part of that knowledge) as the natural consequence and by-product of reading. This, of course, can be construed as the reading to learn part of reading that has been traditionally thought of as what, in Grade 3 or 4, comes AFTER the learning to read stage of reading development. But we need a more ambitious agenda. Learning should be part of the reading equation from the outset of kindergarten and first grade. Kids should always be reading content that is worth knowing, content that promotes the acquisition of knowledge, insight, human understanding, and joy. And they should be writing about things that matter, about those very understandings, insights, and moments of joy. Then, and only then, will they learn that reading and writing are tools for learning—a message some curricula seem hard pressed to promote.

We'd be better off to think of reading, writing and language as tools for learning that we can readily apply to disciplinary learning, and my disciplinary categories are science, social studies, mathematics, and literature. It's better to think of literature (not language arts but literature) as a discipline on a par with the subject areas of schooling. Then the process parts of the language arts (reading, writing, and language) are released from the sole grasp of literature and available for all the disciplines. Think of it as a matrix with disciplines across the top and tools for learning down the side.

Were we to take such a matrix seriously, we would have very different basal reading programs than those currently on the market, because the distribution of disciplines and genres would be much broader in scope than is currently the case. This broader scope would have the side benefit of broadening the appeal of basal content to a wider range of learners than is possible with the literature-centric basals in today's market. But most important, the acquisition of knowledge, understanding, insight, and (yes) joy would always provide a context for honing our language-based learning tools.

When strategy instruction becomes too generic and abstract, too "isolated" from the goal of acquiring knowledge, it is in danger of becoming an end unto itself—what Pearson and Fielding (1991) speculated might become "introspective nightmares" that were more complicated than the ideas that the strategies were supposed to help students acquire. I am not arguing that we should throw out all forms of strategy instruction. To the contrary, I remain committed to high quality strategy instruction, instruction that demonstrates the purpose and utility (what they buy you in terms of learning goals) of strategies at every step along the way. To do that, kids must get instant feedback demonstrating to them that strategies are useful—that pulling out just the right tool to help you over a hurdle at just the right moment makes you a smarter, more effective, and more strategic reader. In a sense, strategies are just like phonics rules. They are only a means to an end. It's when either a phonics rule or a strategy routine becomes an end unto itself that bad things happen. We get mock compliance, but no real uptake. As a result, the strategies remain in a special "school talk" box that is hauled out only when the assignment requires it, and then put back on a shelf well out of reach of everyday reading. The only way to block mock

TABLE 10.1 Reading, Writing, and Language as Tools for Learning

| | | Disciplines | | | |
		Literature	Science	Social Studies	Mathematics
Learning Tools	Reading	✓	✓	✓	✓
	Writing	✓	✓	✓	✓
	Language	✓	✓	✓	✓

compliance is to provide guided apprenticeships that help students learn how, when, and why to apply strategies so that they can see their transparent benefit.

Is this too much of a revolution to hope for? I hope not, for the alternatives are too devastating to contemplate. And if we could really make these things happen, we would be blazing a trail back to the radical middle that I championed in the last edition of this book, and that is the destination toward which I am still trying to guide myself and others.

References

Adams, M.J. (1990). *Beginning to read: Thinking and learning about print.* Cambridge, MA: MIT Press.

Flippo, R.F. (1998). Points of agreement: A display of professional unity in our field. *The Reading Teacher, 52,* 30–40.

Goodman, K.S. (1967). Reading: A psycholinguistic guessing game. *Journal of the Reading Specialist, 4,* 126–135.

McIntyre, E., & Pressley, M. (Eds.). (1996). *Balanced instruction: Strategies and skills in whole language.* Norwood, MA: Christopher-Gordon.

McKeown, M.G., Beck, I.L., & Blake, R.G.K. (2009). Rethinking reading comprehension instruction: A comparison of reading strategies and content approaches. *Reading Research Quarterly, 44*(3), 218–253.

Pearson, P.D. (1996). Reclaiming the center. In M.F. Graves, P. van den Broek, & B.M. Taylor (Eds.), *The first R: Every child's right to read* (pp. 259–274). New York, NY: Teachers College Press.

Pearson, P.D. (1999). An historically-based review of Preventing Reading Difficulties in Young Children. *Reading Research Quarterly, 34,* 231–246.

Pearson P.D., & Fielding, L. (1991). Comprehension instruction. In R. Barr, M.L. Kamil, P. Mosenthal, & P.D. Pearson (Eds.), *Handbook of reading research* (Vol. 2, pp. 815–860). New York, NY: Longman.

Pearson, P.D., & Raphael, T.E. (1999). Toward an ecologically balanced literacy curriculum. In L.B. Gambrell, L.M. Morrow, S.B. Neuman, & M. Pressley (Eds.), *Best practices in literacy instruction* (pp. 22–33). New York, NY: Guilford Press.

Pearson, P.D., Moje, E., & Greenleaf, C. (2010). Science and literacy: Each in the service of the other. *Science, 328,* 459–463.

Snow, C.E., Burns, M.S., & Griffin, P. (Eds.). (1998). *Preventing reading difficulties in young children.* Washington, DC: National Academy Press.

Wilkinson, I.A.G., & Son, E.H. (2011). A dialogical turn in research on learning and teaching to comprehend. In M.L. Kamil, P.D. Pearson, E.B. Moje, & P.P. Afflerbach (Eds.), *Handbook of reading research,* Vol. IV (pp. 359–387). New York, NY: Routledge.

11

POINT OF VIEW: GEORGE SPACHE

Richard D. Robinson

> Reading is more than going rapidly over the lines of print, and it is more than slowly and laboriously plodding along looking carefully at every symbol and form. Rather, reading is a complex of several skills which must function together to produce an amount of comprehension in keeping with the purposes, needs, and methods of the reader.
>
> George Spache and Paul Berg, *The Art of Efficient Reading* (1955)

Over the past several decades, a wide variety of theories, programs, and materials have been developed related to the effective teaching of reading. Each new idea has been recommended as being a better way to teach reading in comparison with what is currently being used in classrooms. Many, if not most, of these changes follow a fairly well-developed scenario that sees their introduction, extended use in classrooms, and then the eventual replacement of these ideas by other "new" concepts and programs. A classic example is the extended use of phonics as a basis for reading instruction—a particular reading philosophy that has come and gone a number of times (see Spache, 1963, 1964, 1972). With each renewal, advocates of the new approach believe it is truly revolutionary, and yet in most cases it is often nothing more than new terminology applied to old ideas and concepts.

An outcome of this continual change in reading instruction has been the development of factional groups of educators who advocate an approach or set of materials that they believe is superior to all others—thus, the historical evolution of cadres of teachers who hold to their way of teaching as being the "gospel truth" without regard to other views or approaches to reading instruction (Spache & Spache, 1969).

Despite these differences in reading education, in terms of both philosophical principles as well as actual teaching practices, it is interesting to note how much overlap there is among experts representing diverse philosophies regarding contexts and practices for teaching reading. This is one of the primary conclusions or outcomes for the Expert Study (Flippo 1998; refer to Chapter 1 in this book).

As Director of the Reading Clinic at the University of Florida, George Spache was interested in determining the degree of effectiveness of a variety of reading programs (Spache, 1961). The results of his work showed that while programs differed in terms of specifics, they had much in common, especially in relationship to fundamental beliefs and practices. A corollary to this work was the conclusion that no single approach to reading was clearly superior to all others.

This chapter presents an interpretation of Spache's reading views, based primarily on his lifetime of professional writing and research on this topic. I take full responsibility for my representation of Spache's ideas and thoughts, acknowledging that there may be differing conclusions and opinions. In line with the Expert Study clustered summary agreements reprinted in Chapter 1, I have organized this analysis into the following sections: Combining Reading with Other Language Processes; Contexts, Environment, and Purposes for Reading; Developing (or Shaping) Students' Perceptions and Expectations; Materials; and Reading Instruction.

Combining Reading with Other Language Processes

Spache's writings demonstrate his long belief that the effective teaching of reading should be in the context of the other language processes (Spache, 1964, 1972). For instance, in describing what he considered to be the characteristics of a good reading program, Spache (1976a) noted that in effective reading instruction "vocabulary, phonic skills, and mechanics of writing—as well as handwriting and the development of speaking, writing, and listening vocabularies—are promoted in multiple uses of the child-produced material" (p. 342). The language efforts described clearly indicate the widest possible use of all aspects of both oral and written language. It should be noted that an important part of this use of language is based fundamentally on "child-produced materials."

A related approach to reading instruction that Spache advocated was the use of individualized reading. Spache (1963) concurred with and cited Veatch's definition of this method of reading instruction:

> An individualized reading program provides each child with an environment which allows him to seek that which stimulates him, choose that which helps him develop most, and work at this own rate of regardless of what else is going on.

p. 150

Spache's view was that, to be successful, school reading programs need to be constantly aware of individual student's interests and desires, and to make every effort to meet those various goals.

Contexts, Environment, and Purposes for Reading

Reading should not be an isolated school experience, but rather needs to be incorporated into the context of the student's environment and purposed for reading (Spache & Berg, 1955). Of particular note was Spache's firm belief in the use of trade books or library materials as a fundamental part of all reading instruction. Spache in fact edited a series of teacher-directed books titled *Good Reading for Poor Readers* (1962–1974). Each of the nine editions contains an extended discussion on how to select the right book for each student, and how to use literature effectively in all classrooms. The series emphasizes the fact that while real reading beyond the classroom is important for all students, it is especially critical for those who are having difficulty learning to read. Spache's view was that reading is not just a classroom subject, but rather should be made functional and a foundation for all future learning activities throughout a person's life.

Developing (or Shaping) Students' Perceptions and Expectations

Spache's work reflects his belief in the importance of reading as a major influence on both the social and intellectual lives of readers (see Spache, 1963, 1976b). Often, young children equate their success or failure in school simply by their perceived abilities in reading (Spache, 1976a). This conclusion says to the effective teacher of reading that, as much as possible, each child's self-image should be enhanced through successful reading. A technique Spache (1963, 1976b) long advocated in helping students develop this positive view of reading as a lifelong activity was the use of bibliotherapy.

Bibliotherapy is "the treatment of personal problems through the medium of reading" (Spache, 1963, p. 323). When using bibliotherapy, readers are able to identify personal characteristics and difficulties in their own lives that are similar to those described in various types of reading. Success in bibliotherapy requires the teacher to have "a wide knowledge of books and a deep understanding of the personal needs of her pupils" (Spache, 1963, p. 324). While there have been some questions as to the competence of classroom teachers in the use of bibliotherapy, there is much evidence to support its use in the classroom: "Teachers are by training perhaps better equipped to initiate and to follow up on this process [bibliotherapy] by helping the child implement insights in constructive action than are most adults" (Spache, 1976b, p. 341).

It is the primary goal of reading instruction to develop in all readers a positive self-image as well as to help them value reading as a lifelong activity (Spache, 1955, 1963, 1976b). These goals were fundamental in Spache's research and teaching, and he considered them most important in the effective teaching of reading.

Materials

The Basal Reader

For the most of Spache's career, the dominant approach to the teaching of reading was use of the basal reader (see Spache, 1963, 1972). Although the basal reader was used by over 90% of schools during that period, it was not without problems. Spache pointed out the following difficulties, evident from almost the beginning of the extensive use of the basal reader: sterility of content, lack of provision for individual differences, and overemphasis on the basal series. Many of these issues apply to "the manner in which basal readers were used rather than against the basal approach itself" (Spache, 1964, p. 73).

Perhaps the most dominant criticism of the basal reader materials is that they are "stereotyped and lacking in vitality, creativity or interest ... sterile, lacking in appeal to boys, and unrealistic, in terms of the common experiences of lower middle class boys and girls" (Spache, 1963, p. 25). While Spache might have seen some basis in these arguments, he found that much of this criticism is based on the false assumption that the only reading material a student would use in learning to read is the basal reader. Spache, along with many contemporaries (see Betts, 1954; Dolch, 1949; Russell, 1944), saw the basal reader as a mere "tool" to introduce students to the much wider world of reading. In his view, if the basal reader is the only reading material being used for instruction, this is not the fault of the materials but rather the fault of the teacher using them in this fashion.

Another serious criticism of the basal reader is that it tends to be written for the average student, and ignores the remedial and gifted individuals—this despite the fact that the authors of all basal series have encouraged individualization of instruction when teachers use their materials. Spache (1963) pointed out,

> It is doubtful in the minds of many reading authorities that any one basal book or series can give training in all of the skills and abilities needed, or give the breadth of reading experiences desired. Nor can it provide for the many stages of reading growth.
>
> *p. 26*

Here, again, the problem is with how the basal is used rather than with the materials themselves. Throughout his career, Spache continually emphasized the fact that the basal reading series is only a tool to encourage further reading, and that it should be used as an introduction to more extensive reading. His *Good Reading for Poor Readers* series details ways in which the classroom teacher needs to move beyond the basal reader into the real world of wide and purposeful reading activities.

It has been said, with some degree of accuracy, that classroom teachers tend to have an overdependence on the extended use of the basal reader. Spache noted the following practices in the use of the basal reader:

> The series is treated as a group of sacred books in which every child must read every page and over learn every basic vocabulary word. In addition, we see the basal workbooks used slavishly without regard to the child's actual needs, an attitude of worship extended to the core vocabulary of the basal series, a stultifying use of the oral reading circle, and an almost complete reliance upon a visual or "look–say" method of teaching reading.
>
> *1963, pp. 27–28*

Practices such as these clearly reflect a fundamental misunderstanding of the primary roll of the basal reader. No basal reading series today claims that the program is the only reading students should do. Basal publishers emphasize that their material is "intended as a tool for teaching children to read, and not as a complete program" (Spache, 1972, p. 35). In fact, publishers have made extra efforts to encourage wide reading in a great variety of materials.

In reaction to this misuse of the basal reader, we see an effort to change teacher practice to the opposite extreme—no use of basal material at all (see Spache, 1963, 1972: Spache & Spache, 1964). For instance, advocates of individualized reading (Jacobs, 1953; Jenkins, 1957; Veatch, 1957, 1960) are often most critical of the basal reader. As noted earlier, much of this criticism rests not on the basal materials themselves, but rather on the unintelligent ways in which they often are used by classroom teachers.

In 1941, Spache noted a number of factors that can enhance reading achievement through the effective use of basal readers: "A reading series should provide … for integration of the reading materials, either though provision of parallel readers, unit reading materials, or books of between-grade difficulty…" (p. 290). Spache believed this to be a fundamental goal of all basal reading instruction.

Workbooks

Accompanying most basal reading textbooks today are supplemental materials, often categorized under the umbrella term "workbooks." There is perhaps no more criticized area related to the use of the basal reader than the use of workbooks. Many critics see the workbook as nothing more than organized "busy work," with little if any value for students. There are certainly many stories about the serious misuse of this material, such as the proud teacher who tells of all the students in her classroom completing every page in the workbook by the end of the year.

Arguments abound on both the positive and negative use of the workbook. For instance, teachers who feel positively about the workbook cite it as a source for helping individual students with specific problems, as well as containing relevant material carefully planned and related to what has been recently read in the basic readers. Those who oppose workbooks point out the "tendency to overdependence of the teacher upon these tools, their disregard of individual needs, their lack of creativity or training in expression or fluency, and their monotonous, repetitive nature" (Spache, 1963, pp. 28–29).

According to Spache (1963), the answer to this problem lies in the manner in which workbooks are used by the classroom teacher, rather than in the workbooks themselves.

Limited Vocabulary

Early in Spache's career, the concept of limited or controlled vocabulary was a dominant theme in most reading materials. This limiting of vocabulary was based on many studies of intensive work counts and other types of vocabulary and concept load. Despite the research support, Spache (1963) opposed this philosophy of reading materials:

> The adherents of a limited vocabulary will hasten to point out that, in all probability, the child does not learn this wider vocabulary in comics and other recreational material. The same breadth of vocabulary could not be used in basal reading, these protagonists say, for the child cannot readily learn this number of words in a short space of time. We agree, but must point out that this is no proof that basal vocabularies cannot possibly extend beyond the child's daily learning rate. Even though learners are limited in the number of concepts they can absorb in a given time, this does not demonstrate that a spoon-feeding process is best. If we put less emphasis upon over learning of a minute basal vocabulary, and broadened the material, deepened its content, and injected greater intrinsic appeal, reading progress might well be even more rapid and enjoyable.
>
> To the best of our knowledge, there is no proof that over learning of a small core vocabulary is the only possible foundation for learning to read. This belief is predicated upon the assumption that a beginning reader must memorize each and every word he meets, or else he will not be able to read other future materials. If this were true, no primary child could read any book that was not completely parallel to his basal book in vocabulary usage. Yet primary children read literally hundreds of recreational books with enjoyment and adequate comprehension, even though these books

collectively introduce many, many new words. This recreational reading begins, in some programs, as early as the preprimer or primer stage—when the child has learned no more than 50–150 words. Does not this ability to read independently refute the claim that over learning of the meager basal vocabulary and memorization of every word encountered are essential?

pp. 30–31

Inflexibility of Method

The dependence on one form or format for erasing instruction has long dominated reading instruction. Whether it was, for example, the "look–say" approach or the extensive use of phonics, teachers tended to follow a particular method to the complete exclusion of all other reading plans.

According to Spache (1963), the effective teacher of reading is the one who is not slavishly tied to one approach or philosophy, but rather chooses from a wide array of possibilities based on what is best for students.

Excessive Oral Reading

Oral reading has been a constant source of difficulty for many years in reading education. More than 45 years ago, Spache (1963) wrote, "Observers in primary classrooms receive the impression that both teachers and pupils apparently believe that there is no real reading activity other than oral reading in a circle" (p. 33). This situation in many classrooms, even today, has not changed a great deal. Students spend significant amounts of time reading orally, apparently so that the teacher can tell whether the readers can say the words correctly. Little effort is given for silent reading as well, or for determining students' understanding of what is being read (Spache & Spache, 1964; Spache, 1972). Extensive research, as well as actual classroom practice, clearly demonstrates that silent reading should take precedence over oral reading (Spache, 1963). As one little boy said about oral reading in a circle, "We starts at the same place, but some of us gets there first. How come we has to keep lookin' if we knows how to read it?"

Reading Instruction

Spache's feelings about reading instruction may be best understood through his own statements over the years:

> [A good reading program is based on] … a well rounded selection of reading experiences. It includes both recreational and work-type reading poetry and prose, factual and fictional matter, informational and entertaining materials that extend the child's ideas and knowledge.
>
> *Spache & Spache, 1964, p. 92*

Reading interest can be fostered or stifled by different classroom practices. Among those with positive values are group discussion of what is read, by panel discussions, debates, reading aloud, choral reading, etc.

Spache, 1962–1974

There is no better tonic for stimulating interest in a [reading] task than recognized success...

Spache, 1941, p. 287

The relative emphasis on phonics has waxed and waned through the years, but heavy doses of it were no panacea for reading failures.

Spache, 1972, p. 153

Only when the teacher sees reading as a dynamic interaction between the personality of the reader and literature will her influence grow beyond a mechanical drilling of skills.

Spache, 1963, p. 323

In addition to the basal and subject-matter vocabularies, most pupils learn many more words from their recreational, supplementary, and casual reading.

Spache & Spache, 1964, p. 91

[Effective reading instruction] ... may also be achieved by abandoning rigid standards of progress in the first three grades. Progress should be a continuum rather than a series of distinct steps. Pupils will be permitted to progress at their own rate and will be given varying amounts of time to complete the primary program.

Spache, 1963, p. 35

It also becomes apparent that reading success is not promoted by separating the act from related language activities, as in over-emphasis upon skill development, or reading lessons carefully isolated in time and content from other language media, or any classroom practice which assumes that simply practicing in reading aloud or silently is the best program for development of the reading act.

Spache & Spache, 1964, p. 36

The Past 10 Years: In Retrospect

1. *What are the most important things that you believe literacy research has shown over the past 10 years? (Positive and/or Negative)*

In the intervening years between the late 1960s, when George Spache's last literacy research and study were completed, and today, his work was to prove insightful in predicting many of the current developments in literacy instruction and research. It is interesting to note that while terminology and descriptions of literacy programs and techniques change with what is promoted as "new," many of the same ideas and concepts have been known and used for many years. In some cases, these literary techniques have not only been known but have also been tried in the past and rejected by teachers as impractical or unworkable in the classroom setting. It is unfortunate to realize that pioneer work by such literacy pioneers as George Spache and others has almost universally has either been rejected or is not known by many of today's literacy teachers and other educators. Thus, it is always important to place in appropriate context current developments in literacy research with the fundamental knowledge gained in the past.

As noted earlier in this chapter, George Spache was a prolific and innovative literacy researcher in many different aspects of this academic field. In the following discussion I have identified what I consider to be some of the most important developments in literacy in the past 10 years, and what I believe Spache would have believed about them.

Government Mandated Literacy Programs

For those of us who have read much of what George Spache wrote, to have known him in person was to know an individual who had firm beliefs and was not hesitant to express them to all. He had great concern for the autonomy of the public school curriculum, and felt outside interference, such as that of the federal government and state agencies, was for the most part clearly inappropriate. He lived and worked at a time when these influences on schools were at a minimum compared to what schools are experiencing today. If he were living today, I am sure he would have encouraged all schools to develop and implement their own unique curriculum efforts in the interests of their students.

Multicultural Education

In his teaching experience both in New York and Florida, George Spache developed and administered reading clinics which were designed to be of assistance to a wide variety of students with many different literacy disabilities. In many cases, these students were from divergent cultural and educational backgrounds. In light of the current emphasis on cultural diversity, George Spache's pioneering work would be of great value. He was truly a pioneer in this work, in his child study clinics, with individuals from many different cultures and backgrounds.

Classroom Literacy Assessment Programs

George Spache was a pioneer in the field of literacy assessment. He was especially critical of the inappropriate use of test results in making pedagogical decisions about individual student learning experiences in the classroom. In numerous papers and books, he cautioned teachers and school administrators about the many problems associated with all academic tests in general and literacy assessments in particular. His comments were in the context of an assessment researcher who had an extensive background in both the development and the administration of a variety of test instruments. While he expressed concern about the uses of these tests in the past, he would have been even more critical today about the latest national and state assessment procedures in place in our public schools.

2. *How do you think this should inform the contexts and practices of reading instruction in the classroom?*

George Spache, in his literacy research and writing, consistently put the classroom and the teacher at the center of all effective instruction. He was especially concerned about the many outside pressures that shape and mold the literacy curriculum on a daily basis. Of particular concern throughout his life were the influences of both formal and informal assessment results on basic teacher decisions related to the teaching of reading and writing.

Current Literacy Curriculum Conditions in Modern Classrooms

The classroom literacy curriculum, in its various forms and developments, is certainly not immune to the effects of outside influences in many different ways. Whether it is government mandated assessment criteria, state and local control issues, or public input at all levels, any classroom literacy instructional program must be dynamic and flexible in response to these external pressures. Perhaps no better example of this current situation is the national classroom literacy response to the "No Child Left Behind" legislation. Schools, in trying to meet the demands of this law, especially in terms of literacy test scores, have made many changes to their existing programs of reading instruction. These adjustments to the literacy curriculum have ranged from the relatively minor, such as various new ways of reporting student scores, to major changes that have fundamentally changed the very "heart and soul" of literacy instruction. The latter have seen classroom teachers adjust their teaching goals and objectives, as well as actual pedagogy, drastically from past practices, primarily to meet presubscribed test criteria. Whole reading instructional programs of materials have been eliminated, and new "government prescribed" reading curriculum books and related products been selected. Often, teachers' choices and preferences in these decisions have been either ignored or drastically altered. In addition, instructional organization and teaching time have been carefully prescribed as to length and content by these governmental laws and policies. In many respects, the day of the autonomous public school in terms of developing and implementing its own literacy teaching curriculum has ended.

In summary, George Spache would view many of the most recent developments in literacy education with reserve and concern. He would not be hesitant to criticize the seemingly endless pressure applied to classroom teachers to mold their literacy teaching to government mandates, publishers' contrived goals and objectives, as well as the public's unrealistic expectations for the current literacy.

References

Betts, E.A. (1954). Three essentials in basic reading instruction. *Education*, 74, 575–582.

Dolch, E.W. (1949). Self-survey of a school program for the teaching of reading. *The Elementary School Journal*, 49, 230–234.

Flippo, R.F. (1998). Points of agreement: A display of professional unity in our field. *The Reading Teacher*, 52, 30–40.

Jacobs, L.B. (1953). Reading on their own means reading at their growing edges. *The Reading Teacher*, 6, 27–32.

Jenkins, M. (1957). Self-selection in reading. *The Reading Teacher*, 11, 84–90.

Russell, D.H. (1944). Opinions of experts about primary grade basic reading programs. *The Elementary School Journal*, 44, 602–609.

Spache, G.D. (1941). New trends in primary-grade readers. *The Elementary School Journal*, 42, 283–290.

Spache, G.D. (1961). Research in reading at the University of Florida, 1950–1960. In E.P. Bliesmer & A.J. Kingston (Eds.), *Phases of college and other adult reading programs*. Tenth yearbook of the National Reading Conference (pp. 141–149). Charlottesville, VA: Jarman Printing Company.

Spache, G.D. (1962–1974). *Good reading for poor readers*. Champaign, IL: Garrard.

Spache, G.D. (1963). *Toward better reading*. Champaign, IL: Garrard.

Spache, G.D. (1964). *Reading in the elementary school*. Boston, MA: Allyn & Bacon.

Spache, G.D. (1972). *The teaching of reading. Methods and results: An overview*. Bloomington, IN: Phi Delta Kappan.

Spache, G.D. (1976a). Investigating the issues of reading disabilities. Boston, MA: Allyn & Bacon.

Spache, G.D. (1976b). *Diagnosing and correcting reading disabilities*. Boston, MA: Allyn & Bacon.

Spache, G.D., & Berg, P.C. (1955). *The art of efficient reading*. New York, NY: Macmillan.

Spache, G.D., & Spache, E.B. (1964). *Reading in the elementary school*. Boston, MA: Allyn & Bacon

Spache, G.D., & Spache, E.B. (1969). *Reading in the elementary school* (2nd ed.). Boston, MA: Allyn & Bacon.

Veatch, J. (1957). Children's interests and individual reading. *The Reading Teacher*, 10, 160–165.

Veatch, J. (1960). In defense of individualized reading. *Elementary English*, 37, 227–233.

12

POINT OF VIEW: PRINCIPLED PLURALISM, COGNITIVE FLEXIBILITY, AND NEW CONTEXTS FOR READING

Rand J. Spiro, Paul Morsink, and Benjamin Forsyth

What follows is the text from the earlier edition of this chapter (Spiro, 2001) in *Reading Researchers in Search of Common Ground* (Flippo, 2001). Its pertinence seems to have increased with developments of the past 10 years. The remarks are written from the perspective of Cognitive Flexibility Theory (CFT; Spiro, Vispoel, Schmitz, Samarapungavan, & Boerger, 1987; Spiro & Jehng, 1990; Spiro, Coulson, Feltovich, & Anderson, 1994). In CFT (a successor of schema theories; Anderson, 1977; Anderson, Spiro, & Anderson, 1978; Spiro, 1980), it has been argued for many years that *all* learning, instruction, mental representation, and knowledge application should be governed by a principled utilization of interlocking multiple representations, multiple methodologies, multiple perspectives, multiple case precedents, multiple analogies, and so on (Spiro, Feltovich, Coulson, & Anderson, 1989; Spiro et al., 1994). CFT was designed for learning in ill-structured domains, where cases of knowledge application are characterized *individually* by complexity, and *across cases* by considerable variability and irregularity in the conditions of knowledge use. Given the complexity of such domains, *single* approaches of *any* kind will be limiting, successful in some contexts, and off the mark in many others. This is so whether the domain is a content area, like history or biology; a process, like reading; or an arena of practical application of knowledge, like medicine or teaching.

CFT is intended to prepare people to flexibly and adaptively apply their knowledge to new cases or situations—situations that are often unlike any they have encountered before. Hence the inappropriateness of old-style schema theory, which depends on the retrieval of a pre-stored schema or template from memory, despite the unlikelihood that one would have a prepackaged schema for everything that might be needed (especially in reading; Spiro & Myers,

1984). CFT argues that when facing a complex new case or situation, you need to *assemble* elements of prior knowledge and past experience and tailor those elements to fit the new situation's needs. This situation-sensitive assembly of multiple perspectives from prior knowledge is the part of *pluralism* that the title of this chapter refers to that is *principled*—it is not just throwing together any old set of theories, methodologies, knowledge elements, and so on. Rather, one must assemble just those aspects that will help in the current situation, while discounting those aspects that are less helpful. Further, the assembled elements must be meaningfully related to each other, and tailored to the specific content of the case at hand. In a sense, one must build a "schema-of-the-moment" (Spiro et al., 1987, 1994; Spiro & Jehng, 1990). For most domains there are strengths and weaknesses of all of the credible approaches, and patterns of com- bined strength and weakness (across approaches) are usually determined by fea- tures of the teaching or learning situation one is facing. The key question for CFT is *which* approaches, theories, methods, content schemas, and so on are *most appropriate for a new situation*, and then *how are they to be put together* (com- bined, coordinated, aligned) to adaptively fit that new context.

It is hard to imagine a domain where these principles would be more appli- cable than in learning to read and in the teaching of reading. Therefore it is heartening to see an increasing tendency towards pluralism in the reading field, towards the advocacy of integration of different theoretical and methodological perspectives (e.g., Pearson, 1996; Flippo, 1999; International Reading Associ- ation, 1999). And, of course, it should not be surprising to see the agreements in the Expert Study (Flippo, 1998), of which I was a part, which indicate a belief that many things that are said to be true of reading and learning to read *are* true—in many but not all situations—for some children, at some times, for some teaching and learning purposes. Furthermore, it will usually be the case that beliefs and practices in the teaching of reading are best applied in combina- tions, and these combinations will also shift according to changing contexts. In other words, the only summary statement that applies to all of reading is: *it all depends*.

The skilled teacher of reading will have a rich repertoire to draw upon, and she or he will examine each teaching situation closely—and, based on that "close reading," assemble a situation-sensitive approach that draws on different elements of knowledge and different prior case experiences. Furthermore, this mix will be fluidly changeable as the reading situation evolves and changes. Similarly, the skilled reader will sometimes rely more on the use of knowledge of phonics, sometimes use whole word approaches; sometimes rely on prior knowledge and contextual information, sometimes accept a premise of novelty and rely less on prior knowledge; sometimes read for accuracy, sometimes skim for gist; and so on—all depending on characteristics of what is being read, why it is being read, and who is doing the reading. And, of course, sometimes these strategies of reading are used in combination rather than in isolation from each other. In these senses, there is a principled pluralism required at the "micro" level (the act of reading) that mirrors that which has been argued for at the "macro" level of the field of reading research and the theory of the teaching of reading.

I believe that these issues of cognitive flexibility and situation-adaptive assembly of multiple perspectives are central to the next generation of educational research, not just in the "Reading Wars" but across the spectrum of learning and teaching. The development of *principled pluralisms of the mind and of pedagogy* is crucial for learning and teaching in *all* complex domains of knowledge acquisition and application—and we are coming to find that more and more domains that we had thought to be relatively simple and orderly actually have crucial properties of complexity and ill structure. Unfortunately, those approaches that work for learning in simple domains are exactly the *opposite* of the ones that are best for dealing with complexity—what helps for one, hurts for the other (e.g., single versus multiple representations, compartmentalized versus interconnected knowledge, knowledge-centeredness versus case-centeredness, retrieval from memory of prepackaged prescriptions for how to think and act versus case-sensitive knowledge assembly (see Spiro et al., 1987, 1994)). Fortunately, we also now possess new theories and theory-based educational technologies to help foster these more difficult kinds of complex learning that have so often resisted our best efforts in the past (see, for example, Spiro, Feltovich, Jacobson, & Coulson, 1992a, 1992b).

One of the most important of the next-generation research questions concerns the manner of operation of "principled pluralisms." How does situation-adaptive assembly of knowledge and experience occur, and how should it be fostered (in teachers and students)? There are at least two key elements in the answer to these questions. The first is a recognition of the centrality of case experience (Spiro et al., 1994). The organizing nexus for assembling multiple perspectives is the *case* (example, occurrence, actual event in the world). In ill-structured domains of real-world practice (e.g., reading, or teaching reading), wide-scope generalizations, abstractions, and schemas do not work. Instead, one must attend to "how the world goes," and learn how to piece together and tailor knowledge to the demands of practice—*there is no "formula."* So it is the case that becomes the organizing focus for knowledge assembly, that provides the guidance for what needs to be part of the schema-of-the-moment and how that assemblage needs to be put together. This contrasts to well-structured domains, where examples or cases are interchangeable illustrations of generic knowledge that spin out in highly routinized ways. In ill-structured domains, the principled basis for adaptive knowledge assembly referred to in the phrase "principled pluralism" is to be found in the landscape of a domain's cases—alignment and coordination of multiple knowledge sources and methods is governed by their fit to the events to which they are being applied, and their usefulness in dealing with those events.

An important implication of this shift in emphasis to the situation-adaptive assembly of schemas-of-the-moment out of multiple perspectives is that the structures of prior knowledge must be conceived differently than they were in schema theory. It is no accident that the situated cognition movement has de-emphasized, and at times been antagonistic to, earlier views that placed abstract cognitive structures in a central place. Such views were notorious for their failures to account for novel transfer, the ability to apply knowledge to new situations that differ from the conditions of initial learning. The situations of the world are too rich to permit wide-scope application of generic cognitive structures. However, the problem is not with knowledge structures per se, but rather with the *kind* of knowledge structure that has typically been proffered. What is required is a *different kind of knowledge structure*, one that works with the jagged and messy contours of situations in the world rather than smoothing them out—*open structures to think with*, rather than closed structures that dictate thought. The goal of CFT is to foster the learning of such open, situation-sensitive structures (Spiro et al., 1987, 1992a, 1992b, 1994).

The second key element of preparing people to assemble knowledge in situation-adaptive ways is the role of new technologies. Certain uses of case-based hypermedia are designed to promote knowledge assembly skills by modeling them across a range of contexts (Spiro & Jehng, 1990; Spiro et al., 1994). The non-linear traversal capability of hypermedia, along with the newly expanded ease of dealing with digital video cases, allows real-world examples to be overlaid by shifting constellations of perspectives and then compared and contrasted in varying ways to illustrate the vagaries of situation-adaptive knowledge assembly across diverse contexts. With this technology it is possible to demonstrate and teach principled pluralism in operation, in all its forms.

Finally, perhaps the most important frontier for next-generation research is that of changing students' and teachers' *habits of mind,* their underlying epistemic stance towards the world, in the direction of ones that are more compatible with the changing circumstances of knowing and doing that characterize our increasingly complex and rapidly evolving modern world of life and work (Feltovich, Spiro, & Coulson, 1989; Spiro, Feltovich, & Coulson, 1996). We often speak of cognitive structures; rarely do we speak of the underlying assumptions and structures that determine the shape of the cognitive structures that get built, the background "lenses" that *prefigure* the shape of knowledge (Feltovich et al., 1989). It is these "prefigurative schemas" that I refer to as habits of mind. There is considerable evidence that the predominant habits of mind are overly simple in a variety of ways (see Spiro et al., 1996) and are thus antithetical to the needs of successful performance in complex domains (such as reading and the teaching of reading). Habits of mind suited to dealing with complexity must be developed; finding ways to do this will be a major challenge of the coming years. Progress in the use of principled pluralisms for the cognitively flexible, situation-adaptive assembly of prior knowledge and experience will be slow until we are able to develop corresponding changes in the underlying habits of mind of teachers and students who would greatly prefer that things were simpler.

In summary, it should be clear to the reader by now what led me to indicate agreement to all of the items in the final lists of the Expert Study in the first edition of *Reading Researchers in Search of Common Ground*. My research has led me to believe that all credible approaches are useful on some occasions, that none are always useful, and that the relevance of one does not preclude the simultaneous relevance of others with which it might be fruitfully combined. This is an inevitable outcome of advocating for a principled pluralism. In the end, it will all depend on an expert teacher making a judgment about which ensemble of approaches and practices to select for a particular student and context. It is the job of those who prepare teachers of reading to insure that those future teachers understand the implications of principled pluralism, and are able to apply knowledge and methods of various types with adaptive flexibility.

The Past 10 Years: In Retrospect

In rereading the chapter I wrote 10 years ago (Spiro, 2001) for the first edition of *Reading Researchers in Search of Common Ground*, I found nothing I said there that I wished to change. This is not to say that I believe nothing important has occurred during this time; quite the contrary. As the answers to the two questions that follow will clearly indicate, I think things have changed radically. However, those changes are extensions along the dimensions I previously wrote about, and they build upon what was in my earlier piece. So my update is, in summary, "Yes, I still agree with our Expert Study findings, but more so." Therefore, I have left the previous chapter as is, and add, with my two new coauthors, a "10 years later" update here, in answering the two questions posed.

1.   *What are the most important things that you believe literacy research has shown over the past 10 years? (Positive and/or Negative)*

Spiro's argument, Cognitive Flexibility Theory (Spiro, Collins, & Ramchandran, 2007), in brief, was that reading is an ill-structured domain where instances of knowledge construction and knowledge application are characterized *individually* by complexity and *across cases* by considerable variability and irregularity. As such, the activity of reading cannot be satisfactorily described—let alone taught or learned—with any single conceptual framework, theoretical lens, or methodological approach. What was advocated instead was a principled pluralism wherein the primary focus is the individual's assembly from relevant prior knowledge, theory, and habitual routines of a "schema of the moment" (Spiro et al., 1987, 1994; Spiro & Jehng, 1990) suitable for a particular situation and purpose. Learners, it was argued, are better off if they do not mechanically apply memorized rules or routines, but instead assemble such schemas of the moment for tasks as varied as deciphering an unfamiliar word or bringing to bear disparate elements of background knowledge on a topic to support the comprehension of a particular text. Similarly, teachers (and their students!) are better off when they do not rigidly adhere to a single pedagogical principle or method, but instead assemble schemas of the moment for different groups of students and learning contexts. At every turn, the principled consultation and utilization of multiple representations, multiple methodologies, multiple perspectives, multiple case precedents, multiple analogies, and so on (Spiro et al., 1989, 1994) is to be preferred to any monological perspective or approach.

Ten years later, we write from much the same CFT perspective, only with even greater conviction and urgency. Trends in reading (and writing), in our view, make a CFT perspective more relevant than ever. These trends derive from the rapid spread of learning technologies and the advent of the Web as a pervasive learning environment (Lehnart et al., 2008), and include the following (to read more about these trends and others, a good set of texts to start with would include Coiro & Dobler, 2007; Coiro et al., 2008; Hartman, 2000; Leu et al., 2007, 2009; Spiro, 2006; Spiro et al., 2007; Spiro & DeSchryver, 2008).

The reading paths readers take across hyperlinked, multimedia texts are increasingly personal and idiosyncratic. Most obviously, hyperlinked texts present readers with a multitude of choices, many of which will literally change the shape of the text being read and, from one moment to the next, alter the scope of the reader's task. When readers acquire advanced Web search skills, more sophisticated search queries make possible an even greater variety of valid choices.

As readers criss-cross the Web, reading becomes increasingly intertextual. Reading a single text in isolation is now unusual; making connections and inferences across texts (whether to augment, contrast, corroborate, or critique) is more and more the norm. Indeed, in a world that allows words, sentences, motifs, themes, etc., to be instantly connected to sources and precursors, the very idea of single, self-contained texts is harder and harder to defend.

Reading is increasingly multimodal. Alphabetic texts are increasingly interspersed—or more complexly interwoven—with images, charts, videos, audio effects, interactive multimedia displays, etc. Readers are challenged to make meaning across modes and media far more frequently than they needed to with traditional text.

Everyday reading experiences are more and more decisively shaped by readers' procedural and strategic knowledge, as well as by their metacognitive and self-regulatory control. Ten years ago, it was a commonplace to say that the reader is an author of his or her understanding. This conformed with a constructive view of reading comprehension in which the text was a "blueprint" for creating meaning (Spiro, 1980). Now, with readers traversing different Web sites to build their understandings of a topic, the need to synthesize those individual understandings from various text fragments—rather than reading a text assembled as a whole by an author or authors—is to a much greater extent an act of "authorship," and it is one that requires new and far more advanced metacognitive skills (especially since the determination of purpose is increasingly under the control of the reader, rather than being shaped by an author—multiple authors from different sites all have their own purposes, often leaving the reader to construct his or her own purposes during the act of reading and then synthesizing those different pieces).

Reading is increasingly interwoven with writing. Reading and writing have, of course, always been intertwined, both literally and figuratively (in the sense that mentally constructing meaning in one's mind while reading constitutes a kind of writing). Twenty-first century technologies and the Web in particular increasingly integrate reading with opportunities to interact, react, and/or reply during reading—to annotate, bookmark, review, share, and post.

Reading is increasingly social and interactive. Readers have more and more technologies at their disposal to share their reading activity, to see what others are reading, to interact or collaborate with others "live" during the act of reading, etc.

How do these trends make a CFT perspective more relevant than ever before? In the first place, they underscore the ill-structuredness of the domain of reading (for teachers, learners, and researchers). If anyone 10 years ago felt tempted to argue (contra CFT) that the learning or teaching of reading can be reduced to an orderly set of concepts, rules, and principles applied consistently across a wide variety of contexts, today the evidence more and more overwhelmingly favors the CFT view that "it all depends"—that how we read and what it means to read a given text all depend on who is reading, for what purpose(s), in what context, etc. With the Web, difference and variety, and the importance of context, are everywhere on display.

The process of assembling what we have called a "schema of the moment" is also today more conspicuously visible than before. This visibility has to do with the choices readers today are explicitly called upon to make as they read, the frequency and variety of these choices, and the way many readers today quite literally and deliberately marshal a variety of reading tools and resources as they read or prepare to read. Beyond the important act of choosing which content to read, a reader also has a rich set of choices in building a schema of the moment for "reading support," which may entail using a text-to-voice tool, a Webpage annotation tool such as Diigo, or an online text summarization tool. Tools such as these and *many* others are relevant and useful on some occasions, and not on others. The reader is, in many ways, and much more so than previously, in the driver's seat.

Many more examples could be offered (and can be found in the texts cited earlier). However, the point should be self-evident: more readers than ever before are in a position where they will discover that central idea of CFT;

namely, that in ill-structured domains prepackaged prescriptions for how to read and how to teach reading, how to think and how to problem-solve are inadequate or worse. Unfortunately, much research has indicated that readers still have a long way to go in this realm, especially in matters of synthesis (see, for example, Coiro & Dobler, 2007).

Fortunately, new research frameworks (Spiro, 2006; DeSchryver & Spiro, 2008; Spiro & DeSchryver, 2008) are pointing to new approaches, ones in which these new kinds of reading environments have been shown to be able to support advanced comprehension outcomes beyond those possible from single texts, deep learning at a rapid rate, and kinds of synthesis of diverse content. Single texts, by contrast, are limited in their capacity to provide a multiplicity of perspectives, and have difficulty supporting a wide-ranging applicability of acquired knowledge to new, real-world contexts. Further, practiced use of new technologies can help to manage the increase in cognitive load that comes with greater task complexity. Yet none of these things is likely to happen without a radical change in mindset. The mindset CFT applies to reading, learning, and teaching in ill-structured domains is outlined in the next section. For the new world of online reading, though, the key *additional* mindset shift has to be from using the Web to find answers, closing down one's searches toward that end, and then terminating them when an answer is found, to going in the opposite direction: opening one's searches, so that the more that is learned, the more one seeks to learn, until a critical mass of interconnected knowledge is built that will support the adaptive construction of schemas of the moment when new readings come along in that area, or when knowledge from that area has to be applied in some other way. Obviously, much more work is needed. It would not be too extreme a move to call for a crash program in basic and applied research, curriculum development, preservice and inservice teacher preparation, and educational policy to meet the challenges and capitalize on the affordances of reading comprehension and reading to learn on the Web. We have barely scratched the surface of what is possible in an environment where so much of the world's knowledge has, only within the past 10 years, become so easily accessible.

2. *How do you think this should inform the contexts and practices of reading instruction in the classroom?*

Until we have more answers from research to the kinds of issues discussed in the answer to Question 1, our recommendation would be that the best thing for now would be for reading comprehension instruction to attempt to inculcate the mindset and associated skills identified throughout the earlier chapter from *Reading Researchers in Search of Common Ground* (Spiro, 2001) on CFT and principled pluralism, as well as the more specialized reconceptualization of reading to learn for synthesis of online materials that we have proposed in detail elsewhere (DeSchryver & Spiro, 2008; Spiro & DeSchryver, 2008). Many problems that teachers and students face will be ameliorated in an increasingly Web-based reading and learning environment. Further, our students will be better prepared for the increasing complexity of life and work in the 21st century, offline as well as on.

Acknowledgements

The author wishes to acknowledge the many helpful comments and great patience of Rona Flippo. The second author was a primary contributor to the second part of the chapter. Responsibility for the first part of the chapter (the one that appeared in the earlier edition of *Reading Researchers in Search of Common Ground* (Flippo, 2001)) remains, for whatever faults it contains, with the first author.

References

Anderson, R.C. (1977). The notion of schemata and the educational enterprise. In R.C. Anderson, R.J. Spiro, & W.E. Montague (Eds.), *Schooling and the acquisition of knowledge* (pp. 415–432). Hillsdale, NJ: Lawrence Erlbaum Associates.

Anderson, R.C., Spiro, R.J., & Anderson, M.C. (1978). Schemata as scaffolding for the representation of information in discourse. *American Educational Research Journal, 15,* 433–440.

Coiro, J., & Dobler, E. (2007). Exploring the comprehension strategies used by sixth-grade skilled readers as they search for and locate information on the Internet. *Reading Research Quarterly, 42,* 214–257.

Coiro, J., Knobel, M., Lankshear, C., & Leu, D.J. (2008). Central issues in new literacies and new literacies research. In J. Coiro, M. Knobel, C. Lankshear, & D.J. Leu (Eds.), *Handbook of research on new literacies* (pp. 1–21). New York, NY: Erlbaum.

DeSchryver, M. & Spiro, R. (2008). New forms of deep learning on the Web: Meeting the challenge of cognitive load in conditions of unfettered exploration. In R. Zheng (Ed.), *Cognitive effects of multimedia learning.* Hershey, PA: IGI Global, Inc.

Feltovich, P.J., Spiro, R.J., & Coulson, R.L. (1989). The nature of conceptual understanding in biomedicine: The deep structure of complex ideas and the development of misconceptions. In D. Evans & V. Patel (Eds.), *The cognitive sciences in medicine* (pp. 113–172). Cambridge, MA: MIT Press.

Flippo, R.F. (1998). Points of agreement: A display of professional unity in our field. *The Reading Teacher, 52* (1), 30–40.

Flippo, R.F. (1999). Redefining the reading wars: The war against reading researchers. *Educational Leadership, 57* (2), 38–41.

Flippo, R.F. (Ed.) (2001). *Reading researchers in search of common ground.* Newark, DE: International Reading Association.

Hartman, D.K. (2000). What will be the influences of media on literacy in the next millennium? *Reading Research Quarterly, 35,* 280–282.

International Reading Association (IRA) (1999). Using multiple methods of beginning reading instruction: A position statement of the International Reading Association [Brochure]. Newark, DE: IRA.

Lenhart, A., Madden, M., Rankin-Macgill, A., & Smith, A. (2008). *Teens and social media: The use of social media gains greater foothold in teen life as they embrace the conversational nature of interactive online media.* Washington, DC: Pew Internet & American Life Project.

Leu, D.J., Zawilinski, L., Castek, J., Banerjee, M., Housand, B., Liu, Y., et al. (2007). What is new about the new literacies of online reading comprehension? In L. Rush, J. Eakle, & A. Berger (Eds.), *Secondary school literacy: What research reveals for classroom practices.* (pp. 37–68). Urbana, IL: National Council of Teachers of English (retrieved December 15, 2009, from www.newliteracies.uconn.edu/docs/whatsnew about online reading comprehension.pdf).

Leu, D.J., McVerry, J.G., O'Bryne, W.I., Zawilinski, L., Castek, J., & Hartman, D.K. (2009). The new literacies of online reading comprehension and the irony of no child left behind: Students who require our assistance the most, actually receive it the least. In L. M. Morrow, R. Rueda, & D. Lapp (Eds.), *Handbook of research on literacy and diversity* (pp. 173–194). New York, NY: Guilford Press.

Pearson, P.D. (1996). Six ideas in search of a champion: What policy-makers should know about the teaching and learning of literacy in our schools. *Journal of Literacy Research, 28,* 302–309.

Spiro, R.J. (1980). Constructive processes in prose comprehension and recall. In R.J. Spiro, B.C. Bruce, & W.F. Brewer (Eds.), *Theoretical issues in reading comprehension: Perspectives from cognitive psychology, linguistics, artificial intelligence, and education* (pp. 245–278). Hillsdale, NJ: Lawrence Erlbaum Associates.

Spiro, R.J. (2001). Principled pluralism for adaptive flexibility in teaching and learning to read. In R.F. Flippo (Ed.), *Reading researchers in search of common ground* (pp. 92–97). Newark, DE: International Reading Association.

Spiro, R.J. (2006). The "New Gutenberg Revolution": Radical new learning, thinking, teaching, and training with technology ... bringing the future near. *Educational Technology, 46* (6), 3–5.

Spiro, R.J., & DeSchryver, M. (2008). Constructivism: When it's the wrong idea and when it's the only idea. In T. Duffy & S. Tobais (Eds.) *Constructivist instruction: Success or failure?* Mahwah, NJ: Lawrence Erlbaum.

Spiro, R.J., & Jehng, J.C. (1990). Cognitive flexibility and hypertext: Theory and technology for the nonlinear and multidimensional traversal of complex subject matter. In D. Nix & R.J. Spiro (Eds.), *Cognition, education, and multimedia: Explorations in high technology* (pp. 163–205). Hillsdale, NJ: Lawrence Erlbaum.

Spiro, R.J., & Myers, A. (1984). Individual differences and underlying cognitive processes in reading. In P.D. Pearson (Ed.), *Handbook of research in reading* (pp. 471–501). New York, NY: Longman.

Spiro, R.J., Vispoel, W.L., Schmitz, J., Samarapungavan, A., & Boerger, A. (1987). Knowledge acquisition for application: Cognitive flexibility and transfer in complex content domains. In B.C. Britton & S. Glynn (Eds.), *Executive control processes* (pp. 177–200). Hillsdale, NJ: Lawrence Erlbaum Associates.

Spiro, R.J., Feltovich, P.J., Coulson, R.L., & Anderson, D. (1989). Multiple analogies for complex concepts: Antidotes for analogy-induced misconception in advanced knowledge acquisition. In S. Vosniadou & A. Ortony (Eds.), *Similarity and analogical reasoning* (pp. 498–531). Cambridge, MA: Cambridge University Press.

Spiro, R.J., Feltovich, P.J., Jacobson, M.J., & Coulson, R.L. (1992a). Cognitive flexibility, constructivism, and hypertext: Random access instruction for advanced knowledge acquisition in ill-structured domains. In T. Duffy & D. Jonassen (Eds.), *Constructivism and the technology of instruction* (pp. 57–75). Hillsdale, NJ: Erlbaum. [Reprinted from a special issue of *Educational Technology on Constructivism.*]

Spiro, R.J., Feltovich, P.J., Jacobson, M.J., & Coulson, R.L. (1992b). Knowledge representation, content specification, and the development of skill in situation-specific knowledge assembly: Some constructivist issues as they relate to cognitive flexibility theory and hypertext. In T. Duffy & D. Jonassen (Eds.), *Constructivism and the technology of instruction* (pp. 121–128). Hillsdale, NJ: Erlbaum. [Reprinted from a special issue of *Educational Technology on Constructivism.*]

Spiro, R.J., Coulson, R.L., Feltovich, P.J., & Anderson, D.K. (1994). Cognitive flexibility theory: Advanced knowledge acquisition in ill-structured domains. In R.B. Ruddell, M.R. Ruddell, & H. Singer (Eds.), *Theoretical models and processes of reading* (4th ed., pp. 602–615). Newark, DE: International Reading Association. [Reprinted from: Tenth Annual Conference of the Cognitive Science Society. Hillsdale, NJ: Erlbaum, 1988.]

Spiro, R.J., Feltovich, P.J., & Coulson, R.L. (1996). Two epistemic world-views: Prefigurative schemas and learning in complex domains [Special issue on reasoning processes]. *Applied Cognitive Psychology, 10,* 51–61.

Spiro, R.J., Collins, B.P., & Ramchandran, A.R. (2007). Reflections on a post-Gutenberg epistemology for video use in ill-structured domains: Fostering complex learning and cognitive flexibility. In R. Goldman, R.D. Pea, B. Barron, & S. Derry (Eds.), *Video research in the learning sciences.* (pp. 93–100). Mahwah, NJ: Lawrence Erlbaum Associates.

PART II

What We Know about Literacy

Revisited

13

MULTICULTURAL CONSIDERATIONS AND DIVERSE STUDENTS

Kathryn H. Au

Christine Tanioka is an experienced fourth-grade teacher in a school in a rural community on the island of Hawaii. Her students are a mix of ethnicities, including Hawaiian, Filipino, European, and Japanese. Most come from low-income families, and speak Hawaii Creole English as their first language. Chris sets up her classroom so that students gain a sense of belonging to a community of readers (for a full description, see Carroll, Wilson, & Au, 1996). In Chris's classroom, the time to teach reading is called the "readers' workshop" (Au, Carroll, & Scheu, 1997), and it begins with sustained silent reading. During this time, Chris and her students spend about 15 minutes silently reading books of their own choosing.

Chris believes she can foster her students' motivation to read by demonstrating her own love of books. One day, she brought in a shopping bag full of books that she had taken from her nightstand. As she pulled each book from the bag, she told the class what it was about and why it was important to her. One book was about flower arranging, one of her hobbies. Another was about swimming, her children's favorite sport. Another was a novel a colleague had recommended. Her collection included several children's books, which she said she loved best of all.

Chris often gives her students several minutes to share their reading with classmates. She and a few students may give book talks, she may recommend books, and the students may recommend books to one another. Sometimes, when she encounters a reluctant reader, Chris chooses a book from her personal collection to lend that student. Chris further motivates her students by reading aloud a chapter a day from a favorite novel.

Chris devotes time each day to improving her students' skills as readers. She presents the whole class with a minilesson (Calkins, 1994), lasting about 5 to 10 minutes, focusing on procedures, the author's craft, or basic skills. During the first half of the school year, she meets with students in small groups for reading instruction, seeing each group at least three times a week. Often, these lessons of up to half an hour will center on guided discussion of a novel or short story, to sharpen students' comprehension, including their ability to construct a theme (Au, 1992).

Later in the year, when students have gained in reading proficiency and independence, especially in comprehending literature, Chris organizes the class in literature circles. Literature circles are discussion groups of about six students who are reading the same novel (Au et al., 1997). Each day, students read a chapter or so in the novel and write an individual response to their reading. Their responses include questions and issues for possible discussion by their literature circle. Discussions are lively, because Chris has her students read books, such as *On My Honor* (Bauer, 1986), that give them many issues to debate. This fourth-grade classroom is an example of a multicultural educational setting in which students are successfully learning to read.

Students of Diverse Backgrounds

From the perspective of multicultural education, nine variables are considered important in shaping an individual's cultural identity (Gollnick & Chinn, 1990): ethnicity, social class, primary language, gender, age, religion, geographic region, place of residence (whether urban, suburban, or rural), and exceptionality. Three variables—ethnicity, social class, and primary language—pose a challenge to schools in terms of students' literacy learning. In the United States, for example, schools often do not succeed in bringing to high levels of achievement students who are African American, Latino, or Native American in ethnicity, from low-income families, and speakers of a first language other than standard English. (This language may be a dialect of English, such as African American language or Hawaii Creole English, or it may be another language, such as Spanish.) I will refer to these students, including those in the classroom just described, as students of diverse backgrounds. Students of diverse backgrounds may be contrasted with students of mainstream backgrounds. In the United States, these students are generally European American in ethnicity, from middle-income families, and speakers of standard English.

Considerable evidence points to a gap between the literacy achievement of students of diverse backgrounds and those of mainstream backgrounds. A major source of evidence is the National Assessment of Educational Progress (NAEP), which has monitored the literacy achievement of US students at three grade levels for more than 25 years. Results for the 1994 reading assessment for Grade 4 (9-year-olds) revealed the following percentages of students performing below a basic level of proficiency: Whites, 29%; African Americans, 69%; and Hispanics, 64% (Nettles & Perna, 1997). Similar differences were seen at Grade 8 (13-year-olds) and Grade 12 (17-year-olds). Although the gap appears to be narrowing somewhat, we continue to see large differences between the literacy achievement of students of diverse backgrounds and that of mainstream students.

Multicultural education offers a perspective for understanding the literacy achievement gap and thinking about how it might be narrowed. The goal of multicultural education is to bring about changes in schools that will enable all students to attain educational equality (Banks, 1995). Banks (1994) highlights three major approaches to multicultural education. In the curriculum reform approach, educators change the curriculum to give greater prominence to the experience of different ethnic, cultural, and gender groups. In the intergroup education approach, educators enhance students' understanding of and positive attitudes toward marginalized groups. If the students are members of marginalized groups, the goal is to enhance their appreciation of their own culture and heritage. In the achievement approach, educators work to improve the academic achievement of students of diverse backgrounds, who traditionally have not been well served by schools.

This chapter focuses on the achievement approach to multicultural education. I discuss ways of improving the school literacy learning of students of diverse backgrounds within the framework provided by the Expert Study (Flippo, 1998; refer to Chapter 1 in this book). The experts were asked to reach agreement about contexts and practices that would either make learning to read difficult or facilitate learning to read for most students. I try to show how these agreements are particularly important to the school literacy learning of students of diverse backgrounds. For this purpose, I organized the experts' agreements into six topics, as shown in Table 13.1. These groupings are similar (but not identical) to those devised by Flippo.

Interpretation of Experts' Agreements

1. Linking All Language Processes

As mentioned earlier, students of diverse backgrounds in the United States often enter school speaking a first language other than standard English. The agreements in the Expert Study do not refer directly to the needs in learning to read of second-language learners. Nevertheless, the literacy learning of second-language learners is promoted when teachers use every opportunity to bring reading, writing, talking, and listening together, so that each process supports the other.

During literature discussions in Chris Tanioka's class, students sometimes express their ideas in Hawaii Creole English. Chris accepts students' ideas without stopping to correct their language, because she does not want to embarrass students and inhibit their participation. However, when she responds to students' ideas, Chris speaks in standard English. In this way, she models standard English syntax and vocabulary for students. As the discussion continues, students will often use the standard English forms that Chris has just modeled for them.

TABLE 13.1 Summary Agreements in the Six Topics

1. Linking All Language Processes

Do

- Use every opportunity to bring together reading/writing/talking/listening so that each feeds off and feeds into the other.
- Instead of deliberately separating reading from writing, plan instruction and individual activities so that, most of the time, students engage in purposeful reading and writing.

Don't

- Teach reading as something separate from writing, talking, and listening.

2. Ownership and Purposes for Reading

Do

- Provide multiple, repeated demonstrations of how reading is done or used.
- Focus on using reading as a tool for learning.
- Make reading functional.
- Give your students lots of time and opportunity to read real books (both narrative and expository), as well as time and opportunity to write creatively and for purposeful school assignments (e.g., to research a topic, to pursue an interest).
- Create environments/contexts in which the children become convinced that reading does further the purposes of their lives.

Don't

- Avoid reading for your own enjoyment or personal purposes in front of the students.

3. Independent Reading

Do

- Encourage children to talk about and share the different kinds of reading they do in a variety of ways with many others.

Don't

- Require children to write book reviews of every book they read.
- Make a practice of not reading aloud very often to children.
- Stop reading aloud to children as soon as they get through the primer level.
- Select all the stories that children read.
- Remove the freedom to make decisions about reading from the learner.

4. Rejection of a Behaviorist Model of Teaching

Don't

- Make sure children do it correctly or not at all.
- Focus on the single best answer.
- Make reading correctly or pronouncing words "exactly right" a prime objective of your classroom reading program.
- Detect and correct all inappropriate or incorrect eye movements you observe as you watch children in your classroom during silent reading.
- Refrain from giving children books in which some of the words are unknown (i.e., words that you have not previously taught or exposed them to in some way).
- Insist on providing lots of training on all the reading skills prior to letting children read a story silently, even if there is not much time left for actual reading.
- Teach the children in your classroom letters and words one at time, making sure each new letter or word is learned before moving on to the next letter or word.
- Emphasize only phonics instruction.
- Drill children on isolated letters and sounds using flashcards, chalk or magnetic boards, computers, or worksheets.
- Assign a few more skill sheets to remedy the problem if a child is not "getting it."

5. High Expectations

Do

- Develop positive self-perceptions and expectations.
- Use silent reading whenever possible, if appropriate to the purpose.

Don't

- Group readers according to ability.
- Tell students who are weak in reading that reading is a difficult and complex process and that you do not expect them to be able to do the more difficult reading work.
- Have the children do oral reading exclusively.
- Have children orally read a story in small groups, allowing one sentence or paragraph at a time for each child, and going around the group in either a clockwise or counterclockwise rotation.
- Focus on children's learning the skills rather than on interpretation and comprehension.
- Make sure children understand the seriousness of falling behind.
- Encourage competitive reading.

continued

TABLE 13.1 continued

6. Reading Materials

Do

- Include a variety of printed material and literature in your classroom so that students are exposed to the different functions of numerous types of printed materials (e.g., newspapers, magazines, journals, textbooks, research books, trade books, library books, menus, directions).
- Use a broad spectrum of sources for student reading materials.

Don't

- Have children read short, snappy texts rather than whole stories.
- Follow your basal's teaching procedures as detailed without making any modifications.
- Use workbooks with every reading lesson.
- Test children with paper-and-pencil tests whenever they complete a new story in their basal, and each time you have finished teaching a new skill.

During the writers' workshop in Chris's classroom, students engage in peer conferences, when they frequently exchange ideas in Hawaii Creole English. Using their first language allows students' thoughts to flow freely, and helps them clarify the ideas they wish to write about. When students have their ideas clearly in mind, they orally rehearse these ideas in standard English. Then they are ready to begin writing down their ideas.

Moll and Diaz (1987) found that Spanish-speaking students showed excellent comprehension of a story read in English when they were allowed to discuss the story in Spanish. The students had many ideas about the story that they were unable to express in English. These investigators concluded that students' comprehension of English texts was being underestimated, because they did not have the opportunity to express their understandings in Spanish.

As these examples suggest, students' proficiency in their first language provides a foundation that teachers can build on to promote reading and writing. The difficulty in schools is that students are often denied the opportunity to use strengths in the first language as the basis for learning to read and write. Research supports the idea that students are best taught to read and write in their first language (Snow, Burns, & Griffin, 1998). Once students have learned to read and write in the first language, usually by the third or fourth grade, the transition is made to reading and writing in the second language. For example, Spanish-speaking students in the United States might first learn to read and write in Spanish, then make the transition to English reading and writing.

In many cases, however, it may not be practical to provide students with initial literacy instruction in the first language. Often the students come from many different language backgrounds or there is a lack of qualified teachers who speak students' first languages. But even when students are learning to read and write in a second language, teachers can take steps to build upon strengths in the first language. For example, a student might be given the opportunity to participate in a literature discussion using the first language. Another student in the class might then translate the first student's points for the teacher and other students. In short, students of diverse backgrounds benefit from literacy learning situations in which all four language processes—reading, writing, listening, speaking—are linked.

2. Ownership and Purposes for Reading

The term "ownership" does not appear in the experts' agreements, but a number of the agreements recognize the importance of students' ownership of literacy. Ownership involves students' valuing of reading and writing at home as well as at school (Au, 1997). Students with ownership use literacy for purposes they set for themselves, and make reading and writing a part of their everyday lives. When Chris Tanioka helps her students find books they will enjoy reading, she is trying to build their ownership of literacy.

In the past, educators focused on proficiency, or skill, as the overarching goal. Of course, students' knowledge of reading strategies and skills remains important. However, we now understand that skill in reading should not be separated from the will to read (Winograd & Paris, 1988). For example, we do not consider the teacher's job to be done if a student becomes a skillful reader but reads only for school assignments and never chooses to read for her own enjoyment or information. Such a student does not yet see reading as personally meaningful, or understand how reading can be used to meet the purposes she has set for herself. When we make students' ownership of literacy the overarching goal, we remind ourselves to encourage not just proficiency but purposeful, self-motivated reading.

When educators recognize the importance of ownership, they try to help students make connections between literacy at home and literacy in school. Research shows that students of diverse backgrounds often have a variety of home experiences with literacy. For example, the inner-city, African American families studied by Taylor and Dorsey-Gaines (1988) read to gain information about current events. Newspapers, and often magazines, were present in the apartments of all these families. In this case, teachers might make the connection to literacy at home by conducting classroom activities involving the newspaper. Depending on the age and interests of the students, teachers might have them read and respond to articles about sports and entertainment, or to editorials and advertisements.

The difficulty appears to be that the home literacy experiences of students of diverse backgrounds may not be those expected by teachers. Teachers may assume that children are entering school with a background in family storybook reading, a type of reading event not experienced by children in all cultures (Heath, 1982). Teachers may not realize that, if family storybook reading has not been part of home routines, students will need many positive school experiences with storybook reading and other mainstream literacy activities in order to see the benefit of these activities for their everyday lives. To provide these experiences, teachers can read aloud storybooks that children will find interesting and engaging. They can help children see connections between the events in stories and events in their own lives, so that children come to regard reading as personally meaningful.

The example set by the teacher may be important in promoting ownership of literacy by students of diverse backgrounds. We saw how Chris Tanioka shared with her class the books she was reading for her own enjoyment and learning. Some of the students in Chris's class may not have witnessed such enthusiasm for books among the adults in their own families. Through Chris's sharing, they caught a glimpse of how the reading of books can be both joyful and informative, at home as well as at school.

Meaningful and motivating activities can lead all students to achieve higher levels of literacy. However, teachers in mainstream classrooms can usually count on students to complete literacy assignments even when they do not know the purpose behind these activities. The reason is that mainstream students realize the importance of complying with teachers' requests and getting good grades. They know they need to graduate from high school and go on to college to have good life opportunities, including high-paying jobs. Students of diverse backgrounds may lack this same understanding because the connection between schooling and life opportunities may not have been illustrated in the histories of their own families (Ogbu, 1981).

Teachers in classrooms with students of diverse backgrounds cannot count on students to complete literacy assignments they find meaningless. Students may fail to show compliance because they neither see the value of schooling nor understand its long-term consequences for their lives. With students of diverse backgrounds, teachers should be aware of providing immediate, as opposed to long-term, reasons for staying in school (D'Amato, 1988). An immediate reason is provided when students know that they will be engaging in meaningful and motivating literacy activities on a daily basis. Such activities may include listening to the teacher read aloud the next chapter of an exciting book, debating the interpretation of a novel with peers, and conducting research on a topic of personal interest.

3. Independent Reading

As shown in Table 13.1, the experts reached agreement on a number of statements highlighting the importance of wide, independent reading. Research points to the benefits of such reading. Wide, independent reading provides students with opportunities to strengthen comprehension, build vocabulary, and orchestrate word-identification skills (Anderson, Wilson, & Fielding, 1988). In addition, the independent reading of self-selected books gives students opportunities to develop their own tastes and interests as readers. Students of diverse backgrounds, like all students, improve their reading abilities when teachers support independent reading.

One of the experts' agreements concerns the importance of having students share the reading they do. Many teachers, such as Chris Tanioka, provide students with a daily time for sustained silent reading of books of their own choosing. Too often, however, teachers do not include time to share reading in connection with sustained silent reading. We have noted how Chris acted as a role model by telling students about the books she was reading. Students can also act as reading role models for one another, if teachers give them the time to share books in class. The sharing of books to celebrate one's own reading and boost the reading of others differs from the typical practice of having students write book reports. The experts agreed that students should not be required to write a review of every book they read. Understandably, students may be reluctant to read if they know they will have to write a book report. Furthermore, the only audience for a book report is usually the teacher.

The sharing of books may take place in informal ways, such as giving students a couple of minutes to discuss their reading with a partner. Or sharing may take place in formal ways, such as having students prepare book talks or book posters to present to the whole class. Sharing activities are especially important in classrooms with students of diverse backgrounds. As pointed out earlier, although students may witness many literacy activities in the home and community, they may not have many avid readers of books as role models. Through the sharing of books, students receive recognition for the reading they are doing, and they gain ideas about what to read next by hearing classmates' recommendations.

The experts agreed that the teacher's reading aloud to students continues to be an important source of inspiration, even when students are able to read many books on their own. Several years ago, I conducted a study in which I interviewed fifth-grade students, most of them of Hawaiian ancestry, about their reading habits. In one of the questions, students were asked about their favorite author. At one school, many students told me that their favorite author was Roald Dahl. Through further questioning, I discovered that these students had all been in the same third-grade classroom. Their teacher loved Roald Dahl and had read aloud two of his books. Inspired by their teacher, the students had gone to the school library and borrowed other Roald Dahl books to read on their own. Clearly, a teacher's enthusiasm can lead students to books they might not have discovered by themselves.

4. Rejection of a Behaviorist Model of Teaching

The experts agreed on 10 statements, listed in Table 13.1, which show their rejection of a behaviorist model of teaching and learning. In a behaviorist model, reading is taught as a series of skills presented in a set sequence. Children learn through a process of direct instruction, in which skills are transmitted by the teacher. Skills earlier in the sequence must be mastered before students proceed to skills later in the sequence. This model assumes that all students can and will learn to read through training in the same set sequence of skills. Lower-level skills, such as phonics, are emphasized, and skills tend to be taught in isolation, apart from the reading of literature. The emphasis is on correct responses, such as giving the right answer to the teacher's question or pronouncing words "exactly right." Mistakes are believed to be harmful, because they indicate that children are practicing the wrong behavior. To prevent mistakes, the teacher provides training on reading skills and unknown words in advance of having children read on their own.

Many critiques of a behaviorist model of reading instruction are available (Shannon, 1989; Weaver, 1990). In this section, I focus specifically on reasons for avoiding use of a narrow, behaviorist model in classrooms with students of diverse backgrounds. First, isolated skill instruction may detract from students' ownership of literacy. As discussed earlier, students of diverse backgrounds need meaningful and motivating literacy learning experiences in the classroom. Isolated skill instruction is likely to be neither. When skills are taught in isolation, it may be difficult for students to see the point of instruction, and they may be less willing to learn skills. Isolated skill instruction may be based on scripted lessons, in which no connections are made to children's own background experiences. Even if skills are learned, students may not understand how to apply these skills to real reading.

Problems of motivation and application can be avoided if skills are taught not in isolation but in the context of meaningful literacy activities, such as the reading of an exciting book or an informational article on a high-interest topic. For example, when children are reading *The Cat in the Hat* (Seuss, 1957), the teacher has the perfect opportunity to teach the -at phonogram. The teacher can explain to children that learning this particular skill will help them read this and other books on their own. Children can find -at words in *The Cat in the Hat* as well as in other books, and the teacher can create a chart listing all the -at words the children have discovered. This is an example of how children can be introduced to a skill in the context of the reading of literature, and then encouraged to apply the skill when they read other books.

Second, students of diverse backgrounds may be prevented from progressing rapidly in learning to read if they are required to proceed through a set sequence of skill instruction in which each skill must be mastered before the next is taught. Research on emergent literacy provides considerable information about how young children develop as readers and writers, but much more remains to be learned, especially about the literacy development of young students of diverse backgrounds (McGee & Purcell-Gates, 1997). We do know that young children growing up in different cultural contexts may develop different understandings of literacy (Heath, 1982). For this reason, among others, it is not the case that one set sequence of skill instruction will be beneficial to all students (Allington, 1997).

Learning to read is not a process of mastering particular skills in a set order. Instead, learning to read appears to be a process of successive approximation (Holdaway, 1979), in which children develop proficiency by engaging in the full processes of reading and writing. For example, children attempt to read books and to write their own stories. While attempting these activities, young children will show behavior that seems sensible to them but that looks unconventional to adults. For example, young children may "read" a story by referring to the pictures, or they may represent a word by writing just its first letter. Such approximations are part and parcel of the literacy learning process.

Children may learn more quickly and develop deeper understandings of literacy if their teacher encourages them to take risks, so they can discover for themselves how reading and writing work. For example, research suggests that children who have the opportunity to invent their own spellings for words become better spellers in the long run than children who learn spelling primarily by rote memorization (Ehri, 1987). The reason is that children who invent their own spellings come to understand for themselves how the English spelling system works; children who do not engage in the process of invention do not develop the same degree of understanding. If children hesitate to read and write because they fear making mistakes, their literacy learning may be slowed. To narrow the literacy achievement gap, we must speed and strengthen the literacy learning of students of diverse backgrounds, by seeing that they are actively engaged in constructing their own understanding of how reading and writing work.

In encouraging children to learn to read and write through a process of successive approximation, teachers such as Chris Tanioka still provide skill instruction (Carroll, Wilson, & Au, 1996). However, teachers determine which skills to teach not by following a set sequence, but by observing children. In this way, the teacher can see which skills children already understand and which skills they are ready to learn next. If children are "reading" pictures instead of print, the teacher can call their attention to the words on the pages of a big book and show them how to track print. If children are writing words using only the first letter, the teacher can show them how to say a word slowly, listen for other sounds, and write down the letters for these other sounds.

Third, use of a behaviorist model of reading instruction in classrooms with students of diverse backgrounds may cause too much time to be given to lower-level skills and too little to higher-level thinking. Research suggests that a considerable amount of the reading instruction in classrooms with students of diverse backgrounds centers on oral reading (Fitzgerald, 1995). Because the focus is on accurate word-calling, students may get the impression that the most important part of reading is to pronounce the words correctly. In classrooms with Spanish-speaking students and other second-language learners, and in classrooms with students who speak a non-mainstream variety of English, teachers may spend considerable amounts of time correcting students' pronunciation of words read aloud (Piestrup, 1973; Fitzgerald, 1995). Moll and Diaz (1987) found that when teachers judged Spanish-speaking students' reading proficiency mainly on the basis of their correct pronunciation of English words, they tended to underestimate their reading achievement. Erickson (1993) suggested that teachers' constant correction of the pronunciation of African American children may signal a denigration of the children's language and communication style. Over time, such signals may contribute to children's unwillingness to participate actively in reading lessons.

Studies demonstrate that the instruction of students of diverse backgrounds tends to be biased toward lower-level skills (Allington, 1991; Darling-Hammond, 1995). Every time the pendulum swings "back to basics," these students are likely to receive an even greater dose of isolated skill instruction. Lack of instruction in higher-level thinking in literacy—including summarization, interpretation, and critical evaluation—leaves students of diverse backgrounds at a disadvantage in comparison to their mainstream peers. If the literacy achievement gap is to be narrowed, students of diverse backgrounds must be given every opportunity to develop higher-level thinking.

5. High Expectations

The experts reached agreement on a number of statements about the importance of teachers having high expectations for students' learning. Although it is difficult to do, teachers must keep expectations high in classrooms with students of diverse backgrounds. Having high expectations for students' literacy learning, in the form of grade-level benchmarks tied to state and national standards, is one factor that can contribute to the improved literacy achievement of these students (Au & Carroll, 1997). Chris Tanioka found grade-level benchmarks useful in guiding her teaching, and in making her expectations clear to students. In schools such as the one in which Chris teaches, teachers must be aware of fighting the tendency to have lower expectations for students.

Students of diverse backgrounds tend to be over-represented in low-track, remedial reading, and special education programs, in which expectations for student learning are not high (Darling-Hammond, 1995). In the elementary classroom, students of diverse backgrounds are often placed in the lowest reading group. Studies show that low (as opposed to middle and high) reading groups present students with qualitatively different instructional experiences (Allington, 1983; Barr & Dreeben, 1991). In low reading groups, teachers emphasize oral reading and accurate word-calling. In high groups, the emphasis is on silent reading and comprehension of the text. When a low-group student reads a word incorrectly, the teacher is likely to jump in quickly with the right word (Allington, 1983). Teachers probably make these rapid corrections with good intentions, to save children from embarrassment. In contrast, when a high-group student misreads a word, the teacher often waits for the child to figure out the word herself. The upshot is that low-group students may have less opportunity than high-group students to learn to correct their own mistakes and to gain confidence in their abilities as readers.

These findings suggest that teachers should be aware of providing students of diverse backgrounds with ample time for silent reading and ample instruction in comprehension and higher-level thinking. Of course, instruction in word identification cannot be neglected if students are not yet fluent readers. However, even with beginning readers, teachers should make sure students understand that the purpose of reading is not just to identify words but also to gain meaning from text.

Students of mainstream backgrounds often expect to compete with other students and strive to be recognized for their superior performance. Individualism, achievement, and competition are all core mainstream values, but these values are not held by all cultural groups in the United States (Spindler & Spindler, 1990). Some students of diverse backgrounds may respond negatively to competitive reading, and may appear unconcerned about "falling behind" as readers. For some students of diverse backgrounds, contributions that benefit family and friends may have higher value than their own individual achievement in school. Rather than competing to be recognized individually, some students may prefer opportunities to work cooperatively with peers, such as in a literature circle. While it is essential to hold all students to the same high standards, instructional strategies responsive to differences in cultural values may be needed to help students of diverse backgrounds meet these standards (Au, 1993).

6. Reading Materials

The experts agree that teachers should make a wide variety of printed materials available to students, and that they should avoid many of the practices associated with traditional basal reading programs. These programs continue to be used in approximately 85% of US classrooms (Goodman, 1994). Chris Tanioka, along with most US teachers, taught for years with basal reading programs. However, the nature of texts and instructional recommendations to teachers do seem to be changing. Increasing numbers of teachers report that they supplement the materials provided by basal reading programs with the use of literature. In addition, literature-based instruction is central to all of the major basal reading programs published in the 1990s. Nearly all the selections in the student anthologies consist of literature, in the form of entire trade books or excerpts. Teachers' manuals appear to be moving away from a single, scripted approach to instruction, toward offering teachers a choice of approaches, including cooperative groups.

For educators interested in improving the literacy achievement of students of diverse backgrounds, these trends are all positive. Certainly, reading literature (rather than contrived texts of the "Dick and Jane" variety) is likely to provide students with challenging, interesting, and motivating reading experiences. Morrow (1992) found that students of diverse backgrounds who participated in a literature-based program outperformed control group students on a variety of literacy and language measures, including those for comprehension, story retelling, and story rewriting.

In particular, students of diverse backgrounds can benefit from the reading of multicultural literature as part of the classroom reading program. Works of multicultural literature, often written by authors of diverse backgrounds, present cultures in an authentic manner (Harris, 1992). The use of literature that accurately depicts the experiences of diverse groups may improve students' literacy achievement by increasing their motivation to read (Spears-Bunton, 1990).

When using multicultural literature, attention should be given to the curricular approach as well as to the selection of books. Using Banks' (1989) hierarchy of approaches in multicultural education, Rasinski and Padak (1990) defined several approaches for using multicultural literature, including the transformation and social action approaches. Teachers who follow these approaches use multicultural literature to guide students in the critical analysis of social issues, and seek to empower students to take action on these issues.

Teachers in classrooms with students of diverse backgrounds must be especially aware of using the suggestions in the teacher's manual in a flexible manner. Teachers have extensive knowledge of their students' backgrounds that can be applied to help students make personal connections to the story. Students in a reading group in Joyce Ahuna-Ka'ai'ai's third-grade class were reading a story in which the main characters are Japanese Americans. Joyce knew that one of her students, Chad, was part Japanese, and she asked him if he had a Japanese name. Chad said that he did, and he was able to compare himself to the children in the story, who also had both English and Japanese names. Joyce remarked that she would not have thought to ask such a question if she had been following a prescribed list of questions in a basal teacher's manual (Center for the Study of Reading, 1991).

The experts agree that workbooks should not be used with every reading lesson. Often, workbook pages center on the practice of lower-level skills. As discussed earlier, it may be more beneficial for students of diverse backgrounds if assignments focus instead on higher-level thinking and comprehension. Researchers have looked at the benefits of having students write in open-ended ways about the literature they are reading (Raphael & McMahon, 1994). Students share their written responses with peers in literature circles. Such purposeful writing for an audience of peers will generally be much more meaningful to students than the completion of workbook pages. With workbook pages, students may be more concerned with getting finished than with improving their reading skills (Scheu, Tanner, & Au, 1986).

Conclusion

The Expert Study points to six topics important in improving the literacy education of students of diverse backgrounds and narrowing the literacy achievement gap. In closing, I put forward some suggestions for educators, based on the agreements on each of these topics:

1. Link reading with writing, listening, and speaking, so that students of diverse backgrounds can use their strengths in all language processes when learning to read.
2. Provide students of diverse backgrounds with motivating, purposeful literacy activities that will promote their ownership of literacy.
3. Give students many opportunities for wide independent reading, and help them develop their own tastes and interests as readers.
4. Reject a behaviorist model of reading instruction and move instead toward approaches that emphasize higher-level thinking with text, promote students' risk-taking as literacy learners, and encourage students' active involvement in developing their own understandings of reading and writing.

5. Hold high expectations for the literacy achievement of students of diverse backgrounds, while realizing that instruction to help students meet these expectations may need to be responsive to their cultural values.
6. Center reading instruction on literature, drawing from knowledge of students' backgrounds to help them make personal connections to literature and encouraging them to share their thoughts about literature in writing and in discussions with peers.

In short, when I looked at the Expert Study from the perspective of the achievement approach to multicultural education, I found that the agreements fit quite well with research and with my own sense of what it will take to narrow the literacy achievement gap.

The Past 10 Years: In Retrospect

1. *What are the most important things that you believe literacy research has shown over the past 10 years? (Positive and/or Negative)*

I follow research about the school literacy learning of students of diverse cultural and linguistic backgrounds. From this perspective, I believe we have seen progress in two broad areas. The first is a vision of classrooms where diverse students are successfully learning to read and write, and the second is whole-school change that can make this vision a reality in more than a handful of classrooms. I see current research in these two areas as reinforcing three themes from my earlier chapter: (1) high expectations for students' literacy learning, (2) constructivist approaches to teaching and learning, and (3) ownership of literacy and literacy instruction.

Vision of Classrooms

In the terms of the vision of classrooms, for the theme of high expectations, research conducted by Taylor and colleagues (Taylor, Pearson, Peterson, & Rodriguez, 2003, 2005) constitutes a valuable contribution to the field. Taylor et al. conducted a series of studies of high-poverty schools that beat the odds, consistently achieving test scores higher than schools with comparable demographics. The theme of high expectations for student learning is reflected in the finding that, in contrast to other teachers, effective teachers ask their students more questions focused on higher-level thinking with text. By asking these questions, they raise the level of cognitive challenge for their students. Taylor et al. use the term "cognitive engagement" to describe the framework emerging from their studies. According to the cognitive engagement framework, teachers should strive to provide students with a challenging, motivating environment for literacy learning, where students have ample opportunity to engage in reasoning with text.

The theme of constructivist approaches to teaching and learning is addressed in the work of Raphael and her colleagues on Book Club Plus (Raphael, Florio-Ruane, & George, 2001). Raphael's recent efforts include adaptations of the Book Club Plus framework to address the literacy learning needs of English-language learners (Au & Raphael, 2010). For example, she described how a fourth-grade teacher of English-language learners (ELLs) uses Book Club Plus to build her students' vocabulary. Students are taught to identify for themselves the words that they would like to learn from their assigned text. They work within their book clubs (small groups of four to six students) to arrive at a list of six words that are central to comprehension of the text, appear repeatedly, and are generally useful. This approach allows the students to participate in in-depth study of 50–75 in each of the chapter books they read in class.

Ownership is shown when students value literacy so much, they make it part of their lives out of school as well as within the walls of the classroom (Au, 1997). The theme of ownership of literacy is emphasized in the work of Guthrie and colleagues on Concept-Oriented Reading Instruction (Guthrie et al., 1996). CORI is based on the concept that, if students are to read at high levels, they need concepts and strategies which they are motivated to use in an intentional manner. Guthrie and colleagues have done much to refocus the attention of literacy researchers on the importance of building students' ownership and motivation through literacy instruction. A comprehensive, authoritative review of engagement and motivation in reading is provided in the chapter by Guthrie and Wigfield (2000).

This research points to the following practical implications for teachers in classrooms serving high proportions of students of diverse cultural and linguistic backgrounds:

- At all grades, provide students with ample instruction focused on reading comprehension and reasoning with text. This instruction must begin at the earliest opportunity, in kindergarten with stories read aloud to children.
- Use constructivist frameworks for instruction, such as Book Club Plus, that are readily adapted to meet the needs of ELLs. The writers' workshop is another framework that provides ELLs with the opportunity to engage actively with text and to construct their own understandings (Au & Raphael, 2010).
- Increase students' motivation to learn and ownership of literacy by involving them with topics and text they find interesting and then incorporating concept and strategy instruction into this engaging context. Note that the idea is to start with interest and follow with skills, not the other way around (Au, 1993).

Whole-School Change in Literacy

Research such as that cited above has helped to make clear a vision of excellence in classroom literacy instruction that will help students of diverse cultural and linguistic backgrounds achieve high levels of literacy. I regard these developments as highly positive. Yet we have numerous studies to show that few students of diverse cultural and linguistic backgrounds are receiving literacy instruction of this nature; these studies provide important negative findings. For example, Glass (2008) outlined the many forces that have worked against students' access to high quality literacy instruction of the type described here. Glass pointed to such obstacles as the rhetoric about the failure of American public education, or what has been described as the manufactured crisis about falling test scores (Berliner & Biddle, 1997). In the era of No Child Left Behind (2001), schools came under increased pressure to raise scores on high-stakes tests. This pressure was felt most acutely in schools in low-income communities, those typically serving a high proportion of students of diverse cultural and linguistic backgrounds. In the rush to raise test scores, these schools relied increasingly on packaged programs to achieve results, including comprehensive reform programs (Correnti & Rowan, 2007). One unfortunate consequence of this chain of events was the narrowing of the curriculum, with increased attention to high-stakes testing and test preparation, a consequence particularly evident in high-minority states (Glass, 2008). Another was the deprofessionalization of teachers, who were increasingly regarded as implementers of packaged programs rather than as creators of curricula tailored to the needs of their students (Dillon, 2003), lending support to the notion of preparing teachers through alternative programs less costly and less rigorous than traditional, university-based, teacher education.

These negative research findings provide a context for understanding why the broad area of whole-school change in literacy is so important. Research must be conducted to show how the vision of successful classrooms, as described above, can be made a reality for many students of diverse backgrounds. We have known for two decades that students of diverse backgrounds require consistent instruction, over a period of 5–7 years, if they are to develop the language and literacy to prosper in school and to advance to college and promising careers (Cummins, 2003). The need for at least 5 years of consistent instruction means that literacy improvement efforts cannot center on individual teachers but must instead focus on schools, building toward coordinated K-12 systems of curriculum, instruction, and assessment.

Literacy researchers are starting to conduct studies of whole-school reform. Work in this area was reviewed by Taylor, Raphael, and Au (2011), who focused on research from seven different projects; six in the US and one in New Zealand. All projects emphasized teachers' professional development as the key to improved literacy achievement, as opposed to implementation with fidelity of a comprehensive reform model. These projects were selected for inclusion because they supported teachers in schools serving students of diverse cultural, linguistic, and socioeconomic backgrounds, demonstrated a positive impact on students' reading achievement, and had published results appearing in recognized archival research sources.

All projects reinforced the theme of high expectations, for both teachers and students. For example, in schools following the Standards-Based Change (SBC)

Process (Au, 2005; Raphael, Au, & Goldman, 2009), teachers focused on developing a shared vision of the excellent reader or writer who graduated from their schools, with a focus on higher-level thinking with text. The SBC Process led to improved student achievement because teachers developed their school's own staircase or coherent curriculum, implemented across the grades. As students moved through the grades, the consistent, coordinated instruction received through the grades enabled teachers to aim for increasingly ambitious end-of-year outcomes. Langer (2004) reported that effective teachers in her project taught students strategies for planning, organizing, completing, and reflecting on the content of their lessons. Effective teachers moved beyond basic concepts to teaching and exploration, leading to rich understandings of text ideas. Students further deepened their understandings through interactions with peers, focused on inquiry and collaboration. In less successful schools and classrooms, students received little strategy instruction, seldom engaged in in-depth discussion of texts, and rarely collaborated with peers.

In terms of the theme of constructivist frameworks, these studies show that such frameworks provide powerful contexts for teacher learning, as well as student learning. All projects had approaches to professional development based on allowing teachers not just to receive new information but also to construct their own understandings through extensive interaction with colleagues and supported application in their classrooms. For example, in successful schools in the School Change in Reading Process, teachers engaged in three-times-a-month study groups. The focus of these groups was on research-based reading topics, such as instruction to develop students' decoding, vocabulary, comprehension strategies, and higher-level thinking (Taylor et al., 2005). The study groups emphasized reflection and change in teaching, with teachers sharing videos of classroom instruction and examining samples of student work. Teachers were supported by school-based literacy coordinators and external facilitators who visited classrooms to model and coach. Teachers learned to reflect upon and improve their teaching by analyzing observational data of their own lessons. In the Minnesota project (Taylor & Peterson, 2007), all teachers met with other teachers in the state-wide project three times a year. A highlight of these meetings was that teachers—not just external literacy experts—presented at sessions and at round tables.

As with the theme of constructivist frameworks, it should be noted that the theme of ownership is applicable to teachers as well as students. In all projects, teachers took ownership of the literacy reform effort because they had the opportunity to shape curriculum, instruction, and assessment in ways that would allow them to improve their students' achievement. For example, in schools successful with the Standards Based Change Process (Au, Raphael, & Mooney, 2008), teachers formed a school-wide professional learning community to develop the elements in the system needed to improve students' reading achievement: a shared vision of the excellent reader or writer, grade-level benchmarks or end-of-year outcomes for student performance, and assessments to monitor students' progress toward meeting benchmarks. Teachers collected student assessment evidence three times per year and shared these results with the whole school, so that each grade would gain an understanding of what every other grade was attempting to accomplish in literacy. Teachers created curriculum guides that included goals for student learning, instructional strategies, instructional materials, and assessments. Finally, they learned to make the literacy curriculum transparent to students through techniques such as I Can statements (Cleland, 1999), student-friendly rubrics, portfolios with student self-assessment (Valencia, 1998), and three-way conferences (Wong-Kam, 1998).

2. *How do you think this should inform the contexts and practices of reading instruction in the classroom?*

The research on whole-school change to improve literacy achievement leads to the following practical implications for schools and classrooms serving many students of diverse cultural and linguistic backgrounds:

- Keep expectations for student performance high, by supporting teachers in creating a staircase curriculum across the grades. Implementation of the staircase curriculum will allow teachers to raise expectations for students' learning, thus boosting their achievement levels.
- Observe constructivist principles in teachers' professional development, allowing teachers ample time to learn about research-based ideas, discuss these ideas with peers, apply them in the classroom, and reflect upon the effectiveness of their implementation. Support teachers in constructing their own understandings of best practices and incorporating these practices in their classrooms. Give teachers opportunities to share what they have learned with teachers at other grade levels, and at other schools.
- Allow teachers to take ownership of literacy improvement efforts by involving them in creating all elements of the system, from the vision of the excellent reader or writer, to grade-level benchmarks, to assessments. Provide teachers with guidance at each step along the way, and show flexibility in increasing time and support as necessary so that teachers can do a quality job.

References

Allington, R.L. (1983). The reading instruction provided readers of differing abilities. *The Elementary School Journal, 83*, 548–559.

Allington, R.L. (1991). Children who find learning to read difficult: School responses to diversity. In E.H. Hiebert (Ed.), *Literacy for a diverse society: Perspectives, practices, and policies* (pp. 237–252). New York, NY: Teachers College Press.

Allington, R.L. (1997). Overselling phonics. *Reading Today*, August/September, pp. 15–16.

Anderson, R.C., Wilson, P.T., & Fielding, L.G. (1988). Growth in reading and how children spend their time outside of school. *Reading Research Quarterly, 23*, 285–303.

Au, K.H. (1992). Constructing the theme of a story. *Language Arts, 69*, 106–111.

Au, K.H. (1993). *Literacy instruction in multicultural settings.* Fort Worth, TX: Harcourt Brace.

Au, K.H. (1997). Ownership, literacy achievement, and students of diverse cultural backgrounds. In J.T. Guthrie & A. Wigfield (Eds.), *Reading engagement: Motivating readers through integrated instruction* (pp. 168–182). Newark, DE: International Reading Association.

Au, K.H. (2005). Negotiating the slippery slope: School change and literacy achievement. *Journal of Literacy Research, 37*(3), 267–286.

Au, K.H., & Carroll, J.H. (1997). Improving literacy achievement through a constructivist approach: The KEEP demonstration classroom project. *The Elementary School Journal, 97*, 203–221.

Au, K., & Raphael, T. (2010). Using workshop approaches to support literacy development of ELLs. In G. Li & P. Edwards (Eds.), *Best practices in ELL instruction* (pp. 207–221). New York, NY: Guilford Press.

Au, K.H., Carroll, J.H., & Scheu, J.A. (1997). *Balanced literacy instruction: A teacher's resource book.* Norwood, MA: Christopher-Gordon.

Au, K., Raphael, T., & Mooney, K. (2008). Improving reading achievement in elementary schools: Guiding change in a time of standards. In S. Wepner & D. Strickland (Eds.), *The administration and supervision of reading programs* (4th ed., pp. 71–89). New York, NY: Teachers College Press.

Banks, J.A. (1989). Multicultural education: Characteristics and goals. In J.A. Banks & C.A.M. Banks (Eds.), *Multicultural education: Issues and perspectives* (pp. 2–26). Boston, MA: Allyn & Bacon.

Banks, J.A. (1994). *An introduction to multicultural education.* Boston, MA: Allyn & Bacon.

Banks, J.A. (1995). Multicultural education: Historical development, dimensions, and practice. In J.A. Banks & C.A.M. Banks (Eds.), *Handbook of research on multicultural education* (pp. 3–24). New York, NY: Macmillan.

Barr, R., & Dreeben, R. (1991). Grouping students for reading instruction. In R. Barr, M.L. Kamil, P.B. Mosenthal, & P.D. Pearson (Eds.), *Handbook of reading research* (Vol. II, pp. 885–910). White Plains, NY: Longman.

Bauer, M.D. (1986). *On my honor.* Boston, MA: Clarion.

Berliner, D.C., & Biddle, B. (1997). *The manufactured crisis: Myths, frauds, and the attack on America's public schools* (College ed.). White Plains, NY: Longman.

Calkins, L.M. (1994). *The art of teaching writing* (2nd ed.). Portsmouth, NH: Heinemann.

Carroll, J.H., Wilson, R.A., & Au, K.H. (1996). Explicit instruction in the context of the readers' and writers' workshops. In E. McIntyre & M. Pressley (Eds.), *Balanced instruction: Skills and strategies in whole language* (pp. 39–63). Norwood, MA: Christopher-Gordon.

Center for the Study of Reading (1991). *Teaching reading: Strategies from successful classrooms.* [Six-part videotape series, available from the International Reading Association, 800 Barksdale Road, PO Box 8139, Newark, DE, 19714–8139].

Cleland, J.V. (1999). We Can charts: Building blocks for student-led conferences. *The Reading Teacher, 52*(6), 588–595.

Correnti, R., & Rowan, B. (2007). Opening up the black box: Literacy instruction in schools participating in three comprehensive school reform programs. *American Educational Research Journal, 44*(2), 298–338.

Cummins, J. (2003). BICS and CALP: Origins and rationale for the distinction. In C. Paulston & G. Tucker (Eds.), *Sociolinguistics: The essential readings* (pp. 322–328). Malden MA: Blackwell.

D'Amato, J. (1988). "Acting": Hawaiian children's resistance to teachers. *The Elementary School Journal, 88*, 529–544.

Darling-Hammond, L. (1995). Inequality and access to knowledge. In J.A. Banks & C.A.M. Banks (Eds.), *Handbook of research on multicultural education* (pp. 465–483). New York, NY: Macmillan.

Dillon, D.R. (2003). In leaving no child behind, have we forsaken individual learners, teachers, schools, and communities? In C.M. Fairbanks (Ed.), *52nd yearbook of the National Reading Conference* (pp. 1–31). Oak Creek WI: National Reading Conference.

Ehri, L.C. (1987). Learning to read and spell words. *Journal of Reading Behavior, 19*, 5–31.

Erickson, F. (1993). Transformation and school success: The politics and culture of educational achievement. In E. Jacob & C. Jordan (Eds.), *Minority education: Anthropological perspectives* (pp. 27–51). Norwood, NJ: Ablex.

Fitzgerald, J. (1995). English-as-a-second-language reading instruction in the United States: A research review. *Journal of Reading Behavior, 27*, 115–152.

Flippo, R.F. (1998). Points of agreement: A display of professional unity in our field. *The Reading Teacher, 52*, 30–40.

Glass, G. (2008). *Fertilizers, pills, and magnetic strips: The fate of public education in America.* Charlotte NC: Information Age Publishing.

Gollnick, D.M., & Chinn, P.C. (1990). *Multicultural education in a pluralistic society* (3rd ed.). Columbus, OH: Merrill.

Goodman, K. (1994). Foreword: Lots of changes, but little gained. In P. Shannon & K. Goodman (Eds.), *Basal readers: A second look* (pp. iii–xxvii). Katonah, NY: Richard C. Owen.

Guthrie, J.T., & Wigfield, A. (2000). Engagement and motivation in reading. In M.L. Kamil, P.B. Mosenthal, P.D. Pearson & R. Barr (Eds.), *Handbook of reading research* (Vol. III, pp. 403–422). Mahwah NJ: Erlbaum.

Guthrie, J.T., Van Meter, P., McCann, A.D., Wigfield, A., Bennett, L., Poundstone, C.C., et al. (1996). Growth of literacy engagement: Changes in motivations and strategies during concept-oriented reading instruction. *Reading Research Quarterly, 31*(3), 306–332.

Harris, V.J. (1992). Multiethnic children's literature. In K.D. Wood & A. Moss (Eds.), *Exploring literature in the classroom: Content and methods* (pp. 169–201). Norwood, MA: Christopher-Gordon.

Heath, S.B. (1982). What no bedtime story means: Narrative skills at home and school. *Language in Society, 11*, 49–76.

Holdaway, D. (1979). *The foundations of literacy.* Sydney, Australia: Ashton Scholastic.

Langer, J.A. (2004). *Getting to excellent: How to create better schools.* New York, NY: Teachers College Press.

McGee, L.M., & Purcell-Gates, V. (1997). So what's going on in research on emergent literacy? *Reading Research Quarterly, 32*, 310–318.

Moll, L.C., & Diaz, 5. (1987). Change as the goal of educational research. *Anthropology and Education Quarterly, 18*, 300–311.

Morrow, L.M. (1992). The impact of a literature-based program on literacy achievement, use of literature, and attitudes of children from minority backgrounds. *Reading Research Quarterly, 27*, 251–275.

Nettles, M.T., & Perna, L.W. (1997). *The African American data book: Preschool through high school education* (Vol. II). Fairfax, VA: Frederick D. Patterson Research Institute.

No Child Left Behind (2001). Public Law No. 107–110, paragraph 115 Stat. 1425, 2002, 2004 (retrieved from www.ed.gov/policy/elsec/leg/esea02/beginning/html).

Ogbu, J.U. (1981). School ethnography: A multilevel approach. *Anthropology & Education Quarterly, 12*, 3–29.

Piestrup, A.M. (1973). Black dialect interference and accommodation of reading instruction in first grade (Vol. IV). Berkeley, CA: University of California.

Raphael, I.E., & McMahon, SI. (1994). Book Club: An alternative framework for reading instruction. *The Reading Teacher, 48*, 102–116.

Raphael, T., Au, K., & Goldman, S. (2009). Whole school instructional improvement through the Standards-based Change Process. In J. Hoffman & Y. Goodman (Eds.), *Changing literacies for changing times: An historical perspective on the future of reading research, public policy, and classroom practices* (pp. 198–229). New York, NY: Routledge.

Raphael, T.E., Florio-Ruane, S., & George, M. (2001). Book Club Plus: A conceptual framework to organize literacy instruction. *Language Arts, 79*(2), 159–168.

Rasinski, T.V., & Padak, N.V. (1990). Multicultural learning through children's literature. *Language Arts, 67*, 576–580.

Scheu, J., Tanner, D., & Au, K.H. (1986). Designing independent practice activities to improve comprehension. *The Reading Teacher, 40*, 18–25.

Seuss, Dr (1957). *The cat in the hat.* New York, NY: Random House.

Shannon, P. (1989). *Broken promises: Reading instruction in twentieth century America.* New York, NY: Bergin & Garvey.

Snow, C.E., Burns, M.S., & Griffin, P. (1998). *Preventing reading difficulties in young children.* Washington, DC: National Academy Press.

Spears-Bunton, L.A. (1990). Welcome to my house: African American and European American students' responses to Virginia Hamilton's *House of Dies Drear. Journal of Negro Education, 59*, 566–576.

Spindler, G., & Spindler, L. (1990). *The American cultural dialogue and its transmission.* London, UK: Falmer Press.

Taylor, D., & Dorsey-Gaines, C. (1988). *Growing up literate: Learning from inner-city families.* Portsmouth, NH: Heinemann.

Taylor, B., & Peterson, D. (2007). *Year 2 report of the Minnesota Reading First Cohort 2 School Change project.* St Paul, MN: University of Minnesota, Center for Reading Research.

Taylor, B., Pearson, P., Peterson, D., & Rodriguez, M. (2003). Reading growth in high-poverty classrooms: The influence of teacher practices that encourage cognitive engagement in literacy learning. *Elementary School Journal, 104*, 3–28.

Taylor, B., Pearson, P., Peterson, D., & Rodriguez, M. (2005). The CIERA School Change Framework: an evidenced-based approach to professional development and school reading improvement. *Reading Research Quarterly, 40*(1), 40–69.

Taylor, B., Raphael, T., & Au, K. (2011). Reading and school reform. In M.L. Kamil, P.D. Pearson, E.B. Moje, & P.P. Afflerbach (Eds.), *Handbook of reading research*, Vol. IV (pp. 594–628). New York, NY: Routledge.

Valencia, S. (1998). *Literacy portfolios in action.* Fort Worth, TX: Harcourt Brace College Publishers.

Weaver, C. (1990). *Understanding whole language: Principles and practices.* Portsmouth, NH: Heinemann.

Winograd, P., & Paris, S.G. (1988). A cognitive and motivational agenda for reading instruction. *Educational Leadership, 46*, 30–36.

Wong-Kam, J. (1998). Sharing responsibility for assessment and evaluation with our students. In T. Raphael & K. Au (Eds.), *Literature-based instruction: Reshaping the curriculum* (pp. 305–329). Norwood, MA: Christopher-Gordon.

14

MOTIVATION TO READ

Jacquelynn A. Malloy and Linda B. Gambrell

There is an extensive body of theory and research-based knowledge about the broad area of motivation to learn. The research on motivation to read, however, having only been initiated in earnest over the past few decades, is comparatively less well developed. In the 1980s and 1990s researchers explored the nature of reading motivation as a construct, and delineated some of the important dimensions and contributing factors. These investigations provided insights about the relationship between reading motivation and reading achievement, and the essential elements of motivating classroom contexts.

What has developed over the recent decade is a focus on the situational aspects of reading motivation that are important to understanding how an individual student's motivation to read is influenced by the nature of the tasks, activities, and interactions that occur in classrooms. Researchers suggest that instruction that creates a situational, temporary, interest in literacy topics may lead to a more stable individual level interest in the activity over time (Ryan & Deci, 2000; Hidi, Bernforff, & Ainley, 2002; Renninger & Hidi, 2002; Guthrie, Hoa, Wigfield, Tonks, & Perencevich, 2006; Nolen, 2007).

This research supports a "community of learners" approach (Pressley, 1998) to promote reading motivation and learning. By creating classroom contexts that include small groups in understanding and creating texts or solving problems, students become engaged in sustained, in-depth, and authentic interactions with texts and online media where each member has opportunities to contribute to the learning of all members. Guthrie and colleagues (1996a, 1996b, 2000, 2001, 2006) present a well-researched model of these communities of learning in their Concept Oriented Reading Instruction (CORI) involving information texts and content learning. Students involved in the CORI model developed questions in response to hands-on authentic activities related to the target content learning, then used a variety of texts and peer interactions to engage in a group investigation of a topic using appropriate comprehension strategies.

In another recent study, reading, writing, and discussion were explored within the context of authentic tasks (Gambrell, Hughes, Calver, Malloy, & Igo, 2011). Specifically, students read books, talked about their interpretations of the books in peer-led discussion groups, and engaged in letter writing about the books with adult pen pals. Findings revealed that students' literacy motivation increased for both boys and girls over the course of a school year, and that the increase was particularly salient for boys. One possible explanation for this finding is that the authentic and purposeful nature of the pen pal exchange with an adult carried a sufficient social significance for boys such that they perceived a utility value for engaging in the reading, discussion, and writing activities. Exchanging ideas with an adult who is personally interested in their thoughts may provide a context for scaffolding the school-related tasks of creating, revising, and communicating personal interpretations of a commonly read book. In addition, the study found that students engaged in important higher-order thinking skills as they talked and wrote about their books. The findings of this investigation suggest that authentic literacy tasks such as pen pal exchanges and small group discussions support and sustain literacy motivation.

Brophy (1999, 2004) suggests that our quest to promote students' motivation to learn—and to read—must begin at the curricular level. Focusing on what we teach in school, Brophy challenges educators to consider the relevance of our curriculum, and to match content to motivational strategies (1999). Students are more likely to become engaged in learning outcomes that connect to their lives and are relevant to their futures (2004). These newer lines of research extend our understanding of the student-level aspects of motivation to read and provide ample fodder for considering how, and for what purposes, we create contexts for reading in school that support and nurture the reading motivation of our students.

The Importance of Motivation

Motivation is of considerable consequence in reading development for a number of reasons. First, motivation often makes the difference between learning that is superficial and shallow, and learning that is deep and internalized (Gambrell, 1996; Guthrie, Wigfield, & VonSecker, 2000; Guthrie, Schafer, & Huang, 2001). Second, we know that children who are motivated and who spend more time reading are better readers (Anderson, Wilson, & Fielding, 1988; Taylor, Frye, & Maruyama, 1990; Morrow, 1992; Guthrie et al., 2001). Third, supporting and nurturing reading motivation and achievement is crucial to improving the educational prospects of all children, and particularly those who find learning to read difficult (Allington, 1986; Smith-Burke, 1989; Chapman & Tunmer,

2003; Morgan & Fuchs, 2007). Teachers have long recognized that motivation is at the heart of many of the pervasive problems we face in teaching young children to read. In a review of 15 studies, Morgan and Fuchs (2007) compared variables such as reading skill and either reading competence or goal orientation and found a moderate correlation between reading ability and motivation. Because of the powerful influence that motivation plays in early literacy learning, teachers are more interested than ever before in understanding the relationships that exist between motivation and literacy development, and in learning how to guide all students toward improved reading ability and motivation.

The value that teachers, as well as reading experts place on motivation is supported by a robust research literature that documents the link between motivation and achievement (Dweck, 1986; Elley, 1992; Gambrell & Morrow, 1996; Flippo, 1998; Guthrie et al., 1998). Highly motivated readers generate their own reading opportunities. They want to read and choose to read for a wide range of personal reasons, such as curiosity, involvement, social interchange, and emotional satisfaction. According to Guthrie and colleagues (1998), highly motivated readers generate their own literacy learning opportunities, and in doing so they begin to determine their own destiny as literacy learners.

Motivation is a construct that is complex; consequently, an ever-increasing number of motivational theories have been put forth in an effort to explain the role of motivation in learning (see Malloy & Gambrell, 2008). Kuhl (1986) describes motivation as all latent and aroused goal states that drive, orient, and select behavior at any given point in time. Wittrock (1986) defined motivation as the process of initiating, sustaining, and directing activity. Maehr (1976) focused on the concept of continuing motivation, which he defined as the tendency to return to and continue working on tasks away from the instructional context in which they were initially presented, and Oldfather and colleagues (Oldfather & McLaughlin, 1993; Oldfather & Dahl, 1994) have defined motivation as the "continuing impulse to learn." More recently, Wigfield (1997) describes an *engagement perspective* that combines motivation to read with use of strategies and background knowledge to describe an involvement with text that is sustained and purposeful.

Contemporary theories of motivation emphasize the importance of self-perception in learning (Dweck, 1986; McCombs, 1989, 2003; Weiner, 1990; Wigfield, 1994; Wigfield & Eccles, 2000). Motivation is viewed as a function of individuals' learned beliefs about their worth, abilities, or competencies. A vast body of research (Bandura, 1977, 1989; Covington, 1985; Dweck, 1986; Weiner, 1990; Eccles, Wigfield, Harold, & Blumenfeld, 1993; Wigfield, 1994; Wigfield & Eccles, 2000) supports the contention that learned self-beliefs, expectations, and goals are critical factors that affect motivation and performance. In the following sections, motivation theories are briefly discussed, relevant research is presented, and theory and research-based recommendations for creating classroom contexts that support motivation to read are described.

Motivation: Theoretical Conceptualizations and Related Research

Fundamentally, motivation refers to what moves people to put forth effort. Motivational theorists, therefore, are concerned primarily with the "whys" of behavior. To understand motivation's influence on literacy behavior, theorists and researchers are interested in the choices students make about the reading they do, the amount of effort they exert on reading tasks, and their degree of persistence in the activity of reading.

There is a vast number of motivational theories that are relevant to the topic of motivation to read. Many of these theories overlap in principles and constructs (Bergin & Lafave, 1998); however, current theories of motivation are in general agreement about the importance of self-concept as a learner, and learning goals. While there are numerous theories of motivation that have direct implications for reading instruction, three overarching theoretical orientations have helped to inform us about motivation and learning: expectancy–value theory, goal orientation theory, and intrinsic and extrinsic theories of motivation.

Expectancy-Value Theory

A number of current theories suggest that self-perceived competence and task value are major determinants of motivation and task engagement (Eccles, Adler, Futterman, Koff, Kaczala, & Meece, 1983; Pintrich & Degroot, 1990; Pintrich, Roeser, & DeGroot, 1994; Wigfield, 1994). Eccles et al. (1983) and Wigfield (1994) have advanced an expectancy–value theory (EVT) of motivation that posits that motivation is strongly influenced by one's expectation of success or failure at a task, as well as the value or relative attractiveness the individual places on the task. The expectancy component of EVT is supported by a number of research studies which suggest that students who believe they are capable and competent readers are more likely to outperform those who do not hold such beliefs (Schunk, 1985; Paris & Oka, 1986; Chapman & Tunmer, 2003; Morgan & Fuchs, 2007).

In a survey-interview study designed to explore EVI, Gambrell (1995) interviewed third- and fifth-grade students and analyzed their responses by reading ability level (above grade level, on grade level, and below grade level). The results revealed a statistically significant difference among reading ability groups with respect to self-concept as a reader (expectancy). Responses of students reading below grade level in both third and fifth grades were lower in self-perceived reading competence. In addition, at the third-grade level, there were ability level differences with respect to self-perceived competence relative to peers, decoding ability, oral reading, and responding to questions about a reading, with the below grade-level students reporting lower self-perceived competence when compared to the on grade-level and above grade-level groups. On the other hand, there were not statistically significant differences among the reading ability groups with respect to the value of reading for either grade level.

In a review of studies on the self-efficacy and self-concepts of young children, Chapman and Tunmer (2003) found that these constructs develop in response to their initial successes or failures with learning to read. Early and repeated experiences where reading is difficult lead some students to view themselves as "poor readers," an attribution that is perceived as being difficult to change, and links between reduced self-efficacy and future valuing of reading as an activity may develop. These findings raise some interesting questions with respect to the EVT of motivation, and suggest that self-concept or expectancy is a critical factor in the reading motivation of young children, and that it can influence the construct of value.

Goal Orientation Theory

In goal orientation theory, learning goals are distinct from performance goals (Dweck & Elliot, 1983). A student with a learning goal in reading might want to learn about the topic of aviation, whereas a student with a performance goal would want to learn about aviation in order to make an "A" on a test. Both types of motivation goals can result in increased effort and attention; however, research suggests that learning goals are more likely to result in high-level learning and increased time devoted to the task.

Students who have literacy learning goals engage in reading tasks for pleasure or in order to acquire knowledge. Teachers who foster literacy learning goals emphasize understanding, enjoyment, and the usefulness of reading and writing rather than making good grades or competition (doing better as compared to others). On the other hand, teachers who emphasize performance goals are more likely to reward correct performance and emphasize task completion, rather than understanding, enjoyment, and the value of literacy learning.

Research by Ames and Archer (1988) suggests that students in classrooms that emphasize learning goals are more likely to have greater use of learning strategies than those in classrooms that emphasize performance goals. In a study with fifth and sixth graders, Meece, Blumenfeld, and Hoyle (1988) reported that students who held learning goals were more likely to report active cognitive engagement in learning tasks, as compared to students who held performance goals. According to Maehr (1976), a learning goal orientation is more likely to foster intrinsic motivation, enjoyment, and continuing impulse to learn.

Intrinsic and Extrinsic Theories of Motivation

Most motivational theorists identify two types of motivation: extrinsic and intrinsic (Deci & Ryan, 1985; Lepper & Hodel, 1989; Ryan & Deci, 2000).

Behavior is said to be extrinsically motivated when done to satisfy some external, separable goal, such as doing well on a spelling test in order to earn the privilege of a Saturday outing. Intrinsically motivated behavior, on the other hand, is characterized by a desire to engage in an activity because doing so brings personal satisfaction. Dichotomous theories of motivation that pit learning as a self-initiated process against learning as a conditioning process provide the context for viewing motivation as either intrinsic or extrinsic.

According to Ryan & Deci (2000) and Csikszentmihalyi (1990), intrinsically motivated actions are performed out of interest, and require no incentive other than the spontaneous experience of enjoyment, interest, and satisfaction that accompanies them. Extrinsically motivated behaviors, on the other hand, are performed for the external incentive or consequence that follows from their performance (Skinner, 1953; Bandura, 1977), although an externalized goal can become autonomized (Ryan & Deci, 2000). When an activity is seen as leading to a valued goal, even if it's not preferred or intrinsically motivating, the activity becomes self-endorsed as necessary to achieve a desired outcome. While other-imposed extrinsic motivators may cause resentment or avoidance of task, auto-momized extrinsic motivators actually increase motivation to engage in activites (Ryan & Deci, 2000).

While the distinction between intrinsic and extrinsic motivation is an important one, a simplistic view of the intrinsic–extrinsic dichotomy has often led to confusion and misinterpretation. While early studies intended to support the view that intrinsic and extrinsic motivation are antagonistic (Deci, 1971, 1972; Lepper, Greene, & Nesbit, 1973), other studies have suggested that, under certain circumstances, extrinsic incentives (tangible and intangible) can enhance intrinsic motivation to learn (McLoyd, 1979; Ryan, Mims, & Koestner, 1983; Ryan & Grolnick, 1986).

Teacher praise and feedback are intangible extrinsic incentives that have been shown to positively influence student attitudes and behavior. Lepper and Cordova (1992) found that verbal rewards in the form of teacher praise that provided verbal scaffolding, support, direction, and additional information led to more motivated, confident problem-solving. In addition, they reported that elaborated or embellished praise was more motivational than tangible incentives.

One of the most important findings in the research on motivation and learning is the facilitating effect of teacher praise and feedback on student achievement (Deci, 1971; Cameron & Pierce, 1994). A notable characteristic of both teacher praise and feedback is that they are, by their very nature, always closely linked to the desired student behavior, while tangible incentives (e.g., gold stars, stickers, toys) are usually unrelated to the desired behavior. While the research provides clear evidence that intangible rewards such as teacher praise and feedback, under certain conditions, enhance intrinsic motivation, the research is less clear about the effects of tangible incentives on student performance. Some studies report a decrease in intrinsic motivation following the receipt of a tangible reward (Deci, 1971, 1972, 1992; Lepper, Greene, & Nesbit, 1973), while others report an increase in motivation (Karnoil & Ross, 1977; Brennan & Glover, 1980).

In a classic study on motivation, McLoyd (1979) examined the effects of high-value versus low-value rewards on children's intrinsic interest in reading a high-interest versus low-interest book. The results of the study revealed that when the amount of time spent reading and the approximate number of words read were used as indices of intrinsic interest in reading, both high- and low-value rewards decreased children's interest in reading the high-interest book. On the other hand, high-value rewards significantly increased children's interest in reading the low-interest book. The results of this study suggest that, in general, rewards undermine reading motivation; however, highly valued incentives may enhance subsequent interest and involvement in tasks that children find relatively uninteresting.

McLoyd's study suggested that the type of reward influenced motivation. Extending this notion, Gambrell (1996) put forth the reward proximity hypothesis that intrinsic motivation is enhanced when a reward or incentive is linked to the desired behavior. For example, if one wants to foster intrinsic motivation to read, appropriate incentives that are clearly linked to the desired behavior of reading might include books, bookmarks, or extra time for reading. The reward proximity hypothesis posits that a person's intrinsic motivation will be enhanced if an incentive not only rewards the desired behavior, but also reflects the value of the behavior and encourages future engagement in the desired behavior (Gambrell & Marinak, 1997).

In a study designed to test the reward proximity hypothesis, elementary students completed an authentic reading task (choosing books for the school library) and then received a reward according to treatment condition: book reward, token reward (erasers, rings, charms, etc.), or no reward (Marinak & Gambrell, 2008). The children were asked to browse a selection of newly published books, choose one, read an excerpt, and offer their opinion regarding whether the book should be purchased for their library. After receiving their "reward" (book, token, or no reward) for helping to select books for the library, the students were allowed to choose from three activities to spend the remaining free time: continue reading, do a puzzle, or do a math game.

In this study, the students who were rewarded with books and the no-reward group were more likely to choose reading as a follow-up activity than students who were given small tokens as a reward. The findings of this study support the reward proximity hypothesis in that rewards unrelated to reading (tokens) resulted in decreased motivation to read, while a reward that was proximal (books) and no reward resulted in increased motivation to read. While research by Deci and colleagues (Deci & Ryan, 1985) demonstrates that overall rewards diminish intrinsic motivation, in the Marinak and Gambrell study (2008) intrinsic motivation to read was not diminished when students received books as a reward. Clearly, there is a need to investigate the role of incentives in the reading curriculum, particulary given the finding by Moore and Fawson (1992) that 95% of elementary teachers use some variation of a reading incentive program in their classrooms.

Wigfield and Guthrie (1997) also investigated how students varying in motivation differed in the amount and breadth of their reading. They measured both intrinsic and extrinsic aspects of motivation, and found that students who were highest in intrinsic motivation read nearly three times as many minutes per day as did the students who were lowest in intrinsic motivation, and those students who were highest in intrinsic motivation did not differ nearly as much on the different measures of the amount and breadth of reading.

Taken together, these motivation theories and related research suggest that motivation is strongly influenced by one's expectations of success or failure at a task, as well as the value or relative attractiveness or usefulness the individual places on the task. Students who believe they are capable and competent readers are more likely to outperform those who do not hold such beliefs (Schunk, 1985; Paris & Oka, 1986). In addition, students who perceive reading as valuable and important and who have personally relevant reasons for reading will engage in reading in a more planned and effortful manner (Dweck & Elliott, 1983; Paris & Oka, 1986; Ames & Archer, 1988; Guthrie et al., 2006).

What Research Reveals about Factors Associated with Reading Motivation

Two lines of research have provided important insights about schooling and reading motivation. One line of research explores the decline in motivation to read as children move up the grades in school. The other, more recent, line of research has focused on classroom factors associated with reading motivation. In studies of school motivation, most researchers have found that children begin school with optimistic beliefs and attitudes related to reading. For many children, these initially positive beliefs and attitudes decline across the elementary years (Stipek, 1988, 1996; Eccles et al., 1993).

In a large-scale longitudinal study, McKenna, Kear, and Ellsworth (1995) documented that positive attitudes toward reading declined as children progressed through the elementary grades. However, in a cross-cultural study of young children's motivation to read, Gambrell, Mazzoni, and Korkeamaki (1996) found that motivation to read increased during first grade on fall-to-spring measures, and began to decline during second grade for both Finnish and US students. Because US students begin first grade at 5 years old and Finnish students begin first grade at 7 years old, this study documents that schooling rather than an age-effect impacts reading motivation. This finding suggests that first grade may be a critical time in the development of motivation to read. Additional research is needed that will explore critical dimensions of motivation to read in first grade.

Research by Turner (1995), Morrow and Gambrell (1998), and Guthrie et al. (1998) suggests that the classroom context plays an important role in reading motivation. Turner's (1995) work in first-grade classrooms suggests the importance of open tasks that support students in choosing books, defining activities, and social interaction. The work of Morrow and Gambrell (1998) suggests the following kinds of classroom activities that have been found to foster motivation to read: materials that are easily accessible; teachers who model, guide and scaffold reading strategies; providing for choice; activities that are meaningful and functional; social collaboration; and opportunities for success (see also Edmunds & Bauserman, 2003). The research conducted by Guthrie et al. (2006) documents teaching practices that foster positive reading motivation, such as conceptual themes, real-world interactions, self-direction, interesting texts, social collaborations, self-expression, cognitive strategy instruction, time for engaged reading, and coherence.

Reading Motivation: Theory, Research, and Expert Agreement

There are several clear themes that run across current theories of motivation and research studies that have focused on classroom factors associated with reading motivation. In addition, the results of Flippo's Expert Study (1998) suggest that there is considerable agreement about the important role of motivation. Many of the points of agreement among the experts in Flippo's study appear to be grounded in the belief that motivated children are more likely to engage in meaningful learning, and that motivation is an important outcome of instruction (Bergin & LaFave, 1998). There appears to be congruence across theoretical perspectives, research findings, and reading experts—representing a range of diversity in their views and orientations toward reading education—that the following classroom characteristics foster motivation to read: access to reading materials, opportunities for self-selection, social interactions about books, and positive self-perception.

Access to Reading Materials

Having access to abundant materials to read—such as books, magazines, and newspapers—is critical to the development of reading motivation. Access to literacy materials encourages students to engage in reading in a voluntary and sustained manner. A number of studies have documented that when children have classroom environments that are book rich, the motivation to read is high (Elley, 1992; Morrow, 1992; Allington & McGill-Franzen, 1993; Lundberg & Linnakyla, 1993; Neuman & Roskos, 1993; Gambrell, 1995; Purcell-Gates, McIntyre, & Freppon, 1995; Guthrie et al., 1996a, 1996b; Edmunds & Bauserman, 2006).

According to Flippo's Expert Study (1998), reading experts agreed on the importance of giving students time and opportunity to read real books, both narrative and expository. Access to materials that are challenging and offer opportunities for success have consistently been found to promote motivation to read. The results of the studies cited above suggest that book access and time to read are significant factors in literacy development, and that greater attention should be devoted to assuring that high quality classroom libraries are a priority in our schools.

Opportunities for Self-Selection

Self-selection of reading materials is strongly linked to motivation to read. The role of choice in motivation in general, and reading motivation in particular, is well documented (McLoyd, 1979; Spaulding, 1992; Gambrell, 1995; Turner, 1995; Edmunds & Bauserman, 2006). Skinner and Bellmont (1993) found that students' intrinsic motivation increased during the academic year when teachers supported student choice of learning tasks and involvement in decision-making about learning activities. In addition, students in classrooms in which teachers supported student choice have demonstrated increased persistence, effort, attention, and intrinsic motivation (Ryan & Grolnick, 1986; Skinner & Bellmont, 1993).

The research related to self-selection of reading material supports the notion that books and stories that students find most interesting are those they have selected for their own reasons and purposes (Palmer, Codling, & Gambrell, 1994; Gambrell & Morrow, 1996). Schiefele's (1991) research revealed that students who were allowed and encouraged to choose their own reading material expended more effort in learning and understanding the material. Turner's (1995) research describes how classroom literacy experiences can be described in terms of task type. Open tasks were those in which students chose books, defined their activities, interacted with their peers, and co-constructed writing assignments. Closed tasks were those in which the teacher determined the reading materials, tasks, and outcomes, and students worked individually. Turner reported that open literacy tasks were more often associated with persistence than closed literacy tasks.

In Flippo's Expert Study (1998), there was consensus among reading experts that student choice and self-selection of reading materials is an important characteristic of classroom contexts that support literacy learning. For example, the reading experts rejected the notion that the teachers should "remove the freedom to make decisions about reading from the learners" and "select all the stories children read," suggesting consensus in recognizing the importance of student choice in learning to read. Clearly, there is congruence and consensus across theory, research, and reading experts that opportunities for choice promote students intrinsic motivation and independence as readers (Spaulding, 1992; Gambrell, 1995; Turner, 1995; Flippo, 2001; Edmunds & Bauserman, 2006; Guthrie et al., 2006).

Social Interactions about Books

Current theories of motivation recognize that learning is facilitated by social interactions with others (McCombs, 1989, 2003; Oldfather, 1993; Guthrie et al., 1998, 2001, 2002; Edmunds & Bauserman, 2006). A classroom environment that fosters social interaction is more likely to foster intrinsic motivation than are more individualized, solitary learning environments (Ames, 1984; Deci & Ryan, 1991; Guthrie, Schafer, Wang, & Afflerbach, 1995). Guthrie et al. (1998) found that students who had opportunities to interact socially with peers during literacy activities were more intrinsically motivated to read, and they read more widely and more frequently than students who were less socially interactive. A number of recent studies have revealed that social interaction promotes intrinsic motivation, achievement, and higher-level cognition (Almasi, 1995, 2001; Edmunds & Bauserman, 2003; Guthrie et al., 2006; Gambrell et al., 2011; see also Malloy & Gambrell, 2009).

There is agreement in the Expert Study (Flippo, 1998) about the importance of the role of social interaction in learning to read. The reading experts support the notion that children should be encouraged to talk about and share the different kinds of reading they do in a variety of ways with many others. Taken together, these studies suggest that motivated readers place a high priority on social interactions associated with the discussions about text, and that intrinsic motivation is enhanced when students perceive the learning context to be socially supportive.

Positive Self-Concept as a Reader

There is wide acceptance of the notion that motivation is strongly influenced by one's expectation of success or failure at a task as well as the value or relative attractiveness the individual places on the task. Learning and motivation are enhanced when students believe they are capable and competent (Schunk, 1985). These notions are in keeping with the view of the experts in the Expert Study (Flippo, 1998) who reported that it is important to develop positive self-perceptions and expectations, and that it is also important to create classroom environments and contexts in which children become convinced that reading furthers their purposes of their lives (Brophy, 1999, 2004).

Summary

There is a general consensus about the importance of motivation and developing an intrinsic desire to read across current theories of motivation, research, and expert opinion. We know a great deal about the construct of motivation, and how to create classroom contexts that support and nurture reading motivation. However, it is worth noting that although there is an extensive theory and research base with respect to achievement motivation, the theory and research on reading motivation continues to develop.

Clearly, there are many issues specifically related to reading motivation that will require our continued attention in order to understand more fully how children acquire motivation to read, and which classroom contexts support continued literacy engagement. There is movement toward developing a better understanding of the situational elements that contribute to reading motivation (Nolen, 2007; Malloy & Gambrell, 2008). Incorporating community-centered learning activities of relevant content for authentic purposes shows promise for developing classrooms where reading growth and motivation can flourish.

References

Allington, R.L. (1986). Policy constraints and effective compensatory reading instruction: A review. In J.V. Hoffman (Ed.), *Effective teaching of reading: Research and practice* (pp. 261–289). Newark, DE: International Reading Association.

Allington R.L., & McGill-Franzen, A. (1993, October 13). What are they to read? Not all children, Mr Riley, have easy access to books. *Education Week, 26*.

Almasi, J.L. (1995). The nature of fourth graders' sociocognitive conflicts in peer-led and teacher-led discussions of literature. *Reading Research Quarterly, 30*, 314–351.

Almasi, J.F., O'Flahavan, J.F. & Arya, P. (2001). A comparative analysis of student and teacher development in more and less proficient discussions of literature. *Reading Research Quarterly, 36*(2), 96–120.

Ames, C. (1984). Achievement attributions and self-instructions under competitive and individualistic goal structures. *Journal of Educational Psychology, 76*, 478–487.

Ames, C., & Archer, J. (1988). Achievement goals in the classroom: Students' learning strategies and motivation processes. *Journal of Educational Psychology, 80*, 260–267.

Anderson, R.C., Wilson, P.T., & Fielding, L.C. (1988). Growth in reading and how children spend their time outside of school. *Reading Research Quarterly, 23*, 285–303.

Bandura, A. (1977). *Principles of behavior modification*. New York, NY: Academic.

Bandura, A. (1989). Human agency in social cognitive theory. *American Psychologist, 44*, 1175–1184.

Bergin, D.A., & LaFave, C. (1998). Continuities between motivation research and whole language philosophy of instruction. *Journal of Literacy Research, 30*, 321–356.

Brennan, T.P., & Glover, J.A. (1980). An examination of the effect of extrinsic reinforcers on intrinsically motivated behavior: Experimental and theoretical. *Social Behavior and Personality, 8*, 27–32.

Brophy, J. (1999). Toward a model of the value aspects of motivation in education: Developing appreciation for particular learning domains and activities. *Educational Psychologist, 34*(2), 75–85.

Brophy, J. (2004). *Motivating students to learn*. Mahwah, NJ: Lawrence Erlbaum Associates.

Cameron, J., & Pierce, W.D. (1994). Reinforcement, reward, and intrinsic motivation: A meta-analysis. *Review of Educational Research, 64*, 363–423.

Chapman, J.W., & Tunmer, W.E. (2003). Reading difficulties, reading-related self-perceptions, and strategies for overcoming negative self-beliefs. *Reading and Writing Quarterly, 19*(1), 5–24.

Covington, M.V. (1985). The motive for self-worth. In C. Ames & R. Ames (Eds.), *Research on motivation in education: The classroom milieu* (pp. 77–113). San Diego, CA: Academic Press.

Csikszentmihalyi, M. (1990). *Flow: The psychology of optimal experience*. New York, NY: Harper Collins.

Deci, E.L. (1971). Effects of externally mediated rewards on intrinsic motivation. *Journal of Personality and Social Psychology, 18*, 105–115.

Deci, E.L. (1972). Intrinsic motivation, extrinsic reinforcement, and inequity. *Journal of Personality and Social Psychology, 22*, 113–120.

Deci, E.L. (1992). The relation of interest to the motivation of behavior: A self-determination theory perspective. In K.A. Renninger, S. Hidi, & A. Krapp (Eds.), *The role of interest in learning and development* (pp. 43–70). Hillsdale, NJ: Erlbaum.

Deci, E.L., & Ryan, R.M. (1985). *Intrinsic motivation and self-determination in human behavior*. New York, NY: Plenum.

Deci, E.L., & Ryan, R.M. (1991). A motivational approach to self: Integration in personality. In R.A. Dienstbier (Ed.), *Perspectives on motivation: Nebraska symposium on motivation* (Vol. 38, pp. 237–288). Lincoln, NE: University of Nebraska Press.

Dweck, C.S. (1986). Motivational processes affecting learning. *American Psychologist, 41*, 1040–1048.

Dweck, C.S., & Elliot, E.S. (1983). Achievement motivation. In E.M. Hetherington (Ed.), *Socialization, personality and social development* (pp. 643–681). New York, NY: Wiley.

Eccles, J.S., Adler, T.F., Futterman, R.B., Koff, S.B., Kaczala, C.M., & Meece, J.L. (1983). Expectancies, values, and academic behaviors. In J.T. Spence (Ed.), *Achievement and achievement motivation* (pp. 75–146). San Francisco, CA: Freeman.

Eccles, J.S., Wigfield, A., Harold, R., & Blumenfeld, P.C. (1993). Age and gender differences in children's self- and task perceptions during elementary school. *Child Development, 64*, 830–847.

Edmunds, K.M., & Bauserman, K.L. (2006). What teachers can learn about reading motivation through conversations with children. *The Reading Teacher, 59*(5), 414–424.

Elley, W.B. (1992). *How in the world do students read?* Hamburg, Germany: International Association for the Evaluation of Educational Achievement.

Flippo, R.F. (1998). Points of agreement: A display of professional unity in our field. *The Reading Teacher, 52*, 30–40.

Gambrell, L.B. (1995). Motivation matters. In W.M. Linek & E.C. Sturtevant (Eds.), *Generations of literacy: Seventeenth yearbook of the College Reading Association* (pp. 2–24). Harrisonburg, VA: College Reading Association.

Gambrell, L.B. (1996). Motivating contexts for literacy learning. In L. Baker, P. Afflerbach, & D. Reinking (Eds.)., *Developing engaged readers in school and home communities*. Mahwah, NJ: Lawrence Erlbaum Associates.

Gambrell, L.B., & Marinak, B.A. (1997). Incentives and intrinsic motivation to read. In J.T. Guthrie & A. Wigfield (Eds.), *Reading engagement: Motivating readers through integrated instruction* (pp. 205–217). Newark, DE: International Reading Association.

Gambrell, L.B., & Morrow, L.M. (1996). Creating motivating contexts for literacy learning. In L. Baker, P. Afflerbach & D. Reinking (Eds.), *Developing engaged readers in school and home communities* (pp. 115–136). Hillsdale, NJ: Erlbaum.

Gambrell, L.B., Mazzoni, S., & Korkeamaki, R.L. (1996, April). *Cross-cultural models of home-school early literacy practices*. Presentation at the Annual Meeting of the American Educational Research Association, New York.

Gambrell, L.B., Hughes, E., Calvert, W., Malloy, J., & Igo, B. (2011). Authentic reading, writing, & discussion: An exploratory study of a pen pal project. *Elementary School Journal* (in press).

Guthrie, J.T., Schafer, W., Wang, Y., & Afflerbach, P. (1995). Relationships of instruction to amount of reading: An exploration of a social, cognitive, and instructional connection. *Reading Research Quarterly, 30*, 8–25.

Guthrie, J.T., Van Meter, P., McCann, A.D., Wigfield, A., Bender, L., Poundstone, C.C, Rice, M.E., Faibisch, F.M., Junt, B., & Mitchell, A.M. (1996a). Growth of literacy engagement: Changes in motivations and strategies during concept-oriented reading instruction. *Reading Research Quarterly, 31*, 306–325.

Guthrie, J.T., McGough, K., Bennett, L., & Rice, M.E. (1996b). Concept-oriented reading instruction: An integrated curriculum to develop motivations and strategies for reading. In L. Baker, P. Afflerbach, & D. Reinking (Eds.). *Developing engaged readers in school and home communities* (pp. 165–190). Hillsdale, NJ: Erlbaum.

Guthrie, J.T., Cox, K., Anderson, E., Harris, K., Mazzoni, S., & Rach, L. (1998). Principles of integrated instruction for engagement in reading. *Educational Psychology Review, 10*, 177–199.

Guthrie, J.T., Wigfield, A., & VonSecker, C. (2000). Effects of integrated instruction on motivation and strategy use in reading. *Journal of Educational Psychology, 92*(2), 331–341.

Guthrie, J.T., Schafer, W.D., & Huang, C. (2001). Benefits of opportunity to read and balanced instruction on the NAEP. *Journal of Educational Research, 94*, 145–162.

Guthrie, J.T., Hoa, L.W., Wigfield, A., Tonks, S.M., & Perencevich, K.C. (2006). From spark to fire: Can situational reading interest lead to long-term reading motivation? *Reading Research and Instruction, 45*, 91–117.

Hidi, S., Berndorff, D., & Ainley, M. (2002). Children's argument writing, interest and self-efficacy: An intervention study. *Learning & Instruction, 12*(4), 429–446.

Karnoil, R., & Ross M. (1977). The effect of performance relevant and performance irrelevant rewards on children's intrinsic motivation. *Child Development, 48*, 482–487.

Kuhl, J. (1986) Introduction. In J. Kuhl & J.W. Atkinson (Eds.), *Motivation, thought and action* (pp. 1–16). New York, NY: Praeger.

Lepper, M.R., & Cordova D.I. (1992). A desire to be taught: Instructional consequence of intrinsic motivation. *Motivation and Emotion, 16*, 187–208.

Lepper, M.R., & Hodell, M. (1989). Intrinsic motivation in the classroom. In C. Ames & R. Ames (Eds.), *Research in motivation in education* (Vol. III, pp. 139–186). New York, NY: Academic Press.

Lepper, M.R., Greene, D., & Nesbit, R.E. (1973). Undermining children's intrinsic interest with extrinsic reward: A test of the overjustification hypothesis. *Journal of Personality and Social Psychology, 28*(1), 129–137.

Lundberg, I., & Linnakyla, P. (1993). *Teaching reading around the world.* Hamburg, Germany: International Association for the Evaluation of Educational Achievement.

Maehr, M.L. (1976) Continuing motivation: An analysis of a seldom considered educational outcome. *Review of Educational Research, 46*, 443–462.

Malloy, J.A., & Gambrell, L.B. (2008). New insights on motivation in the literacy classroom. In C.C. Block & S.R. Paris (Eds.), *Comprehension Instruction* (2nd ed.). New York, NY: Guilford.

Malloy, J.A., & Gambrell, L.B. (2009). The contribution of discussion to reading comprehension and critical thinking. In. R. Allington & A. McGill-Franzen (Eds.). *Handbook of Reading Disabilities Research.* Mahwah, NJ: Lawrence Erlbaum Associates.

Marinak, B., & Gambrell, L.B. (2008). Intrinsic motivation and rewards: What sustains young children's engagement with text? *Literacy Research and Instruction, 47*, 9–26.

McCombs, B.L. (1989). Self-regulated learning and academic achievement: A phenome-nological view. In B.J. Zimmerman & D.H. Schunk (Eds.), *Self-regulated learning and achievement: Theory, research, and practice* (pp. 51–82). New York, NY: Springer-Verlag.

McCombs, B.L. (2003). A framework for the redesign of K-12 education in the context of current educational reform. *Theory Into Practice, 42*(2), 93–102.

McKenna, M.C., Kear, D.J., & Ellsworth, R.A. (1995). Children's attitudes toward reading: A national survey. *Reading Research Quarterly, 30,* 934–956.

McLoyd, V.C. (1979). The effects of extrinsic rewards of differential value on high and low intrinsic interest. *Child Development, 50,* 1010–1091.

Meece, J.L., Blumenfeld, P.C., & Hoyle, R.H. (1988). Students' goal orientations and cognitive engagement in classroom activities. *Journal of Education Psychology, 80,* 514–523.

Moore, S.A., & Fawson, P.C. (1992, December). *Reading incentive programs: Beliefs and practices.* Paper presented at the 42nd Annual Meeting of the National Reading Con-ference, San Antonio, Texas.

Morgan, P.L., & Fuchs, D. (2007). Is there a bidirectional relationship between chil-dren's reading skills and reading motivation? *Exceptional Children, 73*(2), 165–183.

Morrow, L.M. (1992). The impact of a literature-based program on literacy achieve-ment, use of literature, and attitudes of children from minority backgrounds. *Reading Research Quarterly, 27,* 250–275.

Morrow, L.M., & Gambrell, L.B. (1998). How do we motivate children toward inde-pendent reading and writing? In S.B. Neuman & K.A. Roskos (Eds.), *Children achiev-ing: Best practices in early literacy* (pp. 144–161). Newark, DE: International Reading Association.

Neuman, S.B., & Roskos, K.A. (1993). Access to print for children of poverty: Differen-tial effects of adult mediation and literacy-enriched playsettings on environmental and function print tasks. *American Educational Research Journal, 32,* 801–828.

Nolen, S.B. (2007). Young children's motivation to read and write: Development in social contexts. *Cognition & Instruction, 25* (2), 219–270.

Oldfather, P. (1993). What students say about motivating experiences in a whole lan-guage classroom. *The Reading Teacher, 46,* 672–681.

Oldfather, P., & Dahl, K. (1994). Toward a social constructivist re-conceptualization of intrinsic motivation for literacy learning. *Journal of Reading Behavior, 26,* 139–158.

Oldfather, P., & McLaughlin, J. (1993). Gaining and losing voice: A longitudinal study of students, continuing impulse to learn across elementary and middle school contexts. *Research in Middle Level Education, 17,* 1–25.

Palmer, B.M., Codling, R.M., & Gambrell, L.B. (1994). In their own words: What ele-mentary children have to say about motivation to read. *The Reading Teacher, 48,* 176–179.

Paris, S.G., & Oka, E.R. (1986). Self-regulated learning among exceptional children. *Exceptional Children, 53,* 103–108.

Pintrich, P.R., & DeGroot, E.V. (1990). Motivational and self-regulated learning com-ponents of classroom academic performance. *Journal of Educational Psychology, 82,* 33–40.

Pintrich, P.R., Roeser, R.W., & DeGroot, E.A.M. (1994). Classroom and individual differences in early adolescents' motivation and self-regulated learning. *Journal of Early Adolescence, 14,* 139–161.

Pressley, M. (1998). *Reading instruction that works: The case for balanced teaching.* New York, NY: Guilford.

Purcell-Gates, V., McIntyre, E., & Freppon, P.A. (1995). Learning written storybook language in school: A comparison of low-SES children in skills-based and whole language classrooms. *American Educational Research Journal, 32,* 659–685.

Renninger, K.A., & Hidi, S. (2002). Student interest and achievement: Developmental issues raised by a case study. In A. Wigfield & J. Eccles (Eds.), *The development of achievement motivation* (pp. 173–195). San Diego, CA: Academic Press.

Ryan, R.M., & Deci, E.L. (2000). Intrinsic and extrinsic motivations: Classic definitions and new directions. *Contemporary Educational Psychology, 25,* 54–67.

Ryan, R.M., & Grolnick, W. (1986). Origins and pawns in the classroom: Self-report and projective assessments of individual differences in children's perceptions. *Journal of Personality and Social Psychology, 45,* 736–750.

Ryan, R.M., Mims, V., & Koestner, R. (1983). Relation of reward contingency and interpersonal context to intrinsic motivation: A review and test using cognitive evaluation theory. *Journal of Personality and Social Psychology, 45,* 735–750.

Schiefele, U. (1991). Interest, learning, and motivation. *Educational Psychologist, 26*(3–4), 299–323.

Schunk, D.H. (1985). Self-efficacy and school learning. *Psychology in the Schools, 22,* 208–223.

Skinner, B.F. (1953). *Science and Human Behavior.* New York, NY: Free Press.

Skinner, E.A., & Bellmont, M.J. (1993). Motivation in the classroom: Reciprocal effects of teacher behavior and student engagement across the school year. *Journal of Educational Psychology, 85,* 571–581.

Smith-Burke, T.M. (1989). Political and economic dimensions of literacy: Challenges for the 1990's. In S. McCormick & J. Zutell (Eds.), *Cognitive and social perspectives for literacy research and instruction* (pp. 1–18). Chicago, IL: National Reading Conference.

Spaulding, C.L. (1992). *Motivation in the Classroom.* New York, NY: McGraw-Hill.

Stipek, D.J. (1988). *Motivation to learn: From theory to practice.* Englewood Cliffs, NJ: Prentice Hall.

Stipek, D.J. (1996). Motivation and instruction. In D.C. Berliner & R.C. Calfee (Eds.), *Handbook of educational psychology* (pp. 85–113). New York, NY: Macmillan.

Taylor, B.M., Frye, B.J., & Maruyama, G.M. (1990). Time spent reading and reading growth. *American Educational Research Journal, 17,* 351–362.

Turner, J. (1995). The influence of classroom contexts on young children's motivation for literacy. *Reading Research Quarterly, 30*(3), 410–441.

Weiner, B. (1990). History of motivational research in education. *Journal of Educational Psychology, 92,* 616–622.

Wigfield, A. (1994). *Dimensions of children's motivations for reading: An initial study.* Paper presented at the annual meeting of the American Educational Research Association, New Orleans, Louisiana.

Wigfield, A. (1997). Children's Motivations for Reading and Reading Engagement. In J.T. Guthrie and A. Wigfield, (Eds.), *Reading Engagement: Motivating Readers Through Integrated Instruction.* Newark, DE: International Reading Association.

Wigfield, A., & Eccles, J. (2000). Expectancy-value theory of achievement motivation. *Contemporary Educational Psychology, 25*(1), 68–81.

Wigfield, A., & Guthrie, J.T. (1997). Relations of children's motivation for reading to the amount and breadth of their reading. *Journal of Educational Psychology, 89*(3), 420–432.

Wittrock, M.C. (1986). Students' thought processes. In M.C. Wittrock (Ed.), *Handbook of research on teaching* (pp. 297–314). New York, NY: Macmillan.

15

EMERGENT WRITING DEVELOPMENT AND SECOND-LANGUAGE LEARNERS

David B. Yaden and Joan M. Tardibuono

Young children make attempts to write in a variety of ways: some may use scribbles, shapes, or mock letters, and others may opt for sticks, circles, and pictures (Hildreth, 1936; Dyson, 1982; Harste, Woodward, & Burke, 1984; Sulzby, 1985). As Clay (1975) pointed out early on, the development of these figural aspects of early writing attempts are important in demonstrating the variety of strategies that young children employ to gain control over not only the symbols of the written language system, but also the uses to which they may be put. At the same time, however, it has been noted by many of these same researchers (e.g., Dyson, 1986, 1993a; Sulzby, 1986; Dyson & Freedman 2003), as well as others (e.g., Ferreiro & Teberosky, 1982; Ferreiro, 1985, 1986; Fang, 1999; Vernon & Ferreiro, 1999), that observation alone of the increasing conventionality of graphic forms does not reveal the nature of the sociocognitive processes that underlie children's understanding of the symbolic role played by written language. It is important, then, for researchers to apply methodological techniques that are designed to elicit from children their understandings of the written language as an artifact of culture, as well as the processes used to gain mastery over its forms, structures, and purposes.

The primary purpose of this chapter, therefore, is to share the results of a Piagetian-inspired clinical analysis (see National Research Council (2001) for a recent appraisal of this methodology) in which 4-year-old Spanish-speaking children were engaged in a variety of writing tasks and then given the opportunity to interpret the meanings of their written productions. This particular study, which adopts a constructivist, socio-psychogenetic perspective on writing (cf. Ferreiro & Teberosky, 1982; Valsiner, 1992; Rocco, 1998; Tolchinsky & Teberosky, 1998; Vernon & Ferreiro, 1999), was nested within a larger emergent literacy intervention in which the preschool children participated in a variety of emergent activities, involving weekly shared readings, big books, extensive classroom libraries, writing centers, a home library component, and teachers who regularly engaged them in book conversations and other language activities (for more detailed information, see Yaden et al., 2000a; Yaden & Brassell, 2002; Yaden, Madrigal, & Tam, 2003).

This discussion has the additional purpose of demonstrating the close tie-in between findings from Rona Flippo's Expert Study (1998, 2001) and the types of classroom environments and instructional strategies that support creative, risk-taking reading and writing behavior by young English-language learners (ELLs). As Au (2001) points out, even though the consensus statements of 11 well-known literacy scholars about the "contexts and practices" that support healthy reading and writing growth do not explicitly mention the needs of children learning English as a second language, these statements nonetheless accurately describe the environmental, social, and instructional conditions that have been underscored as essential for second-language literacy learning (see, for example, Stefanakis, 1998; Donato, 1999; Reyes, Scribner, & Scribner, 1999). The remarkably close agreement between the general principles of sound literacy instruction espoused by researchers in the Expert Study (Flippo, 1998) and more specific suggestions for ELLs made by investigators such as Reyes et al. (1999) will be discussed more specifically in later portions of the chapter.

Review of Literature

Extant Research Trends in Emergent Writing

In a recent review of emergent writing research primarily from the United States, Yaden, Rowe, and MacGillivray (2000b) suggested that while early writing research has waned somewhat in the past 10 years (cf. also Farnan & Dahi, 2003), two theoretical emphases can still be noted: one taking a sociocultural, sociohistorical, or cultural-historical view of young children's writing, based upon principles derived from Vygotsky (Vygotsky, 1931/1997, 1934/1987); the other portraying children's writing processes as being constructivist, developmental, psychogenetic, or sociogenetic, following particularly the tenets of Piagetian or neo-Piagetian theory (Demetriou, Shayer, & Efklides, 1992; see also Piaget, 1962; van der Veer & Valsiner, 1993; Rocco, 1998 for discussions comparing both approaches). Though the oft-drawn contrast between the two theories in emergent literacy research (see, for example, Spodek & Saracho, 1993; McGee & Richgels, 2000; Katz, 2001) has created an unfortunate polarization between the two perspectives, we will point out some important, complementary aspects of both theories that inform the present research to be discussed. A detailed analysis of the goals of Piaget's and Vygotsky's research programs and the methodological techniques developed to gather data regarding children's developing conceptualizations is not possible in the present chapter, and thus only a few points of comparison will be touched upon.

The Cultural-Historical Perspective on Children's Emergent Writing

The "cultural-historical" (Davydov & Radzikhovskii, 1985; van der Veer & Valsiner, 1993), "sociohistorical" (Moll, 1990) or "sociocultural" (Smagorinsky, 1995) line of research into emergent writing comprises by far the bulk of the US investigations in the 1990s. Several researchers have studied the powerful influences exerted upon the development of children's writing by their social environment, including peers, family members, teachers, home, and school, as well as television and movies. These social and cultural catalysts to children's thinking about and development of writing behaviors have been comprehensively discussed by many authors (e.g., Goodman, 1984; Dyson, 1985, 1992, 1993a, 1993b, 1995; 1997; Daniels, 1990; Glazer & Burke, 1994; Rowe, 1994; Purcell-Gates, 1995; Richgels, 1995; Sulzby, 1996; Geekie, Cambourne, & Fitzsimmons, 1999; McGee & Richgels, 2000).While North American researchers such as Dyson (1986, 1997, 2002), Rowe (1994), Sulzby (1986), and Sulzby and Teale (1991, 2003) have noted developmental characteristics in the nature of children's early writing behavior (see also Templeton & Bear, 1992), they have been careful not to suggest that the levels observed follow one another in any strict or clear developmental order. Rather, the common view is that even the earliest, nascent stages of reading and writing develop simultaneously with one another and with other sociocultural aspects of the child's environment. When development is mentioned, it is usually framed within a discussion of the zone of proximal development (Vygotsky, 1934/1987), where a more competent peer or adult provides a scaffold for the child to demonstrate abilities that are not evident if the child attempts the same tasks him/herself (for representative statements, see Goodman, 1986; Teale & Sulzby, 1986; Clay, 1987; Sulzby & Teale, 1991; Glazer & Burke, 1994; Campbell, 1996; Reynolds, 1997; Neuman & Roskos, 1998; Gee, 2000; Dickinson & Tabors, 2001). For the most part, however, the definition of "development" (e.g., Dyson, 2002), in the present authors' view, is what Vygotsky (1931/1997) identified as a "descriptive" analysis of development, as opposed to an "explanatory" analysis such as he was conducting that had the potential "to disclose the real causal-dynamic relations and connections that lie at the base of any phenomenon" (p. 68).

However, it is exactly this explanatory analysis of development (or, as he termed it, "conditional-genetic-analysis"; Vygotsky, 1931/1997, p. 69), which has been ignored by most US literacy researchers, that formed the very core of Vygotsky's research program. This omission of the search for the psycho- and sociocognitive origins, structure, and emergence of children's concepts about written language is particularly unfortunate, since van der Veer and Valsiner (1993) have emphasized that "Vygotsky's consistent developmental perspective stands as a worthwhile contribution to psychology" (p. 398). Reflecting a similar view, Joseph Glick (1997) writes:

Within the European tradition of the time, the major analytic thrust was precisely to "differentially diagnose" and examine the complex layering of different developmental strata underlying behavior. The analytic metaphors were geological ... Careful reading of The History the Development of Higher Mental Functions will show that this is precisely the tack that Vygotsky takes throughout, often providing strikingly illuminating insights derived from this orientation to a complex developmental geology.

p. xiv

Vygotsky's focus on the gradual and rule-governed development of children's concept development was also recognized by Piaget (1962):

When Vygotsky concluded from his reflections on my earliest books that the essential task of child psychology was to study the formation of scientific concepts in following step by step the process unfolding under our eyes, he had no inkling that such was exactly my program.

p. 9

Not surprisingly, the clearest statements of this focus on the evolution of the higher mental functions were made by Vygotsky himself. For example, speaking of the psychological processes involved in child development, he stated that this could be only understood

by taking into account that it is a complex dialectical process that is characterized by complex periodicity, disproportion in the development of separate functions, metamorphoses or qualitative transformation of certain forms into others, a complex merging of the process of evolution and involution, a complex crossing of the external and internal factors, a complex process of overcoming difficulties and adapting.

Vygotsky, 1931/1987, p. 99

Interestingly, this statement by Vygotsky, as well as others throughout his work, foreshadows much of the same thinking, which undergirds present-day discussions of complexity or chaos theory (see Taylor, 2002, for an explanation of chaos theory as applied to Jackson Pollock's painting). Van der Veer and Valsiner (1993) make explicit this connection by noting, "in contemporary terms, we might find Vygotsky to be a forerunner of the present-day fascination with fractals, minimal Gestalts of which complex structures are formed" (p. 310). In particular, the systemic nature of Vygotsky's understanding of cognitive development is a feature that is fundamental to our own interpretations of how children grapple with mastering the structural and semiotic aspects of the written language system.

A Socio-psychogenetic Perspective on Young Children's Writing

The second line of inquiry in literacy studies, in which we primarily place our own approach, includes researchers who have studied literacy from a Piagetian, "psychogenetic" (Ferreiro, 1985, 1996) or "sociogenetic" (Bearison, 1991) point of view that stems initially from the research of Ferreiro and Teberosky (1982) in Latin America. (Recently, it has been noted by Rocco (1998) that Alexander Luria, one of Vygotsky's closest collaborators, conducted similar writing research with children as early as the 1920s!) In her extensive research into children's writing processes, only a portion of which is available in English, Ferreiro (1984, 1985, 1986, 1994, 1996; Vernon & Ferreiro, 1999) has demonstrated that in the process of becoming literate, children evidence definite but continually evolving conceptualizations of the writing system and its symbols that represent at first a direct or "first-order" syncretistic relationship with the child's world, where writing and drawing are barely distinguished from one another.

These initial conceptualizations are then followed by a focus on the topological properties of script, which often mirror selected properties of the actual object or person being referred to, such as size, shape, or quantity of features (cf. Levin & Korat, 1993). It is only relatively late in the preschool and primary grades that children frame written language as an "object of knowledge" of which primary referents are portions of the spoken language itself (see Luria (1929/1998) for a "cultural-historical" interpretation of these same characteristics). Other research drawing either in part or whole upon Piagetian principles and methodology can also be found in Besse (1996), Pontecorvo, Orsolini, Burge, and Resnick (1996), Pontecorvo and Zucchermaglio (1988), Roberts (1992), Rocco (1998), Temple, Nathan, Temple, and Burns (1993), Tolchinsky (2001), Tolchinsky Landsman (1991), Tolchinsky Landsman and Levin (1985, 1987), Tolchinsky and Teberosky (1998), and Yaden, Smolkin, and MacGillivray (1993).

Despite the frequent and incorrect perception (see Lourenço & Machado (1996) for 10 of the most common criticisms and their rebuttal) that Piaget ignored the social aspect of learning, Ferreiro has made it clear that a psychogenetic view of conceptual development systematically incorporates the child's social environment, the people with whom the child interacts, and the cultural activities in which the child is engaged. According to Ferreiro (1985), one of Piaget's fundamental principles is that

> cognitive development is an interactive process. The construction of knowledge always implies a part that is contributed by the object (with its physical, social, and cultural properties) and a part that is contributed by the subject (with his or her assimilation schemata).
>
> *p. 218*

As Piaget (1970, 2001) himself said over a half century ago,

> The human being is immersed right from birth in a social environment, which affects him just as much as his physical environment. Society, even more, in a sense, than the physical environment, changes the very structure of the individual, because it not only compels him to recognize facts, but also provides him with a ready-made system of signs, which modify his thought; it presents him with new values and it imposes on him an infinite series of obligations.
>
> *p. 171*

Thus, both Ferreiro (1985) and others (see Bearison, 1991; Valsiner, 1992; Wertsch, 1992; Kohl de Oliveira & Valsiner, 1998), pursuing similar constructivist theories of human learning, have warned researchers against assuming that this type of perspective discounts the fact that children learn about written language (as they do other things) through immersion in a social community, supportive instructional environments, and especially from their experiences with immediate and extended family members. These and related assumptions are explored briefly in the next subsection.

Selected Assumptions Regarding Socio-Psychogenetic Development

In this section, we will mention only two aspects of Piagetian theory of particular importance to the present study. One key feature of constructivist theory, which Ferreiro (see Ferreiro, 1986; Ferreiro & Pontecorvo, 2002) and others working within neo-Piagetian traditions (cf. Case, 1992; Valsiner, 1992) have reiterated, is that children transform environmental stimuli according to their own internalized cognitive structures. In other words, statements or comments meant by parents, teachers, or others to "inform" children about conventional ways of thinking or behaving, for instance, are never taken at face value, but are reformed and reinterpreted according to the child's idiosyncratic views of the world (cf. also Yaden, 2003). As Valsiner (1992) has pointed out, "the transformational nature of the internalization process guarantees that the internalized version of the external (social) experience is not an 'internal replica' of the latter, but a transformation of it into a novel form" (p. 68). Thus, in order to evaluate and interpret the outcome of a child's early writing performance, for example, it is important not to make the final comparison with the conventional task parameters that the child was to follow, but rather to seek to understand the outcome according to the internal sociocognitive schema, as it were, from which the outward performance emanated (Valsiner, 1992, p. 73). And it is for the purposes of trying to understand these internalized conceptions or "assimilation schemes" that the clinical protocol or "inquiry method" was originally developed (see Ferreiro & Teberosky, 1982, pp. 13, 21). (See also Vygotsky (1931/1997) for an extended discussion of this type of analysis.)

A second important feature of the socio-psychogenetic perspective is that the growth of knowledge does not proceed in a cumulative fashion—in other words, it does not grow by accretion but rather is systemic, moving forward in somewhat erratic spurts and comprising multiple conceptualizations, rather than passing through well-defined stages (cf. Piaget, 1975, 1985). This type of process has been described by Ferreiro and Teberosky (1982):

> In Piaget's theory, objective knowledge appears as the end result rather than as an initial piece of information. The path toward this objective knowledge is not linear. We do not move toward it step-by-step, adding bits of knowledge one on top of another. We reach it through great global reconstructions, some of which are erroneous (with respect to the ultimate goal) but constructive (in the sense that they allow us to reach it).
>
> *p. 16*

Following this notion, as Ferreiro has further pointed out, "pedagogic practice in accordance with Piagetian theory must not fear error" (p. 17). For it is in the examination of the very processes of these "errors" (or "processes" of externalization, as opposed to their "products") through which the workings of the child's assimilative schemes or systems of reconstruction may be revealed. While using similar methods in the present study, the next section discusses some important distinctions between the population of Spanish-speaking children here in the United States as compared to Ferreiro's original sample in Argentina.

Investigative Focus of the Current Study

Other Research

Although the research conducted by Ferreiro and Teberosky (1982) took place nearly 30 years ago, few studies have attempted to confirm their findings in the United States with English-speaking children—none with second-language learners. One such study, conducted by Kamii, Long, Manning, and Manning (1991), was designed to investigate if similar spelling patterns emerged for English-speaking kindergartners as identified by Ferreiro and Teberosky (1982), and if the syllable emerged as the salient segment of language to which children first associated graphic forms. In clinical interviews with a sample of 192 African- and Euro-American children of both middle- and lower-class backgrounds, the researchers discovered that while similar developmental levels could be identified, the English-speaking children seemed to focus on consonants rather than syllables when exhibiting knowledge of the grapheme/phoneme relationships in

English. This latter finding supports research done in languages other than English (see Tolchinsky, 2001), in which contributors suggest that the target language itself may determine which aspects of the phonological system become salient in accomplishing the "phonetization of script" (Gelb, 1963).

Sample Differences between the Los Angeles and Argentinean Samples

As the present study was being designed, however, we recognized several differences between the earlier sample and our own. First of all, while the Argentine sample included children ranging from 4 to 6 years of age, our sample would only include 4-year-olds. Second, the South American sample included children from two social classes, lower and middle, while, according to our estimates (based upon agency and other demographic statistics), our Los Angeles sample would be exclusively of low socioeconomic status. Nonetheless, we understood that historical differences between the two data collection periods, and the generally better living conditions in the United States, meant that our population of children from low-income areas in Southern California may have many more opportunities than their Argentinean counterparts to interact with print, as our subsequent results seem to suggest. Similarly, while Ferreiro and Teberosky do not give specific statistics for the level of parent education in their study, we knew that the parents in our Southern California sample had an average sixth-grade level of schooling in their home countries, with many completing secondary schooling as well.

Third, while Ferreiro and Teberosky described their population as monolingual Spanish, the Los Angeles sample, while primarily speaking Spanish at home, was exposed to spoken English from several sources, including bilingual parents and extended family, older siblings in English-only classrooms, visitors to the preschool center, and English speakers in the community. Even though we have not attempted to measure the degree of English exposure or developing bilingualism or biliteracy, it is obvious from working with the children in the preschool center that many of them are acquiring English and using it more frequently, especially in the spring of the school year. In a few cases, some children have even requested to be addressed in English only. In this discussion, however, we will focus exclusively on writing performance in Spanish.

Design Differences

Finally, we initiated a few additional changes in design. Ferreiro and Teberosky had suggested that the "syllabic hypothesis" would be more evident in the children's name-writing than in writing familiar words or sentences. We added a name-writing component (cf. Bloodgood, 1999) to explore this hypothesis, in addition to having more general writing tasks. Also, all of the testing with the

Argentine sample was done at one point in time, whereas writing samples in the present study were elicited three times during a 5-month period (February–June, 2000). The general questions guiding the writing component of the larger study were as follows:

- How do 4-year-old Latino preschoolers primarily exposed to Spanish literacy instruction interpret their own writing?
- Do children's interpretations of their own writing follow a pattern of development?
- Does developmentally appropriate instruction assist children in moving conceptually toward conventional understandings of the writing process?

Methodology

Population and Setting

Located east of downtown Los Angeles in an area known as "skid row" (Rivera, 1999), Para Los Niños (PLN) is a comprehensive childcare center and family services support center whose stated mission is "raising children out of poverty into a brighter future." Approximately 98.7% of the over 2000 families served by the agency each year have incomes below the federal poverty level, with the most frequent family unit being a single mother with three to four children. The majority of parents in our sample worked in the downtown garment industry, where the monthly wage ranged between $584 and $1030. While Spanish was the primary language of communication in the home and preschool classrooms, teachers and aides spontaneously addressed the children in English when appropriate.

During the year in which the writing data were gathered (2000), 126 children, almost all Latino, ages 18 months to 4 years, were enrolled in the center's all-day preschool program. The writing study and the larger intervention, however, were conducted in the two classrooms for 4-year-olds, one having 32 children, the other 24. The final sample consisted of 47 children, for whom both pre- and post-tests were available. Further, all tasks were administered either in the child's own classroom or an adjoining one. These classrooms, however, were separated by a short 4-foot wall so that each individual teacher could see the children in adjacent classes. At all times during the clinical interviews the children were in familiar spaces surrounded by familiar people—including the investigators, who had already spent several months in the center interacting with the children.

Procedures and Materials

Initially, 56 4-year-olds were assessed individually in Spanish at three points in time: February, April, and June of 2000. In February and June, the children were asked to participate in a series of general writing (GW) tasks (cf. Ferreiro

& Teberosky, 1982, p. 179). Each child was given an unlined, 8×11 sheet of blank paper and asked to write his or her name, the names of parents or other family members, four high-frequency words (mama, papá, oso [bear], nene [baby]), three familiar but less frequently heard words (sapo [toad], mapa [map], pato [duck]), and one sentence (Mi nena toma sol [My little girl sits in the sun]). The children were instructed to write each word with a different colored marker so as to clearly indicate where it was written on the page. If some of the children refused to write, or stated that they did not know how, the examiner encouraged them to write it in their own way. Any attempt by the children was accepted. After they wrote each word, they were asked to read what they had written. The researcher then continued with follow-up questions, as is characteristic of the clinical method, and queried the children about the nature of their interpretation.

In April of 2000, using the same interview procedures as before, the children were also asked to write and interpret their name only, but this time they were asked to interpret the name after selected parts were covered by the researcher with a 3×5 index card. After the children wrote their names to the best of their ability without assistance, the researcher first asked them to read what they had written, then covered the first part of their name with the index card and asked them to read the uncovered part. This process was then repeated with the last part of the name covered.

While only one child refused to write her name, some signatures contained completely unconventional graphic markings. We departed from Ferreiro and Teberosky's (1982) procedure by accepting these markings as a valid representation, and therefore did not provide movable letters to be manipulated by the child or researcher. Our rationale for this adaptation was based on Ferreiro and Teberosky's comment that some children believe that they can only read what they write, that they cannot read what others write, and that they are not able to use conventional letters. Therefore, we felt that if the children could produce any variant of their own name using any marks at all, then their interpretations could be analyzed.

Analysis

Based on the classification system used by Ferreiro and Teberosky (1982), the children's interpretations of their writing on the general writing tasks (GW) and the name-writing (NW) task were evaluated and classified into one of five hierarchical general writing and name-writing levels. The majority of the coding was done by the second author. However, when questions arose concerning the proper classification, both authors analyzed the writing sample and decided jointly upon the level to which it should be assigned. Rather than discuss the classification system in the abstract, we will describe each category in our discussion of results, using the child's writing to illustrate the various features which were used to evaluate the level of the writing. In addition, pseudonyms are used to identify the children's first and/or surnames in Figures 15.1, 15.3, and 15.5–15.9. The written surnames (as in Figures 15.11 & 15.12) are spelled incorrectly and are missing letters, thus preserving identity.

Results

General Writing Tasks (GW)

GW Level 1

Like Ferreiro & Teberosky, we discovered children who did not identify writing as a means of recording or transmitting information, and those who believed that they couldn't read any writing other than their own. For example, Jovanny writes strings of unconnected characters for words or sentences (Figure 15.1); his characters, composed of curved and straight lines, are similar to those described by Ferreiro and Teberosky for children in their sample at this level. Writing left to right, Jovanny also used the width of the page to mark word and sentence boundaries. As illustrated in Figure 15.1, Jovanny also interspersed drawing with writing, including a picture to represent the word "sol" in the sentence "mi nena toma sol."

Interestingly, a slightly more advanced variation at Level 1 was observed among children who used conventional letters to write, but who assigned more than one meaning to the same written string. In Figure 15.2, when Dilsy was asked to interpret the first string she had just written for her name, she indicated that it said "mama." When asked to write her own name again, she produced exactly the same sequence of characters, only this time she indicated that the

"mapa"

"pato"

"mi nena tomo sol"

FIGURE 15.1 Jovanny (4 years), general writing, level 1

graphic array said her name, "Dilsy." When asked by the examiner whether she thought the strings were different or the same, she said they were "diferente." Thus, while interpreting the strings globally, children writing in this manner reveal that their intent can be used to differentiate meaning even when no graphic difference (at least to the adult eye) exists.

GW Level 2

According to Ferreiro and Teberosky, Level 2 is characterized by children who understand that writing must contain a certain number of characters and that these characters need to vary as the meaning of their referent changes. At both this level and the previous one, the children interpret their writings globally or iconically, in that the total meaning is ascribed either to the whole string or any portion of it. However, the important distinction is that at Level 2, children begin to focus on aspects of the graphic image itself when signaling a difference in meaning. Although Alfredo uses a limited number of graphic characters in different orientations, he varies these symbols in order to distinguish words and the names of family members. For example, in Figure 15.3, reading from bottom to top, Alfredo writes his name, his mother's name, his father's name, nene, and oso by using various combinations of three known letters. This type of recombinatory strategy was used by several children at Level 2, although the total number of characters used varied from three to eight among the children.

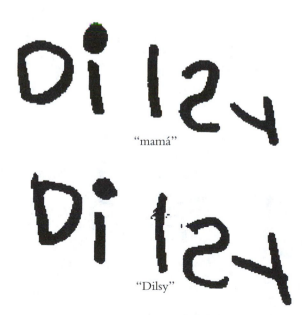

"mamá"

"Dilsy"

FIGURE 15.2 Dilsy (4 years), general writing, level 1

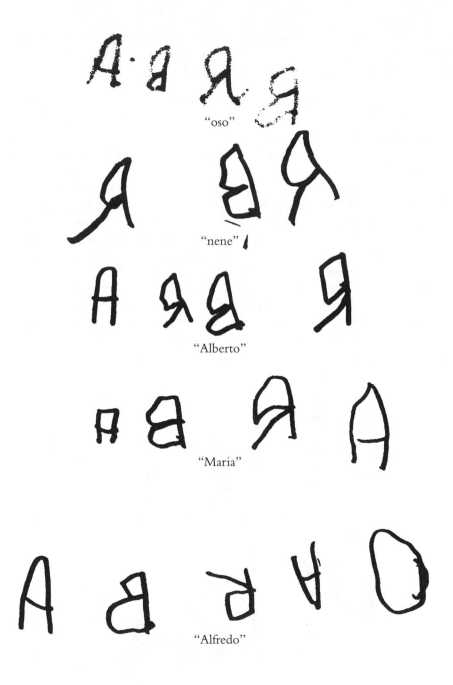

"oso"

"nene"

"Alberto"

"Maria"

"Alfredo"

FIGURE 15.3 Alfredo (4 years), general writing, level 2

GW Level 3

At Level 3, the children make "attempts at assigning a sound value to each of the letters that compose a piece of writing" (Ferreiro & Teberosky, 1982, p. 197), exhibiting what is known as the "syllabic hypothesis." The child's interpretation of the written string is no longer global, or figurally based, but reflects awareness of a specific correspondence between each syllable and graphic marking. When Alexis was asked to write several two-syllable words (Figure 15.4), "nene," "oso," and "pato," he pronounced each word while assigning one graphic character to each syllable. For example, "Ai" = /ne-ne/, "mo" = /o-so/, and "op" = /pa-to/. However, even at this level, children still exhibit some global interpretations of fixed strings (cf. Ferreiro & Teberosky, 1982, p. 202). For example, Alexis wrote his name, and then "momo" and "papa" for his parent's names, Yolanda and Roberto (pseudonyms), respectively (see Figure 15.4).

GW Levels 4 And 5

At these levels, children continue to advance from the syllabic hypothesis to assigning phonemes to each grapheme, and, ultimately, to conventional writing. No children in our study demonstrated these advanced levels of conceptualization in the general writing tasks.

FIGURE 15.4 Alexis (4 years), general writing, level 3

Name-writing Task (NW)

NW Level 1

As mentioned earlier, the name-writing task required the children to interpret what they had written while parts of the writing were covered by the examiner with an index card. At this level, children cannot read and write their name in a conventional way. When they read their name, it is not apparent that they use featural information such as letter shape or length to assist them. Therefore, they may read their first and last name when only the first name is written, and vice versa. Furthermore, when part of their name is covered, they still interpret the remaining symbols as designating their whole name.

In Figure 15.5, Martha scribbled her name using one continuous line in an up-and-down manner, resembling multiple "Ms" (see Harste, Woodward, & Burke, 1984, for a discussion of the choice of style for initial writing). She read her name as "Martha Rojo." When the first half and then the second half were covered, she still read it as "Martha Rojo." Another example of NW Level 1 is illustrated in Figure 15.6. While Marlena wrote her name with letter-like forms, she responded like Martha did when either half of her name was covered, indicating that any portion represented her name.

Juan provided a final example of Level-1 name-writing, when he wrote his name using horizontal and vertical sticks (Figure 15.7). When asked to read his name, however, he read it as "Mickey Mouse." The examiner told him that she thought he was going to write his name. He then pointed to the same writing and called it "Juan." (For a similar case, see the discussion above on Dilsy's work.)

NW Level 2

Children at this level may or may not know how to write their name conventionally. The defining characteristic of this level is that children begin to look at the quantity and variation of written symbols as designating different meanings, or attempt to assign a portion of their name to each mark or cluster of marks. For instance, Berenice wrote her name using the same three letters (O, B, and E) in varying order (see Figure 15.8). She read the whole string as "Berenice Rosa." When the last part of her name was covered (OBE//////////), she

"Martha Rojo"

FIGURE 15.5 Martha (4 years), name writing, level 1

"Marlena"

FIGURE 15.6 Marlena (4 years), name writing, level 1

read the remaining letters as "Berenice." When the first part was covered, she read it as "Rosa."

Another example of this level comes from Roberto (Figure 15.9), who wrote his name conventionally and read it as "Ro-ber-to." When the first part of his name was covered (////////rto), he pointed to each remaining letter (r, t, o) successively and assigned it a name part—"Roberto ... Alfredo ... Alcala ..." A final example of NW Level 2 is provided by Teresa (see Figure 15.10). When the examiner covered the last part of Teresa's name (Ter////) and asked "what does it say," Teresa replied that it didn't say "Teresa," because part of it "está tapado" (is covered up).

First reading: "Mickey Mouse"
Second reading: "Juan"

FIGURE 15.7 Juan (4 years), name writing, level 1

NW Level 3

The distinguishing characteristic of this level is the emergence of the syllabic hypothesis. When reading the parts of their names, children will assign a syllabic value to each of the conventional or unconventional letters. Ferreiro and Teberosky have subdivided this level into Level 3a (children who assign a syllabic value when the first part of their name is visible, but not when only the last part is visible), and Level 3b (children who assign a syllabic correspondence to the first and last parts of their names). For the following examples, see Figures 15.11 and 15.12.

"Berenice Rosa"

FIGURE 15.8 Berenice (4 years), name writing, level 2

"Roberto"

FIGURE 15.9 Roberto (4 years), name writing, level 2

"Teresa"

FIGURE 15.10 Teresa (4 years), name writing, level 2

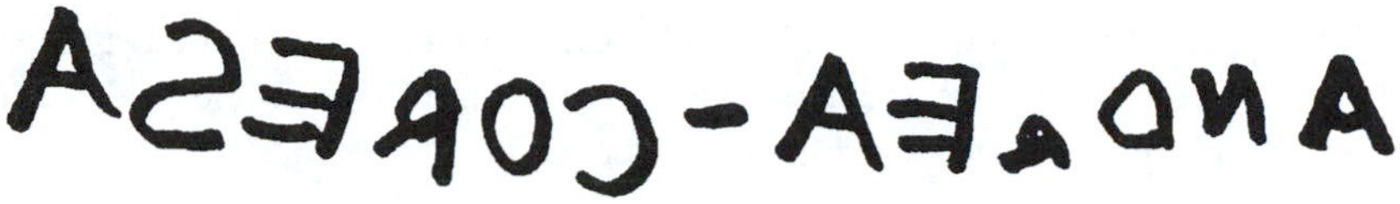

"Andrea"

FIGURE 15.11 Andrea (4 years), name writing, level 3a

"Diana"

FIGURE 15.12 Diana (4 years), name writing, level 3b

NW Level 3a

In Figure 15.11, Andrea wrote her first and last names from right to left, in a mirror image. She also read her name from right to left as "Andrea Coresa." When all was covered but /////// DNA, she pointed and assigned a syllabic value to each visible letter, reading right to left, "An ... dre. .. a." Similarly, /////// RDNA was read as "An ... dre ... a ... co," with one syllable per letter.

NW Level 3b

Diana wrote her first and last names conventionally (Figure 15.12). When the last part of her first name was covered (Di///////), she read it as "Di ... an." When the first part of her last name was covered (///////uez), she read it as "quez."

NW Level 4

At this level, the children begin to use the alphabetic principle in addition to the syllabic hypothesis. In Figure 15.13, Raul wrote his name conventionally

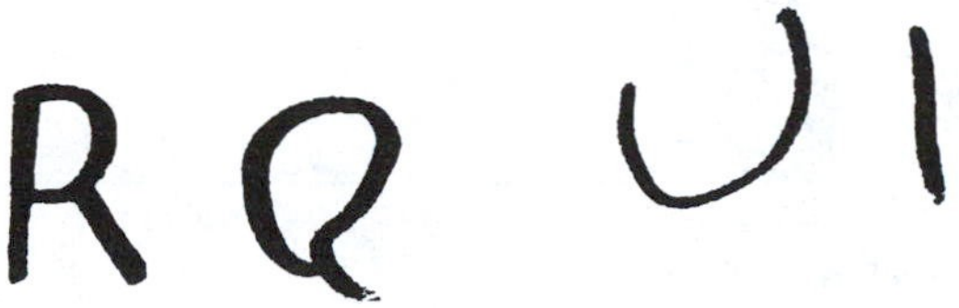

"Raul"

FIGURE 15.13 Raul (4 years), name writing, level 4

and read it as "Raul." For Ra////, he read "Ra." However, when the last three letters were uncovered one at a time (////l, ////ul and ////aul), he read them all as "úl," placing him at Level 4 instead of Level 5.

NW Level 5

At this final level, the children are able to assign a sound value to each letter and interpret it alphabetically, although many graphemes still retain unstable sound values. At the time of our study, no child in our sample could really be said to have attained this level.

Comparisons with the Latin American Sample

General Writing

With regard to the general writing tasks, the middle-class 4-year-olds in the Ferreiro and Teberosky study were mostly classified at Level 2, whereas their lower-class counterparts were mainly classified at Level 1. Ferreiro and Teberosky attributed this difference to middle-class parents' ability to provide high quality, private preschool programs for their children, while the lower-class children did not have the same access to high quality early childhood education. In our sample, we found that the 4-year-old children who were provided with bilingual literacy activities were classified at levels similar to those of the middle-class children in the Ferreiro and Teberosky (1982) study.

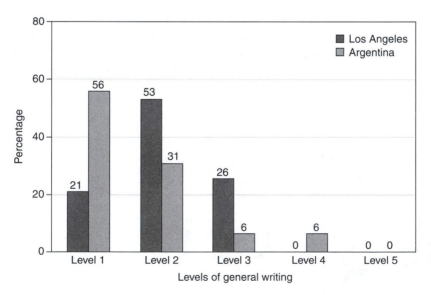

FIGURE 15.14 Comparison of general writing levels of middle- and lower-class 4-year-olds in Argentina with 4-year-old children in Los Angeles

Figure 15.14 compares the distribution of children from Los Angeles with that of a combined sample of middle- and lower-class 4-year-olds from the Argentinean study. From this graph, it can be seen that there are far fewer children from the present study in Level 1 than there are from the Argentine sample, and comparatively more children represented at Levels 2 and 3. When comparing these same groups of children at 5 years of age, however, the distributions are less disparate (see Figure 15.15), with the exception that Ferreiro and Teberosky classified a few children at the most advanced levels, whereas we did not find any 4-year-olds at this level. Interestingly, the patterns of distribution (Figure 15.15) for both samples, now separated by nearly three decades, are strikingly similar, suggesting the stability of these levels of conceptualizations over time among these populations of young children. While the relatively high levels of literacy exposure among the lower-class 4-year-olds in the Los Angeles study hastened these children's progression toward conventional understanding, the developmental aspects that were originally identified by Ferreiro and Teberosky are evident in the Los Angeles sample as well.

Name-writing

According to Ferreiro and Teberosky (1982), most 4-year-old middle- and lower-class children stated that they did not know how to write their names, or that they were unable to write their names conventionally. Only half of the lower-class 5-year-old children in Ferreiro's and Teberosky's study were able to

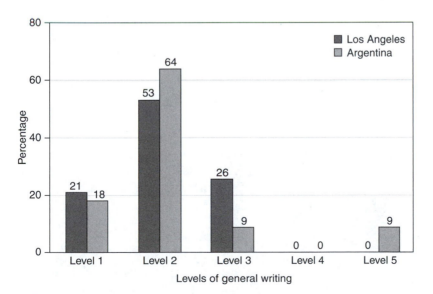

FIGURE 15.15 Comparison of general writing levels of middle- and lower-class 5-year-olds in Argentina with 4-year-old children in Los Angeles

write their names, while, in contrast, 71% of the children in our study were able to write their names at the end of the year. The 4-year-old children in the Los Angeles sample also functioned at a slightly higher level of conceptualization in name-writing than their same-age counterparts in Latin America. In fact, 40% of the 4-year-old children in our study had reached the syllabic hypothesis, as compared to 24% of the South American 4-year-olds; in the Ferreiro and Teberosky study, it was primarily the middle-class 5- and 6-year-old children (75%) who had reached this level (see combined percentages for Levels 3 and 4 in Figure 15.16).

Ferreiro and Teberosky (1982) noted as well that many children attain a high level of conceptualization in name-writing before applying that knowledge to writing other words and sentences. This same phenomenon was evidenced in our study. When the name performance of the combined sample of middle- and lower-class 4-year-olds from Argentina is compared with that of the children in Los Angeles, the pattern of distribution is striking, as both samples demonstrate four levels of conceptualization (see Figure 15.16).

Discussion

In order to further elaborate on the central findings of the study for both theory and practice, the following discussion is divided into four major sections, touching upon aspects of diagnosis, instruction, and theory building. In the section immediately following, we suggest some of the diagnostic implications related to interpreting young children's writing performances in the classroom

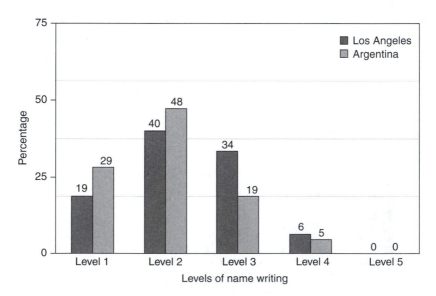

FIGURE 15.16 Comparison of name writing levels between 4-year-old children from Los Angeles and Argentina

when using clinical analysis, the importance of not underestimating the capabilities of children normally viewed as "at risk," and the dynamic, sociopsychological processes that children undergo in fully mastering written language structures. In the second and third sections, we use the findings of the Expert Study (Flippo, 1998) and other research with Latino populations (Ortiz, 1998; Reyes et al., 1999) to underscore the types of instructional environments, activities, and professional development proven to support the learning of young second-language learners. Finally, we present a model of learning that draws upon both psychogenetic and sociohistorical theory in order to help explain the deep complexities underlying early literacy growth as manifested through children's writing.

Conventional Representations May Not Indicate Conventional Understandings

It is important for teachers and educators to realize that even though a child may not be able to produce conventional letter characters, their understanding of how the written language system works may be developing at a normal pace. Similarly, even though a child may be able to produce conventional letters early on, this ability does not necessarily indicate a more advanced level of understanding than in a child who doesn't produce them. Thus, what seems clear from our studies as well as others (Ferreiro & Teberosky, 1982; Tolchinsky & Teberosky, 1998) is the fact that there is not a clear or proportionate correlation between the ability to produce adult-like graphic forms, and an understanding that the majority of those markings actually refer to segments of speech. However, a clinical analysis such as the one described in this chapter may be more useful for determining how children actually understand the process of writing and the graphic codings used therein, giving teachers and researchers additional insight into instructional strategies that can foster children's learning about written language instead of confusing them by assuming conceptualizations that do not yet exist.

Secondly, the present study also sheds light on the steadily emerging capabilities of young children from high-poverty, multilingual environments when exposed to emergent literacy activities and adults who encourage them to explore writing through a wide variety of literacy interactions. One of the key findings in the Ferreiro's and Teberosky (1982) study was that instruction in Latin America in the late 1970s did not match children's conceptualizations of the writing process. The tasks that were typically required in beginning reading classes included "deciphering" in reading, and "copying" in writing. In other words, pedagogical assumptions were being made that, first of all, children already knew that the processes of reading and writing involved the use of conventional graphic characters as second-order symbols for representing the meanings and sounds of language, and, second, that the connections between sound and letter would become automatic through repetitive drilling.

In order to understand this type of instruction (aside from any question of whether it creates the conditions for learning), it is first necessary for children to understand (if implicitly, for the most part) that language itself can be viewed as an "object" of metalinguistic focus (cf. Luria, 1929/1998; Sinclair, Jarvella & Levelt, 1978; Bakes, 1980; Downing & Valtin, 1984; Tunmer, Pratt, & Herriman, 1984; Yaden & Templeton, 1986; Blachrnan, 2000); that is, that manipulable acoustic and semantic components occur in a systematic order that can be further represented by graphic markings, which in turn can be organized in varying combinations from which an interpretation of both sound and meaning can be drawn. According to Ferreiro and Teberosky (1982), this complicated intellectual understanding takes years to fully acquire, and is only achieved by a process of active discovery, from engagement in innumerable situations of trial and error, and multiple opportunities to observe more-literate others applying the written system in many different contexts (pp. 12–15, 272–275). Given that the lower-class children in their study had fewer opportunities to attend private preschool or to observe adults engaged in various literate behaviors, most made very little progress in understanding the writing system, even after attending school for a year. The authors also go on to point out that the growth in literacy knowledge among middle-class children who began the year at higher levels of conceptualizations was due less to instruction than it was to a rehearsal of what they already knew from their extracurricular encounters with print and literate others.

Creating Environments for Discovery and Learning

The research literature on emergent literacy (see Sulzby & Teale, 2003; Yaden, Rowe, & MacGillivray, 2000b, for reviews) repeatedly has shown that early literacy growth is promoted by programs that

> draw children in as socially competent partners, allow them to experiment without undue duress, provide them with a variety of adulthood and peer-mediated dialogue about literature and ways to read and write and create any number of opportunities for them to practice their unconventional, yet emerging skills.
>
> *p. 443*

Nowhere is the above statement more strongly supported than in the conclusions of the literacy experts from Flippo's (1998, 2001) 10-year study. These conclusions do indeed provide a common ground of understanding for how instruction in early reading and writing should take place. In response to these findings of the Expert Study and applying them to second-language learners, Kathryn Au (2001, p. 115) summarizes the agreements as follows:

- Link reading with writing, listening, and speaking, so that students of diverse backgrounds can use their strengths in all language processes when learning to read.
- Provide students of diverse backgrounds with motivating, purposeful literacy activities that will promote their ownership of literacy.
- Give students many opportunities for wide independent reading, and help them develop their own tastes and interests as readers.
- Reject a behaviorist model of reading instruction and move instead toward approaches that emphasize higher-level thinking with text, promote student risk-taking as literacy learners, and encourage students' active involvement in developing their own understandings of reading and writing.
- Hold high expectations for the literacy achievement of students of diverse backgrounds while realizing that instruction to help students meet these expectations may need to be responsive to their cultural values.
- Center reading instruction on literature, drawing from our knowledge of students' backgrounds to help them make personal connections to literature and encouraging them to share their thoughts about literature in writing and in discussions with peers.

These agreements were very much a part of the emergent literacy program in which the children who provided our writing samples participated (see Yaden & Brassell [2002] and Yaden et al. [2000a], for complete details on implementation). The full-day preschool provided continual access to writing materials, children's literature, and sociodramatic play areas where scenarios involving literacy artifacts (e.g., menus, personal letters, grocery lists) were acted out several times a week. In addition, both teachers and aides modeled literate activities, served as an appreciative audience for various literacy performances by the children, and worked alongside the children, supporting and guiding their nascent efforts to master the complications that the written system presents to any novice.

Specific Instructional Principles for Second-Language Learners

Findings derived from the research of Reyes et al. (1999) on the learning environments created by eight schools in Texas with predominantly Latino populations align very closely with the experts' agreements in Flippo's study (1998). Given the space limitations of this chapter, we can only list the broad categories of pedagogical assumptions and activities that supported each of the elementary, middle, and secondary schools and were seen as providing the conditions for successful academic achievement (see also Donato, 1999; Ortiz, 1998). According to Scribner and Reyes (1999, p. 192), the conceptual framework adopted by these high-performing schools can be defined as having the following four "action dimensions":

Action Dimension I. Community and family involvement are essential to the development of a high-performing community for Hispanic students.

Action Dimension II. High-performing learning communities for Hispanic students depend upon leadership at all levels that supports collaborative governance that enables every student to succeed.

Action Dimension III. Culturally responsive pedagogy is required for students to succeed in a high-performing learning community for Hispanic students.

Action Dimension IV. Advocacy-oriented assessment that motivates the individual learning of the student is crucial to sustaining a high-performing learning community for Hispanic students.

The findings of the Expert Study and the Action Dimensions listed above are clearly connected by the themes of holding high but individually motivating expectations for students; using a culturally-relevant pedagogy that capitalizes on students' individual strengths and community connections; employing well-trained and supportive teachers who follow a flexible, dynamic approach to instruction; and maintaining a learning environment in which students and teaching staff respect each others' voices and participate in decisions that further encourage learning. Thus, while the suggestion (see August & Hakuta, 1997; Snow, Burns, & Griffin, 1998) should be heeded that additional research is needed to further illuminate the processes involved in acquiring second-language literacy, the broad parameters of those processes, both conceptual and methodological, have already been sketched out and agreed upon by a wide range of scholars working in the field.

Second-Language Literacy Develops Dynamically Over Time

Implicit, we believe, in the findings of the Expert Study and of other studies of second-language and literacy acquisition is the fact that literacy growth does not proceed in a systematic manner, nor does it move forward uniformly upon all fronts. In commenting on the parameters of an "Indeterminate Constraints Model," which is consistent with both sociopsychogenetic and cultural-historical theory, Valsiner (1992) states that

> this model treats developmental process as partially indeterministic (hence unpredictable to a large extent) depending upon the limiting conditions in organismic-environmental relations (hence the emphasis on "constraints"), and does not assume predetermined unilinear progression (unilinearity) in development.

p. 66

Therefore, even though we have been able to identify different types of conceptualizations that children reveal in learning to write, adjacent conceptualizations overlap and exist simultaneously, have their own pace of development, and incorporate a wide range of inputs on the way to a conventional view of the written language system. Au (2001, p. 111) has summarized the experts' statements well in saying that teachers should "reject a behaviorist model of reading instruction" that discourages students' critical thinking, risk-taking, and experimentation with written language, for it is only through these processes and within the full range of methods for displaying and using written language that children will be able to master the complex learning necessary to become literate in this society.

Conclusion

In this chapter, we have primarily attempted to do two things: first, to demonstrate that even within an environment where experimentation with written forms is encouraged, children's understanding of the forms and functions of written language undergoes a complex evolution, moving through increasingly sophisticated levels of conceptualization before reaching the final realization that a pattern of graphic markings, while denoting meaning, is first and foremost a mapping of the manipulable parts of spoken language. Second, we have attempted to show that the type of instructional environment, theory, and practice unanimously accepted by leaders in the field of literacy education (see Flippo, 2001), and which is most facilitative of nurturing healthy progress toward conventional functioning, is the very foundation upon which reading and writing instruction for young second-language learners must be based.

Our own caveat is that in its earliest stages, the development of writing takes time and a great deal of mental energy and coordination, and develops unevenly. Thus, while it is crucial to create the appropriate instructional environment, this is only one part of the learning equation. Children are simultaneously influenced by their family background, language interaction patterns, cognitive capabilities, behavioral habits, and, no doubt, many other subtle forces that are invisible to their adult mentors. As educators of young children, therefore, we must be patient, understanding, tolerant of less-than-"correct" performance, and professionally astute enough to distinguish between outcomes that look conventional but really aren't, and unconventional outcomes that are actually indications of healthy progress toward a full understanding of the complexities of written language.

The Past 10 Years: In Retrospect

1. *What are the most important things that you believe literacy research has shown over the past 10 years? (Positive/Negative)*

For the field of emergent literacy, at least, we think one of the more positive trends is the repeated confirmation, through major meta-analyses of experimental and quasi-experimental research done throughout the past 15 years, of many of the early case study findings in the 1970s and 1980s (cf. reviews by Teale & Sulzby, 1986; Yaden & Templeton, 1986) that engagement in early writing and emergent reading behaviors and multiple experiences with printed materials during the preschool years is predictive of acquiring conventional reading and spelling ability early in elementary school. Most recently, for example, findings from the meta-analyses of the National Early Literacy Panel (NELP, 2008) identified several early literacy behaviors, in addition to alphabet knowledge and phonological awareness, which were consistent predictors of learning how to read and spell, including name-writing and invented spelling, knowledge of print conventions, concepts of word, and oral language proficiency. The general finding is that it is not only one skill (such as phonological awareness) that enhances early literacy ability, but rather a broad set of experiences in which children are given regular opportunities to explore, experiment with, and talk about written language as its varied forms occur across multiple contexts.

Another positive trend is the broadening of early literacy research to include aspects of human development as a part of young children's response to the written language environment. In particular, the findings of Rowe and Nietzel (2010) that children's "personal interest orientations were related to ways they participated in emergent writing activities" highlight the importance of personality development as a mediator for both engagement in early literacy behavior as well as the types of engagement preferred. This research is notable as well for its target population—2- and 3-year-olds—since the vast majority of emergent literacy research has been done with children at least 4 years old. This study and others by Rowe and colleagues challenge the traditional field of early literacy to become less parochial and exhibit more interdisciplinarity by studying literacy growth within the broader field of early childhood development, and identifying key precursors of literacy instead of looking only at reading and writing behavior at ages just prior to kindergarten when important developmental milestones of early childhood have already passed.

2. *How do you think this should inform the contexts and practices of reading instruction in the classroom?*

For young children, at least, but perhaps for anyone learning how to read and write, models of literacy instruction should be characterized by a bioecological perspective (Bronfenbrenner, 2005). First fully delineated by Urie Bronfenbrenner in 1979 in *The Ecology of Human Development: Experiments by Nature and Design*, this perspective recognizes that learning and development of any kind is influenced at different times by both proximal (e.g., parents, caregivers, immediate family) as well as distal (e.g., neighbors, teachers, household adults' workplace, social status, and civic, state or national policies) influences. In other words, any individual's growth develops within a framework, a network of others' development as well, and all are influenced by social, economic, and political contexts. Therefore, expressions of this growth—literacy growth in our case—will reflect many of these influences at various times in different degrees in response to particular topics or circumstances that instruction introduces.

As mentioned earlier, young children begin to learn about written language before adults acknowledge certain behaviors as being literate. Children begin to form notions and understandings about the symbols of written language in situ, and the manifestation of these understandings either in talk or expressions on paper, computer, artistic mediums, etc., may look nothing like what is considered to be conventional literacy forms. The upshot is that teachers of young children must be flexible in drawing out these unconventional literacy expressions, and insightful as to their possible origins given the environment in which the child is developing. It is, for the most part, a long time before most children grasp fully what it means to be a literate person—and an instructional overemphasis on form or adult notions may decidedly delay the very understanding which adults' seek to observe.

As the National Early Literacy Panel discovered, conventional literacy is predicted by a wide range of experiences a child has, not just direct instruction in one or two skills. Further, as Rowe and Nietzel (2010) point out, literacy instruction is shaped, transformed, and given meaning by personality itself. Thus, the content of any literacy instruction should be broadly focused, rather than narrow, and it should seek to tap into some familiar experience of the learner, such that what is to be learned benefits from the strength of personal motivation. These are hardly new ideas, but perhaps too easily dismissed in the press for accountability and results. Our belief is that literacy educators must always defend the idea that literacy instruction must mirror the complexities of human development, challenging the simplistic notions that more assessment will produce the results which only humane, sophisticated, and deeply informed instruction is capable of doing.

References

Au, K.H. (2001). What we know about multicultural education and students of diverse backgrounds. In R.F. Flippo (Ed.), *Reading researchers in search of common ground* (pp. 101–117). Newark, DE: International Reading Association.

August, D., & Hakuta, K. (Eds.). (1997). *Improving schooling for language-minority children: A research agenda.* Washington, DC: National Academy Press.

Bakes, D.T. (1980). *The development of metalinguistic abilities in children.* Berlin: Springer-Verlag.

Bearison, D.J. (1991). Interactional contexts of cognitive development: Piagetian approaches to socio-genesis. In S. Strauss (Series Ed.) & L.T. Landsmann (Vol. Ed.), *Human development*, Vol. 4: *Culture, schooling and psychological development* (pp. 56–70). Norwood, NJ: Ablex.

Besse, J. (1996). An approach to writing in kindergarten. In C. Pontecorvo, M. Orsolini, B. Burge, & L. Resnick (Eds.), *Children's early text construction* (pp. 127–144). Mahwah, NJ: Erlbaum.

Blachrnan, B.A. (2000). Phonological awareness. In M.L. Kamil, P.B. Mosenthal, P.D. Pearson, & R. Barr (Eds.), *Handbook of Reading Research* (Vol. 3, pp. 483–502). Mahwah, NJ: Erlbaurn.

Bloodgood, J.W. (1999). What's in a name? Children's name writing and literacy acquisition. *Reading Research Quarterly*, 34, 342–367.

Bronfenbrenner, U. (1979). *The ecology of human development: Experiments by nature and by design*. Cambridge, MA: Harvard University Press.

Bronfenbrenner, U. (Ed.). (2005). *Making human beings human: Bioecological perspectives on human development*. Thousand Oaks, CA: Sage.

Campbell, R. (1996). *Literacy in nursery education*. Stoke-on-Trent, UK: Trentham Books.

Case, R. (1992). The role of central conceptual structures in the development of children's scientific and mathematical thought. In A. Demetriou, M. Shayer, & A. Efklides (Eds.), *Neo-Piagetian theories of cognitive development: Implications and applications for education* (pp. 52–64). New York, NY: Routledge.

Clay, M. (1975). *What did I write?* Auckland, NZ: Heinemann.

Clay, M. (1987). *Writing begins at home: Preparing children for writing before they go to school.* Auckland, NZ: Heinemann.

Daniels, H.A. (1990). Young writers and readers reach out: Developing a sense of audience. In T. Shanahan (Ed.), *Reading and writing together: New perspectives for the classroom.* (pp. 99–125). Norwood, MA: Christopher-Gordon.

Davydov, V.V., & Radzikhovskii, L.A. (1985). Vygotsky's theory and the activity-oriented approach in psychology. In J.V. Wertsch (Ed.), *Culture, communication, and cognition: Vygotskian perspectives* (pp. 35–65). Cambridge, UK: Cambridge University Press.

Demetriou, A., Shayer, M., & Efklides, A. (1992). *Neo-Piagetian theories of cognitive development: Implications and applications for education.* New York, NY: Routledge.

Dickinson, D.K., & Tabors, P.O. (Eds.). (2001). *Beginning literacy with language.* Baltimore, MD: Paul H. Brookes Publishing Co.

Donato, R. (1999). Hispano education and the implications of autonomy: Four school systems in southern Colorado, 1920–1963. *Harvard Educational Review*, 69, 117–149.

Downing, J., & Valtin, R. (Eds.). (1984). *Language awareness and learning to read.* New York, NY: Springer-Verlag.

Dyson, A.H. (1982). The emergence of visible language: Interrelationships between drawing and early writing. *Visible Language*, 16, 360–381.

Dyson, A.H. (1985). Individual differences in emerging writing. In M. Farr (Ed.), *Advances in writing research*, (Vol. 1, pp. 59–125). Norwood, NJ: Ablex.

Dyson, A.H. (1986). Children's early interpretation of writing: Expanding research perspectives. In D. Yaden & S. Templeton (Eds.), *Metalinguistic awareness and beginning literacy: Conceptualizing what it means to read and write* (pp. 201–218). Portsmouth, NH: Heinemann.

Dyson, A.H. (1992). Whistles for Willie, lost puppies, and cartoon dogs: The sociocultural dimensions of young children's composing. *Journal of Reading Behavior*, 24, 433–462.

Dyson, A.H. (1993a). *Social worlds of children learning to write in an urban primary school.* New York, NY: Teachers College Press.

Dyson, A.H. (1993b). From invention to social action in early childhood literacy: A reconceptualization through dialogue about difference. *Early Childhood Research Quarterly*, 8,409–425.

Dyson, A.H. (1995). Writing children: Reinventing the development of childhood literacy. *Written Communication, 12,* 4–46.

Dyson, A.H. (1997). *Writing superheroes: Contemporary childhood, popular culture, and classroom literacy.* New York, NY: Teachers College Press.

Dyson, A.H. (2002). Writing and children's symbolic repertoires: Development unhinged. In S.B. Neuman & D.K. Dickinson (Eds.), *Handbook of early literacy research* (pp. 126–141). New York, NY: Guilford Press.

Dyson, A.H., & Freedman, S.W. (2003). Writing. In J. Flood, D. Lapp, J.R. Squire, & J. Jensen (Eds.), *The handbook of research on teaching the English language arts* (2nd ed., pp. 967–992). Mahwah, NJ: Erlbaum.

Fang, Z. (1999). Expanding the vista of emergent writing research: Implications for early childhood educators. *Early Childhood Education Journal, 26,* 179–182.

Farnan, N., & Dahl, K. (2003). Children's writing: Research and practice. In J. Flood, D. Lapp, J.R. Squire, & J.M. Jensen (Eds.), *The handbook of research on teaching the English language arts* (2nd ed., pp. 993–1007). Mahwah, NJ: Erlbaum.

Ferreiro, E. (1984). The underlying logic of literacy development. In H. Goelman, A. Oberg, & F. Smith (Eds.), *Awakening to literacy* (pp. 154–173). Portsmouth, NH: Heinemann.

Ferreiro, E. (1985). Literacy development: A psychogenetic perspective. In D.R. Olson, N. Torrance, & A. Hildyard (Eds.), *Literacy, language and learning: The nature and consequences of reading and writing* (pp. 217–228). Cambridge, UK: Cambridge University Press.

Ferreiro, B. (1986). The interplay between information and assimilation in beginning literacy. In W.H. Teale & E. Sulzby (Eds.), *Emergent literacy: Writing and reading* (pp. 15–49). Norwood, NJ: Ablex.

Ferreiro, E. (1994). Literacy development: Construction and reconstruction. In D. Tirosh (Ed.), *Implicit and explicit knowledge: An educational approach* (pp. 169–180). Norwood, NJ: Ablex.

Ferreiro, E. (1996). The acquisition of cultural objects: The case of written language. *Prosects (BIE-UNESCO), 26,* 131–140.

Ferreiro, E., & Pontecorvo, C. (2002). Word segmentation in early written narratives. *Language and Education, 16,* 1–17.

Ferreiro, E., & Teberosky, A. (1982). *Literacy before schooling* (K.G. Castro, Trans.). Portsmouth, NH: Heinemann. (Original work published 1979.)

Flippo, R.F. (1998). Points of agreement: A display of professional unity in our field. *The Reading Teacher, 52,* 30–40.

Flippo, R.F. (Ed.). (2001). *Reading researchers in search of common ground.* Newark, DE: International Reading Association.

Gee, J.P. (2000). Discourse and sociocultural studies in reading. In M.L. Kamil, P.B. Mosenthal, P.D. Pearson, & R. Barr (Eds.), *Handbook of Reading Research* (Vol. 3, pp. 195–208). Mahwah, NJ: Erlhaum.

Geekie, P., Cambourne, B., & Fitzsimmons, P. (1999). *Understanding literacy development.* Stoke-on-Trent, UK: Trentham Books.

Gelb, I.J. (1963). *A study of writing* (2nd ed.). Chicago, IL: University of Chicago Press.

Glazer, S.M., & Burke, E.M. (1994). *An integrated approach to early literacy.* Boston, MA: Allyn and Bacon.

Glick, J. (1997). Prologue. In R.W. Rieber (Ed.), The collected works of L.S. Vygotsky: Vol. 4: *The history of the development of higher mental functions* (pp. v–xvi). Trans. by M.J. Hall. New York, NY: Plenum Press.

Goodman, Y. (1984). The development of initial literacy. In H. Goelman, A. Oberg & F. Smith (Eds.), *Awakening to literacy* (pp. 102–109). Portsmouth, NJ: Heinemann.

Goodman, Y. (1986). Children coming to know literacy. In W. Teale & E. Sulzby (Eds.), *Emergent literacy: Writing and reading* (pp. 1–14). Norwood, NJ: Ablex.

Harste, J., Woodward, V., & Burke, C. (1984). *Language stories and literacy lessons.* Portsmouth, NH: Heinemann.

Hildreth, G. (1936). Developmental sequences in name writing. *Child Development, 7,* 291–303.

Kamii, C., Long, R., Manning, M., & Manning, G. (1991). Spelling in kindergarten. In C. Kamii, M. Manning, & G. Manning (Eds.), *Early literacy: A constructivist foundation for whole language* (pp. 69–82). Washington, DC: National Education Association.

Katz, J.R. (2001). Playing at home: The talk of pretend play. In D.K. Dickinson, & P.O. Tabors (Eds.), *Beginning literacy with language* (pp. 53–74). Baltimore, MD: Paul H. Brookes Publishing Co.

Kohl de Oliveira, M., & Valsiner, J. (1998). *Literacy in human development.* Stamford, CT: Ablex.

Levin, I., & Korat, O. (1993). Sensitivity to phonological, morphological, and semantic cues in early reading and writing in Hebrew. *Merrill-Palmer Quarterly, 39,* 233–257.

Lourenço, O., & Machado, A. (1996). In defense of Piaget's theory: A reply to 10 common criticisms. *Psychological Review, 103,* 143–165.

Luria, A. (1998). The development of writing in the child. In M.K. de Oliveira & J. Valsiner (Eds.), *Literacy in human development* (pp. 15–56). Norwood, NJ: Ablex. (Original work published 1929.)

McGee, L., & Richgels, D. (2000). *The beginnings of literacy: Supporting young readers and writers* (3rd ed.). Boston, MA: Allyn and Bacon.

Moll, L.C. (Ed.). (1990). *Vygotsky and education: Instructional implications and applications of sociohistorical psychology.* Cambridge, UK: Cambridge University Press.

National Early Literacy Panel (2008). *Developing Early Literacy: Report of the National Early Literacy Panel.* Jessup, MD: National Institute for Literacy.

National Research Council (2001). *Eager to learn: Educating our preschoolers.* Washington, DC: National Academy Press.

Neuman, S., & Roskos, K. (1998). *Children achieving: Best practices in early literacy.* Newark, DE: International Reading Association.

Ortiz, M.F. (Ed.). (1998). *Literacy instruction for culturally and linguistically diverse students.* Newark, DE: International Reading Association.

Piaget, J. (1962). *Comments.* Cambridge, MA: The MIT Press.

Piaget, J. (1970). *Introduction to genetic epistemology.* New York, NY: Columbia University Press (original work published 1950).

Piaget, J. (1985). *The equilibration of cognitive structures: The central problem of intellectual development.* Trans. by T. Brown & K.J. Thampy. Chicago, IL: The University of Chicago Press. (Original work published 1975.)

Piaget, J. (2001). *The psychology of intelligence.* Trans. by M. Piercy & D.E. Berlyne. New York, NY: Routledge. (Original work published 1950.)

Pontecorvo, C., & Zucchermaglio, C. (1988). Modes of differentiation in children's writing construction. *European Journal of Psychology of Education, 4,* 371–385.

Pontecorvo, C., Orsolini, M., Burge, B., & Resnick, L. (Eds.). (1996). *Children's early text construction*. Mahwah, NJ: Erlbaum.

Purcell-Gates, V. (1995). *Other people's words: The cycle of low literacy*. Cambridge, MA: Harvard University Press.

Reyes, P., Scribner, J.D., & Scribner, A.P. (Eds.). (1999). *Lessons from high-performing Hispanic schools: Creating learning communities*. New York, NY: Teachers College Press.

Reynolds, B. (1997). *Literacy in the preschool: The roles of teachers and parents*. Stoke-on-Trent, UK: Trentham Books.

Richgels, D. (1995). A kindergarten sign-in procedure: A routine in support of written language learning. In K.A. Hinchman, D.J. Leu, & C.K. Kinzer (Eds.), *Perspectives on literacy: Research and practice: 44th Yearbook of the National Reading Conference* (pp. 243–244). Chicago, IL: National Reading Conference.

Rivera, C. (1999, May 26). Zoning chief vows action on skid row "crime magnets." *Los Angeles Times*, B1 & B3.

Roberts, B. (1992). The evolution of the young child's concept of word as a unit of spoken and written language. *Reading Research Quarterly, 27*, 124–139.

Rocco, M.T.F. (1998). Parallels between the perspectives of Alexander Luria and Emilia Ferreiro. In M. Kohl de Oliveira & J. Valsiner (Eds.), *Literacy in human development* (pp. 57–78). Norwood, NJ: Ablex.

Rowe, D. (1994). *Preschoolers as authors: Literacy learning in the social world of the preschool*. Cresskill, NH: Hampton Press.

Rowe, D.W., & Nietzel, C. (2010). Interest and agency in 2- and 3-year-olds' participation in emergent writing. *Reading Research Quarterly, 28*, 304–333.

Scribner, J.D., & Reyes, P. (1999). Creating learning communities for high-performing Hispanic students: A conceptual framework. In P. Reyes, J.D. Scribner, & A.P. Scribner (Eds.), *Lessons from high-performing Hispanic schools: Creating learning communities* (pp. 188–210). New York, NY: Teachers College Press.

Sinclair, A., Jarvella, R.J., & Levelt, W.J.M. (1978). *The child's conception of language*. Berlin, Germany: Springer-Verlag.

Smagorinsky, P. (1995). The social construction of data: Methodological problems of investigating learning in the zone of proximal development. *Review of Educational Research, 65*, 191–212.

Snow, C.E., Burns, M.S., & Griffin, P. (Eds.). (1998). *Preventing reading difficulties in young children*. Washington, DC: National Academy Press.

Spodek, B., & Saracho, N. (Eds.). (1993). *Yearbook in Early Childhood Education*, Vol. 4. Language and literacy in early childhood education. New York, NY: Teachers College Press.

Stefanakis, E.H. (1998). *Whose judgment counts? Assessing bilingual children, K-3*. Portsmouth, NH: Heinemann.

Sulzby, E. (1985). Kindergarteners as readers and writers. In Farr, M. (Ed.), *Advances in writing research*, Vol. 1: *Children's early writing development* (pp. 128–199). Norwood, NJ: Ablex.

Sulzby, E. (1986). Children's elicitation and use of metalinguistic knowledge about word during literacy interactions. In D. Yaden & S. Templeton (Eds.), *Metalinguistic awareness and beginning literacy: Conceptualizing what it means to read and write* (pp. 219–234). Portsmouth, NH: Heinemann.

Sulzby, E. (1996). Roles of oral and written language as children approach conventional literacy. In C. Pontecorvo, M. Orsolini, B. Burge, & L. Resnick (Eds.), *Children's early text construction* (pp. 25–46). Mahwah, NJ: Erlbaum.

Sulzby, E., & Teale, W. (1991). Emergent literacy. In R. Barr, M. Kamil, P. Mosenthal, & P.D. Pearson (Eds.), *Handbook of Reading Research* (Vol. 2, pp. 727–757). New York, NY: Longman.

Sulzby, E., & Teale, V.H. (2003). The development of the young child and the emergence of literacy. In J. Flood, D. Lapp, J.R. Squire, & J.M. Jensen (Eds.), *Handbook of research on teaching the English language arts* (2nd ed., pp. 300–313). Mahwah, NJ: Erlbaum.

Taylor, R.P. (2002). Order in Pollock's chaos. *Scientific American, 287*, 116–121.

Teale, W., & Sulzby, E. (1986). *Emergent literacy: Writing and reading.* Norwood, NJ: Ablex Publishing Corporation.

Temple, C., Nathan, R., Temple, F., & Burns, N.A. (1993). *The beginnings of writing* (3rd ed.). Boston, MA: Allyn and Bacon.

Templeton, S., & Bear, D.R. (1992). *Development of orthographic knowledge and the foundations of literacy: A memorial festschrift for Edmund H. Henderson.* Mahwah, NJ: Erlbaum.

Tolchinsky, L. (2001). Developmental perspectives on writing. In G. Rijlaarsdam (Series Ed.) & L. Tolchinsky (Vol. Ed.), *Studies in writing: Vol. 8. Developmental aspects in learning to write* (pp. 1–12). Dordrecht, The Netherlands: Kiuwer Academic Publishers.

Tolchinsky Landsmann, L. (1991). The conceptualization of writing in the confluence of interactive models of development. In L. Tolchinsky Landsmann (Ed.), *Culture, schooling, and psychological development* (pp. 87–111). Norwood, NJ: Ablex.

Tolchinsky Landsmann, L., & Levin, I. (1985). Writing in preschoolers: An age related analysis. *Journal of Applied Psycholinguistics, 6*, 319–339.

Tolchinsky Landsmann, L., & Levin, I. (1987). Writing in four- to six-year-olds: Representation of semantic and phonetic similarities and differences. *Journal of Child Language, 14*, 127–144.

Tolchinsky, L., & Teberosky, A. (1998). The development of word segmentation and writing in two scripts. *Cognitive Development, 13*, 1–24.

Tunmer, V.E., Pratt, C., & Herriman, M.L. (1984). *Metalinguistic awareness in children: Theory, research, and implications.* New York, NY: Springer-Verlag.

Valsiner, J. (1992). Social organization of cognitive development: Internalization and externalization of constraint systems. In A. Demetriou, M. Shayer, & A. Efklides (Eds.), *Neo-Piagetian theories of cognitive development: Implications and applications for education* (pp. 65–78). New York, NY: Routledge.

van der Veer, R., & Valsiner, J. (1993). *Understanding Vygotsky: A quest for synthesis.* Oxford, UK: Blackwell Publishers.

Vernon, S., & Ferreiro, E. (1999). Writing development: A neglected variable in the consideration of phonological awareness. *Harvard Educational Review, 69*, 395–414.

Vygotsky, L.S. (1987). *The collected works of L.S. Vygotsky: Volume 1: Problems of general psychology.* R.W. Rieber & A.S. Carton (Eds.). New York, NY: Plenum Press. (Original work published 1934.)

Vygotsky, L.S. (1997). *The collected works of L.S. Vygotsky: Volume 4: The history of the development of higher mental functions.* R.W. Rieber (Ed.) & M.J. Hall. (Trans). New York, NY: Plenum Press. (Original work published 1931.)

Wertsch, J.V. (1992). Sociocultural setting and the zone of proximal development: The problem of text-based realities. In S. Strauss (Series Ed.) & L. Tolchinsky Landsmann (Vol. Ed.), *Human development*, Vol. 4: *Culture, schooling and psychological development* (pp. 71–86). Norwood, NJ: Ablex.

Yaden, D.B. Jr. (2003). Storybook reading as a Complex Adaptive System. Or "Is an igloo a house for bears?" In A. van Kleeck, S. Stahl, & E. Bauer (Eds.), *On reading to children: Parents and teachers* (pp. 336–362). Mahwah, NJ: Erlbaum.

Yaden, D.B. Jr, & Brassell, D. (2002). Enhancing emergent literacy with Spanish-speaking preschoolers in the inner-city: Overcoming the odds. In C. Keating (Ed.), *Comprehensive reading instruction across the grade levels* (pp. 20–39). Newark, DE: International Reading Association.

Yaden, D.B. Jr, & Templeton, S. (Eds.). (1986). *Metalinguistic awareness and beginning literacy: Conceptualizing what it means to read and write.* Portsmouth, NH: Heinemann.

Yaden, D.B. Jr, Smolkin, L., & MacGillivray, L. (1993). A psychogenetic perspective on children's understanding about letter associations during alphabet book readings. *Journal of Reading Behavior, 25,* 43–68.

Yaden, D.B. Jr, Tam, A., Madrigal, P., Massa, J., Brassell, D., Altamirano, L.S., & Armendariz, J. (2000a). Early literacy for inner-city children: The effects of reading and writing interventions in English and Spanish during the preschool years. *The Reading Teacher, 54,* 186–189.

Yaden, D.B. Jr, Rowe, D., & MacGillivray, L. (2000b). Emergent literacy. A matter (polyphony) of perspectives. In Kamil, M.L., Mosenthal, P.B., Pearson, P.D., & Barr, R. (Eds.), *Handbook of Reading Research* (Vol. 3, pp. 425–454). Mahwah, NJ: Erlbaum.

Yaden, D.B. Jr, Madrigal, P., & Tam, A. (2003). Access to books and beyond: Creating and learning from a book lending program for Latino families in the inner-city. In G. Garcia (Ed.), *English learners: Reaching the highest level of English literacy* (pp. 357–386). Newark, DE: International Reading Association.

16

COMMUNICATION AND COLLABORATION WITH PARENTS, FAMILIES, AND COMMUNITIES

Timothy V. Rasinski

From my perspective, the major finding from Flippo's study of common ground in literacy (Flippo, 1998) is that the perceived gulf that exists between orientations to research and practices in literacy education by literacy researchers and scholars may not be as large as it may seem. Moreover, at the foundation for all approaches, regardless of theoretical or pragmatic orientation, there is a common core value—the desire to improve the efficacy of literacy education so that all learners may be able to attain full and functional levels of literacy. This should be looked on as good news. There is more that we, as a body of literacy scholars, researchers, and practitioners, agree on than we disagree on.

Although consensus among literacy professionals is something to be applauded, there is still much work to be done if we take the notion of consensus seriously. Clearly, there is lack of consensus between literacy professionals, whether researchers or practitioners, and the general public, specifically parents of children who receive instruction in literacy. Parents and their families may themselves have distinct differences in the way they look at literacy, and how literacy is best taught, from literacy scholars. Indeed, parents and their families are likely to manifest distinct differences among themselves about literacy. Heath's (1983) classic study of language and literacy learning in two culturally different communities separated by only a few miles demonstrates how differences exist. If differences (read, lack of consensus) exist between and among families, think of the lack of consensus that must inevitably exist between literacy professionals and families.

Nearly any literacy professional who has spent time in a classroom has viewed the disconnect that exists between school and home, especially when it comes to literacy education. Teachers come across many parents who don't seem to care about their children's reading and who don't want to be involved in their children's literacy development. Of course, to be fair, there are many parents who view teachers as not interested in what parents know about their children's literacy development and what parents do and can do to foster their children's growth in reading.

Yet, despite this lack of consensus and collaboration, this apparent disconnect between schools and parents, the importance of parents in children's literacy learning is widely recognized and supported by a growing body of research. In March 2009, newly inaugurated President Barack Obama spoke about the importance of parents in children's learning:

> The bottom line is that no government policies will make any difference unless we also hold ourselves more accountable as parents. Because government, no matter how wise or efficient, cannot turn off the TV or put away the video games. Teachers, no matter how dedicated or effective, cannot make sure your children leave for school on time and do their homework when they get back at night. These are things only a parent can do. These are things that our parents must do.
>
> *Taking on Education, 2009*

At the same, two significant research studies from the past (Durkin, 1966; Postlethwaite & Ross, 1992) have clearly documented the importance of parental involvement. More recent research, conducted in just the past decade, continues to affirm the importance of parental and family involvement in, among other things, fostering children's growth in reading and writing, including vocabulary, phonemic awareness, and comprehension; improving general knowledge and overall academic achievement; increasing attendance in school; developing more positive attitudes toward school and motivation for reading; improving parental confidence in their own abilities to help their children learn; and improving teacher morale (Fan & Chen, 2001; Epstein et al., 2002; Henderson & Mapp, 2002; National Middle School Association, 2003; Padak & Rasinski, 2003; Wherry, 2009).

The question has turned from what is the potential of parental involvement in children's literacy development, to how can teachers of literacy gain consensus and collaboration with parents—how can teachers of literacy help parents improve their children's literacy, and how can parents help teachers become more effective in teaching literacy to their children? In the remainder of this chapter, I will explore ways that literacy educators at all levels, classroom teachers to teachers of literacy education in higher education, can achieve higher levels of consensus and collaboration.

Principles for Effective Communication and Collaboration with Parents and Families

For effective collaboration to occur, groundwork of basic principles needs to be established. Rasinski, Padak, and Fawcett (2010) identify several essential elements that lay the basis for effective parent involvement in literacy education. The first is simply that whatever advice and suggestions be given to parents must be *proven effective* through scientific investigation. In literacy education, we have come to the recognition that our field needs to have a scientific basis. This is not only true for what we do in the classroom; it is also true for what we ask parents to do, in the name of literacy education, with their children.

Not only does literacy education need to be scientific, it also needs to be authentic. It is abundantly clear that the more reading a person does, the better reader he or she becomes. Whatever we ask parents to do must be rooted in the authentic literacy experiences that one might normally find in homes—*real reading*. High levels of engagement are necessary to insure student learning and long-term involvement. When we make *reading and reading activities enjoyable*, parents and children will want to be involved. Certainly, authentic reading is very enjoyable. But there are other ways to insure enjoyment and engagement. Word games, list making, letter writing, and reading are simple literacy activities that are authentic in nature, and enjoyable and fulfilling in their implementation.

Parents are not trained in literacy education. For parent involvement to work, parents need to have *ongoing training and support* from educators who are the experts in literacy education. Life for parents and families seems to constantly become more complex. Time is critical, and so is ease of implementation. Whatever we ask parents to do with their children in the name of literacy needs to be *easy and consistent* in its implementation. Overly complex activities, or activities that change radically from one day to the next, or activities that require large investments of time will simply not be done by parents on a regular basis. Effective parent involvement needs to be *consistent over the long term*. One-shot parent initiatives may be fun, but they are unlikely to have the desired effect. When parents and their children work daily on reading, even if for a few minutes per day, that daily work will have a dramatic impact on their children's growth as readers. Ten minutes each evening given to reading between parent and child will be much more effective than an hour-long activity done only once a week. Making parent involvement activities easy and simple to do will help to insure consistent implementation. *Providing parents with texts and other instructional materials* will also help to insure consistent implementation. If parents have to hunt down the books and find the materials needed to be used in a literacy activity with their children, many will find the preparation for the activity too cumbersome to try. Teachers are not only experts in literacy instruction, they are also experts in the kinds of reading texts and other materials needed for effective instruction. Teachers need to use their expertise to assist parents. More and more these days, teachers are being held accountable for the academic achievement of their students. Parents, too, may be asked to be accountable for the support they provide their children in literacy. Providing parents with a way to *document their work with their children* not only asks parents to be accountable for their children's literacy development, it also provides parents a tacit encouragement and reminder to work with their children consistently over the long term. Documentation of parent involvement allows teachers to determine the effectiveness of their parent involvement program. If implementation is high and students are progressing, teachers can assume that their parent involvement initiative is effective.

Achieving Consensus and Collaboration with Parents and Families

With these ground rules for parent involvement as a guide, how might educators actually work to make parent collaboration and consensus work?

Parent Involvement in Teacher Education

Undergraduate and graduate coursework in literacy are among the initial opportunities for the latest research into methods of literacy instruction and issues related to literacy education to be presented to teachers. We have courses on reading methods at every level of schooling, and for various kinds of learners. We have courses on literacy and literature, literacy and drama, literacy and coaching, literacy and phonics, literacy and the various content areas, multicultural issues related to literacy, gender issues related to literacy, literacy and assessment. Interestingly, however, in very few colleges of education are there courses offered on involving parents in children's literacy education.

Despite a growing body of research into the importance and effectiveness of parental and family involvement, there is not an instructional vehicle in most colleges for delivering information about parental involvement to teachers-in-training. Although information about parental involvement may be integrated into existing courses, by the very nature of these topics and issues being subsumed into other coursework it suggests that they are of, at best, secondary importance in the grand scheme of things. I think it is time that we seriously consider making the issue of parental involvement in literacy education a topic worthy of deep, intense, and sustained study. Certainly there is enough information available on parents and families and literacy development to sustain a regular course on the topic.

Parent Involvement in Schools and Classrooms

Bringing parents into the schools is perhaps the best way to guide and support parents in their children's literacy development. Regular programs of information dissemination to parents can help parents develop the knowledge necessary to help their own children. Through a series of well-planned and regularly scheduled meetings, parents can learn about the importance of reading to children, reading with children, developing a literate environment at home, "can't miss" books for children, word games to play at home, summer reading, etc. They can also share their own insights on helping children grow as readers.

Parents who have the time can also take on more active roles in the school. Schools are always in need of volunteers who can provide additional assistance and tutoring in school to those children who may benefit from it. Again, a well-planned and expertly managed parent volunteer literacy program can make a world of difference in children's growth as readers (see, for example, Wilfong, 2008). Moreover, parents who learn the skills and strategies of effective literacy education while working in such programs are more likely to use those same skills and strategies at home with their own children. Indeed, I know of more than one parent involved in such programs being so moved by their involvement as to pursue careers as teachers themselves.

Parent Involvement at Home

The most natural venue for parents to help their children in literacy is at home. There is much that educators can do to help parents be more effective in their literacy interactions with children. Beyond the standard "read to your children" teachers can design research-based approaches, in collaboration with parents, for parents to implement with their children on a regular basis.

One parent literacy program for young readers I have had the opportunity to work on is called *Fast Start* (Rasinski, 1995; Padak & Rasinski, 2004, 2005, 2006; Rasinski & Stevenson, 2005). In each daily 10-minute home lesson, parents read a short poem or rhyme to their child, read the same poem with their child, and eventually listen to and celebrate their child reading the same poem to them. This is then followed with a very brief game-like activity on some aspect of the poem, most often a focus on interesting words or word parts embedded in the poem. Our research into the program has found that parents and children find the activity easy, enjoyable, and worthwhile, and that parents and children who engage in Fast Start regularly make significantly greater progress in reading and various reading skills than children who are not involved in such a program. There is nothing magical about Fast Start. It is simply a literacy involvement program for parents that is based on the principles of effective parent and family involvement identified earlier. Other programs that are equally effective can be developed by teachers committed to parent and family communication and collaboration in literacy.

Community Connections

The local community can be viewed as the family writ large. Schools that work to involve the local community in children's literacy learning at school not only can impact children's literacy development in a positive way, but also will make stronger ties between the schools and the communities they serve and upon which they depend for support. The local community is filled with resources that can play a positive role in communicating and collaborating with schools to improve literacy (Tooms, Padak, & Rasinski, 2007). These include governmental agencies, community libraries, local businesses, community service organizations (e.g., Rotary, American Legion, local councils of the International Reading Association), local foundations, retirement homes, and even other schools.

These agencies and organizations are filled with people (many of whom are parents themselves) who would benefit from information on literacy development, who could be organized to provide volunteer tutorial assistance to children in need, and who could provide financial and other tangible assistance (e.g., books and other literacy materials) to the school literacy program. Moreover, these agencies and organizations could provide venues for students to use their literacy skills to serve their communities. I know of some communities where students perform patriotic readers' theater scripts, read patriotic poetry, and sing patriotic songs in local American Legion and VFW halls around Veterans Day and Memorial Day each year. I know businesses that love to have students' artwork and literacy work (such as stories and poems) put on display so that customers can see the wonderful work done by students and teachers in the local schools. I know of retirement homes where students visit regularly, not only to perform for residents but also to take oral histories of them in order to learn about times past and also about aging. I know of many newspapers that regularly publish students' stories and letters. I know of several local councils of the International Reading Association that sponsor and celebrate "Literacy Day" at the local mall or shopping center.

Children learn to read and write by using reading and writing for authentic and organic purposes. Communicating and collaborating with the local community can provide opportunities for making reading and writing authentic and organic. There is no question that such work can be difficult. Connecting with the community and working with community organizations to find ways to make collaboration work is time consuming, and often fraught with dead ends—lots of effort that seems to go nowhere. Nevertheless, it is through such literacy collaborations that we can achieve the connection between school and society that Dewey (1991) argued was essential for schools to achieve their ultimate potential.

The research is clear. When parents and families (and communities) are involved in the literacy lives and education of students, the students, parents, families, teachers, and community benefit (Padak & Rasinski, 2003). Without doubt, involving parents can be a challenging and often frustrating task. Equally clear, however, is that teachers and schools cannot do the task of growing readers on their own. If we ever hope to achieve the goal of developing a full literate society, then the literacy education community must work to achieve consensus, communication, and collaboration with the larger public community it serves.

The Past 10 Years: In Retrospect

1.   *What are the most important things that you believe literacy research has shown over the past 10 years? (Positive and/or Negative)*

From my perspective, literacy research has provided two important insights into parental involvement. First, research continues to confirm the importance of parental involvement in their children's literacy development. When parents and families are actively involved in their children's literacy development, children are more likely to be successful in achieving their full potential as literacy learners. Second, research has shown that reading fluency is critical to children's literacy development. Moreover, the methods for teaching reading fluency are simple enough that parents can easily be trained to implement them effectively with their children in a matter of minutes per day. My own research on Fast Start (see, for example, Rasinski & Stevenson, 2005), a parental involvement program in fluency, has demonstrated that parents can make a significant impact on their children's growth in reading with 10–15 minutes per day devoted to fluency work.

2.   *How do you think this should inform the contexts and practices of reading instruction in the classroom?*

I think that it is critical that schools, school administrators, and teachers make a concerted, dedicated, and long-term commitment to developing and implementing systemic parental involvement programs in the literacy education of their children. The research is clear that if we are interested in growing readers, then parents and families must be involved—not in one time, hit-and-miss "make it and take it"-like activities, but in systemic programs based on research findings of the critical elements of effective reading instruction.

References

Dewey, J. (1991). *The school and society and the child and the curriculum* (Centennial Publications of The University of Chicago Press). Chicago, IL: University of Chicago Press.

Durkin, D. (1966). *Children who read early*. New York, NY: Teachers College Press.

Epstein, J.L., Sanders, M.G., Simon, B.S., Salinas, K.C., Jansorn, N.R., & Van Voorhis, F.L. (2002). *School, community, and community partnerships: Your handbook for action* (2nd ed.). Thousand Oaks, CA: Corwin Press.

Fan, X.T., & Chen, M. (2001). Parental involvement and students' academic achievement: A meta-analysis. *Educational Psychology Review, 13*, 1–22.

Flippo, R.F. (1998). Points of agreement: A display of professional unity in our field. *The Reading Teacher, 52*, 30–40.

Heath, S.B. (1983). *Ways with words: Language, life, and work in communities and classrooms*. New York, NY: Cambridge University Press.

Henderson, A.T., & Mapp, K.L. (2002) *A new wave of evidence: The impact of school, family, and community connections on student achievement.* Austin, TX: National Center for Family & Community Connections with Schools.

National Middle School Association (2003). *This we believe: Successful schools for young adolescents.* Westerville, OH: Author.

Padak, N., & Rasinski, T. (2003). *Family literacy programs: Who benefits?* Available online at http://literacy.kent.edu/Oasis/Pubs/WhoBenefits2003.pdf.

Padak, N., & Rasinski, T. (2004). Fast Start: A promising practice for family literacy programs. *Family Literacy Forum, 3,* 3–9.

Padak, N., & Rasinski, T. (2005). *Fast start for early readers: A research-based, send-home literacy program.* New York, NY: Scholastic.

Padak, N., & Rasinski, T. (2006). Home-school partnerships in literacy education: From rhetoric to reality. *The Reading Teacher, 60,* 292–295.

Postlethwaite, T.N., & Ross, K.N. (1992). *Effective schools in reading: An exploratory study.* The Hague, The Netherlands: International Association for the Evaluation of Educational Achievement.

Rasinski, T.V. (1995). Fast Start: A parental involvement reading program for primary grade students. In W.M. Linek & E.G. Sturtevant (Eds.), *Generations of literacy: Seventeenth yearbook of the College Reading Association* (pp. 301–312). Harrisonburg, VA: College Reading Association.

Rasinski, T., & Stevenson, B. (2005). The effects of Fast Start Reading, a fluency based home involvement reading program, on the reading achievement of beginning readers. *Reading Psychology: An International Quarterly, 26,* 109–125.

Rasinski, T., Padak, N., & Fawcett, G. (2010). *Teaching children who find reading difficult* (4th ed.). Columbus, OH: Pearson.

Taking on education. (2009) Available online at www.whitehouse.gov/blog/09/03/10/Taking-on-Education/.

Tooms, A., Padak, N., & Rasinski, T. (2007). *Principal's Essential Guide to Literacy in the Elementary School.* New York, NY: Scholastic.

Wilfong, L.G. (2008). Building fluency, word-recognition ability, and confidence in struggling readers: The Poetry Academy. *The Reading Teacher, 62*(1), 4–13.

Wherry, J.H. (2009). *Selected parent involvement research.* Available online at www.parent-institute.com/educator/resources/research/research.php.

17

LITERACY INSTRUCTION

Toward a Comprehensive, Scientific, and Artistic Literacy Curriculum

Nancy Padak and Timothy V. Rasinski

Literacy scholars appear to have reached consensus that a balanced approach to reading instruction holds the greatest promise for improving reading achievement among students. Following the lead of the National Reading Panel (2000), curricular manifestations of a balanced reading program include instructional components in phonics or word decoding, fluency, vocabulary, and comprehension. While agreeing with the concept of a balanced approach to literacy instruction, we feel that the issue of balance in literacy is considerably more complex than the current models may suggest. In this chapter, we argue that a more comprehensive consideration of literacy instruction is needed. We present examples of issues that need to be considered in the development of a balanced and comprehensive approach to literacy education. In particular, we argue for the need of reading instruction to be both artistic as well as scientific.

Remarkably, as the first decade of the new millennium has passed, literacy educators appear to have achieved some degree of consensus. After years of wrangling over which approaches to reading instruction are more effective—whole language or phonics, skills-based or literature-based instruction, comprehension-oriented classrooms or word-based classrooms—the field seems to have concluded that they are all important, and that they all need to be taught. This movement toward a compromise position is echoed in the first edition of this volume (Flippo, 2001) and in the words of literacy scholars like David Pearson, who calls himself a member of the "radical middle" (Pearson, 2001, p. 78), and Rand Spiro, who describes his situation-sensitive assembly of multiple perspectives as "principled pluralism" (Spiro, 2001, p. 92).

And this movement seems to make sense. There does appear to be research evidence that the various and eclectic approaches to reading instruction, argued over for years, do produce positive results in students' development as readers and writers. For example, in the spring of 2000, the National Reading Panel issued its long-awaited report, which appears to confirm what advocates of a balanced approach to literacy instruction have been saying—we need to try to provide students with a comprehensive approach to reading instruction, one that is more than authentic and holistic and more than skills-based. The panel noted that phonemic awareness, phonics and decoding, fluency in reading; vocabulary acquisition; and reading comprehension are important parts of the total reading process in the elementary grades, and need to be emphasized in instruction.

Literacy curriculum projects that have attempted to embody this balanced instructional approach have had very positive outcomes. For example, Cunningham, Hall, and Defee's "Four Blocks" approach (1998; Cunningham, 2006) has been demonstrated to lead to significantly positive outcomes in the primary grades. In the Four Blocks, students spend 2 hours per day in the reading curriculum. The 2-hour block of time is divided into 30-minute segments that are devoted to self-selected reading, guided reading, word study, and writing.

Timothy Shanahan has developed a somewhat different balanced literacy framework that is aligned more closely with the conclusions of the National Reading Panel. In his balanced framework, which also consists of four blocks, Shanahan substitutes reading fluency instruction for self-selected reading. Shanahan has implemented his framework in a number of schools, and has achieved remarkably positive results (Shanahan, 2000, 2006). Balanced approaches may indeed offer a form of reading instruction that produces effective literacy learning. Moreover, planning instruction in terms of large blocks of time is an efficient and effective tool for curriculum development. Instructional programs that combine aspects from more than one theoretical or conceptual framework have been found to result in positive learning outcomes.

A More Complex View of Balance

As appealing as a balanced approach to literacy instruction may be, it seems to us that the notion of balance is considerably more complex than it may appear at the outset. The concept of balance may seem simple—"give students everything that has been demonstrated to work"—but in reality, a truly balanced approach needs to be considered as a complex and unified system. A balanced program is more than the simple conglomeration of disparate approaches to literacy instruction—in a truly balanced system, one element influences other parts of the curriculum, and that interrelationship of parts needs to be considered.

For example, the simple notion of weighting needs to be considered. When balancing feathers with marbles, a one-to-one correspondence won't work: several feathers will be needed to balance against one marble. This analogy applies in a balanced reading program as well. While it may be appealing to think that 30 minutes devoted to word decoding and phonics balances against an equal amount of time devoted to guided reading, this may not produce the optimal results that are hoped for. In sixth grade, for example, it may be wise to give additional weighting to guided reading and less weighting to decoding and phonics, so that perhaps 50 minutes per day is given to guided reading while 10 minutes is spent focused on decoding or phonics. Both guided reading and decoding are being taught; however, appropriate balance in the intermediate and middle grades may require greater emphasis on negotiating meaning in text.

Of course, "the devil is in the detail," particularly when considering a balanced reading curriculum. In this chapter, then, we wish to go beyond the surface-level consensus on balanced reading and explore some of the other issues that reading scholars, curriculum developers, and teachers need to consider as they move toward and beyond a balanced literacy curriculum. We feel that the notion of a comprehensive literacy curriculum better captures the complexity and integrated nature of the sort of literacy curriculum we ought to be aiming for.

Balance in Instructional Grouping

What does it mean to achieve balance when it comes to grouping practices? Certainly, one-to-one or small-group instruction offers teachers the opportunity to provide direct and targeted instruction aimed at students' needs. But is it a good idea to keep lower-achieving students grouped with one another for long periods of time? Won't these students begin to feel a sense of failure and frustration as they recognize their status in the classroom? Won't these students be negatively affected by being segregated from the more advanced students, who could act as models and help explain more challenging ideas and strategies to them? Moreover, when a teacher works with an individual or small group, what happens to students not in those groups? These students may not be as fully engaged in productive reading activity than if they were receiving instruction from the teacher.

So, is whole group instruction better? In Cunningham and Hall's Four Block model, whole group instruction is the order of the day. Students receive direct instruction for the maximum amount of time possible. However, there may be problems associated with this decision. Whole group instruction is usually aimed at the middle of the group: students who are at either end of the achievement continuum receive instruction that is either too easy or overly frustrating. Some students may be "taught" things they already know, and others may be presented with content they are not yet ready to learn. Is it possible to differentiate instruction according to instructional needs and achievement levels in a large-group situation?

Moreover, in a large-group situation, it is too easy to ignore the quiet student, or the student who only appears to understand the lesson on the surface. Some students are even quite adept at appearing to pay attention while their minds wander. Researchers have begun to offer advice regarding group size and composition. Marzano, Pickering, and Pollock (2001), for example, report results of meta-analyses of studies comparing small-group instruction to whole group or individual instruction. In general, children achieve significantly more when instruction is organized around small, cooperative groups. What does it mean, then, to achieve balance when it comes to grouping students for instructional purposes?

In one of our local schools, teachers have come up with a novel way of grouping, called Circle Reading. During the guided reading period, a "SWAT Team" made up of the reading specialist and two or three highly trained instructional aides invades each primary grade classroom. With four or five teachers present, the class can be divided into four or five small groups. Every reading group receives direct instruction for the entire 30-minute guided reading block. During other times of the day, the teachers in these classrooms have students work individually, in pairs, in heterogeneous small groups, and in large groups. Balance is achieved, instructional time is maximized, and students learn.

Balance in Text Types

What sorts of texts should students read in a balanced and comprehensive literacy program? In the 20th century, narrative fiction, or stories, tended to predominate. Children learned to read on a literary diet that was rich in stories but often short in other kinds of materials to read. Similarly, writing instruction also tended to be oriented toward the writing of stories (Daniels, 1990; Shanahan, 1990). While it may be true that narrative is a "primary act of the mind" (Hardy, 1978), a literacy curriculum that focuses on one type of text genre to the near exclusion of others cannot be considered balanced or comprehensive.

Surely, in a balanced literacy program, non-fiction, informational text and poetry should hold primary positions along with narrative. But even this triumvirate too restrictively limits the kinds of reading and writing students should be asked to engage in. The reading study sponsored by the International Association for the Evaluation of Education (Postlethwaite & Ross, 1992), for example, found that students who created newspapers in their classrooms or for their schools were more likely to be successful in learning to read than in places where such opportunities were not afforded students. Newspapers are not only a distinct genre, but also have embedded within them a variety of subforms, from world to national to local news, and from opinions to advice to advertisements and propaganda. The variety of other text genres that students can read and emulate in their writing is huge—magazines, personal journals, learning logs, scripts, dialogue journals, personal letters, business letters, and greeting cards, as well as charts, tables, figures, and maps. And let's not forget electronic texts. In a balanced and comprehensive literacy program, a much larger variety of text types and genres needs to be considered. The questions, then, should be what texts ought to be used in reading instruction, and in what weighting?

Cognition and Affect

When Mark Twain stated that "those who don't read good books have no advantage over those who cannot," he captured a more comprehensive goal than we normally hold for literacy instruction. Most of us maintain that the goal of literacy instruction is to help students learn to read and write. While there is probably universal agreement with such a goal, a comprehensive view of literacy should take an even larger view of literacy and literacy instruction—that the ultimate goal of reading instruction is to help children learn to read and write, and to become lifelong readers and writers. The second part of this goal suggests a definite affective component to literacy instruction. When we nurture lifelong reading and writing in students, we help them see that reading and writing are more than a set of skills to be mastered in order to make it through school; rather, we help students see that reading is a way to enrich one's life—a means to earning a better living, to be sure, but also a means to participate in and appreciate some of the more esthetic aspects of life.

Affect is important for another reason, too. If given a choice, most of us avoid doing what we don't like to do and choose instead what we do enjoy. Moreover, fluency and proficiency in reading and writing are linked to actual practice of reading and writing (see, for example, Postlethwaite & Ross, 1992; US Department of Education, 1996). So students who like to read and write will read and write more, and, as a consequence of reading and writing, develop fluency and grow as readers and writers. A truly balanced and comprehensive literacy program, then, must help develop in students a love of and appreciation for reading, writing, and the written word—a love that will span the school years and remain with students into their adult lives. This is no easy task, yet it is essential to a comprehensive literacy approach.

Yet more often than not, this affective dimension of reading is missing from school literacy programs. Even so-called "balanced" reading programs do little to promote the affective dimension of reading. Some may say that having students engage in self-selected reading helps develop a reading habit that will span students' lifetimes. But what message does it send to students when, during self-selected reading, the teacher chooses not to read, but instead confers with students about their reading assignments and does quick assessments of their reading progress? "Pleasure reading is important for you students, but not for me—I don't have the time."

In a truly balanced and comprehensive literacy program, it is critical for teachers to find the time to nurture students' love for reading and writing. Time needs to be spent daily in self-selected reading where the teacher and students read material of their own choosing. Time needs to be spent daily with the teacher reading the very best children's literature—fiction, non-fiction, poetry—to students. Time needs to be spent daily with the teacher talking with students about books they are reading and how they are enjoying them. Time needs to be spent daily with the teacher sharing his or her own reading and writing life with students—helping students see that reading and writing are ways to create richer and more satisfying lives for themselves.

Struggling Readers and Other Readers

In any classroom, not all students are equal when it comes to literacy. Some students excel, some develop along more normal trend lines, and others struggle mightily with reading and writing. Some models of balanced literacy instruction suggest that all students receive the same amount of instruction, regardless of how they may be faring in reading and writing. Some models of balanced literacy suggest that all students be grouped together regardless of their level of achievement. We disagree. A balanced, comprehensive, and equitable program must provide differentiated instruction to students—and a fundamental source of differentiation needs to be time. Students who struggle need more instructional time, more of the teacher's direct scaffolding and support, than those students who are developing in literacy without major difficulties. A balanced and comprehensive literacy program gives greater instructional attention and time to those students who struggle. Students who do not experience severe difficulties in learning to read are more likely to progress through their own independent and guided reading. Not so for struggling readers and writers.

Allington (2001) notes that one of the best predictors of progress in reading is the amount of reading that students do. Allington reports that struggling readers read fewer words during instructional periods, and, since most struggling readers read at a slower rate than more advanced readers, they also read fewer words when reading independently. Thus, if the amount of time given to reading instruction and reading is equal for all readers, struggling readers will invariably read less. In such a scenario, they will never catch up with their peers. Indeed, the gap between struggling readers and more advanced readers is likely to increase if the time given to literacy instruction is equal for all students. Equal is not necessarily equitable or balanced. Reutzel (1998–1999) points out that New Zealand conceived of balanced literacy programs long before the notion became popular in the United States, and the balanced program that evolved in New Zealand included provisions for providing additional and intensive instruction for students who were identified as at risk for reading failure. This led to the development of Reading Recovery, a program to help struggling first-grade readers catch up to their peers through intensive and systematic reading instruction.

Given the finite number of hours in a school day, it may be difficult for teachers to address the needs of struggling readers while at the same time addressing other curriculum concerns. It may require thinking "outside of the box" to solve this and the other concerns we identify in this chapter.

In one elementary school, the first-grade teachers begin their school day 45 minutes early, 3 days a week. On those three days, they work with the four or five students in each of their classrooms who are experiencing the most difficulty in their reading development in an intervention program they call "reading workshop." Because they are the regular classroom teachers for these classrooms, these teachers are able to correlate their instruction to the instruction that the children will receive later in the day. Because they know the children so well, they are also able to more closely match instruction to the children's identified reading needs. It may cost the school district a little more to provide this extra instruction for those students who need it, but in the long run it is worth it. The teachers report that throughout the school year they "graduate" students out of the program as they catch up with their normal achieving classmates and new students are added to the reading workshop.

Reading and Writing and Other Areas of the Curriculum

In a truly balanced and comprehensive literacy program, reading and writing should carry equal weight. Reading and writing are equally important, and instruction in one benefits the other. Yet, in most literacy programs, and most balanced literacy programs with which we are familiar, instruction in reading significantly outweighs writing instruction. In the four blocks models that we mentioned earlier, the ratio of authentic reading to writing instruction is at least two to one.

We feel that writing instruction deserves equal weighting with reading instruction. Indeed, in this particular case, we feel that reading and writing are so related that it may be best to teach them in an integrated fashion. We agree with Smith's (1992) assertion that the best way to become a good writer is to read a lot, and, conversely, the best way to become a good reader is to write a lot. All reading assignments and activities should have a writing component, and all writing assignments and activities should involve some external reading.

When students read a text they should be asked to respond to their reading through writing—responding in a journal, composing a poem that reflects their thoughts on the piece, developing a written script on the text that will later be performed for an audience, or writing their own version of the story by changing one aspect of the story and keeping the other factors constant. Similarly, writing assignments should be preceded by opportunities to read and discover the writer's craft through reading exemplary writing and then emulating that writing on their own. A balanced literacy program may include separate and roughly equal times for reading and writing instruction, but integrated within each should be opportunities to do the other.

A balanced and comprehensive literacy program needs to address other areas of the curriculum. Reading and writing are not subject areas in the same sense that social studies, science, and mathematics are discrete, content-oriented subject areas. Reading and writing could more aptly be described as vehicles that students and scholars use to discover the other subject areas. Moreover, concept learning, writing needs, and comprehension or learning strategies vary by content area. The literacy abilities that historians use, for example, differ from those used by scientists.

Thus, in a balanced, comprehensive, and authentic literacy approach, students constantly use reading and writing to explore and discover in other content areas. Students use reading and writing often and intensely for the very same reasons that non-students use reading and writing—to learn about their worlds.

Balance across the School Day: School and Home

Most models for balanced literacy are classroom-specific; that is, they focus on reading and writing development in the classroom only. Yet, we all know that students spend the greater part of each day at home. Moreover, research into the influence of the home and parents has established beyond doubt that the home connection is critical to students' success in learning in general, and in literacy learning in particular (Epstein, 1984; Henderson, 1988; Padak & Rasinski, 1998). The research is truly quite remarkable. Postlethwaite and Ross (1992) found that parental involvement was the most significant predictor of student reading achievement in their worldwide survey of literacy development in Grades 2 and 8. Even simple interventions that require a small amount of time can result in substantial gains in students' literacy learning at nearly any stage of development (Rasinski, 1995; Rasinski & Padak, 2000; Padak & Rasinski, 2004; Rasinski & Stevenson, 2005).

A truly balanced and comprehensive literacy program needs to take into account home-based literacy activities, and to support parents in helping their children learn to read. Parental involvement needs to be fostered even before students begin formal schooling. Preschool children develop basic literacy concepts and understandings of basic literacy conventions, as well as the all-important notion of phonemic awareness. Durkin (1966) found that children who learned to read before beginning school required the assistance and support of engaged parents—indeed, Durkin also noted that the small advantage children had when they began school expanded as they continued through the elementary school years.

In addition to the fact that home-parent involvement is central to success in early literacy development, we must also recognize that it is in the early grades that parents are most likely to be involved in their children's school experience. If we want parents to be involved in the upper elementary through secondary school years, we must make them feel welcome and wanted, and provide them the necessary support during their children's preschool and primary grades.

The nature of the involvement can vary, but our own experience suggests that reminding parents to read to their children is a necessary but insufficient condition for children's development. Parents want more information and support, and if they don't get it from their schools, they'll look elsewhere. We recommend that a truly balanced and comprehensive literacy program includes a significant home-parent component. Moreover, the home-parent component needs to be time efficient and include specific recommendations and support for parents, as well as the materials parents need to work with their children. The very best home–school literacy programs are ones in which the home component reinforces what goes on in the classroom. That said, teachers need to recommend activities that tie directly into the content, skills, and strategies that are being taught in the classroom. If children are reading particular poems and practicing particular word families in the classroom, those same poems and word families should be practiced at home with the children. Or, teachers may develop special activities that help children make the connection between the learning they do in school with the activities they engage in with their parents at home. For this to happen, the teacher needs to be fairly direct in what he or she would like parents to do. Our experience suggests that parents appreciate the specific and concrete suggestions they receive from their children's teachers.

Balance needs to cross the boundaries of the school day. For that to happen, and for reading instruction to really work for the benefit of all students, we need to put forth greater efforts to involve parents in the education of their children.

Balance Across the Year: School and Summer Vacation

A study of reading achievement in the Baltimore public schools (Entwisle, Alexander, & Olson, 1997) found that regardless of where children went to school, whether in affluent neighborhoods or poverty-stricken areas, their reading progress during the school year was about the same. During the summers, however, significant differences in educational progress manifested themselves. In the more affluent areas of town, students were most likely to improve in their reading development during the summer. In the lower-income parts of town, students were most likely to regress in their reading development over the summer. Entwisle and colleagues suspect that the cumulative effect of this phenomenon over the first several years of a child's schooling may explain the significant differential that is often seen in literacy achievement in various schools and neighborhoods throughout the country.

Balance and comprehensiveness in literacy learning need to cross the boundaries of the school year into the summer and other vacation periods. A balanced and comprehensive literacy program needs to find ways to keep children engaged in reading throughout the entire year, not just during the portion of the year in which school is in session. We need to help parents and community leaders keep students reading. As good and as well intentioned as public library summer reading programs may be, this means going well beyond such programs. Schools need to move beyond one-shot programs that are meant to bring attention to reading as much as they are meant to inspire student reading and community involvement. In Ohio, the former governor launched an effort to encourage community members to become volunteers involved in children's reading; he also created a quasi-governmental structure to support this work. This sort of institutionalization of community involvement in literacy development is a good start toward making reading instruction and support an all-year, all-the-time activity.

Teachers and school personnel may find that community organizations are eager to offer assistance. In our local community, for example, the Rotary is planning to support schools' implementation of Reading Millionaires (O'Masta & Wolf, 1991), a relatively simple school-wide reading "contest" to accumulate a million minutes of independent reading over a school year. Rotary volunteers will help schools keep track of minutes read, and financial support from Rotary will be used for incentives to keep children reading.

Balanced and comprehensive literacy means involving community and community organizations in developing and implementing a systemic, multi-faceted, and integrated plan for keeping students reading when not in school. Balance and comprehensiveness in literacy needs to go beyond the school, into children's homes and even their communities.

Teaching Reading as an Art and a Science

One of the most significant movements in literacy education in the first decade of the 21st century has been the recognition that the study of reading and reading instruction is a science. Scientifically validated methods of instruction have been identified and have been mandated in programs of literacy instruction. While generally the movement toward treating reading as a science has been good, the movement has left in its wake the understanding that the teaching of reading is an art and that teachers of reading are artists (Rasinski, 2008).

The near total reliance on only scientifically tested instructional materials and approaches has turned reading and its instruction into mechanical tasks that are scripted for teachers and students. Students have come define reading as little more than reading fast, and teachers have had to come to grips with such scientific jargon as "response to intervention" and various "tiers of instruction."

Gone from many classrooms now is the sheer joy in reading, the esthetic pleasure and satisfaction that comes from reading a book, performing a poem, singing a song, acting out a play. We can't help but wonder if we may now be teaching more children to read, but at a price: the desire to read.

A balanced and comprehensive approach to reading and reading education must embrace the artistic as well as the scientific dimensions of reading. Teachers must be given the freedom, opportunity, and resources to create reading instruction that is both efferent and esthetic (Rosenblatt, 1994).

Conclusions

Yes, balance may be the new consensus in literacy education. But simplistic notions of balance will only take us so far. We need to go further. We need to think more broadly and comprehensively about what balance in instruction means. We need to understand more fully what it means to be a literate person, and how we can help students achieve the type of literacy we envision for them. We call for literacy instruction to become comprehensive in its approach and implementation. To be comprehensive, literacy needs to be integrated within the literacy curriculum itself: literacy needs to be integrated within all facets of the classroom and school, literacy needs to be integrated with the home, and literacy needs to be integrated into the life of the community itself.

The goal of literacy education should be literate lives for all students, both now and in their futures. Achieving that goal requires a consensus that literacy education is more than a curricular balancing act.

The Past 10 Years: In Retrospect

1. *What are the most important things that you believe literacy research has shown over the past 10 years? (Positive and/or Negative)*

The Report of the National Reading Panel (2000) was released 10 years ago. Although the scholarly community argued for a while about which studies were (and should have been) reviewed, the No Child Left Behind Act of 2002 (NCLB) and Reading First soon affected the extent to which primary education was influenced by the Report, particularly the focus on the "five essentials": phonemic awareness, decoding, fluency, vocabulary, and comprehension. Thus, research and policy/politics commingled in a way that is unprecedented in US history.

We see both positives and negatives in this turn of events. On the positive side, schools and teachers have a useable set of instructional foci for teaching young children to read. Moreover, we think the Report of the NRP brought needed attention to fluency and vocabulary as critical aspects of effective reading. On the negative side, despite some publishers' and test-makers' assertions to the contrary, nothing in teaching children to read is "teacher-proof," or easy, for that matter.

A second major scholarly contribution over the past decade has been the increasing number of meta-analyses that provide practical guidance for teachers and curriculum leaders. Some of these are statistical in nature, such as Marzano and colleagues' (2001) study of effective learning routines and Sénéchal's (2006) study of effective parent–child literacy interactions in the home. Others are more informal, such as Dick Allington's (2001) synthesis of studies about supporting struggling readers. We believe that the effects of this sort of research are (or can be) singularly positive. Few professionals have the time to read and synthesize all the literacy research our very active field produces. Researchers who can apply scientific principles to synthesize research results provide guidelines that can be applied to practice.

2. *How do you think this should inform the contexts and practices of reading instruction in the classroom?*

Although the proverbial "grain of salt" is always a good ingredient, we believe that schools and districts can find much to guide their literacy improvement plans in recent research. What difference might these findings make, for example?

- Marzano and colleagues' (2001) finding about the power of instructional activities that focus on similarities and differences.
- Sénéchal's (2006) finding that at-home reading that a brief instructional activity "attached" to parents' reading aloud is six times more powerful than simply parental read aloud.
- Allington's (2001) list of four elements that can really help struggling readers (time to read, access to books, focus on fluency, focus on comprehension).

We think that teacher educators and professional development leaders should find ways to make meta-analyses, whether formal or informal, accessible to teachers. Results of this kind of research have direct implications for classroom practice and school policy.

References

Allington, R.L. (2001). *What really matters for struggling readers*. New York, NY: Addison Wesley Longman.

Cunningham, P.M. (2006). High-poverty schools that beat the odds. *The Reading Teacher, 60* (4), 382–385.

Cunningham, P.M., Hall, D.P., & Defee, M. (1998). Nonability grouped, multilevel instruction: Eight years later. *The Reading Teacher, 44*, 566–571.

Daniels, H. (1990). Young readers and writers reach out: Developing a sense of audience. In T. Shanahan (Ed.), *Reading and writing together: New perspectives for the classroom*, (pp. 99–124). Norwood, MA: Christopher-Gordon.

Durkin, D. (1966). *Children who read early*. New York, NY: Teachers College Press.

Entwisle, D., Alexander, K.L., & Olson, L.S. (1997). *Children, schools, and inequality.* Boulder, CO: Westview.

Epstein, J. (1984). School policy and parent involvement: Research results. *Educational Horizons, 62,* 70–72.

Flippo, R.F. (Ed.) (2001). *Reading researchers in search of common ground.* Newark, DE: International Reading Association.

Hardy, B. (1978). Narrative as a primary act of the mind. In M. Meed, A. Warlow, and G. Barton (Eds.), *The cool web: The pattern of children's reading.* New York, NY: Atheneum.

Henderson, A.T. (1988). Parents are a school's best friend. *Phi Delta Kappan, 70,* 148–153.

Marzano, R., Pickering, D., & Pollock, J. (2001). *Classroom instruction that works.* Alexandria, VA: Association for Supervision and Curriculum Development.

National Center for Educational Statistics National Assessment of Educational Progress. Available online at http://nces.ed.gov (accessed October 29, 2003).

National Reading Panel (2000). *Report of the National Reading Panel: Teaching children to read.* Washington, DC: National Institute of Child Health and Human Development.

O'Masta, G.A., & Wolf, J.A. (1991). Encouraging independent reading through the reading millionaires project. *The Reading Teacher, 44,* 656–662.

Padak, N., & Rasinski, T. (1998). *Family literacy: Who benefits?* Kent, OH: Ohio Literacy Resource Center. Retrieved September 29, 2009, from http://literacy.kent.edu/Oasis/Pubs/WhoBenefits 2003.pdf.

Padak, N., & Rasinski, T. (2004). Fast Start: A promising practice for family literacy programs. *Family Literacy Forum, 3,* 3–9.

Pearson, P.D. (2001). Life in the radical middle: A personal apology for a balanced view of reading. In Flippo, R.F. (Ed.), *Reading researchers in search of common ground* (pp. 78–83). Newark, DE: International Reading Association.

Postlethwaite, T.N., & Ross, K.N. (1992). *Effective schools in reading: Implications for educational planners.* The Hague: International Association for the Evaluation of Educational Achievement.

Rasinski, T.V. (1995). Fast Start: A parental involvement reading program for primary grade students. In W. Linek & E. Sturtevant (Eds.), *Generations of literacy: 17th Yearbook of the College Reading Association* (pp. 301–312). Harrisonburg, VA: College Reading Association.

Rasinski, T.V. (2008). Teaching fluency artfully. In R. Fink & S.J. Samuels (Eds.), *Inspiring reading success: Interest and motivation in an age of high-stakes testing* (pp. 117–140). Newark, DE: International Reading Association.

Rasinski, T., & Padak, N. (2000). *Effective reading strategies: Teaching children who find reading difficult* (2nd ed.). Columbus, OH: Merrill/Prentice-Hall.

Rasinski, T., & Stevenson, B. (2005). The effects of Fast Start Reading, A fluency based home involvement reading program, on the reading achievement of beginning readers. *Reading Psychology: An International Quarterly, 26,* 109–125.

Reutzel, R. (1998–1999). On balanced reading. *The Reading Teacher, 52,* 322–324.

Rosenblatt, L. (1994). *The reader, the text, the poem: The transactional theory of the literary work.* Carbondale, IL: Southern Illinois University Press.

Sénéchal, M. (2006). *The effect of family literacy interventions on children's acquisition of reading.* Portsmouth, NH: RMC Research Corp.

Shanahan, T. (1990). *Reading and writing together: New perspectives for the classroom.* Norwood, MA: Christopher-Gordon.

Shanahan, T. (2000). *Frameworks for literacy instruction.* Paper presented at the Annual Kent State University Reading Conference, Kent, OH.

Shanahan, T. (2006). Developing fluency in the context of effective literacy instruction. In T. Rasinski, C. Blachowicz, & K. Lems (Eds.), *Fluency instruction: Research-based best practices* (pp. 21–38). New York, NY: Guilford.

Smith, F. (1992). Learning to read: The never-ending debate. *Phi Delta Kappan, 73,* 432–441.

Spiro, R. (2001). Principled pluralism for adaptive flexibility in teaching and learning to read. In Flippo, R.F. (Ed.), *Reading researchers in search of common ground* (pp. 92–97). Newark, DE: International Reading Association.

US Department of Education, National Center for Educational Statistics (1996). *Almanac: Reading from 1984–1994.* Washington, DC: Author.

PART III

Toward a Common Ground

Revisited

18

A FOCUS ON POLICY-DRIVEN LITERACY PRACTICES, THE MEDIA, AND THE WORK OF READING PROFESSIONALS

Maryann Mraz and Richard T. Vacca

Debates over literacy instruction and pedagogy have occurred across the decades. The philosophical pendulum has swung routinely from one extreme to the other for over a hundred years: from the use of the whole word method in early reading, to the use of the letter-sound method (Smith, 2002); from a focus on child-centered teaching and learning practices, to program-driven instructional practices (Shannon, 2007); from a holistic, context-based approach, to an emphasis on the systematic acquisition of isolated skills. Until the 1990s, however, discussions about literacy practices were largely confined to professionals within the educational establishment (Reutzel & Mitchell, 2005).

Traditionally, policy matters related to literacy education were left to the discretion of educators, usually those at the local level. The backlash associated with the whole language movement of the 1980s and 1990s moved the debate about literacy education, and the decisions that followed, into the hands of politicians and policy-makers at the state and federal levels. In fact, prior to 1997, no federal legislation had specifically addressed literacy instruction as a policy issue. That changed with the 2000 presidential campaign, when George W. Bush touted his gubernatorial record on literacy education and spoke of reading as "the new civil right" (Davenport & Jones, 2005, p. 45). By the early 2000s, legislation had been passed in 48 statehouses around the country mandating the use of systematic, explicit phonics instruction in early literacy education, an implicit mandate echoed in the federally authorized No Child Left Behind Act of 2002 (NCLB).

Beginning in the 1990s and continuing in the first decade of the 21st century, the discretionary powers held by reading professionals in making curricular and instructional decisions were gradually eroded in the name of systematic education reform and accountability in the United States. A major tool used by top-level policy-makers—accountability through the use of high-stakes assessment—has attained enormous importance in literacy learning, and has influenced literacy practice in classrooms, schools, and districts. In this chapter, we provide an overview of major policy developments in literacy education. We examine the complex and interlocking relationship between policy-driven literacy practices and the role of the media in shaping public perceptions of education in general and literacy learning in particular, and we discuss the impact of recent policy decisions on literacy teaching and learning.

The Reading Crisis: Perspectives Through Time

The media are the main vehicle for dissemination and commentary in relation to national and state reports on education, and collectively affect the way the public thinks about literacy achievement and literacy learning. In turn, politicians and policy-makers, ever responsive to public opinion and concerns, have made reading achievement and learning to read as much a political issue as an educational one by enacting legislation that undergirds modern education reform. According to Reutzel and Mitchell (2005),

> Literacy instruction is seen as a panacea for social ills and preventing future economic calamity ... politicians, the press, and the public have gradually seized upon illiteracy as a significant factor highly related to a plethora of social problems including poverty, crime, and social dependency.
>
> *p. 606*

The role of the media in shaping public perceptions of literacy in the United States has been a strong catalyst in reform efforts across the decades. In 1983, the National Commission on Excellence in Education's well-publicized report, *A Nation at Risk*, painted a dire picture of the failure of American schools to develop a literate student body capable of competing economically with other technologically advanced countries. Other government-sponsored reports on literacy learning followed. These included *Beginning to Read: Thinking and Learning about Print* (Adams, 1992); *Preventing Reading Difficulties in Young Children* (Snow, Burns, & Griffen, 1998); *Thirty Years of Reading Research: What We Now Know about How Children Learn to Read* (Grossen, 1997), and *The Report of the National Reading Panel* (National Reading Panel, 2000). Subsequent legislation, most recently the No Child Left Behind Act of 2002, sought to respond to the concerns and challenges raised in these reports.

The concept of a "national reading crisis" in the United Stated did not begin with NCLB, or even in the decade that immediately preceded it. The US public's preoccupation with a national reading crisis first became evident in the late 1950s with the publication of Rudolf Flesch's 1955 bestseller, *Why Johnny Can't Read—And What You Can Do About It*. Although Flesch was not considered a reading professional or an "expert" in the field, he wrote a stinging commentary on the "whole-word method" of teaching reading, also commonly known as the "look–say" method. *Why Johnny Can't Read* was one of the first books on reading to have a major impact on the public's perception of how reading is taught in US schools. Not only was it on *The New York Times* bestseller list for 37 weeks, but it also rekindled the controversy on how children should be taught to read.

Flesch's book made an impassioned plea for an emphasis on phonics in the teaching of reading. However, he allowed his emotional appeal in favor of phonics to go too far, "and his book was discounted among reading profession-als as the work of a crank" (Yarrington, 1978, p. 7). Nevertheless, *Why Johnny Can't Read* brought the teaching of reading into the public consciousness in a way that had not been done before. For the first time in US history, a popular book on reading practices in schools was read by a mass audience and was widely covered by the print media. The *Saturday Review*, for example, featured Flesch's beliefs about teaching reading, and suggested that his book "may be ranked as the most important contribution to the betterment of public-school teaching methods in the past two decades" (Morris, 1955, p. 21).

Flesch's book had little, if any, substantive impact on the work of reading professionals. Because it was dismissed by the educational establishment as the emotional rants of a malcontent, the controversy over how to teach reading soon faded from the public's eye. Not until Jeanne Chall, a much respected Harvard University educator and member of the reading establishment, wrote *Learning to Read: The Great Debate* (1967) did the controversy over how to teach children to read surface again. Although Chall's book had a major impact on the field of reading and led to some changes in the development of basal reading materials, the controversy over how to teach reading was confined primarily to the world of academe. While much has changed in the field of reading since the publication of these two books, the controversy first kindled by them later developed into what came to be known as the "Reading Wars" of the 1990s.

The Reading Wars were a media-driven phenomenon waged along several battlefronts: in the media, in legislatures, and in school districts. As Flippo (1999) explained, the wars were not really between reading researchers but "against the reading-research community" (p. 38). The message delivered by the media and by some politicians was that whole language practices contribute to reading failure, and Flippo cited the ill-effects of sensationalism in numerous headlines that appeared in newspapers and magazines throughout the US when news coverage reached its peak in the mid-1990s (Flippo, 1997). In 1995, the headline on the front page of a Los Angeles newspaper proclaimed the end of an "educational fad" (whole language) as state legislators voted to approve a new instructional framework for teaching reading in California schools. The article (Robinson, 1995) accompanying the headline described the "failure" of the whole language movement and championed the return of phonics in the teaching of reading. What was troubling to many reading researchers was the simplistic pitting of an important philosophy of literacy learning (whole language) against an important instructional tool in learning to read and spell (phonics).

When William Clinton was elected 42nd President of the United States in 1996, he identified reading as the centerpiece of his education policy and reform proposals. In the 1996 presidential campaign, education was *the* major domestic concern on the minds of most US citizens, and reading became the "poster child" for educational reform.

That same year, at the height of the Reading Wars, chapter coauthor Rich Vacca served as the president of the International Reading Association. As IRA president, he recalled receiving numerous phone calls from newspaper reporters as well as "talk radio" show hosts throughout the county asking him to comment on issues and concerns related to reading and learning to read. In the wake of highly publicized state reading initiatives and reform efforts in California and Texas, those media interviews often revolved around two questions: (1) Why the decline in reading achievement among US school children? (2) Is phonics better than whole language as an approach to teaching reading? Often, as Vacca quickly discovered, attempts to explain the myths and misperceptions associated with the first question and the theoretical and practical complexities inherent in the second question were often sidestepped by reporters and radio commentators who appeared to be more concerned with short, terse statements—"sound bites"—than involved explanations. Some seemed to already have developed a "story angle" based on personal bias, preconceived notions, or limited research on reading and learning to read. At times, it appeared that reporters around the United States were reading one or two articles on the Web and essentially recycling the ideas they encountered for their local newspaper audiences. The legendary "legwork" and rigor that news reporters traditionally put into a story seemed to be missing.

One of the most dramatic and potentially positive outcomes to emerge from the portrayal of the Reading Wars in the media was the emergence of an emphasis on balance in the teaching of reading. Combining explicit strategy instruction with literature and language-rich activities called for a mix of different instructional approaches in a balanced literacy program. The combination of instructional methods and approaches was not an entirely new concept. It was supported by one of the most influential and ambitious undertakings in reading research during the 20th century: The United States Cooperative First-Grade Studies (Bond & Dykstra, 1967). The First-Grade Studies compiled data from 27 individual research projects examining the effects of instructional approaches on beginning reading and spelling achievement. The First-Grade Studies found that *no instructional approach was superior to the others* for students at either high or low levels of readiness. Instead, the findings suggested that "although no single method proved best, combinations of methods were associated with the highest achievement" (Shanahan & Neuman, 1997, p. 643).

The First-Grade Studies, more than anything else, underscored the importance of the "teacher variable" in children's reading achievement. Teachers make a difference. The more informed and knowledgeable the reading professional, the more influential he or she will be in dealing with the complexities of learning to read. Highly effective classroom teachers and reading specialists weave approaches and strategies into a seamless pattern of instruction. The growing body of reading research that followed the Reading Wars supported the view that while phonics is an important instructional tool, it is not a comprehensive method for teaching reading; that if literacy skills are taught out of context, they must also be put into a meaningful context so that readers understand how to apply skills. In other words, readers need opportunities to engage in real reading for real purposes.

During this time, reading professionals advocated combining explicit strategy instruction with literature and language-rich activities and called for a mix of different instructional approaches in a balanced literacy program. By contrast, some legislators and policy-makers called for balanced literacy programs as a means of ensuring that children received systematic instruction in the "basic skills." As a result, a narrow view of balanced instruction often linked politically and educationally to accountability in the wake of systematic reform efforts (Johns & Elish-Piper, 1997). And accountability was increasing measured by scores on mandates, high-stakes tests.

Policy Initiatives Raise New Concerns

On January 7, 2002, the No Child Left Behind Act of 2001 was signed into law with the stated purpose of helping "…states and local educational agencies utilize scientifically-based reading research to implement comprehensive reading instruction for children in kindergarten through third grade" (US Department of Education, 2002, p. 10). Notable features of NCLB include the following:

- Accountability requirements by which students must demonstrate Adequate Yearly Progress (AYP) as measured by standardized indicators
- Consequences for schools that fail to meet AYP and providing students in these schools with the option to attend a higher performing school within the same district
- Application of "scientifically-based reading research" (SBRR) to educational programs and instructional practices
- Requirements that teachers meet "highly qualified" credentialing criteria (Mills, 2008)

Many groups, including legislators, unions, and advocacy organizations, supported the NCLB initiative. In doing so, as Shaker and Heilman (2008) explain, "The stage was set for this radical, top-down meddling in the profession by years of disinformation propagated to the public" (p. 27). NCLB supports the use of strategies and professional development based on "scientifically-based reading research" (SBRR), where SBRR is defined as experimental or quasi-experimental designs in which research participants or programs have been assigned to different conditions and with controls in place to assess the effects of the condition in question.

Policy initiatives of the 2000s focused on providing literacy instruction to children from high-risk environments by integrating scientifically-based reading researched with instructional practices and materials. While supporting sentiments about the importance of reading instruction, literacy professionals cautioned policy-makers against prescribing the use of particular instructional methods or programs. All too often, however, those concerns fell on deaf ears as districts sought to meet NCLB's litany of mandates in order to qualify for badly needed funding provided under the legislation.

Literacy researchers raised concerns about the research to inform policy decisions: What research was used to support policies and practices? How was that research interpreted? How were the findings applied? What research was omitted from the conversation? What difference might its inclusion have made in policy discussions and decisions? For example, Coles (2000) found that, in studies where findings were interpreted as "indisputable, scientific evidence" (p. ix) that systematic, directed teaching methods were more effective than holistic instructional methods, frequently a causal relationship was assumed where only a correlation was found. Shaker and Heilman (2008) assert that the narrow definition of research "threatens to roll back a generation of work broadening the field of research in education ... No single paradigm of research is capable of presenting a whole truth or offering silver bullets for school improvement" (p. 28).

Grossen's (1997) *Thirty Years of NICHD Research* report also came under scrutiny. The report outlined instructional recommendations, most of which promoted a direct, explicit, systematic approach to early literacy instruction, and the report was widely quoted as drawing upon research sponsored by the NICHD, thus adding legitimacy to its claims. When Allington and Woodside-Jiron (1999) conducted their own analysis of the report, they found that both NICHD-supported research and non-NICHD supported research had been used to substantiate Grossen's recommendations. Furthermore, their independent analysis of the NICHD-supported studies that were cited in Grossen's report found that none of the report's recommendations were adequately supported by the NICHD research cited. The implications of the disparity of interpretations of research were significant, because reports such as this were used routinely to decide and defend educational policy decisions at both state and federal levels. If the interpretations of the research were flawed, then the policy decisions that followed from them could also be in question.

Similarly, questions were raised by reading researchers about the methodology used to compile the NRP Report. Faced with the prospect of having to review over 100,000 studies on reading education, the National Reading Panel chose to include in its analysis only those studies of reading that used experimental and quasi-experimental designs. Correlational studies and qualitative designs were excluded from the Panel's analysis, even though literacy researchers pointed out that many literacy education issues cannot be ethically studied using experimental methods (Strickland, 2001). The findings of the excluded research might have challenged some of the Panel's conclusions and the implications that followed from them.

Also of concern in the portrayal of the purported education crisis de jour has been the interpretive spin put on data from state reading proficiency tests, national assessments of reading, and international comparisons. Throughout the past decade, researchers have raised questions about the reasons behind student gains on some state-mandated assessments. They often found that some of these gains could be attributed to factors such as lowering required pass scores, manipulation of scores, and increased instructional time spent on test preparation, other than actual achievement (Koretz & Barron, 1998). One of the most high-profile examples of test-score manipulation concerned the Texas Assessment of Academic Skills (TAAS), and the now debunked "Texas Miracle" that supposedly sprang from it. Like many states, the Texas education reform effort emphasized accountability and mandated high-stakes testing. And, following the implementation of state mandated literacy instructional practices and assessment, viola! 91% of third-grade students passed the state reading test in 2004, compared with 76% in 1994 (Davenport & Jones, 2005). While TAAS reading tests scores had risen dramatically over several years, students' performance on the NAEP test had not. NAEP scores, in fact, reflected only marginal gains. This led researchers to question whether student gains on the TAAS reflected a real improvement in students' reading achievement, or whether gains were inflated as a consequence of other factors, such as teachers teaching to the test, or to a larger proportion of low-scoring students being exempted from taking the test in order to avoid the sanctions connected with low test scores (Klein, Hamilton, McCaffrey, & Stecher, 2000).

While the use of high-stakes testing is believed by many policy-makers to be a key to increasing reading achievement, researchers continue to raise concerns about it. In the National Reading Conference Policy Brief, *High-Stakes Testing and Reading Assessment*, Afflerbach (2004) cites several concerns:

- No research exists to link increased testing with increased reading achievement.
- A single assessment is limited in its ability to accurately describe a student's reading achievement and potential.
- The inordinate amount of time required for test preparation is disruptive to high quality teaching and learning.

- Test administration demands the significant allocation of time and money that could otherwise be used to improve reading achievement.
- Often, high-stakes tests come with caveats pertaining to the accuracy of scores and cautions about the interpretation of the scores. Too often, these caveats are ignored.

If the education catch-phrase in 1990s political and media circles was "scientifically-based-reading-research," the catch-phrase of the 2000s was "achievement gap." A report by McKinsey and Company (2009) focused on educational achievement gaps on many fronts and found that African American and Latino students in the US were approximately 2–3 years behind Caucasian students of the same age; that achievements gaps exist between racial groups in terms of both test scores and graduation rates; that the US lags behind other advanced nations in educational performance; and that the gap in performance between American students and international students widens as the school years proceed.

The report concluded that achievement gaps "impose the economic equivalent of a permanent national recession" (p. 6). The findings of reports such as this have been widely publicized in the popular press. The April 27, 2009, headline in *Time Magazine*, for example, warned: "How to Raise the Standard in America's Schools: Our Students are Falling Behind their Counterparts in the Rest of the World, Threatening the US's Economic Future. Why National Education Standards are the Only Way to Fix the System" (Isaacson, 2009).

This led to assertions by some literacy professionals that public schools were continuing to be scapegoats for policy-makers and journalists who attributed the cause of the achievement gap to ineffective instructional practices and who believed that the gap could be closed by bringing schools under the control of authorities who would mandate test-driven accountability (Shaker & Heilman, 2008). While policy-makers and journalists have been quick to attribute the achievement gaps to "failing schools," researchers suggest that the blame for the achievement gap is misplaced. Berliner's (2009) research found that six out-of-school factors have been clearly linked to lower achievement among low SES students. These factors include: non-genetic parental influences, medical care, food insecurity, environmental pollution, family breakdown and stress, and neighborhood norms and conditions. He recommends an approach to school improvement that would demand, "a reasonable level of societal accountability for children's physical and mental health and safety" (p. 40).

Similarly, Hoover (2000) examined both school variables (over which schools have some control) and non-school variables (over which schools have no control) in relation to scores on state-mandated tests. He found that student achievement was most consistently related to the socioeconomic living conditions and experiences of the student, rather than to any variable which the schools could control: the higher the student's SES, the higher the test score;

the lower the student's SES, the lower the test score. Other researchers have echoed this finding, and have cautioned that policy initiatives such as NCLB cannot improve the quality of education in the US until the issues of poverty, social class, and parental involvement are addressed (Kastle, 2008).

Looking Forward

What is feared missing from current policy discussions are the voices of literacy educators who engage in the day-to-day work of developing a literate citizenry in unprecedented diverse and challenging conditions. Concerns about government intrusion in the day-to-day work of educators abound. Gallagher (2008) explains:

> Public schools today are less in the direct control of those who spend their days in them, or those immediately affected by them, than ever before … We cannot expect schools to contribute to the functioning of our democracy if they are denied freedom and self-determination through remote control and bullying policy making.
>
> *p. 340*

One representative of a national literacy organization attributed conflicts, in part, to agenda and communication differences between the literacy and policy communities. While the policy community is about outcomes, the reading community talks about processes. Some special interest groups have offered plain, bold assertions in response to policy-makers' questions about how to improve literacy education. In contrast, literacy professionals tended to respond to the same questions by emphasizing the complexity of the issues. "As educators," he explained, "we are taught to write deep, dense prose, not spiffy little sound bites" (Mraz, 2004, p. 32). The policy and literacy communities often have different languages, different definitions, different expectations.

When asked who he believed influenced the views of policy-makers, one state legislator cited popular radio and television personalities, noting:

> They (radio and TV hosts) have had a huge influence on what people think about education. I mean they (legislators) listen to these people. The result is that they've bashed this public education system so badly that they people are willing to say, "Gosh, if it's that bad, we'd better go in and just change the whole complexion of it."
>
> *Mraz, 2002, p. 103*

As a new administration moves in a new era to revise NCLB, and likely change the name of that legislation, many believe that the federal role in literacy education policy will grow (Dillon, 2009). The Obama administration has challenged states to set "world-class standards" and to stop lowering standards to ensure higher pass-rates on standardized assessments. Five pillars of the new education reform effort have been proposed:

> Enhance early childhood initiatives
> Develop and implement effective standards and assessments
> Recruit, prepare, and reward outstanding teachers
> Promoting innovation and excellence
> Provide every American with a quality higher education

Secretary of Education Arne Duncan (Cruz, 2009) explains that the Race to the Top initiative "marks a new federal partnership in education reform with states, districts, and unions to accelerate change and boost achievement." Additionally, citing the large number of schools considered as needing corrective action or restructuring, the Obama administration is urging states to replace their individual standards with a common set of national standards, known as the Common Core State Standards Initiative. The *Washington Post* (Glod, 2009) reports that the pursuit of common core standards, led by the National Association of Governors (NGA) and the Council of Chief State School Officers (CCSSO), will seek to provide a uniform definition of success in schools by establishing common standards nationwide in reading and mathematics. In addition to establishing a set of common core standards, the group plans to align text curricula and assessment with the standards, hold systems and schools accountable to the higher standards, and use international standards to measure state-level education performance. As of this writing, every state except Texas has signed on to participate.

Yet even in the midst of these new initiatives, familiar concerns resound. To date, the role of major professional literacy organizations in the development of these standards has been peripheral at best. The National Council of Teachers of English (NCTE), for example, was not initially consulted in forming the English language arts standards that will comprise the Common Core. The International Reading Association (IRA), while monitoring the development of the standards, has not been asked to play a meaningful role in their development (IRA, 2009). The NCTE Board was asked to review an initial draft of the document and offer recommendations. The extent to which those recommendations will be considered remains unknown. Also unknown are answers to questions raised, such as: Why are NGA and CCSSO leading the Common Core Standards effort? Why are content experts from corporate and assessment organizations like Achieve, Inc, and the College Board assigned to develop the standards, while nationally respected researchers are asked only to give feedback? Why are prominent members of professional literacy organizations, such as IRA, NCTE, the National Reading Conference (NRC), and the Association of Literacy Educators and Researchers (ALER) not engaged as content experts in framing these standards? (Stahl, 2009). Other concerns about the detail of the proposed plan have been raised, including the provisions that require states to remove laws limiting the number of charter schools, agree to common standards, and remove legal barriers to linking student test scores with teacher performance in order to obtain funding.

The findings of the Expert Study (Flippo, 1998) make clear that the field of reading is not as fractious as has been reported in the media, and that reading professionals have much to contribute to policy conversations. The findings serve to identify a set of core literacy practices that would tend to make learning to read difficult for students, and a set of core literacy practices that would tend to facilitate learning to read. Why are the points of agreement by reading experts important to the work of reading professionals? Flippo (1997) responds to the question this way:

> We must use our expertise and the findings of research ... to shape the public's understanding. Educational philosophies, in any area of the curriculum, should not become the scapegoats for our politicians' inability to solve the economic and sociocultural problems of our states. Nor can we simply shed our belief systems in order to "fit in" with a more currently acceptable political viewpoint.
>
> *p. 304*

Concluding Thoughts

Literacy professionals have an important role to play in shaping the progress of literacy education. As a representative of a national literacy organization noted:

> There's a lot of discussion about how public schools are about to go down the tubes ... but I don't see a whole lot of concrete suggestions about what it is that we need to do to close the achievement gap. And that's what the politicians will say, "Well, tell me what to do then. These other guys have told me what to do. You haven't." I think that's a real Achilles heel of a profession. We have such fun debating among ourselves, that we never get the unity to turn around and say. "Here's a legislative educational program we all support," and have the good sense to politic with our parents and instructional colleagues to get their support for that as well.
>
> *Mraz, 2002, p. 105*

The media will no doubt continue to play an influential role in shaping the perceptions (and misperceptions) of the public toward education generally, and reading specifically. In turn, US politicians at national, state, and local levels will continue to respond to educational issues though legislative action. All of this, of course, will continue to affect the work of reading professionals.

State and national literacy organizations have called for more substantive inclusion of professional educators in the policy-making process. Literacy professionals can contribute their voices to these efforts. As Davenport and Jones (2005) suggest,

> If politics is the art of the possible, the changed political climate creates new possibilities for literacy. Literacy is of fundamental importance. And it seems important to take advantage of this opportunity for some consensus on literacy policy and renewed efforts to improve the ability of our children to read.

p. 57

While thought-provoking and often necessary, these high-profile "tussles" among prominent educational researchers questioning one another's methods and interpretations has not helped to raise the view of educational research among policy-makers (Henig, 2008).

Perhaps if there is a glimmer of hope in this new, and yet somehow familiar, era of literacy education reform it is that there is growing acknowledgement by some policy-makers and some journalists that school reform alone cannot improve student achievement. The tired, but ever present, political mantras of "hold teachers accountable" and "raise test scores" must be balanced by policy discussions and policy decisions which reflect that, all too often, the problems for which educators are held "accountable" lie, as Berliner (2009) says, "outside of their zone of influence" (p. 6). The educational challenges of our time are broader than teacher accountability and test scores. The solutions must be broader as well.

References

Adams, M. (1990). *Beginning to read: Thinking and learning about print.* Cambridge, MA: MIT Press.

Afflerbach, P. (2004). *National Reading Conference policy brief: High-stakes testing and reading assessment.* Oak Creek, WI: National Reading Conference.

Allington, R.L., & Woodside-Jiron, J. (1999). The politics of literacy teaching: How "research" shaped educational policy. *Educational Researcher, 28*(8). 4–13.

Berliner, D. (2009). *Poverty and potential: Out-of-school factors and school success.* East Lansing, MI: Great Lakes Center for Education Research and Practice.

Bond, G., & Dykstra, R. (1967). The cooperative research program in first-grade reading instruction. *Reading Research Quarterly, 2,* 135–142.

Chall, J. (1967). *Learning to read: The great debate.* New York, NY: McGraw-Hill.

Coles, G. (2000). *Misreading reading: The bad science that hurts children.* Portsmouth, NH: Heinemann.

Cruz, G. (2009). Can Arne Duncan (and $5 billion) fix America's schools? *Time Magazine, 174,* 25–29.

Davenport, D., & Jones, J.M. (2005). The politics of literacy. *Policy Review, 106,* 45–57.

Dillon, S. (2009). Education standards likely to see toughening. *New York Times,* April 15 (retrieved from www.nytimes.com/2009/04/15/education/15educ.html?_r=1).

Duncan, A. (2009). Education reform's moon shoot. *Washington Post,* July 24 (retrieved from www.washingtonpost.com/wp-dyn/content/article/2009/07/23/AR200907230 3881.html?hpid=topnews).

Flesch, R. (1955). *Why Johnny can't read—And what you can do about it.* New York, NY: Harper & Brothers.

Flippo, R.F. (1997). Sensationalism, politics, and literacy: What's going on? *Phi Delta Kappan, 79,* 301–304.

Flippo, R.F. (1998). Points of agreement: A display of professional unity in our field. *The Reading Teacher, 52,* 30–40.

Flippo, R.F. (1999). Redefining the Reading Wars: The war against reading researchers. *Educational Leadership, 57,* 38–41.

Gallagher, C.W. (2008). Democratic policy making and the arts of engagement. *Phi Delta Kappan, 89,* 340–346.

Glod, M. (2009). 46 states, D.C., plan to draft common education standards. *Washington Post,* May 31 (retrieved from http://www/washingtonpost.com/wp-dyn/content/ article/2009/05/31/AR20090531102339.html?referrer=emailartcile).

Grossen, B. (1997). *30 years of research: What we now know about how children learn to read: A synthesis of research on reading from the National Institute of Child Health and Development.* Santa Cruz, CA: The Center for the Future of Teaching and Learning.

Henig, J.R. (2008). The evolving relationship between researchers and public policy. *Phi Delta Kappan, 89,* 357–360.

Hoover, R.L. (2000). *Forces and factors affecting Ohio Proficiency Test performance: A study 593 Ohio school districts.* Unpublished manuscript, Youngstown State University.

International Reading Association (2009) Focus should be on teachers in common core initiative. *Reading Today, 27*(1), 1, 7.

Isaacson, W. (2009, April 27). How to raise the standard in America's schools. *Time Magazine, 89,* 32–37.

Johns, J.L., & Elish-Piper, L. (1997). *Balanced reading instruction: Teachers' visions and voices.* Dubuque, IA: Kendall-Hunt.

Kastle, K.D. (2008). Educators must rally for reform. *Phi Delta Kappan, 90,* 38–39.

Klein, S.P., Hamilton, L.S., McCafferey, D.F., & Stecher, B.M. (2000). *Issue paper: What do test scores in Texas tell us?* Santa Monica, CA: RAND.

Koretz, D., & Barron, S.T. (1998). *The validity of gains in scores on the Kentucky Instructional Results Information System.* Santa Monica, CA: RAND.

McKinsey & Company (2009). *The economic impact of the achievement gap in America's schools* (retrieved from www.mckinsey.com/clientservice/socialsector/achievementgap.asp).

Mills, J.I. (2008). A legislative overview of No Child Left Behind. In T. Berry & R.M. Eddy (Eds.). *Consequences of No Child Left Behind for educational evaluation. New Directions for Evaluations, 117,* 9–20 (retrieved from www.interscience.wiley.com DOI: 10.1002/ev.248).

Morris, W. (1955). Teaching Johnny to read. *Saturday Review, 38,* 21.

Mraz, M. (2002). *Factors that influence policy decisions in literacy: Perspectives of key policy informants.* Unpublished dissertation, Kent State University.

Mraz, M. (2004). Factors that influence policy decisions in literacy: Perspectives of key policy informants. *Reading Research and Instruction, 43*(3), 20–36.

National Commission on Excellence in Education (1983). *A nation at risk: The imperatives for educational reform.* Washington, DC: US Department of Education.

National Reading Panel (2000). *Report of the National Reading Panel: Teaching children to read, an evidence-based assessment of the scientific research literature on reading and its implications for reading instruction.* Washington, DC: National Institute of Child Health and Human Development.

Reutzel, D.R., & Mitchell, J. (2005). High-stakes accountability themed issue: How did we get here from there? *The Reading Teacher, 58*(7), 606–608.

Robinson, M. (1995). Last rites for an educational fad. *Los Angeles Times,* December 12, p. 1.

Shaker, P.S., & Heilman, E.E. (2008). Scapegoating public schools. *School Administrator, 65*(6), 27–29.

Shanahan, T., & Neuman, S.B. (1997). Literacy research that makes a difference. *Reading Research Quarterly, 32,* 636–647.

Shannon, P. (2007). *Reading against democracy: The broken promises of reading instruction.* Portsmouth, NH: Heinemann.

Smith, N.B. (2002). *American reading instruction.* Newark, DE: International Reading Association.

Snow, C.E., Burns, M.S., & Griffen, P. (Eds.). (1998). *Preventing reading difficulties in young children.* Washington, DC: National Academy Press.

Stahl, N. (2009, July 29). Questions Common Core Standards message posted to the National Reading Conference electronic mailing list, archived at NRCLIST@listserv.nrconline.org.

Strickland, D.S. (2001, April). *Trends and issues in literacy education.* Pre-conference Institute Address presented at the annual International Reading Association Convention. New Orleans, LA.

US Department of Education (2002). The No Child Left Behind Act of 2001 (retrieved from www.ed.gov/offices/OESE/esea/NCLBexecsumm.pdf).

Yarrington, D.J. (1978). *The great American reading machine.* Rochelle Park, NJ: Hayden.

19

A FOCUS ON THE NAEP DATA

Jay R. Campbell

The contexts and practices identified in the Expert Study (Flippo, 1998; refer to Chapter 1 in this book) that would facilitate learning to read are probably not surprising to most educators. Most of the statements that represent agreement among the experts have been confirmed by research and classroom practice. Many are also consistent with findings from the National Assessment of Educational Progress (NAEP), a large-scale assessment and survey of fourth, eighth, and twelfth graders across the United States. This chapter provides an examination and discussion of the connections that can be made between NAEP data and several key findings from the Expert Study.

NAEP is a project of the National Center for Education Statistics within the US Department of Education. As a monitor of student achievement in the United States for three decades, NAEP has provided educators and policy-makers with an abundance of information regarding the status of student learning and the factors associated with achievement. The NAEP assessments provide information on the performance of groups and subgroups of students in a variety of subject areas; the performance of individual students is not analyzed or reported. The most recently developed NAEP reading assessment was administered in 1992, 1994, and 1998 to national samples of fourth, eighth, and twelfth graders, and to samples of fourth and eighth graders within individual states.

Results from the NAEP reading assessment, administered three times during the 1990s, have been used at both the national and state levels to inform educational policy initiatives and school reform. The NAEP results include not only students' scores on the assessment, but also information regarding the background and instructional experiences of students. This information is collected through questionnaires administered to students and their teachers. Given the importance of the NAEP data and the implications of the results, it is instructive to examine closely the nature of the assessment instrument and its framework, the background and instructional data collected by NAEP that are associated with achievement, and the degree of interpretation that is warranted by NAEP's findings.

This examination is made particularly meaningful in light of results from the Expert Study indicating that experts from different theoretical perspectives can agree on many ideas for supporting and advancing the reading achievement of students. In fact, much of what has been reported by NAEP from the reading assessments of the 1990s is consistent with findings from the Expert Study— providing some empirical support for what the experts agree contributes to student achievement in reading.

The NAEP Reading Framework and Assessment Content

As with all frameworks that underlie NAEP assessments, the NAEP reading assessment framework was developed through a national consensus process that was responsive to the voices of a variety of educators, curriculum experts, researchers, and concerned members of the general public. Developed during the early 1990s, the current reading framework describes reading broadly, using the term "reading literacy" to describe knowing when to read, how to read, and how to reflect on reading. More specifically, the *Reading Framework for the National Assessment of Educational Progress: 1992–1998* sets forth six important characteristics of good readers that distinguish them from less proficient readers. According to the National Assessment Governing Board (1997, p. 9), good readers

1. possess positive habits and attitudes about reading;
2. read with enough fluency so that they can focus on the meaning of what they read;
3. use what they already know to understand what they read;
4. form an understanding of what they read and extend, elaborate, and critically judge its meaning;
5. use a variety of effective strategies to aid their understanding and to plan, manage, and check the progress of their reading;
6. can read a variety of texts and can read for different purposes.

The consistency between these characteristics of good readers set forth in the NAEP framework and points of agreement in the Expert Study is worth noting (refer to Chapter 1 in this book): the experts agree that students should "develop positive self-perceptions and expectations," similar to the NAEP framework's description of good readers' positive habits and attitudes about reading; also, the experts agree that students should be exposed to "a broad spectrum of sources for student reading materials" and should be engaged in "purposeful reading," similar to the NAEP framework description of good readers as those who read a variety of texts and read for different purposes.

A shared vision of reading education goals is also evident in the type of assessment called for by the NAEP framework and the experts' common ground. For example, the NAEP reading assessment presents students with texts that are authentic and not written specifically for instruction or assessment; that is, they are drawn from reading materials that are typically available to students in and out of school. The texts are reproduced in test booklets in a manner that replicates as closely as possible the way they appeared in their original source. NAEP's emphasis on assessing reading with authentic reading materials is consistent with the experts' agreement that students should be given opportunities to read real books.

The NAEP reading framework also calls for the assessment of students' ability to read a variety of text types. In recognition that reading is an interactive and constructive process that varies depending on the type of text being read and the purpose for reading, the NAEP reading assessment measures students' ability to read and understand different types of texts. The assessment includes texts written for literary experiences, for providing information, and for describing how to perform a task. Once again, this would appear to be consistent with the experts' agreement that students should be exposed to a broad spectrum of sources for student reading material and the different functions of numerous types of printed materials.

Yet another similarity between the NAEP reading assessment and the experts' common ground may be seen in the emphasis placed on integrating reading and writing activities. Although the NAEP reading assessment is distinct from the writing assessment, over half of the comprehension questions on the reading assessment require written answers. Students are asked to demonstrate the ability to construct and extend their understanding of texts in answering what are referred to as constructed-response questions. With short constructed-response questions, complete answers typically require one or two sentences. With extended constructed-response questions, a paragraph or more is often required to demonstrate extensive understanding of the text. Thus, the ability to construct written interpretations of text is clearly valued and emphasized on the NAEP reading assessment.

It should, perhaps, be of no surprise that a national assessment framework developed through a process of national consensus building on what is valued in reading education should be so well aligned with the shared values of a group of national reading experts. The NAEP assessments are intended to represent commonly held objectives for student achievement. In some sense, they are based not only on what the experts can agree on, but on what most educators and concerned citizens believe should be the goal of education.

NAEP Findings on Factors Associated with Reading Achievement

As described earlier, the NAEP assessments include not only measures of achievement in various subject areas, but also survey questionnaires completed by students and their teachers about a variety of experiences and activities that are thought to be related to achievement. Students' and teachers' responses to these questionnaires provide a context for understanding students' performance on the NAEP assessments. In the area of reading, the three assessments conducted during the 1990s collected information through these survey questionnaires about reading and literacy-related activities in and out of school. Because the students who took the assessment also responded to the survey questions, as did their teachers, it is possible to use NAEP data to examine the relationship between reading achievement and a variety of school and home activities. A brief overview of some of the major findings from these assessments provides support for many of the findings in the Expert Study. In order to facilitate a comparison between findings from the NAEP reading assessments and the Expert Study, the following discussion is framed according to the clustered categories of statements agreed to by the reading experts in the Expert Study.

Combining Reading with Other Language Processes

The experts seem to agree on the importance of integrating the language arts in students' instructional experiences. Writing about reading and talking about reading are two ways to provide for integrated instruction that are mentioned in the experts' agreements. Findings from the NAEP assessments support this conclusion. Results from the 1998 assessment indicated that fourth, eighth, and twelfth graders who were asked on a weekly or monthly basis to write extended answers to questions about what they read scored higher on the NAEP reading assessment than did students who reported being asked to do so only a few times a year or less (Donahue, Voelkl, Campbell, & Mazzeo, 1999). Also, findings from the 1994 assessment indicated that fourth- and eighth-grade students whose teachers used classroom assessment practices that included paragraph-length responses to reading had higher scores, on average, than did students whose teachers never or hardly ever assessed reading this way (Campbell, 1997).

Results from both the 1994 and 1998 assessments revealed a positive relationship between student achievement and integrating reading, talking, and listening through discussing or explaining ideas in reading materials. Students in Grades 8 and 12 who were given opportunities on at least a weekly basis to explain their understanding or to discuss various interpretations of what they read had higher reading scores than students who did so less frequently (Campbell, Donahue, Reese, & Phillips, 1996).

Contexts, Environment, and Purposes for Reading

The experts' agreements in this area emphasize multiple reading experiences, frequent opportunities to read, and purposeful reading. The NAEP results support these conclusions. For example, data collected in 1998 indicated that the amount of reading done each day had a positive relationship with reading achievement. Students in Grades 4, 8, and 12 who indicated reading more than 10 pages each day had higher reading scores, on average, than did students who read fewer pages (Donahue et al., 1999). Also, fourth graders in 1992 who said they read silently in class almost every day had higher scores than students who did not (Mullis, Campbell, & Farstrup, 1993).

Developing (Or Shaping) Students' Perceptions and Expectations

According to the experts, learning to read is facilitated by developing a sense of one's self as a reader and recognizing that reading is integral to daily life. Several findings from the NAEP reading assessments are consistent with these ideas. For example, students in Grades 4, 8, and 12 who said they frequently read for fun had higher reading scores than students who did so rarely (Campbell et al., 1996). It is likely that students who read for fun daily or weekly have acquired a positive perception of themselves as readers, and expect reading to be a rewarding or enjoyable experience. Spending time talking to family and friends about reading may also be an indication that these important affective traits are developing. Students at all three grades who reported frequent discussions about what they read had higher reading scores than students who said that they rarely had such discussions (Donahue et al., 1999).

Materials, and Reading Instruction

The experts' agreements related to the types of materials and instructional contexts and practices that facilitate reading development suggest that a broad range of materials and opportunities to read for a variety of purposes is advantageous. In 1992, NAEP asked the teachers of fourth graders how much emphasis they placed on literature-based instruction in their classrooms. Nearly half of the fourth graders were taught by teachers who said that they placed heavy emphasis on this instructional practice. The students of these teachers had higher reading scores than the students whose teachers indicated only moderate emphasis and little or no emphasis on literature-based instruction (Mullis, Campbell, & Farstrup, 1993). If literature-based reading instruction involves the use of varied and multiple reading materials, this NAEP finding supports the experts' agreements in these clusters. A related instructional activity is allowing students to read books of their own choosing in the classroom. At the fourth-grade level this activity had a positive relationship with reading achievement, according to the NAEP findings. More frequent opportunities to read self-selected books as a part of instruction were associated with higher reading scores (Donahue et al., 1999).

Interpreting Data from the NAEP Reading Assessments

The NAEP reading assessment is a measure of the reading comprehension skills and abilities of groups of students across the country and within states that have chosen to participate in NAEP's state-by-state assessments. It provides for the reporting of average scores for the groups of students that are sampled and assessed. For example, results from the assessment indicate the level of achievement attained by all fourth graders in the country or in a state. Results are also reported for subgroups of students within a particular grade. For example, the average reading scores of male students can be compared to those of female students, and the average scores of African American students can be compared to those of white students. Scores for individual students cannot be analyzed and reported.

The fact that the NAEP assessment is a group assessment, rather than an individual assessment, makes it possible for the assessment to be administered across the country and within states without the pressures of typical high-stakes assessments that report individual scores and are often used for accountability monitoring. This makes the assessment less likely to be one that has been the subject of direct teaching and preparation; that is, it is unlikely that teachers are "teaching to the test." Because the framework is intended to represent a national consensus on reading objectives for each grade assessed, it is broadly defined to fit with a variety of curricula and instructional approaches. It is expected that the objectives of the NAEP assessment represent shared goals for schools and districts across the nation.

Although these aspects of the NAEP assessment make it a valuable instrument for assessing students from across the country who are involved in a range of curricular programs, they present some limitations to how the findings can be interpreted. Because the assessment provides information about both achievement and the contextual factors related to achievement, these two components of NAEP findings, and the degree or type of interpretation warranted by both, are discussed below.

Interpretations of Student Achievement from NAEP Data

The first important aspect of any assessment that must be considered in interpreting its results is a clear understanding of what the assessment was intended to measure. The NAEP reading assessment is an assessment of reading comprehension. The test is constructed of authentic, intact texts. Students are asked to demonstrate their understanding of the texts through responses to both multiple-choice and constructed-response questions. The questions are written to elicit the processes of constructing and extending meaning from texts. The performance of students on each individual question is analyzed, and the results are summarized on a 0 to 500 scale. The average scale score attained by a particular group of students is an indication of how well students are able to comprehend the texts that have been selected as age- and grade-appropriate.

Thus, it would be inappropriate to interpret these results as an indication of any other aspect of student learning and achievement. For example, although written responses represent a majority of the types of answers provided by students taking the assessment, these responses are scored strictly on the basis of evidence of understanding the text, not on criteria related to writing ability. Likewise, it would be inappropriate to infer directly from the NAEP reading results that students who scored low on the assessment were necessarily deficient in phonics or phonemic awareness skills. The assessment is intended to measure comprehension skills, not phonics skills. Although students who demonstrate lower reading comprehension proficiency may also demonstrate lower proficiency in phonics skills, the link between these two skills is not addressed by the NAEP assessment.

This may be a particularly important point for state policy-makers who use NAEP data from the state-by-state assessments to gauge the effectiveness of literacy and reading education programs. For example, if the fourth graders assessed in a state performed lower on the NAEP assessment one year than did fourth graders who were assessed in the same state during an earlier year, it is likely to concern policy-makers and the citizens of that state. If a subsequent assessment shows further trends toward lower performance among fourth graders, there may be a call for action on the part of educators and policy-makers. It is important to keep in mind that the NAEP reading assessment is a single assessment of a specific academic skill-reading comprehension. The factors related to achievement in reading comprehension are multiple and varied, and are not entirely addressed by the NAEP assessment alone. Although the NAEP results may point to possible weakness in the curriculum or school policies, they should be considered along with other sources of information in determining the most appropriate actions to be taken.

Another aspect of the assessment that must be considered in interpreting the achievement results is one mentioned earlier—that the NAEP assessment does not provide for the reporting of individual students' scores, only average scores for groups and subgroups of students. This is an important point, because the average score attained by a certain group or subgroup of students does not show the range of performance within that group or subgroup. Thus, when NAEP results indicate that the average scale score of white students is higher than that of African American students, this clearly is not an indication that every white student outperformed every African American student.

The fact that NAEP data represent averages rather than findings for individual students is a relatively obvious and easily understood constraint on the interpretation of results. Other aspects of the assessment and the data collected may present less obvious limitations to interpreting NAEP data. For example, interpretations of NAEP data must also account for the fact that the average scores are estimates of the average performance of students. Although NAEP data indicate the average reading score for fourth, eighth, and twelfth graders, these scores are estimates based on representative samples of students in each grade. Every fourth, eighth, or twelfth grader in the nation or in a particular state did not take the assessment—only a representative sample of these students were assessed. The reports that are published based on NAEP results take into account the degree of uncertainty associated with data based on samples rather than the entire population, and only indicate differences between the average scores of students in various groups, or changes in performance across time, when those differences or changes are statistically significant.

A final consideration in the interpretation of NAEP achievement data relates to the "low-stakes" nature of this assessment. The fact that individual scores are not reported for students may be an advantage, because a long-standing criticism of large-scale standardized tests—that teachers may narrowly fit their teaching to the contents of the test—is likely not a problem with the NAEP assessment. Teachers know that they will not be held directly accountable for the performance of students in their classrooms.

Despite this advantage, the reporting of only group scores for the nation and for states may present a disadvantage that must be considered. If students know that they are not receiving individual scores for their performance on the assessment, there is the possibility that they will not try their hardest. There is some indication that this is a potential problem, particularly among the older students. As a part of the questionnaires administered to students who take the NAEP assessment, students are asked to indicate how important it is to them to do well on the assessment. Students' responses to this question in the 1998 reading assessment indicated that 86% of fourth graders, 58% of eighth graders, and only 31% of twelfth graders felt it was important or very important to them that they did well (Donahue et al., 1999). Thus, although most of the fourth graders sampled indicated that they wanted to do well on the assessment, this was true for less than one-third of the twelfth graders.

Interpreting NAEP Results on Factors Associated with Achievement

The responses of students in the NAEP assessment and their teachers to questionnaires provide an important context for interpreting the achievement scores. Because NAEP collects this information for students who are assessed, it is possible to examine the relationship between students' home and school experiences, and the reading scores attained by students on the assessment. As described in the previous section of this chapter, many of the NAEP findings on factors associated with achievement are consistent with the experts' agreements on what facilitates learning to read. Nevertheless, it is important to understand the limitations of interpreting NAEP results in this area, and to acknowledge that some findings would appear to be inconsistent with those of the experts.

An example of one NAEP finding that may be inconsistent with findings from the Expert Study can be found in results from the 1994 assessment (Campbell et al., 1996). Based on fourth graders' reports of how frequently they were asked by their teachers to work in a reading workbook or on a worksheet, this instructional activity had a positive relationship with achievement. That is, students who said they did this almost every day had higher scores, on average, than students who said they did this less frequently. This would appear to be inconsistent with the experts' agreement that using "workbooks with every reading lesson" would make learning to read difficult.

The relationship between this activity and reading achievement was different, however, when it was examined using teachers' responses to the same question. Based on the responses of the students' teachers, this activity was negatively associated with achievement. That is, students who were taught by teachers who said they had their students work in workbooks or on worksheets almost every day had lower average scores than students who were taught by teachers who indicated that they engaged students in this activity less frequently.

This discrepancy between results based on students' responses and those based on teachers' responses points to one limitation of NAEP findings on factors associated with achievement. Two possible explanations must be considered. It is possible that fourth graders are not able to accurately describe the frequency of an instructional activity such as working in workbooks or on worksheets. Thus, the analysis of their responses may be less valid than the analysis of responses provided by their teachers. A second explanation, though less appealing, must be considered. It is also possible that teachers responding to questionnaires may estimate the frequency of such activities in a manner that favors the socially desirable response. If this is true, it would not be unique to teachers; it is a well-documented fact of survey-type research. In either case, the conclusiveness of findings based on self-reported information from students or teachers should be interpreted cautiously.

Beyond the limitation of self-reported information about instructional experiences, another serious constraint on interpretations of NAEP results is the fact that the questionnaires are asking students and teachers to describe current classroom practices. Because the NAEP assessment is administered in late winter of the school year, the students assessed have been with their current teachers less than 6 months. Thus, the activities and instructional approaches described by students' and teachers' responses to the questionnaires reflect only the last 5–6 months of students' schooling. The questionnaires do not capture the educational experiences of students prior to the current school year. It must be assumed that the school years preceding the current one have had a substantial impact on students' current academic achievement. Therefore, if a particular instructional approach described by teachers in their responses to the questionnaire does not show a relationship to reading scores, it may be due to the fact that it only represents a few months of the students' entire school history.

A final limitation to interpreting NAEP results on factors related to achievement concerns the nature of the relationship. It is important to recognize that these relationships should be interpreted as correlations, not causal relationships. Although the NAEP data may indicate a statistically significant relationship between a certain classroom activity and students' reading achievement, the underlying cause for the relationship cannot be determined from NAEP data alone. A number of contextual factors may contribute to any one significant finding. For example, the NAEP finding described earlier—that frequent reading of self-selected books had a positive relationship with achievement—may have several explanations. First, it is possible that this activity does have a direct impact on reading development. There is some evidence from other research that supports this interpretation (Guthrie & Alvermann, 1999). Nevertheless, other interpretations must be considered. One alternate explanation is that teachers who frequently allow students to choose their own books also support students' reading development through related activities that have a greater impact on their achievement. These may include having students talk about their reading in small groups, assigning projects or reports based on their reading, or having students keep reading logs and journals to record their reading experiences. Yet another alternate explanation may be that teachers who have higher-performing students are more likely to allow reading of self-selected books than are teachers who have lower-performing students. In this case, it would not be the frequency of the activity that causes higher achievement; it would be students' higher achievement that causes the teacher to use this activity frequently. Clearly, the most appropriate way to interpret NAEP findings on factors associated with achievement is in the context of other research, and with an understanding of classroom practices.

Implications of NAEP Data and the Expert Study

This examination of the NAEP reading assessment and findings from the Expert Study suggest several implications for those who seek to increase students' reading achievement. First, it is clear that there are many contexts, practices, and objectives for reading instruction that are shared not only by the experts in the Expert Study, but also by a broad national constituency—like the one that developed the NAEP reading assessment framework. Reaching consensus on a topic as hotly debated as "reading instruction" is not a small accomplishment. Nevertheless, both the findings from the Expert Study and the broad view of reading embodied in the NAEP reading framework indicate that it is possible. Perhaps it can be concluded that discussions about teaching reading do not always have to regress into highly politicized, vitriolic debates that result in the exclusion of voices and a narrow view of reading. Moreover, when efforts are made to include as many voices as possible and to build consensus among an array of perspectives, it results in a valuable resource for educators and policy-makers.

The similarities between NAEP's perspective on reading and the experts' agreements reinforce the notion that there is a common ground for agreement among most reading educators, which is not just a collection of platitudes or abstract ideas. This common ground includes very specific contexts and practices, approaches, activities, and uses of materials that have direct implication for classroom practice and policy-setting. As described earlier, there are a number of limitations on the degree of interpretations that can be made based on NAEP data. Although the NAEP findings point to several activities and instructional approaches that have a positive relationship with reading achievement, NAEP data alone do not provide conclusive evidence of what works in classrooms. Reviewing the NAEP results, however, in light of the findings of the Expert Study is one way to begin to use the NAEP data to determine best practices and effective approaches. If a diverse group of experts who have extensive experience in classrooms and knowledge of research agree on a number of specific contexts and practices that facilitate learning to read, and if data like that collected by NAEP are consistent with their shared recommendations, it may be that the field of reading has a core knowledge base for informing school policies and practices.

A final implication of this examination of NAEP and the Expert Study is that our abilities to agree on a core set of best practices, and the possibility that what we agree on can be confirmed through research and large-scale collections of data, cannot be considered the final goal we are striving toward. Any one particular context, practice, activity, or objective for teaching reading or supporting students' literacy development can only be considered effective when it has had a direct impact on an individual student's learning. The Expert Study and the NAEP reading assessment reflect and support the true work that takes place in classrooms and homes every day. It is, however, in the efforts of teachers and parents that truly effective practices can be observed and measured. Researchers, experts, and large-scale educational programs like NAEP should seek to provide the most useful and relevant information to guide and reinforce the efforts of those directly responsible for helping children learn to read.

The Past 10 Years: In Retrospect

1.   *What are the most important things that you believe literacy research has shown over the past 10 years? (Positive and/or Negative)*

In 2009, a new NAEP reading assessment was administered that had been developed based on a new framework. Advances in research and assessment methodologies during the nearly two decades that spanned the use of the previous framework, informed the writing of the new framework and led to the design and development of a new assessment. The NAEP reading assessment frameworks are developed through a national consensus process, and represent widely held understandings about the nature of reading and how it should be assessed. As such, a brief overview of the differences between the two frameworks might illuminate some of the shifts that have occurred during the past decade in the area of reading.

The new framework calls for an expansion of the types of texts to be represented on the assessment, and more clearly delineates those types at each grade. For example, poetry has been introduced to the fourth-grade assessment with the new framework. While the previous framework described the ways in which students interact with text as stances/aspects of reading, the new framework places more emphasis on the cognition of reading, describing three types of cognitive targets to be assessed. In addition, the new framework calls for a more focused measurement of vocabulary, defining the construct as "meaning vocabulary" in order to emphasize the relationship between word meaning and text comprehension. The assessment continues to emphasize asking students to demonstrate comprehension through constructed responses (i.e., written responses), as well as with multiple-choice questions. And the use of authentic stimulus material in the selection of assessment passages continues to be a requirement (National Assessment Governing Board, 2008).

When the new assessment was administered in 2009, the previous assessment was also administered in order to allow for the possibility of building an analytic bridge between the two instruments, thus allowing for the reporting of trends in students' reading performance across the previous and new assessment frameworks. When the 2009 results were released, they showed a one-point gain for eighth graders and no change for fourth graders since the previous assessment in 2007. At the fourth grade, this was the first time in the three assessment cycles since 2005 that NAEP did not report a significant gain in reading achievement. The lack of progress since 2007 among fourth graders was pretty much across the board—spanning the five reported racial/ethnic groups and the performance distribution. At Grade 8, the overall average one-point gain was accompanied by gains in all five racial/ethnic groups, and among lower-and middle-performing students (National Center for Education Statistics, 2009).

2.   *How do you think this should inform the contexts and practices of teaching instruction in the classroom?*

In addition to describing student performance based on the reading assessment, NAEP collects information from students and their teachers related to reading practices and policies. While examining the patterns of responses to these survey-type questions and their relationship to students' performance can help to place the assessment results in some context, and may be of particular interest to those responsible for the contexts and practices of reading instruction, it is important to keep in mind the limitations in interpreting these results. For example, as NAEP is not an experimental study with control groups, causal interpretations are not warranted. The data may still be useful, however, for illuminating current practices or trends in those practices across time. Moreover, although these are self-reported data, they are based on a representative sample, which could make them of interest from a broad policy standpoint—especially when they confirm or are consistent with other research.

Among the instructional and contextual findings from the 2009 assessment that may be of interest to policy-makers and educators are those related to the amount of reading students are doing. For example, approximately one-fifth of fourth graders reported in 2009 that they only read five or fewer pages per day in school and for homework. Perhaps not surprisingly, these students scored on average lower than students who reported greater amounts of reading. Similarly, the amount of time students reported that they spent reading for fun demon-strated a positive relationship to reading achievement. Fourth graders who said they read for fun almost every day scored higher on average than their peers who said they did so less frequently. Also, fourth graders whose teachers reported giving their students at least sometime each day to read books of their own choosing had higher average scores than students whose teachers reported doing so less frequently (National Assessment of Educational Progress, 2009).

This quick snapshot of some of the findings from the 2009 assessment—both performance results and contextual findings—demonstrates how the NAEP assessment continues to contribute to the body of reading research. Policy-makers and educators often look to NAEP results to consider how the policies and practices of reading instruction affect the reading performance of students. As an overall indicator of reading achievement across populations and groups of students, NAEP plays in important role in monitoring the success of our col-lective efforts to reach educational goals. Of course, NAEP cannot provide the kinds of causal answers that may be sought to explain why achievement may or may not be increasing, but by shedding light on how students across the nation are performing, it does serve a unique and invaluable role.

References

Campbell, J.R. (1997). *NAEP facts: Reading assessment in the nation's fourth- and eighth-grade classrooms*. Washington, DC: National Center for Education Statistics.

Campbell, J.R., Donahue, P.L., Reese, C.M., & Phillips, G.W. (1996). *NAEP 1994 reading report card for the nation and the states*. Washington, DC: National Center for Education Statistics.

Donahue, P.L., Voelkl, K.E., Campbell, J.R., & Mazzeo, J. (1999). *NAEP 1998 reading report card for the nation and the states*. Washington, DC: National Center for Education Statistics.

Flippo, R.F. (1998). Points of agreement: A display of professional unity in our field. *The Reading Teacher, 52,* 30–40.

Guthrie, J.T., & Alvermann, D.E. (Eds.). (1999). *Engaged reading: Processes, practices, and policy implications.* New York, NY: Teachers College Press.

Mullis, I.V.S., Campbell, J.R., & Farstrup, A.E. (1993). *NAEP 1992 reading report card for the nation and the states.* Washington, DC: National Center for Education Statistics.

National Assessment Governing Board (1997). *Reading framework for the National Assessment of Educational Progress: 1992–1998.* Washington, DC: Author.

National Assessment Governing Board (2008). *Reading framework for the 2009 National Assessment of Educational Progress.* Washington, DC: Author.

National Assessment of Educational Progress (2009). National Center for Education Statistics (retrieved from http://nationsreportcard.gov/reading_2009/context_5.asp).

National Center for Education Statistics (2009). *The nation's report card: Reading 2009* (NCES 2010–458), Washington, DC: Author.

20

A FOCUS ON LITERACY TRENDS AND ISSUES TODAY

Jack Cassidy and Corinne Valadez

Just as Rona Flippo was completing her landmark study (1998, 1999, 2001) interviewing literacy experts about their shared beliefs, another survey of literacy leaders was beginning (Cassidy & Wenrich, 1997). Entitled *What's Hot, What's Not* in literacy, the annual survey has appeared at the beginning of each calendar year since 1997 in *Reading Today*, published by the International Reading Association (IRA). In addition to being cited in book chapters and journal articles (Nagy & Scott, 2000; Berne & Blachowicz, 2008; Jakobs, 2008; Bean & Harper, 2009; Hull, Zacher, & Hibbert, 2009), the survey has been translated into Spanish, summarized in *Education Week*, and replicated in the United Kingdom and Romania. Longer analyses of the findings have also appeared in a variety of venues (Cassidy, 2002; Cassidy & Cassidy 2004; Cassidy, Garrett & Barrera, 2006; Cassidy & Wenrich, 1998/1999).

In 2004, Cassidy's and Cassidy's comparative analyses of the *What's Hot* and Expert Study findings (Flippo 1999, 2001) yielded ironic results. For example, a focus on comprehension, word/meaning/vocabulary, which received consensus as being important to development of children's reading in the Expert Study, had not received attention or was not indicated as particularly *hot* at that time in the *What's Hot* 2001 survey. Therefore, in this volume revisiting Flippo's Expert Study, it is appropriate once again to provide an in-depth analysis of the trends and issues affecting literacy research and instruction using the 2010 *What's Hot* list (Cassidy & Cassidy 2009/2010) and relate it to the Expert Study findings.

Purpose of *What's Hot, What's Not*

The purpose of the annual survey of 25 literacy leaders (22 for the first survey) has always been to provide readers with a quick look at the issues involving literacy instruction that are currently receiving attention, as well as those that once had received attention but were now receiving less notice. Included in the survey are not only topics that are favored by researchers, but also issues being discussed in the popular media and by legislators. Unlike the Flippo Expert Study (1999, 2001), the annual survey does not seek consensus among the respondents, neither does it try to identify the issues that are "important." In fact, readers often have to be reminded that *hot* is not synonymous with *important*. By making educators more aware of the current trends and issues, the authors hope that educators can investigate the topics in more depth, and perhaps take advantage of resources that may be available.

Constructing the Survey

The original *What's Hot* survey was constructed by perusing professional journals, noting the frequent topics at conferences, looking at popular magazines, and listening to various reports on television and radio. The newly developed list was then given to the IRA's then Director of Research to suggest any changes. Each subsequent year's list of topics was developed by sending the previous year's list to the previous year's respondents and asking them to add, subtract or modify the list of topics. Table 20.1 gives the list of topics for 2010, along with the aggregated responses of those interviewed. The key at the bottom explains the meaning of the symbols.

Design and Method

Each year 25 (22 the first year) literacy leaders are interviewed orally either in person or by phone. Each is read a standard 178-word paragraph defining *hot* and *not hot*. They are then asked to say whether the topic is *hot* or *not hot*. Those interviewed are cautioned that their biases for or against a given topic should not interfere with their ratings. After 2000, the respondents were also asked if the topic *should be hot* or *should not be hot*. Obviously, for these questions, the respondents' biases are more likely to appear. The researchers record and then compile the responses. The whole survey is done orally because often those interviewed will make comments about why they gave a certain response, although they are not required to explain their reasoning. These unsolicited responses provide some valuable qualitative insights into the responses, and are often used anonymously in the *Reading Today* articles. Occasionally, new respondents will use the word *important*, and must be reminded that the word *hot* is not synonymous with the word *important*.

Selecting the Respondents

The 25 respondents are selected each year on a number of criteria. The most important criterion is probably that they have a broad national or international perspective on literacy. Therefore, often chosen are board members of international organizations like the IRA, the National Reading Conference, and the Association of Literacy Educators and Researchers. Editors of various journals related to literacy are prime respondents. Almost every year, the researchers have interviewed at least one of the editors of the IRA's three major journals, *The Reading Teacher, Journal of Adolescent and Adult Literacy*, and *Reading Research Quarterly*. The geographical location of those interviewed is another factor in choosing the respondents. The researchers decided to use the IRA's demographic/geographic membership data when choosing those to be interviewed from each region.

Another factor in choosing respondents is the positions of those interviewed. The researchers try to get teachers, administrators, independent consultants, and personnel from major educational organizations. However, the major criterion is having a national or international perspective. Thus, the majority of respondents are invariably college professors.

In the 14 years that the *What's Hot* survey has been conducted, 77 different people have been interviewed. Many of them would probably not consider themselves national or international experts in literacy. However, because of their positions at the time, they all had access to information about the literacy issues and trends. Some of those interviewed are indeed recognized experts in the field of reading/literacy education.

What's Hot 2010 vs 2001

The first decade of the new millennium has seen significant changes in the issues gaining attention in the field of literacy. Table 20.2 shows the contrast between 2001 and 2010. For both years, eight topics were rated *very hot*. However, only two of the topics are the same for both years—*early intervention* and *high-stakes assessment*.

Three topics that appeared on the 2001 survey were actually dropped from the list. These deletions occurred because a significant number of a given year's respondents suggested that removal. *Balanced reading* was probably dropped because there was too much confusion over the definition of the term (Cassidy & Wenrich, 1998/1999). *Decodable text* appeared on the list for only a few years, at a time when some states began mandating that beginning reading texts must have a high percentage of words that are decodable according to the skills students had been taught. Unfortunately, that requirement sometimes resulted in very artificial narratives. Many authorities felt that the term *guided reading* was really not that much different from earlier strategies, such as the directed reading thinking activity (DRTA) advocated by Stauffer (1969) and others.

Three topics that were rated *very hot* in 2001 are rated *not hot* according to the 2010 survey (*phonemic awareness, phonics*, and *research-based practice*). *Phonemic awareness* was a *hot* topic when the *What's Hot* survey began in 1997, and

TABLE 20.1 Results of What's Hot Survey for 2010

	What's Hot	What's Not	Should be Hot	Should Not be Hot
1. Adolescent literacy	✓✓		✓✓	
2. Adult literacy (−)	✓✓	✓✓✓	✓✓	
3. Comprehension (+)	✓✓		✓✓✓	
4. Critical reading and writing		✓	✓✓	
5. Curriculum-based assessment	✓		✓	
6. Differentiated instruction★	✓		✓✓	
7. Early intervention (+)	✓✓		✓✓	
8. English as a second language/English language learners	✓✓		✓✓✓	
9. Fluency (−)		✓		✓
10. High-stakes assessment	✓✓			✓✓
11. Informational/non-fiction texts	✓		✓✓	
12. Intertextuality/reading multiple texts★		✓✓	✓✓✓	
13. Literacy and adolescent boys		✓✓	✓	
14. Literacy coaches/reading coaches	✓✓		✓✓	
15. Motivation/engagement		✓✓	✓✓	
16. New literacies/digital literacies (+)	✓		✓✓	

17. Phonemic awareness   ✓✓
18. Phonics   ✓✓
19. Political/policy influences on literacy
20. Preschool literacy instruction/experiences (+)
21. Professional development (inservice) (–)
22. Response to intervention
23. Scientific evidence-based reading research & instruction (–)
24. Struggling/striving readers (grade 4 & above) (+)
25. Teacher education for reading (preservice) (+)
26. Vocabulary/word meaning
27. Writing (–)

Key
✓ Indicates that more than 50% of the respondents were in agreement (*hot* or *not hot*)
✓✓ Indicates that at least 75% of the respondents were in agreement (*very hot* or *cold*)
✓✓✓ Indicates that all the respondents were in agreement (*extremely hot* or *extremely cold*)
(+) indicates the topic was hotter for 2010 than 2009
(–) indicates the topic was less hot for 2010 than 2009
(*) indicates new topic for 2010.

TABLE 20.2 Comparison of Very Hot Topics: 2001 vs 2010

2001 Very Hot Topics	2010 Very Hot Topics
• Balanced reading instruction	• Adolescent literacy
• Decodable text	• Comprehension
• **Early intervention**	• **Early intervention**
• Guided reading	• Literacy coaches/reading coaches
• **High-stakes assessment**	• **High-stakes assessment**
• Phonemic awareness	• English as a second language/English-language learner
• Phonics	• Response to intervention
• Research-based practice	• Struggling/striving readers (Grade 4 & above)

Note
Topics in **bold-face** are the same.

remained a *very hot* topic through 2005. *Phonics* became *very hot* in 1998, and remained *very hot* through 2006. In 2010, both of these topics were judged *not hot*. Why the change? In 2001, the findings from the *Report of the National Reading Panel* (National Institute of Child Health and Human Development (NICHD), 2000) had a significant effect on the reading curriculum. That report identified five areas about which there was enough quality scientific evidence-based research to draw some conclusions about instruction. Those five topics were phonics, phonemic awareness, fluency, comprehension, and vocabulary. The *Report of the National Reading Panel* (NICHD, 2000) never stated that these were the only important areas. However, many administrators, publishers, and policy-makers quickly began to identify these topics as the "five pillars of reading instruction." The mortar that propped up these five pillars was *research-based practice* (later to be modified as *scientific, evidence-based reading research and instruction* on the *What's Hot* list). The first two "pillars" (*phonics, phonemic awareness*) had already received a great deal of attention (Cassidy & Wenrich, 1998), and they became a focus of the Reading First funding for schools. Books, teaching materials, state standards, and professional development seminars dealing with these two "pillars" suddenly appeared. By 2003, a third "pillar"—fluency—became *very hot*. Then, in 2008, came a report from the Institute of Education Sciences at the Department of Education which conducted the evaluation of Reading First projects.

> Reading First did not improve students' reading comprehension. The program did not increase the percentages of students in grades one, two, or three, whose reading comprehension scores were at or above grade level. In each of the three grades, fewer than half of the students in the Reading First schools were reading at or above grade level.
>
> *Gamse, Bloom, Kemple, and Jacob, 2008, xiv*

This disappointing finding heralded a returned focus on comprehension. *Comprehension* was now *very hot* and *vocabulary* also was *hot*. Perhaps there had been too much focus on *phonics*, *phonemic awareness*, and *fluency*, and not enough on *comprehension* and *vocabulary*. Interestingly, Flippo's experts (1998) had already cautioned against a focus on phonics.

Thus, as the first decade of the new millennium draws to a close, we thought it would be appropriate to take a closer look at the literacy topics receiving attention. What are the forces that have determined the *very hot* literacy trends and issues for 2010, and how have these areas of focus changed since 2001? Perhaps this chapter can then provide a resource for future scholars who might want to update Pearson's (2002) chronicle of American reading instruction, which stopped at the year 2000.

Adolescent Literacy and Struggling/Striving Readers (Grade 4 and Above)

Adolescent literacy made its debut on the *What's Hot, What's Not* survey in 2001(Cassidy & Cassidy, 2000/2001). It was *hot* in 2001, became *very hot* in 2006, and continues to be *very hot* in 2010. *Struggling/striving readers (Grade 4 and above)* appeared in slightly different forms on earlier lists, but it was not until 2009 that the topic was stated using its present terminology. It was *hot* in 2009, and became *very hot* in 2010. The topic could really be considered a subset of the more general term, *adolescent literacy*. Undoubtedly, many find it troubling that the concerns of fourth graders are being lumped with those of older adolescents.

The Carnegie Corporation's *Time to Act, a Comprehensive Report* (Carnegie Council on Advancing Adolescent Literacy, 2010) is the latest in a series of high-profile reports delineating concerns with the literacy achievement of adolescents. In fact, this report pinpointed adolescent literacy as the cornerstone of the education reform movement, and concluded "that adolescents need a higher level of literacy than ever before, both for college-readiness and employment in the new global knowledge economy" (p. x). An earlier report *Reading next—A vision for action and research in middle and high school literacy* (Biancarosa & Snow, 2004) drew many of the same conclusions.

The Reading First provisions of the No Child Left Behind Act (2001) resulted in focused efforts to improve reading education in the primary grades. These efforts forced many to realize that the focus to improve reading education must be expanded to include middle and high school years. Many students who had been "excellent third-grade readers began to falter or failed in later-grade academic tasks" (Biancarosa & Snow, 2006, p. 1) as they transitioned from elementary to middle and high school. Furthermore, Biancarosa and Snow noted that literacy development for students in the middle and high school years was a difficult task on two fronts. First, the literacy demands associated with adolescent literacy were much more complex and content-specific. Second, adolescents tended to be less motivated to improve their literacy skills.

Even though adolescent literacy has been *hot* for 10 years now, there is still more to be done. For example, findings from the most recent reading section of the National Assessment of Educational Progress showed that 70% of 17-year-olds achieved the basic level of reading proficiency, and less than 10% achieved the most advanced level (Lee, Grigg & Donahue, 2007). These data suggested that adolescents are leaving high school and entering college or the workforce with a basic level of reading proficiency. This sobering statistic could be one reason why adolescent literacy has progressed from *hot* to *very hot*.

It will also be interesting to see if Fertig's (2009) popular account of the fates of three struggling/striving readers has the same effect as Rudolf Flesch's landmark expose *Why Johnny Can't Read* (1955). If so, we may see another swing toward intensive phonics instruction for all students, but particularly *struggling/ striving readers Grade 4 and above*.

Comprehension

Prior to 2003, comprehension was *not hot*. From 2003 to 2010 comprehension wavered between *hot* and *very hot*, and the survey respondents overwhelmingly agreed that it should be *hot*. Comprehension has always been a topic of importance to reading educators. However, prior to the 1976 establishment of the Center for the Study of Reading at the University of Illinois, very little research had been done on how to teach comprehension. One of the most meaningful investigations to emanate from the University of Illinois was Durkin's landmark (1978/1979) study, which revealed that less than 1% of instructional time focused on comprehension. Since Durkin's study there has been a myriad of research on various aspects of comprehension (Raphael & Pearson, 1985; Pearson & Dole, 1987; Pressley et al., 1992). A recent study (Zunker, 2009), using a Delphi technique employed by Flippo (1999, 2001) in her study, found eight comprehension studies identified by experts as the most influential; several were from research done by those at the Center for the Study of Reading. The plethora of comprehension research between 1976 and 1991 perhaps contributed to the fact that comprehension was not a *hot* topic in the field until 2003 - although, in 1998, Flippo's Expert Study findings indicated consensus among the experts that a focus on comprehension was very important to reading development.

One of the challenges for teaching comprehension has been the ever-changing and increasing expectation for higher levels of literacy. In order to fully prepare students for the increasing demands of literacy comprehension, instruction should include "text that students encounter today" (Godin, Weber, Pearson, & Raphael, 2009, pp. 3, 50). Perhaps, because of these increased expectations and the findings of the Reading First Impact Study (Gamse, Bloom, Kemple, & Jacob, 2008), *comprehension* is once again receiving increased attention in 2010. It is *very hot*.

Early Intervention

Early intervention, a relatively new concept in the history of reading instruction, has been a *very hot* topic on the *What's Hot, What's Not* list beginning with the very first survey (Cassidy & Wenrich, 1997). Early intervention is a shift away from remediation—educators, parents, and even pediatricians are encouraged to give careful consideration to the early signs that "may place a child at risk for the acquisition of literacy skills" (Roth, Paul, & Pierotti, 2006, p. 2). Some of those signs include persistent baby talk, difficulty understanding simple directions, lack of alphabetic knowledge, and difficulty learning letters in the child's own name. *Early intervention* became a *hot* topic long before the advent of the *What's Hot* list. A major impetus for this focus in the late 1980s and early 1990s was the Reading Recovery program (Clay, 1993) from New Zealand. That program, an intensive one-on-one tutoring program for struggling first graders, was widely popular in the United States; however, because of its expense and because of several high-profile critiques of the claims of positive results (Shanahan & Barr, 1995), for most of its time on the *What's Hot* list Reading Recovery was *not hot*. Reading Recovery last appeared on the survey in 2001. Ironically, the What Works Clearinghouse, in its review of 36 supplemental programs studied, found that it was the only program to have positive effects across all four of the domains reviewed—alphabetics, fluency, comprehension, and general reading achievement (What Works Clearinghouse, 2008).

The importance of "intervening early and effectively has been established among educators and service providers" (Strickland, 2003, p. 325) and is not a new concept. Stanovich's study (1986), *The Matthew effects in reading*, used the poor-get-poorer analogy to explain some aspects of reading failure. Juel's study (1988) concluded that most first-grade students who are poor readers will still be poor readers by the time they reach fourth grade. These classic studies illustrated the primary reason for early intervention—learning achieved during the early years is the foundation for future literacy acquisition.

The National Early Literacy Panel (NELP) was formed in 2002 and was charged, much like the National Reading Panel, with summarizing scientific evidence on early literacy development, and on home and family influences on that development. The panel's primary purpose was to synthesize research to contribute to decisions in educational policy and practice that affect early literacy development, and to determine how teachers and families could support young children's language and literacy development (NELP, 2006, p. iii).

The panel identified six variables that had a strong relationship with later conventional literacy skills. The six variables included: alphabet knowledge, phonological awareness, rapid automatic naming (RAN) of letters or digits, RAN of objects or colors, writing or writing name, and phonological memory.

Most educators would agree with the importance of early intervention; however, there are some concerns. The most serious concern associated with early intervention is the misidentification of students, or "false alarms" (Scarborough, 2003). Half of the children who are identified as at risk and receive some type of intervention will not be in need of it. As of yet, the potential "negative educational and psychological consequences of mislabeling 'false alarms' are not known" (Scarborough, 2003, p. 108). Another concern, voiced by Hiebert and Taylor (2000), deals with the long-term effects of early reading interventions. They recommended further research to investigate how early interventions could be parlayed into success with adolescent readers.

For all these reasons, *early intervention* was *very hot* in 2001, still *very hot* in 2010, and will probably still be *very hot* in 2021. Educators will continue to look for means to prevent young children from experiencing reading failure.

English as a Second Language/English-Language Learners

With 4 million students designated as English-language learners and accounting for 8% of the total public school enrollment in the 2003–2004 academic year (National Center for Education Statistics, 2006), it is not surprising that *English as a second language and English-language learners* (ELL) has been a *hot* topic in reading research since 2002 (Cassidy & Cassidy, 2002). According to the PEW Hispanic Center (Fry, 2008), ELL students were "less much less likely than white students to score at or above the state's proficient level" (p. 1). In addition to low scores on standardized tests, ELLs who do not learn to read and write proficiently in English "cannot participate fully in American schools, workplace, or society. They face limited job opportunities and earning power" (August & Shanahan, 2006, p. 1).

The National Literacy Panel on Language-Minority Children and Youth, much like the National Reading Panel, was charged with producing a comprehensive report on the research regarding the education of ELLs with regard to literacy attainment. A few of the recommendations made by the panel were as follows:

- Reading instruction for ELLs should include the five pillars of reading as identified by the National Reading Panel (NICHD, 2000).
- Oral proficiency in English is critical to the development of reading and writing.
- Oral proficiency in the ELLs' primary language should continue to be developed and used to develop proficiency in English.
- Individual differences contribute significantly to English literacy development.
- Assessment should be ongoing to identify individual strengths and weaknesses of English-language learners.

Much like the old pedagogical debate of whole language versus phonics is the current controversy about whether or not instruction for ELLs should be provided in their primary language or should be English only (Viadero, 2009). The National Literacy Panel on Language-Minority Children and Youth recommended that oral proficiency in a child's primary language be used to develop proficiency in English. However, this recommendation was based upon a review of research only of 17 studies. Viadero found the pool of research on English-language learners to be shallow in comparison to other areas of education. A recent subject search of English as a second language in *The Reading Teacher, The Journal of Adolescent and Adult Literacy*, and the *Reading Research Quarterly* between the years of 2001 and 2009 yielded a total of only 51 results, thus seeming to support Viadero's claim.

While ESL and ELL have been *hot* topics since 2002 (Cassidy & Cassidy) in reading education, they have not been the subject of a great deal of research. Until there is that body of research, *English as a second language / English-language learners* will continue to be a *very hot* topic.

High-Stakes Assessment

High-stakes assessment has been a *very hot* topic on the annual survey since it first appeared in 2001. Generally, the term refers to the use of a single test to make major decisions about a student's achievement or lack thereof. These decisions can affect students' admissions, promotion, or graduation. Such judgments can also affect the fate of teachers, administrators, schools, and districts. Although indictments of standardized tests have been prevalent for some time (Allington, & McGill-Franzen, 1992; McGill-Franzen & Allington, 1993; Jones et al., 1999), the negative effects of such testing on the reading curriculum were discussed thoroughly in a highly prophetic 2001 article entitled "High-stakes testing in reading: Today in Texas, tomorrow?" (Hoffman, Assaf, & Paris, 2001). Since then, there have been many articles, reports, and books detailing the horrendous consequences of high-stakes assessment (Amrein & Berliner, 2002; Nichols & Berliner, 2007; Assaf, 2008; Ullucci & Spencer, 2009). Probably for that reason, most of the respondents in 2010 agreed that *high-stakes assessment* should not be a *hot* topic. Likewise, Flippo's experts (1998) indicated that the forced testing of children using paper and pencil tests would make learning to read difficult.

Despite the concerns voiced by educators, two-thirds of the public still support annual testing of students, according to a recent Gallup/PDK poll (Bushaw & McNee, 2009). The same poll also found that two-thirds of the public would prefer that a single national test be used. Given the public support of high-stakes testing, it is doubtful if this phenomenon will disappear in the near future. Policy-makers generally attend more to the voices of the public than to the findings of researchers. A recent report found that policy-makers are skeptical of scientific research about education (Nelson, Leffler, & Hansen, 2009). Therefore, educators would be wise to try to reconcile the conflicts that exist between quality *differentiated instruction* (another *hot* topic in 2010) and mandated *high-stakes assessment* (Brimijoin, 2005)

Literacy Coaches

The Reading First Initiative of *NCLB* (2001) stipulated the hiring of a full-time reading coach to provide mentoring, coaching, training, and demonstration lessons to the classroom teacher. This Act has brought literacy coaches to the attention of reading researchers for the past few years. Literacy coaches first appeared on the *What's Hot, What's Not* 2005 survey (Cassidy & Cassidy, 2004/2005) as *very hot*, and has continued to be *very hot* each and every year. A recent subject search of *The Reading Teacher* and *The Journal of Adolescent and Adult Literacy* produced a total of 684 results between the years 2004 through 2009. With this many results for a single subject search, it is no wonder that literacy coaches have been a *very hot* topic.

The IRA issued a position statement regarding the role and qualifications of the reading coach (IRA, 2004). The IRA recognized the "changing roles … and variety of new titles, such as *reading coach* and *literacy coach*, and … the variability in the job descriptions for these coaches" (p. 2). According to the IRA (2004), reading coaches must have been excellent classroom teachers, have in-depth knowledge of the reading processes, have experience working with teachers, be excellent presenters, and have experience in observing and providing feedback to classroom teachers.

Reading coaches have primarily been associated with elementary schools; however, school districts "have begun to invest in middle and high school literacy coaches" (Carnegie Council on Advancing Adolescent Literacy, 2010, p. 26). The RAND study (Marsh et al., 2008) showed that literacy coaches improved student literacy achievement when schools used coaches over extended periods of time; when schools hired coaches who were more experienced; and when coaches, along with faculty, reviewed assessment data on a regular basis.

While many schools have hired literacy coaches in an effort to increase the academic achievement of their students, other schools have chosen not to hire literacy coaches (Mangin, 2009). Some of the reasons given were the economic downturn resulting in decreased funding for new programs; satisfactory test scores in some schools; and a reluctance to eliminate existing roles (e.g., reading specialists). Schools were cautioned against discarding the role of the reading specialist in favor of literacy coaches, given the financial investments made to develop that role. McKenna (2009) also warned that literacy coaches could disappear as quickly as they appeared.

Response to Intervention

The Individuals with Disabilities Education Act (IDEA) was rewritten and signed into law in 2004. This Act reflected new ideas around learning disabilities, and the concept of a pre-identification strategy called Response to Intervention (RTI). While IDEA was signed into law in 2004, it was not until 2006 that the final regulations were published and made effective. In 2007, RTI made its first appearance on the *What's Hot, What's Not* survey as a *hot* topic, and quickly moved to *very hot* the following year.

According to the RTI Action Network (n.d.), RTI is a multi-tiered approach in both general and special education designed to implement evidence-based intervention for students who experienced difficulty in learning to read. Students' responsiveness to evidence-based interventions is closely monitored in order to determine the nature and intensity of the intervention (Mesmer & Mesmer, 2008). The assumption is that such initiatives will prevent some students from being identified as learning disabled by providing intervention as concerns emerged. There are a variety of models for RTI, which use a three-tier framework (Klingner & Edwards, 2006). In the first tier, all students receive quality instruction in the general education classroom and are screened on a periodic basis in order to identify struggling readers who may require additional support. Students who do not make adequate progress and require intensive instruction are moved into the second tier of the intervention model. The third tier is designed to address the needs of students experiencing significant problems and who have been unresponsive to the interventions received in the first and second tiers of the model.

Allington (2008) suggested that there was not substantive research to support the implementation of RTI. He criticized proponents of RTI for identifying students who were not responsive to the various interventions as "treatment resistors," rather than re-evaluating the intervention. In addition, the reluctance of schools to re-evaluate interventions was viewed as proof that schools continue to put their faith in a program, rather than in the expertise of a highly qualified reading teacher.

Some Conclusions

So what can we conclude from all these surveys? One possible conclusion from looking at the results in Table 20.1 is that most of the *very hot* topics for 2010 are ones that literacy leaders believe *should be hot*. Perhaps the field as a whole is directing its attention to those topics crucial for student success. *Comprehension*, which many consider synonymous with reading, is one of the *very hot* topics in 2010. In 2001, *comprehension* was one of the coldest topics, as was *vocabulary*—also a topic considered crucial for reading success. In 2010, *vocabulary* is also a *hot* topic. Generally, when areas are receiving much attention, publishers develop materials to address these areas. Staff development is also directed toward them.

Another possible conclusion is that attention is no longer directed solely to young readers. Although *early intervention* is still *hot*, policy-makers are beginning to realize that older students also need help. Now, with the disappointing results of the Reading First evaluations, policy-makers are realizing that some funding must be directed toward *struggling/striving readers in Grades 4 and beyond*. Perhaps we are really moving toward an era where the foci identified by literacy leaders in the field are the ones that will be getting attention. Hopefully, this should impact the contexts and practices of reading instruction in our classrooms.

References

Allington, R. (2008). Allington on rti [Audio podcast] (retrieved from www.reading. org/General/Publications/Podcasts.aspx).

Allington, R.L., & McGill-Franzen, A. (1992). Unintended effects of educational reform in New York State. *Educational Policy* 6(4), 396–413.

Amrein, A.L., & Berliner, D.C. (2002). High-stakes testing, uncertainty, and student learning. *Education Policy Analysis Archives* 10(18) (retrieved October 14, 2009 from http://epaa.asu.edu/epaa/v10n18/).

Assaf, L.C. (2008). Professional identity of a reading teacher: Responding to high-stakes testing pressures. *Teachers and Teaching 14*(3), 239–252.

August, D., & Shanahan, T. (2006). *Developing literacy in second-language learners: Report of the national literacy panel on language-minority children and youth.* Mahwah, NJ: Lawrence Erlbaum Associates.

Bean, T.W., & Harper, H. (2009). The "adolescent" in adolescent literacy: A preliminary review. In K.D. Wood & W.E. Blanton (Eds.), *Literacy instruction for adolescents: Research-based practice* (pp. 37–53). New York, NY: Guilford.

Berne, J.I., & Blachowicz, C.L.Z. (2008). What reading teachers say about vocabulary instruction: Voices from the classroom. *The Reading Teacher, 62*(4), 314–323.

Biancarosa, G., & Snow, C.E. (2004). *Reading next—A vision for action and research in middle and high school literacy: A report to Carnegie Corporation of New York.* Washington, DC: Alliance for Excellent Education.

Biancarosa, C., & Snow, C.E. (2006). *Reading next—A vision for action and research in middle and high school literacy: A report to Carnegie Corporation of New York* (2nd ed.).Washington, DC: Alliance for Excellent Education.

Brimijoin, K. (2005). Differentiation and high-stakes testing: An oxymoron? *Theory into Practice 44*(3), 254–261.

Bushaw, W.J., & McNee, J.A. (2009). *The 41st annual Phi Delta Kappa/gallup poll of the public's attitudes toward the public schools* (retrieved October 13, 2009 from www.docstoc. com/docs/10425651/Phi-Delta-KappaGallup-Poll-of-the-Public%E2%80%99s-Attitudes-Toward-the-Public-Schools).

Carnegie Council on Advancing Adolescent Literacy (2010). *Time to act: An agenda for advancing adolescent literacy for college and career success.* New York, NY: Carnegie Corporation of New York.

Cassidy, J. (2002). Literacy 2001: What is and what should be. Presidential address. In W.M. Linek, E.G. Sturtevant, J.R., & P.E. Linder (Eds.), *Celebrating the voices of literacy: 23rd yearbook of the College Reading Association* (pp. 2–6). Commerce, TX: Texas A&M–Commerce: College.

Cassidy, J., & Cassidy, D. (2000/2001). What's hot, what's not for 2001? *Reading Today, 18*(3), 1, 18.

Cassidy, J., & Cassidy, D. (2002). What's hot, what's not for 2003. *Reading Today, 20*(3), 1, 18.

Cassidy, J., & Cassidy, D. (2004). Literacy trends and issues today: An on-going study. *Reading and Writing Quarterly, 20* (1), 11–28.

Cassidy, J., & Cassidy, D. (2004/2005). What's hot, what's not for 2005? *Reading Today, 22*(3), 1, 8.

Cassidy, J., & Cassidy, D. (2005/2006). What's hot, what's not for 2006. *Reading Today, 23*(1), 1, 8–9.

Cassidy, J., & Cassidy, D. (2009/2010). What's hot, what's not for 2010. *Reading Today, 28*(1), 1, 8–9.

Cassidy, J., & Wenrich, J. (1997). What's hot and what's not for 1997: A look at key topics in reading research and practice. *Reading Today, 14* (4), 34.

Cassidy, J., & Wenrich, J. (1998/99). Literacy research and practice: What's hot, what's not, and why. *The Reading Teacher, 52*, 402–406.

Cassidy, J., Garrett, S.D., & Barrera IV, E.S. (2006) What's hot in adolescent literacy: 1997–2006. *Journal of Adolescent & Adult Literacy 50*(1), 30–39.

Clay, M. (1983). *The early detection of reading difficulty. The use of Marie Clay's "diagnostic survey and recovery procedures" with first-grade children.* Paper presented at the meeting of the International Reading Association, Anaheim, CA (retrieved October 15, 2009 from www.eric.ed.gov/ERICDocs/data/ericdocs2sql/content_storage_01/0000019b/80/1e/34/d1.pdf).

Clay, M. (1993). *Reading recovery: A guidebook for teachers in training.* Portsmouth, NH: Heinemann.

Durkin, D. (1978/1979). What classroom observations reveal about reading comprehension instruction. *Reading Research Quarterly*, 14(4), 481–533.

Fertig, B. (2009). *Why cant u teach me 2 read? Three students and a mayor put our schools to the test.* New York, NY: Farrar, Strauss and Giroux.

Flesch, R. (1955). *Why Johnny can't read—And what you can do about it.* New York, NY: Harper & Brothers.

Flippo, R.F. (1998). Points of agreement: A display of professional unity in our field. *The Reading Teacher, 52*, 30–40.

Flippo, R.F. (1999). What do the experts say: Helping children learn to read. Portsmouth, NH: Heinemann.

Flippo, R.F. (Ed.). (2001). *Reading researchers in search of common ground.* Newark, DE: International Reading Association.

Fry, R. (2008). *The role of schools in the English language learner achievement gap.* Washington, DC: PEW Hispanic Center.

Gamse, B.C., Bloom, H.S., Kemple, J.J., & Jacob, R.T. (2008). *Reading First Impact Study: Interim Report.* Institute for Educational Sciences, US Department of Education (retrieved October 15, 2009 from http://ies.ed.gov/ncee/pdf/20084016.pdf).

Godin, S.M., Weber, C.M., Pearson, P.D., & Raphael, T.E. (2009). Comprehension: The means, motive, and opportunity for meeting the needs of diverse learners. In L.M. Morrow, R. Rueda, & D. Lapp (Eds.), *Handbook of research on literacy and diversity* (pp. 337–365). New York, NY: Guilford Press.

Hiebert, E., & Taylor, B. (2000). Beginning reading instruction: Research on early interventions. In M. Kamil, P. Mosenthal, P.D. Pearson, & R. Barr (Eds.), *Handbook of reading research* (Vol. 3, pp. 455–482). Mahwah, NJ: Lawrence Erlbaum Associates.

Hoffman, J., Assaf, L.C., & Paris, S. G. (2001). High-stakes testing in reading: Today in Texas, tomorrow? *The Reading Teacher, 54*, 482–492.

Hull, G., Zacher, J., & Hibbert, L. (2009). Youth, risk and equity in a global world. *Review of Research in Education, 33*, 117–159.

Individuals With Disabilities Act of 2004, P. L. 108–466.

International Reading Association (2004). *The role and qualifications of the reading coach in the United States: A position statement of the International Reading Association.* Newark, DE: International Reading Association.

Jakobs, V.A. (2008) Adolescent literacy: Putting the crisis in context. *Harvard Educational Review, 78* (1), 7–39.

Jones, G.M., Jones, B.D., Hardin B., Chapman, L., Yarbrough, T., & Davis, M. (1999). The impact of high-stakes testing on teachers and students in North Carolina. *Phi Delta Kappan, 81*(3), 199–203.

Juel, C. (1988). *Learning to read and write: A longitudinal study of fifty-four children from first through fourth grade.* Paper presented at the Annual Meeting of the American Educational Research Association, April 1988, New Orleans.

Klingner, J.K., & Edwards, P.A. (2006). Cultural considerations with response to intervention models. *Reading Research Quarterly, 41*(1), 108–117.

Lee, J., Grigg, W., & Donahue, P. (2007). *The nation's report card: Reading 2007.* Washington, DC: National Center for education Statistics, Institute for Education Sciences, US Department of Education.

Mangin, M. (2009). *To have or not to have? Factors that influence district decisions about literacy coaches* (retrieved October 15, 2009 from www.literacycoachingonline.org/briefs/Factors_district_decisions.pdf).

Marsh, J., McCombs, J., Lockwood, J.R., Martorell, F., Gershwin, D., Naftel, S., et al. (2008). *Supporting literacy across the sunshine state: A study of Florida middle school reading coaches.* Santa Monica, CA: Rand Corporation.

McGill-Franzen, A., & Allington, R.L. (1993). Flunk'em or get them classified: The contamination of primary grade accountability data. *Educational Researcher, 22*(1), 19–22, 34.

McKenna, M. (2009). *The literacy coaching challenge.* Paper presented at the 54th annual conference of the International Reading Association, May 2009, Minneapolis, MN.

Mesmer, E.M., & Mesmer, H.E. (2008, December). Response to Intervention (RTI): What teachers of reading need to know. *The Reading Teacher, 62*(4), 280–290.

Nagy, W.E., & Scott, J.A. (2000) Vocabulary processes. In M.L. Kamil, P.B. Mosenthal, P.D. Pearson, & R. Barr (Eds.), *Handbook of reading research: Volume III.* Mahwah, NJ: Lawrence Erlbaum Associates.

National Center for Education Statistics (2006). *Public elementary and secondary students, staff, schools, and school districts: School year 2003–04, NCES 2006–307.* Washington, DC: NCES.

National Early Literacy Panel (2006). *Developing Early Literacy: Report of the National Early Literacy Panel.* Jessup, MD: National Institute for Literacy.

National Institute of Child Health and Human Development (NICHD) (2000). *Report of the National Reading Panel. Teaching children to read: An evidence-based assessment of the scientific research literature on reading and its implications for reading instruction: Reports of the subgroups* (NIH Publication No. 00–4754). Washington, DC: US Government Printing Office.

Nelson, S.R., Leffler, J.C., & Hansen, B.A. (2009). *Toward a research agenda for understanding and improving the use of research evidence.* Portland, OR: Northwest Regional Education Laboratory.

Nichols, S.L., & Berliner, D.C (2007). *Collateral damage: How high-stakes testing corrupts America's schools.* Cambridge, MA: Harvard Educational Press.

No Child Left Behind Act of 2001, EPL 107–110, 115 Stat. 1425, 20 USC §§ 6301 *et seq.*

Pearson, P.D. (2002). American reading instruction since 1967. In N.B. Smith, *American reading instruction* (Special ed., pp. 419–486). Newark, DE: International Reading Association.

Pearson, P.D., & Dole, J.A. (1987). Explicit comprehension instruction: A review of research and a new conceptualization of instruction. *Elementary School Journal, 88*(2), 151–165.

Pressley, M., El-Dinary, P.B., Gaskins, I. Scuder, T., Bergman, J. Almasi, J., et al. (1992). Beyond direct instruction: Transactional instruction of reading comprehension strategies. *Elementary School Journal, 92*, 513–555.

Raphael, T.E., & Pearson, P.D. (1985). Increasing student's awareness of sources of information for answering questions. *American Educational Research Journal, 22*, 217–236.

Roth, F.P., Paul, D.R., & Pierotti, A.M. (2006). *Let's talk for people with special communication needs.* American Speech-Language-Hearing Association (retrieved October 15, 2009 from www.asha.org/public/speech/emergent-literacy.htm).

RTI Action Network. (n.d.). *What is rti?* (retrieved October 8, 2009 from www.rtinetwork.org/Learn/What/ar/WhatIsRTI).

Scarborough, H. (2003). Connecting early language to later reading (dis)abilities. In S. Neuman & D.K. Dickinson (Eds.), *Handbook of early literacy research* (pp. 97–109). New York, NY: Guilford Press.

Shanahan, T., & Barr, R. (1995). Reading recovery: An independent evaluation of the effects of an early intervention for at-risk learners. *Reading Research Quarterly, 30*, 958–997.

Stanovich, K.E. (1986). Matthew effects in reading: Some consequences of individual differences in the acquisition of literacy. *Reading Research Quarterly, 21*(4), 360–407.

Stauffer, R.G. (1969). *Teaching reading as a thinking process.* New York; Harper & Row.

Strickland, D. S. (2003). Early intervention for African American children considered to be at risk. In S. Neuman & D.K. Dickinson (Eds.), *Handbook of early literacy research* (pp. 322–332). New York, NY: Guilford Press.

Ullucci, K., & Spencer, J. (2009). Unraveling the myths of accountability: A case study of the California high school exit exam. *Urban Review 41(*2), 161–173.

Viadero, D. (2009, January). Delving deep: Research hones focus on ELLs. *Education Week 28*(17) (retrieved October 14, 2009 from www.cal.org/qualitycounts/quality_counts_cal.pdf).

What Works Clearinghouse (2008). *Reading recovery* (retrieved October 15, 2009 from http://ies.ed.gov/ncee/wwc/pdf/wwc_reading_recovery_120208.pdf).

Zunker, N. (2009). *A modified delphi study to identify the significant works pertaining to the understanding of reading comprehension and content analysis of the identified works.* Unpublished doctoral dissertation, Texas A&M University—Corpus Christi.

21

A FOCUS ON STRUGGLING READERS

A Comparative Analysis of Expert Opinion and Empirical Research Recommendations

Cindy D. Jones, D. Ray Reutzel, and John A. Smith

Reading is the great emancipator. It unlocks knowledge from the past and present, and places it in the hands, heart, and mind of the reader. The ability to read has been coined the "New Civil Right" (NASBE, 2006). Given the critical role of reading ability to impact a child's future (Stanovich, 1986; Juel, 1988) and our national competitiveness in a world economy, reading instruction continues to be the focus of intense discussion, investigation, and research to determine what constitutes effective, efficient reading instruction that meets the needs of all students (National Commission on Excellence in Education, 1983; Task Force on Education for Economic Growth, 1983).

Insights from "Expert Opinion" on Helping Struggling Readers

Flippo (2001) captured "expert opinion" during one of the most tumultuous times in the history of reading instruction and research—a time referred to by many as the Reading Wars. Stanovich (2000) recommended that several steps be taken to resolve the continuing conflict of the Reading Wars—most importantly, "to look for points of agreement between opposing positions" (p. 398). This was precisely the contribution offered by the work of Dr Rona Flippo through her Expert Opinion Studies. Her book, *Reading Researchers in Search of Common Ground* (2001), was a contribution intended to heal the wounds of a deeply divided profession and provide a "display of professional unity" during an era of passionate political and public scrutiny around the teaching of reading. From Flippo's Expert Study, we gained insights into the professional judgments of an evolving profession wrestling to answer vexing societal, educational, and instructional problems.

Since those tumultuous times, the federal government has mandated the use of evidenced-based practices (No Child Left Behind Act of 2001, 2002). Nelson, Leffler, and Hansen (2009) emphasized that educational decisions and practice should be based on compelling and persuasive evidence—a "burden of proof" presented to substantiate a claim. Stanovich and Stanovich (2003) identified three standards of evidence for making educational decisions: publication of findings in refereed journals, duplication of results by a number of investigators, and consensus from a body of studies. Education as a science is a process of wide dissemination that moves incrementally forward. Educators must first look to the empirical research base to inform decisions and then to the best information available, professional judgment grounded in general research evidence, for practices that do not have an established research base. This firm dedication to evidence-based instructional practices will serve to build and establish "common ground."

In this chapter, we look to the standards of evidence from recent reading research reports of empirical evidence and from professional judgment detailed in the Expert Study (Flippo, 1998, 2001) with an eye toward helping readers who struggle. From the Expert Study, we identify 10 General Principles of Ineffective Reading Instruction and 10 General Principles of Effective Reading Instruction. Next, we identify recommendations for effective reading instruction found in three national reading research reports (National Institute of Child Health and Human Development (NICHD), 2000; August & Shanahan, 2006; National Early Literacy Panel (NELP), 2008). We then compare findings of the selected research reports with the Expert Study (Flippo, 1998, 2001) to identify points of convergence or divergence. Finally, we synthesize the opinions of the "experts" with instructional recommendations from the national reading research reports to create a new set of instructional recommendations, supported by both expert opinion and the national reading research reports, to facilitate learning to read.

Expert Opinion on Making Learning to Read Difficult

At the outset of the review, we, like Flippo (1998), were struck with the fact that more agreement was reached among experts on practices that would make learning to read more difficult than on those that would facilitate it. This finding should not be a surprise, as the Report of the National Reading Panel (NICHD, 2000) validated only a few reading instructional practices based on high quality, replicable, scientific research. From our re-examination of the Expert Study findings, we identified 10 discrete general principles of ineffective reading instruction. We then connected specific instructional practices and contexts thought by the experts to make learning to read difficult to these 10 general principles of ineffective instruction (Table 21.1).

TABLE 21.1 The "Expert Study" on Practices and Contexts that Make Learning to Read Difficult for Struggling Readers and Writers

General Principles for Making Learning to Read Difficult	Specific Practices for Making Learning to Read Difficult
Isolated instruction	Teach reading separate from writing, listening, or speaking.
	Teach letters and sounds in isolation, using flashcards, letter boards, etc.
	Teach only phonics.
Skill drill and mastery	Follow the teacher's edition script with fidelity during instruction.
	Use worksheets and workbooks as practice for every skill and lesson.
	Use more worksheets and workbooks to help struggling readers.
	Teach letters and words one at a time until each is mastered before moving on to new letters or words.
	Focus on skill instruction, not on comprehending the text.
Control	Teacher controls selection and discussion of all reading materials.
	Use short, choppy selections with controlled vocabulary.
	Use texts that contain no new, previously untaught words.
Competition	Learning to read may become a contest with winners and losers.
Implicit instruction and modeling avoidance	Avoid reading aloud to students.
	Stop reading aloud to students after they complete the primer-level books.
	Do not model reading for your own purposes or enjoyment.

Error avoidance	Do it right or not at all. Focus instruction on getting the single, best answer. Detect and correct inappropriate eye movements. Pronounce all words in oral reading exactly correctly.
Negative and lowered expectations	Communicate negative reading attitudes and expectations to students. Emphasize the high stakes and serious consequences for falling behind in reading progress.
Grouping practices	Place children into static reading ability groups for instruction.
Rote accountability	Submit written book reports for every story or text read. Use paper-and-pencil tests and skill practice sheets following the reading for each story or text.
Mode of reading practice—oral reading	Oral reading practice is preferred over silent reading practice. Oral reading practice should be accomplished in a "round robin" or "barber shop style" reading circle.

Isolated Instruction

The experts viewed isolating reading instruction as a prescription for making learning to read difficult, be it reading instruction that was isolated from writing, listening, and speaking, or reading skills/strategies instruction that was isolated from application in reading text. However, there is a substantial research base on the effects of isolated reading instruction using direct instruction narrowly focused on reading skill acquisition (Guthrie, 1977; Rosenshine, 1979; Brophy & Good, 1986). Carnine, Silbert, and Kameenui (1997) indicated that for low-income, primary-grade children, programs focused on direct instruction of essential reading skills are the most effective and efficient manner for assuring student progress. A meta-analysis summary by Forness (2001) reported a large effect size of 0.85 for direct instruction in reading, and a 1.13 effect size for teachers who had received training in implementing direct instruction. It should be noted there is longitudinal research indicating that isolated, narrowly focused, direct-skill instruction has negative long-term effects on children's academic, intellectual, and social development (Marcon, 1992, 1995; Schweinhart & Weikart, 1997). Of course, more research is needed to determine how or if struggling readers' progress and achievement is adversely or positively affected by isolated vs integrated reading instruction, both in the short and long term.

Skill Drill and Mastery

The experts took a dim view of drilling student reading skills and strategies using paper-and-pencil worksheets or workbook pages. Allington (1983) reported that low-achieving readers typically spend more time on worksheets and isolated activities than on reading texts and comprehension tasks. Yet time spent in completing seatwork has been shown to negatively correlate with reading achievement gains (Rupley & Blair, 1987). Teaching each literacy skill one at a time until mastery has been achieved—and withholding the teaching of new literacy skills until then—were also believed to make learning to read more difficult. An overemphasis on skill teaching to the complete exclusion of reading-connected texts for constructing meaning was another point of convergent opinion among the experts. The experts' views on teaching reading skills through drill and mastery were cautiously qualified, however, with specific terms such as an "overemphasis" or "exclusive focus." Once again, we are reminded that a focus on reading skills may be useful for struggling readers during the initial phases of their reading development, but the long-term effects of continued drill to mastery on reading skills, one at a time, may in fact produce undesirable long-term effects on struggling readers' growth and motivation.

Exclusive Teacher Control

The experts likewise agreed that certain types of "control" would make learning to read difficult. Whether it was controlling the language in reading materials (resulting in "short, choppy texts") or making sure students only encountered words in print they had already been taught, these experts seemed to believe that controlling the language in reading materials would only make learning to read more difficult. On the issue of choice of reading materials, the experts agreed that total teacher control would also make learning to read difficult. This agreement seemed to ignore research that demonstrated an unmistakable link between controlling task difficulty and subsequent positive effects on student achievement and motivation (Juel, 1994; Swanson & Hoskyn, 1998; Allington, 2001; Pressley et al., 2003). In fact, a lack of teacher control has been viewed as "a prescription for failure" as struggling readers may regularly face tasks they view as impossible to complete (Margolis & McCabe, 2006). Research has shown that struggling readers may develop negative reading attitudes, behaviors, and habits without teacher control (Worthy & Broaddus, 2001; Stahl, 2004; Chua, 2008). Blair, Rupley, and Nichols (2007) recently noted that varying degrees of control are required for different learning tasks. It remains to be determined, however, which types of control are most helpful for struggling readers at various points in their development of reading acquisition.

Competition

Experts expressed disapproval for treating students' reading progress as a contest or competition. Sorting or labeling students as "winners" and "losers" to motivate or accelerate their reading progress, especially those students who struggle, is at the heart of the experts' concern around making learning to read competitive. Children's persistence and success in learning to read has been linked to their perceptions of their own abilities, their own and others' expectations, and their own efficacy as learners or readers (Wigfield & Guthrie, 1997; Pressley, 2002; Guthrie et al., 2007; Morgan et al., 2008). Readers who lack motivation will not put forth the sustained efforts needed to learn to read, nor persist in the face of challenges and difficulties (Wigfield, 1997; Lutz et al., 2006). Linnenbrink and Pintrich (2003) emphasized that students are more likely to engage in tasks in which they believe they can complete with effort, and that failure at a task is attributable to something the student can change. Reading competitions remove the locus of control from the individual student to an external factor. Such practices doom some students to failure in spite of their best efforts, and some students to success regardless of little expended effort.

Implicit Instruction and Modeling Avoidance

The experts also saw avoiding modeling as a means for creating contexts and encouraging practices as contributing to making learning to read more difficult for struggling students. Explicit teacher modeling of thought processes, procedures, and decisions related to successful reading have proven to be valuable for all children, including those students who struggle (Duffy et al., 1987; Duffy, Roehler, & Herrmann, 1988; Taylor, Pearson, Peterson, & Rodriguez, 2005; Pollard-Durodola & Simmons, 2009). Explicit modeling is recognized as an important component of effective instruction for word recognition, fluency, vocabulary, and comprehension (Coyne et al., 2009; Ehri, Satlow, & Gaskins, 2009; Rasinski, Homan, & Biggs, 2009). In contrast, the effects of implicit modeling of reading behaviors and personal valuing of reading by the teacher (such as the teacher reading books during silent sustained reading) have been difficult to document, and teachers have been encouraged to be active, explicit models of what it means to be a reader rather than passive, implicit models (Levine, 1984, Gambrell, 1996; Gambrell & Almasi, 1996).

Error Avoidance

Error avoidance in tasks such as spelling, pronunciation of words while reading, and test-taking was an agreed upon instructional prescription for making learning to read difficult. Expert opinion is in harmony with current Vygotskian views on the place and value of errors in learning to read. Mistakes and errors are held as evidence of student learning attempts, risk-taking, and persistence, and as such are not to be discouraged (Dixon-Krauss, 1996; Fosnot, 1996). Savage et al. (2001) labeled reading errors as "an important window" into a child's reading strategies. In fact, error analysis can tell a great deal about the skills of a reader, and is used in reading assessments such as Running Records (Clay, 2002) to identify instructional interventions for struggling readers.

Low Expectations

Low expectations, communicating the complexity and difficulty of learning to read, labeling students and placing them into static ability groups, and instilling concern about falling behind other students were seen by the experts as behaviors, contexts, and practices that would make learning to read difficult. Through the work of Rosenthal and Jacobson (1968), the affirming or adverse influence of teacher expectations and communication on student achievement is well known and regarded (Rist, 1970). More effective teachers consistently have higher expectations of students than less effective teachers (Johnson, Livingston, Schwartz, & Slate, 2000; Bohn, Roehrig, & Pressley, 2004).

Ability Grouping

The use of static ability groups has been found to be harmful in a variety of ways for students who struggle learning to read (Weinstein, 1976; Allington, 1980, 1983; Oakes, 1992). Recently, Poole (2008) reported that struggling readers in heterogeneous grouping for reading instruction experience many of the same negative effects as they do in homogenous low-ability grouping. In contrast, flexible skills-based grouping is a way to target instruction for students who share similar needs and challenges (Opitz, 1998; Reutzel, 1999), and is believed to mitigate negative influences on students' progress, self-image, and achievement (Reutzel & Cooter, 2000).

The three-tiered model of reading instruction, Response to Intervention (RTI), has been highlighted by several reports as a way to address the needs of struggling readers (Coyne, Kame'enui, & Simmons, 2001; Al Otaiba & Fuchs, 2002; McMaster, Fuchs, Fuchs, & Compton, 2005). Central to this model is small-group, homogeneous skill-based instruction. Prior research has supported the value of small-group instruction, and it has been shown that small-group instruction is more prevalent in the classrooms of the most effective teachers (48 minutes per day) than in the classrooms of the least effective teachers (25 minutes per day) (Taylor et al., 2005). Systematic progress monitoring documents student progress and informs instruction. The US Department of Education reports that all states are currently attempting to implement RTI policy at the state level (Westat & Abt, 2007).

Rote Accountability

Requiring students to write book reports was viewed as a means of making learning to read difficult. This agreement by the experts is a case where a particular practice, writing book reports, has long been condemned, but for which there is no evidence to demonstrate the harmful effects asserted. Although intuition or experience may suggest harmful results from continually writing reports about texts or books read, in all fairness one must also question the potential negative effects on students' achievement and attitudes toward reading when writing in response journals is expected after each reading. This is an area where research is needed to determine the conditions, nature, and frequency of reporting or responding to books so that students' reading progress and motivation are supported as well as the need for student accountability for time spent reading.

Oral Reading Practice

According to these experts, silent reading practice is to be preferred over oral reading practice where appropriate. This convergence of opinion needs to be tempered by an understanding of the developmental and differential aspects of learning to read. In the earliest stages of reading acquisition, oral reading serves as a window for teachers to scaffold and support students' reading processes. In fact, oral reading practice in shared reading experiences (Holdaway, 1979) or oral recitation lessons (Hoffman, 1987) provides excellent contexts for all children to make progress in learning to read (Reutzel, Hollingsworth, & Eldredge, 1994). Conversely, Reutzel and Hollingsworth (1993) and Eldredge, Reutzel, and Hollingsworth (1996) found that oral reading in a Round Robin or "barbershop style" lesson produced significantly lower reading gains in decoding, vocabulary, comprehension, and fluency when compared with other forms of oral reading practice in second-grade classrooms. These findings are quite easily explained by the fact that children do not read as much in Round Robin oral reading practice as they do in other oral reading instructional and practice configurations (Allington, 1983). Wilkinson, Wardrop, and Anderson (1988) reanalyzed Leinhardt, Zigmond, and Cooley's (1981) data in which silent reading practice was assumed to be the preferred mode for reading practice for all readers, including those who struggle. This reanalysis found that silent reading was not preferred over oral reading practice for students who struggle learning to read. Wilkinson and colleagues hypothesized that oral reading may be of greater value for struggling readers because it requires an overt response and places greater demands on these often-reluctant students for participation. Thus, oral reading is useful for different purposes and at different developmental stages than is silent reading. One should not conclude, however, that a single mode of reading practice (oral or silent) is preferred at all times over another, particularly given the recent evidence on the value of oral reading practice for novice and struggling readers.

Expert Opinion on Facilitating Learning to Read

Next, we focused our re-examination of Flippo's Expert Study (1998, 2001) on finding agreements that would facilitate learning to read. From this re-examination of expert opinion, we identified 10 general principles of effective instruction believed to facilitate learning to read. We connected specific instructional practices and contexts thought by the experts to facilitate learning to read to one of these 10 general principles of effective instruction (Table 21.2).

Modeling and Scaffolding Instruction

In terms of facilitating learning to read, the experts agreed that modeling how one reads, what one reads, and why one reads is a fundamental element of effective reading instruction (Bandura, 1986; Dowhower, 1987; Rasinski, 1990).

As discussed earlier, the teacher's explicit modeling of reading processes and strategy applications has a well-established positive impact on student progress, especially among those students who struggle. The reading experts also agreed

TABLE 21.2 The "Expert Study" on Practices and Contexts that Facilitate Learning to Read for Struggling Readers and Writers

General Principles to Facilitate Learning to Read	Specific Practices to Facilitate Learning to Read
Modeling and scaffolding	Model skilled, fluent reading through teacher Read Aloud. Model functional utility of reading as a tool to learn and to use information. Model specific use of skills and strategies for successful reading.
Academic time on task	Provide adequate time for reading instruction and independent practice.
Volume of reading	Provide daily allocated time for reading practice.
Student choice of reading materials	Provide opportunity for children to select personal reading materials.
Discussion and dialogue	Talk about the purposes for and variety of materials the children are reading.
Integration of the language arts	Teach together the modes of language—reading, writing, speaking and listening.
Access to a variety of reading materials	Provide a wide variety of types and levels of narrative and expository reading materials in school and classroom libraries.
Motivation	Cultivate positive student reading attitudes and expectations.
Print-rich classroom environments	Create a literacy-rich and purposeful classroom environment.
Mode of reading practice—silent reading	Prefer silent reading over oral reading where appropriate.

that providing instructional support or scaffolds was an important part of facilitating learning to read. Stone (1998) asserted that the positive effects of scaffolding reading instruction with children at risk are limited by the dynamics of the discourse between the teacher and the student. For instructional scaffolding to be effective, students must be able to share their teacher's perspectives about the purposes and goals of instruction through making appropriate inferences (Palincsar, 1998; Smagorinsky, 1998). As a consequence, the importance of instructional scaffolding with children at risk may be highly dependent upon each student's ability to make inferences to understand the teacher's goals and perspectives (Bishop, 1997; Westby, 1999). Taylor, Pearson, Clark, and Walpole (2000) reported scaffolding is not characteristic of most reading instruction. Because modeling and scaffolding are important components of effective instruction, recent studies have focused on modeling and scaffolding to teach important reading skills (Clark & Graves, 2005; Cole, 2006; McGee & Ukrainetz, 2009; Ranker, 2009).

Academic Time on Task

A second point of agreement focused on the value of time on task or academic learning time (Fisher & Berliner, 1985; Snow, Burns, & Griffin, 1998). Since academic and behavior problems are positively associated (McEvoy & Welker, 2000), it is important to identify instructional practices that impact students' time on task. Taylor et al. (2005) reported that students maintained on-task, engaged behavior 96% of the time under the direction of effective teachers, while students under the direction of less effective teachers exhibited on-task, engaged behavior 63% of the time. Previous research has also shown a relationship between students' time on task and the difficulty level of the task. On average, all students, including struggling readers, exhibit more on-task behavior when the reading task is at the instructional level than at the independent or frustrational level (Gickling & Armstrong, 1978; Treptow, Burns, & McComas, 2007). Gest and Gest (2005) demonstrated that individual tutoring for struggling readers that increased reading skills also led to significant increases in student time on task for classroom practices. Identification of instructional practices that impact students' time on task is important, as individual differences in time-on-task behaviors contribute to individual differences in academic achievement (Gest & Gest, 2005).

Volume of Reading in Appropriately Challenging Books

Experts uniformly agreed upon a third instructional principle for facilitating learning to read. This principle highlights the volume of student reading, in school and out (Anderson, Wilson, & Fielding, 1988; Allington & McGill-Franzen, 1989). Simply stated, increased reading volume results in accelerated reading progress (Allington, 2001). Teachers, parents, and administrators need to be sure adequate time is allocated on a daily basis for students to read, in and out of school, to increase the volume of reading. However, not all practice is equally effective (Stahl, 2004). Recent research (Topping, Samuels, & Paul, 2007) has emphasized that a combination of both high volume and success in reading comprehension is necessary for high achievement gains in reading. They assert, "The mere allocation of time to independent reading might have little impact upon reading achievement" (p. 262).

Encouraging Student Choice of Reading Materials

The value of encouraging student choice in selecting reading materials was yet another instructional principle around which there was broad expert consensus. Choice can be a motivating factor that increases student engagement (Allington & Johnston, 2001; Pintrich & Schunk, 2002). However, unguided choice can become a negative force. Research has shown that struggling readers, those most in need of reading practice, typically select reading material that is either very easy or difficult (Stahl, 2004; Kelley & Clausen-Grace, 2006). Controlling task difficulty to assure the optimal level of challenge and chance for success, especially among readers who struggle, may be of greater importance in accelerating the progress of struggling readers than is the opportunity to make unguided choices. Teacher guidance in helping students learn to recognize material that is of interest and at an appropriate level of difficulty will increase the quality and the quantity of reading practice for struggling readers.

Discussion and Dialogue About Reading

Experts uniformly felt that talking and interacting with teachers and peers about reading were important features of high quality reading instruction likely to facilitate learning to read. Social interactions about reading are highly important in motivating struggling readers to read more frequently (Gambrell, 1996; Gambrell & Almesi, 1996; Beck & McKeown, 2001; Worthy & Broaddus, 2001; Parr & Maguiness, 2005). Discussions about text also increased appreciation and understanding of literature and reading achievement (Lee-Daniels & Murray, 2000; Atwell, 2007; Garan & DeVoogd, 2008). The research literature on practices such as response groups, book clubs, literature study circles, and grand conversations show that students' critical thinking, self-reflection on the text, and engagement with the text are increased through dialogue and discussion.

Integrated Instruction

Integrating the language modes of reading, writing, listening, and speaking during instruction was another global instructional principle around which there was strong agreement among the reading experts in Flippo's study. Although experts have long advocated the merit of integrating the language arts during reading instruction, there is only a "small but encouraging base" of research support for this recommendation (Gavelek, Raphael, Biondo, & Wang, 2000, p. 594). Smith (1987) argued that isolating reading instruction and focusing too much on skill acquisition constitutes an "insult to intelligence." In evidence of this claim, Smith offered the failed experience of the Chicago Public School's efforts to implement mastery learning, such as that suggested by Bloom (1956). Effective reading instruction includes both the teaching of isolated skills and use of those skills in authentic texts. Taylor, Pearson, Clark, and Walpole (1999) emphasized that most teachers taught phonic skills in isolation and then supported transfer of the skills to real reading situations. Pressley et al. (2003) reported that exemplary teachers carefully balance skill instruction within the context of real reading and writing. In a study directly comparing isolated and contextual word training for young readers, Martin-Chang and Levy (2005) reported that although both groups showed transfer benefits, contextual training resulted in greater increases. For struggling readers, each of the parts (phonemic awareness, phonics, fluency) contributes to the "braided strand" of reading comprehension (Rupley, 2009). The National Reading Panel Report (NICHD, 2000) frequently cautioned that while it is important to teach the individual skills, students must also be taught to apply the skills in reading and writing tasks within and across the curriculum.

Access to a Wide Variety of Reading Materials

The experts also agreed that struggling readers and writers need access to a wide variety of reading materials. Access to reading materials is receiving renewed attention among reading researchers (Neuman, 1999; Duke, 2000; Allington, 2001). It is widely accepted that children will not and cannot learn to read if they do not have access to books in well-organized and adequately stocked classroom and school libraries (Reutzel & Fawson, 2002). For this reason, the International Reading Association (2000a) has recommended that classroom libraries have 7 books per child, and school libraries have 20 books per child.

Student Motivation

Encouraging high student motivation and engagement to facilitate learning to read was another area of convergent agreement among the experts surveyed. Teachers who cultivate positive self-perceptions, attitudes, and expectations toward reading among their students have long noted an increase in students' motivation to read and learn to read. Research has shown a direct link between students' motivation and engagement in reading, and their achievement, attitudes, and persistence (Gambrell, 1996; Gambrell & Almasi, 1996; Wigfield & Guthrie, 1997; Guthrie & Wigfield, 2000). If struggling readers are to learn to read successfully, a classroom context must be present in which students are led to believe in their own abilities to learn to read, persist when the going gets rough, and fully expect to be successful in learning to read.

Print-Rich Classroom Environments

Creating classroom environments that "call out" or invite students to use reading and writing for the purposes of learning and living was another broad area of consensus among the experts. Many authors have long advocated the importance of developing classrooms replete with literacy materials and props arranged in such a way as to be accessible, appropriate, authentic, and useful (Weinstein, 1977; Strickland & Morrow, 1989; Morrow, 1993; Reutzel & Wolfersberger, 1996). Neuman and Roskos (1990, 1992) showed that students' interaction changed from mainly imaginative play to literacy-centered play when literacy props were inserted into kindergarten classroom environments. Thus, the mere presence or absence of literacy props in the classroom environment influenced students' dialogue, activities, play, and interactions differently than when literacy props were absent. Situated cognition theory emphasizes the role that place or context plays in shaping what and how something is learned (Kirschner & Whitson, 1997). As Spivak (1973) indicated some time ago, a setting in which the physical environment fails to support the activities and needs of students' may very well result in "setting deprivation." It is clear from this literature that all children, but especially struggling readers, cannot be expected to accelerate their progress in classroom environments where they do not engage with literacy tools in rich and authentic situations for learning.

Silent Reading Practice

Expert opinion converged on the value of silent reading practice, which was the preferred form of practice where appropriate. The amount of time spent engaged in independent, silent reading practice has long been a strong correlate of reading achievement (Anderson et al., 1988). However, less is known about the causal effects of daily independent silent reading practice on students' reading achievement. Although expert opinion converged on the value of silent reading practice, the report of the National Reading Panel (NICHD, 2000) questioned the value of time spent in independent silent reading in the early years of literacy instruction insofar as this practice directly impacts students' reading achievement. It instead recommends that younger students receive guided oral reading practice, since there is sufficient scientific research to support guided oral reading practice in the early years over independent silent reading practice. More recently, scholars have roundly criticized the unstructured, unaccountable conditions of practice often associated with independent silent reading (Stahl, 2004; Kelley & Clausen-Grace, 2006; Reutzel, Jones, Fawson, & Smith, 2008).

Instructional Recommendations: Comparing "Expert Opinion" and Other Reading Research Reports

Within the past several years, several major influential reading research reports have been released. We selected three research reports to form a comparative context for further analysis of the Expert Study findings (Flippo, 1998, 2001): (1) *Report of the National Reading Panel: Teaching Children to Read* (NICHD, 2000); (2) *Developing Literacy in Second-Language Learners: Report of the National Literacy Panel on Language-Minority Children and Youth* (August & Shanahan, 2006); and (3) *Developing Early Literacy: Report of the National Early Literacy Panel* (NELP, 2008). The best practices recommended for providing effective reading instruction found in these reports are based upon scientific research studies, determined to be of sufficient quantity and quality in design and scope to offer clear, replicable, and reliable results. The instructional recommendations found in each of the reading research reports are summarized in Table 21.3.

Where the Expert Study and Other Reading Research Converged

A comparison of expert opinion and other reading research reports (NICHD, 2000; August & Shanahan, 2006; NELP, 2008) revealed a substantial consensus about those practices and contexts likely to facilitate learning to read. Reading research reports and expert opinion agreed on the value of effective instruction through explicit modeling, guided practice, and progress monitoring. Teacher scaffolding of reading skills, thinking processes, and reading dispositions were uniformly recognized as critical in helping children learn to read—especially those students who struggle.

Expert opinion and national reading research reports also agreed that developing students' oral language concepts would facilitate learning to read. The use of discussion to elaborate understandings, analyze text, express feelings and emotions, and seek necessary clarification was viewed as a way to increase proficiency in oral language, receptive and expressive vocabulary, and background knowledge. The basic components and sequencing of reading instruction aligned across the reports. Expert opinion and national reading research reports agreed that while decoding and word recognition skills are important precursor skills, the ultimate goal of reading instruction must focus on comprehension of text. The Expert Study and the reading research report recommendations converged on the importance of teaching children to write as well as to read.

Expert opinion and the instructional recommendations of the selected national reading research reports also agreed on the need for students to read widely and in large amounts. Print-rich classrooms and availability of texts was a point of "common ground." Students cannot learn to read well without access to a wide variety of reading materials, both narrative and expository (Duke,

2000). Struggling readers are particularly dependent upon access to reading materials because they need to read a larger than average volume of varying types, high interest, and appropriately challenging reading materials to accelerate their progress (Greenleaf et al., 2001; Parr & Maguiness, 2005; Trudel, 2007; Reutzel et al., 2008).

Finally, expert opinion and the instructional recommendations of the national reading research reports also converged on the value of parents and educators cultivating students' positive motivation and high engagement in reading. Students who have skills in reading are unlikely to use these skills if they have not become intrinsically motivated to read. Learning the skills of reading is highly dependent upon each student's level of motivation. Without expectations for success, substantial individual effort, and persistence, many students will not learn to read successfully. Fostering motivation and engagement in literacy tasks are needed to facilitate learning to read.

Where Expert Opinion and Other Reading Research Diverged

Our comparison of expert opinion (Flippo, 1998, 2001) to the three selected reading research reports (NICHD, 2000; August & Shanahan, 2006; NELP, 2008) also revealed areas of divergence about those practices and contexts likely to facilitate learning to read. The experts placed considerable value upon two practices that were not emphasized as instructional recommendations of the national reading research reports: increasing silent reading practice over oral reading practice, and utilizing classroom environments that invite students to experience the authentic uses of reading in their lives.

On the other hand, the reading research reports identified specific instructional elements crucial for facilitating learning to read, including the teaching of oral language, phonemic awareness, concepts of print, alphabet knowledge, systematic and explicit phonics, sight words, fluency, vocabulary, and comprehension strategies. The reports emphasized the value of early assessment to identify at-risk students, and targeted skill-based intervention for at-risk students. The reading research reports also addressed necessary accommodations, adaptations, and resources to accelerate the progress of struggling readers. Additionally, the use of flexible and dynamic grouping strategies and the value of progress monitoring to inform instructional decisions were added to the instructional practices and contexts recommended by the experts to facilitate learning to read.

Instructional Recommendations of the Expert Study and Other Reading Research for Accelerating Struggling Readers' Progress

Struggling readers have a right to receive intensive instruction provided by reading specialists and teachers with expertise in methods proven to develop the necessary reading skills and understandings (IRA, 2000b). Educational decisions and practice

TABLE 21.3 National Reading Research Reports Recommended Instructional Practices

I. Report of the National Reading Panel: Teaching Children to Read

Key Findings about Best Practices Recommended in the Report as "Research Validated"

- Alphabetics
  - o Letter name recognition and production
  - o Phonemic Awareness
    - PA "causes" reading achievement and spelling development
    - Continuous assessment is pivotal to children's success and teaching effectiveness
- Phonics Instruction
  - o Should focus on letter/sound correspondences
  - o Five different types of phonics instruction
    - Synthetic
    - Analytic
    - Analogy
    - Embedded
    - Phonics through spelling
  - o Cautions about phonics instruction
    - Instruction that focuses on letter/sound correspondences and not on blending is likely to be ineffective
    - Instruction is most effective when children practice and apply oral blending in decodable books
    - Adapt to meet individual needs
    - Instruction tied to assessment yields better results
- Fluency
  - o Accuracy, rate, and expression are components of fluency
  - o Fluency is critical factor that facilitates reading comprehension
  - o Acquired through guided oral repeated readings
  - o Guidance from parents, teachers, and more proficient peers has a positive impact on word recognition, fluency, and comprehension
  - o Guidance helps good and struggling readers

- o Sustained silent reading may help build fluency
- Vocabulary and Comprehension
  - o Vocabulary improves comprehension
  - o Vocabulary should be taught directly and through expansive/wide reading
  - o Teaching a combination of reading comprehension strategies is most effective
  - o Include such strategies as reciprocal teaching, graphic and semantic organizers, text structures, oral and written summarization, comprehension monitoring, cooperative learning groups, question–answer relationships (QAR)
  - o More research is needed to determine best ways of teaching comprehension

II. Developing Literacy in Second-Language Learners: Report of the National Literacy Panel on Language-Minority Children and Youth

Key Findings about Best Practices Recommended in the Report for Providing Effective Reading Instruction

- Instruction that provides substantial coverage in the key components of reading has clear benefits for language–minority students (Phonemic awareness, Phonics, Fluency, Vocabulary, Comprehension, Writing)
- Extensive oral English development must be incorporated into successful literacy instruction
  - o Literacy programs that provide instructional support of oral language development in English, aligned with high-quality literacy instruction are the most successful.
- Basic sequencing of teaching is likely to be the same for language-minority students and native English speakers
  - o Students must first acquire precursor skills
    - ▪ Decoding
    - ▪ Word recognition
  - o Greater attention to word-level skills early in the process
  - o Direct attention to reading comprehension later
  - o Vocabulary and background knowledge targeted intensively throughout
- Oral proficiency and literacy in the first language can be used to facilitate literacy development in English
  - o First-language literacy is related to literacy development in word reading, comprehension, spelling, and writing
  - o Students instructed in their native language and in English perform better than students instructed only in English
- Individual differences contribute significantly to English literacy development
  - o Reading difficulties among language-minority students may be a function of individual differences than of language-minority status

continued

TABLE 21.3 continued

- o Reading difficulties seem to be caused by phonological awareness and working memory deficits as opposed to language-minority status
- • Adequate assessments are essential for placement decisions and instruction
  - o Letter naming and phonological awareness tests in English were good predictors of performance in English reading
- • Becoming literate in a second language depends on the quality of teaching
  - o Content coverage
  - o Intensity or thoroughness of instruction
  - o Methods used to support the special language needs of second-language learners
  - o Progress monitoring
  - o Teacher preparation
- • Home language experiences can have a positive impact on literacy achievement

III. Developing Early Literacy: Report of the National Early Literacy Panel

Key Findings about Best Practices Recommended in the Report for Providing Effective Reading Instruction

- • Six Early Literacy Skills correlated with later literacy achievement and maintained medium to large predictive power after accounting for other variables (e.g., SES, IQ)
  - o Alphabet Knowledge
  - o Phonological Awareness
  - o Rapid Automatic Naming (RAN) of letters or digits
  - o RAN of objects or colors
  - o Writing Letters in isolation or Writing One's Own Name
  - o Phonological Memory
- • Five Early Literacy Skills moderately correlated with later literacy achievement but predictive power may not be maintained after accounting for other variables or predictive power has not been evaluated by research
  - o Concepts About Print
  - o Print Knowledge

- o Reading Readiness
- o Oral Language
- o Visual Processing
- Analytical Categories of Instructional Practices that Enhance Early Literacy Skills
  - o Code-Focused Interventions
    - Designed to teach skills to crack the alphabetic code
    - Usually included phonological awareness instruction
    - These produced moderate to large effects across a broad spectrum of early literacy outcomes
  - o Shared-Reading Interventions
    - Simple shared reading
    - Various forms of reader–child interactions
    - These produced moderate effects on print knowledge and oral language skills
  - o Parent and Home Programs
    - These produced moderate to large effects on oral language skills and general cognitive abilities
  - o Preschool and Kindergarten Programs
    - These produced moderate to large effects on spelling and reading readiness
  - o Language-Enhancement Interventions
    - These produced moderate to large effects on oral language skills
- Additional Findings
  - o When age-level comparisons were possible, the intervention appeared effective with both preschool and kindergarten students
  - o In general, variables such as age, SES, and race did not alter the effectiveness of the intervention
  - o Interventions that produced large and positive effects were usually conducted as one-on-one or small-group instructional activities

TABLE 21.4 Instructional Recommendations for Providing Effective Reading Instruction for all Children and for Accelerating the Progress of Struggling Readers

Effective Teaching Behaviors	• Explicitly teach, model, and think aloud for students a variety of effective reading strategies and when to apply those strategies • Scaffold instructional process to make otherwise transparent tacit reading processes visible and accessible to learners • Model the purposes, behaviors, skills, and dispositions of fluent, strategic, and engaged readers • Use dynamic, flexible grouping to meet student needs • Interactively read aloud books and other print materials to students • Discuss texts before, during, and after reading aloud • Use playful language activities that focus on the sounds and letters of spoken language as well as oral and book language for expanding students' oral language development • Use both oral and silent reading practice at appropriate levels of students' development and for appropriate purposes
Curriculum for Reading Instruction	• Teach a comprehensive reading curriculum including: Oral language skills, Letter recognition and production, Phonological awareness, Concepts of print, Phonics, Fluency and sight words, Vocabulary, Comprehension, and Writing
Practice and Volume of Reading	• Increase the amount of time spent on reading instruction and practice • Increase the volume of reading in-school and out-of-school

Supportive Contexts for Reading Instruction
- Integrate reading instruction with language arts instruction
- Create and sustain "print-rich" classroom environments
- Establish strong home-school partnerships

Assessment for Reading Instruction
- Identify at-risk readers early
- Use on-going assessment to inform instructional decisions

Additional Resources for Reading Instruction
- Provide access to a wide variety of reading materials including varying levels of challenge, genres, and topics

Motivating and Engaging Readers
- Encourage positive attitudes and motivation for learning to read
- Provide students opportunity to select their independent reading materials from among appropriately challenging and interesting texts

School Reforms and Restructuring to Improve Reading Instruction
- Intervene early and intensively with those readers identified as at-risk
- Provide intensive, individually targeted instruction of high quality
- Teach LEP children to read in their native language where possible. If not possible, focus on developing children's oral language facility in English before teaching to read
- Focus on the coherence and consistency of reading instruction and assessment across grade levels within the school
- Add necessary resources to reduce class size, offer increased teacher professional development opportunities and provide expanded supplemental reading instructional service in the early years of instruction
- Retain the services of a reading specialist to assist classroom and other special service teachers in helping struggling readers learn to read

should be based on compelling and persuasive evidence. Our re-examination of expert opinion (Flippo, 1998, 2001) and the three selected reading research reports (NICHD, 2000; August & Shanahan, 2006; NELP, 2008) utilizes the three standards of evidence (Stanovich & Stanovich, 2003) to identify an empirical, rather than a consensus, framework of "common ground" for reading instructional practices. Taken together, the Expert Study and the three reading research reports offer a more inclusive set of research-based and expert-supported recommendations for providing effective reading instruction, contexts, and practices to help struggling readers succeed. In summary, we offer a list of instructional recommendations for providing effective reading instruction for all children and for accelerating the progress of struggling readers (see Table 21.4).

The national reading research reports added substantially to the experts' opinions to produce richer and broader common ground for making instructional recommendations to guide teachers, parents, and policy-makers as each play their respective roles in education. We end by quoting the late Jeanne S. Chall and her colleagues:

> It is common today, as in the past, to look elsewhere than to educational research for an understanding of the literacy problems of low-income children and for ways of solving these problems. Currently, cultural and political theories are offered as reasons for the low achievement of poor children and for the lag between mainstream and at-risk children. Although cultural and political explanations may help us understand the broader picture, in the end they must be translated, in practical terms, into what can be done in schools and in homes. Such translation ought to consider the historical [and current] educational research—that good teaching improves achievement and thereby can empower all children and especially those at risk.
>
> *Chall, Jacobs, and Baldwin, 1990, p. xi*

The results of this comparative analysis reveal how the opinions of the reading experts in the Expert Study complement the findings and recommendations of contemporary reading research reports in search of broader common ground to help all children learn to read—especially those children who struggle!

References

Allington, R.L. (1980). Teacher interruption behaviors during primary grade oral reading. *Journal of Educational Psychology, 72*, 371–372.

Allington, R.L. (1983). The reading instruction provided readers of differing reading abilities. *Elementary School Journal, 83*, 548–559.

Allington, R.L. (2001). *What really matters for struggling readers: Designing research based programs.* New York, NY: Addison Wesley Longman.

Allington, R.L., & Johnston, P.H. (2001). What do we know about effective fourth-grade teachers and their classrooms? In C. Roller (Ed.), *Learning to teach reading: Setting the research agenda* (pp. 150–165). Newark, DE: International Reading Association.

Allington, R.L., & McGill-Franzen, A. (1989). School response to reading failure: Instruction for Chapter 1 and special education students in grades 2, 4, and 8. *Elementary School Journal, 89,* 529–542.

Al Otaiba, S., & Fuchs, D. (2002). Characteristics of children who are unresponsive to early literacy intervention. *Remedial and Special Education, 23,* 300–316.

Anderson, R.C., Wilson, P.T., & Fielding, L.G. (1988). Growth in reading and how children spend their time outside of school. *Reading Research Quarterly, 23*(3), 285–303.

Atwell, N. (2007). *The reading zone: How to help kids become skilled, passionate, habitual, critical readers.* New York, NY: Scholastic.

August, D., & Shanahan, T. (Eds.). (2006). *Developing literacy in second-language learners: A Report of the National Literacy Panel on Language-Minority Children and Youth.* Mahwah, NJ: Lawrence Erlbaum Associates, Inc.

Bandura, A. (1986). *Psychological modeling: Conflicting theories.* Chicago, IL: Aldine-Atherton.

Beck, I.L., & McKeown, M.G. (2001). Text talk: Capturing the benefits of read-aloud experiences for young children. *The Reading Teacher, 55*(1), 10–20.

Bishop, D.V.M. (1997). *Uncommon understanding: Development and disorders of language comprehension in children.* East Sussex, UK: Psychology Press.

Blair, T.R., Rupley, W.H., & Nichols, W.D. (2007). The effective teacher of reading: Considering the "what" and "how" of instruction. *The Reading Teacher, 60,* 432–439.

Bloom, B. (1956). *Taxonomy of educational objectives.* New York, NY: David McKay.

Bohn, C.M., Roehrig, A.D., & Pressley, M. (2004). The first days of school in the classrooms of two more effective and four less effective primary-grade teachers. *Elementary School Journal, 104*(4), 269–287.

Brophy, J., & Good, T. (1986). Teacher behavior and student achievement. In M. Wittrock (Ed.), *The handbook of research on teaching* (3rd ed., pp. 328–375). Riverside, NJ: Macmillan.

Carnine, D., Silbert, J., & Kameenui, E.J. (1997). *Direct instruction reading* (3rd ed.). Upper Saddle River, NJ: Merrill: Prentice Hall.

Chall, J.S., Jacobs, V.A., & Baldwin, L.E. (1990). *The reading crisis: Why poor children fall behind.* Cambridge, MA: Harvard University Press.

Chua, S.P. (2008). The effects of the sustained silent reading program on cultivating students' habits and attitudes in reading books for leisure. *Clearing House, 81*(4), 180–184.

Clark, K.F., & Graves, M.F. (2005). Scaffolding students' comprehension of text. *The Reading Teacher, 58*(6), 570–580.

Clay, M.M. (2002). *An observation survey of early literacy achievement* (2nd ed.). Portsmouth, NH: Heinemann.

Cole, A.D. (2006). Scaffolding beginning readers: Micro and macro cues teachers use during student oral reading. *The Reading Teacher, 59*(5), 450–459.

Coyne, M.D., Kame'enui, E.J., & Simmons, D.C. (2001). Prevention and intervention in beginning reading: Two complex systems. *Learning Disabilities Research & Practice, 16,* 62–73.

Coyne, M.D., Zipoli R.P. Jr, Chard, D.J., Faggella-Luby, M., Ruby, M., Santoro, L. E., & Baker, S. (2009). Direct instruction of comprehension: Instructional examples from intervention research on listening and reading comprehension. *Reading & Writing Quarterly, 25*(2), 221–245.

Dixon-Krauss, L. (1996). *Vygotsky in the classroom: Mediated literacy instruction and assessment.* New York, NY: Longman Publishers.

Dowhower, S. (1987). Effects of repeated readings on second-grade transitional readers' fluency and comprehension. *Reading Research Quarterly, 22*, 389–406.

Duffy, G.G., Roehler, L.R., Sivan, E., Radcliffe, G., Book, C., Meloth, M.S., et al. (1987). Effect of explaining the reasoning associated with using reading strategies. *Reading Research Quarterly, 22*, 347–368.

Duffy, G.G., Roehler, L.R., & Herrmann, B.A. (1988). Modeling mental processes helps poor readers become strategic readers. *The Reading Teacher, 41*(8), 762–767.

Duke, N. (2000). 3.6 minutes per day: The scarcity of informational texts in first grade. *Reading Research Quarterly, 35*(2), 202–224.

Ehri, L.C., Satlow, E., & Gaskins, I. (2009). Grapho-phonemic enrichment strengthens keyword analogy instruction for struggling young readers. *Reading & Writing Quarterly, 25*(2), 162–191.

Eldredge, J.L., Reutzel, D.R., & Hollingsworth, P.M. (1996). Comparing the effectiveness of two oral reading practices: Round-Robin reading and the shared book experience. *Journal of Literacy Research, 28*(2), 201–225.

Fisher, C.W., & Berliner, D.C. (1985). *Perspectives on instructional time.* New York, NY: Longman.

Flippo, R.F. (1998). Points of agreement: A display of professional unity in our field. *The Reading Teacher, 52*, 30–40.

Flippo, R.F. (2001). *Reading researchers in search of common ground.* Newark, DE: International Reading Association.

Forness, S.R. (2001). Special education and related services: What have we learned from meta-analysis? *Exceptionality, 9*, 185–197.

Fosnot, C.T. (1996). *Constructivism: Theory, perspectives and practice.* New York, NY: Teacher's College Press.

Gambrell, L. (1996). Creating classrooms that foster reading motivation. *The Reading Teacher, 50*(1), 14–25.

Gambrell, L.B., & Almasi, J.F. (1996). *Lively discussions: Fostering engaged reading.* Newark, DE: International Reading Association.

Garan, E.M., & DeVoogd, G. (2008). The benefits of Sustained Silent Reading: Scientific research and common sense converge. *The Reading Teacher 62*(4), 336–344.

Gavelek, J.R., Raphael, T.E., Biondo, S.M., & Wang, D. (2000). Integrated literacy instruction. In M.L. Kamil, P.B. Mosenthal, P.D. Pearson, & R. Barr (Eds.), *Handbook of reading research* (Vol. 3, pp. 587–608). Mahwah, NJ: Lawrence Erlbaum Associates.

Gest, S.D., & Gest, J.M. (2005). Reading tutoring for students at academic and behavioral risk: Effects on time-on-task in the classroom. *Education & Treatment of Children, 28*(1), 25–47.

Gickling, E.E., & Armstrong, D.L. (1978). Levels of instructional difficulty as related to on-task behavior, task completion, and comprehension. *Journal of Learning Disabilities, 11*, 32–39.

Greenleaf, C.L., Schoenbach, R., Cziko, C., & Mueller, F.L. (2001). Apprenticing adolescent readers to academic literacy. *Harvard Educational Review, 71*, 79–127.

Guthrie, J. (1977). Follow through: A compensatory education experiment. *The Reading Teacher, 31*(2), 240–244.

Guthrie, J.T., & Wigfield, A. (2000). Engagement and motivation in reading. In M.L. Kamil, P.B. Mosenthal, P.D. Pearson, & R. Barr (Eds.), *Handbook of reading research* (Vol. 3, pp. 403–424). Mahwah, NJ: Lawrence Erlbaum Associates.

Guthrie, J.T., Laurel, A., Hoa, W., Wigfield, A., Tonks, S.M., Humenick, N.M., et al. (2007). Reading motivation and reading comprehension growth in the later elementary years. *Contemporary Educational Psychology, 32,* 282–313.

Hoffman, J.V. (1987). Rethinking the role of oral reading in basal instruction. *Elementary School Journal, 87*(3), 367–374.

Holdaway, D. (1979). *The foundations of literacy.* Exeter, NH: Heinemann.

IRA (2000a). *Providing books and other print materials for classroom and school libraries: A position statement.* Newark, DE: International Reading Association.

IRA (2000b). *Making it different, honoring children's rights to excellent reading instruction: A position statement.* Newark, DE: International Reading Association.

Johnson, J.P., Livingston, M., Schwartz, R.A., & Slate, J.R. (2000). What makes a good elementary school? A critical examination. *Journal of Educational Research, 93,* 339–345.

Juel, C. (1988). Learning to read and write: A longitudinal study of 54 children from first through fourth grades. *Journal of Educational Psychology, 80,* 437–447.

Juel, C. (1994). *Learning to read and write in one elementary school.* New York, NY: Springer-Verlag.

Kelley, M., & Clausen-Grace, N. (2006). R5: The Sustained Silent Reading makeover that transformed readers. *The Reading Teacher, 60* (2), 148–156.

Kirschner, D., & Whitson, J.A. (1997). *Situated cognition: Social, semiotic, and psychological perspectives.* Mahwah, NJ: Lawrence Erlbaum Associates.

Lee-Daniels, S.L., & Murray, B.A. (2000). DEAR me: What does it take to get children reading? *The Reading Teacher, 54,* 154–159.

Leinhardt, G., Zigmond, N., & Cooley, W. (1981). Reading instruction and its effects. *American Educational Research Journal, 18,* 343–361.

Levine, S. (1984). USSR: A necessary component in teaching reading. *Journal of Reading, 28,* 394–400.

Linnenbrink, E.A., & Pintrich, P.R. (2003). The role of self-efficacy beliefs in student engagement and learning in the classroom. *Reading & Writing Quarterly: Overcoming Learning Difficulties, 19,* 119–137.

Lutz, S.L., Guthrie, J.T., & Davis, M.H. (2006). Scaffolding for engagement in elementary school reading instruction. *Journal of Educational Research, 100*(1), 3–20.

Marcon, R.A. (1992). Differential effects of three preschool models on inner-city 4-year-olds. *Early Childhood Research Quarterly, 7,* 517–530.

Marcon, R.A. (1995). Fourth-grade slump: The cause and cure. *Principal, 74,* 16–20.

Martin-Chang, S.L., & Levy, B.A. (2005). Fluency transfer: Differential gains in reading speed and accuracy following isolated word and Context training. *Reading and Writing: An Interdisciplinary Journal, 18*(4), 343–376.

Margolis, H., & McCabe, P.P. (2006). Improving self-efficacy and motivation: What to do, what to say. *Intervention in School & Clinic, 41*(4), 218–227.

McEvoy, A., & Welker, R. (2000). Antisocial behavior, academic failure, and school climate: A critical review. *Journal of Emotional and Behavioral Disorders, 8,* 130–140.

McGee, L.M., & Ukrainetz, T.A. (2009). Using scaffolding to teach phonemic awareness in preschool and kindergarten. *The Reading Teacher, 62*(7), 599–603.

McMaster, K., Fuchs, D., Fuchs, L.S., & Compton, D.L. (2005). Responding to non-responders: An experimental field trial of identification and intervention methods. *Exceptional Children, 71,* 445–463.

Morgan, P.L., Fuchs, D., Compton, D.L., Cordray, D.S., & Fuchs, L.S. (2008). Does early reading failure decrease children's reading motivation? *Journal of Learning Disabilities, 41*(5), 387–404.

Morrow, L.M. (1993). *Literacy development in the early years: Helping children read and write* (2nd ed.). Englewood Cliffs, NJ: Prentice Hall.

NASBE (2006). *Reading at risk: The state response to the crisis in adolescent literacy.* Alexandria, VA: National Association of State Boards of Education.

National Commission on Excellence in Education (1983). *A nation at risk: The imperatives for educational reform.* Washington, DC: US Department of Education.

National Early Literacy Panel (2008). *Developing Early Literacy: Report of the National Early Literacy Panel.* Jessup, MD: National Institute for Literacy.

National Institute of Child Health and Human Development (NICHD). (2000). Report of the National Reading Panel. *Teaching children to read: An evidence-based assessment of the scientific research literature on reading and its implications for reading instruction: Reports of the subgroups* (NIH Publication No. 00–4754). Washington, DC: US Government Printing Office.

Nelson, S.R., Leffler, J.C., & Hansen, B.A. (2009). *Toward a research agenda for Understanding and improving the use of research evidence.* Portland, OR: Northwest Regional Educational Laboratory.

Neuman, S.B. (1999). Books make a difference: A study of access to literacy. *Reading Research Quarterly, 34*(3), 286–311.

Neuman, S.B., & Roskos, K. (1990). Play, print, and purpose: Enriching play environments for literacy development. *The Reading Teacher, 44*(3), 214–221.

Neuman, S.B., & Roskos, K. (1992). Literacy objects as cultural tools: Effects on children's literacy behaviors in play. *Reading Research Quarterly, 27*(3), 203–225.

No Child Left Behind Act of 2001 (2002). Public Law No. 107–110, paragraph 115 Stat. 1425.

Oakes, J. (1992). Can tracking research inform practice? *Educational Researcher, 21*(4), 12–21.

Opitz, M. (1998). *Flexible grouping in reading: Practical ways to help all students become better readers.* New York, NY: Scholastic.

Palincsar, A.S. (1998). Keeping the metaphor of scaffolding fresh—A response to C. Addison Stone's "The metaphor of scaffolding: It's utility for the field of learning disabilities." *Journal of Learning Disabilities, 31*, 370–373.

Parr, J.M., & Maguiness, C. (2005). Removing the silent from SSR: Voluntary reading as social practice. *Journal of Adolescent and Adult Literacy, 49*(2), 96–107.

Pintrich, P.R., & Schunk, D.H. (2002). *Motivation in education: Theory, research and applications* (2nd ed.). Englewood Cliffs, NJ: Prentice Hall Merrill.

Pollard-Durodola, S.D., & Simmons, D.C. (2009). The role of explicit instruction and instructional design in promoting phonemic awareness development and transfer from Spanish to English. *Reading & Writing Quarterly, 25*(2), 139–161.

Poole, D. (2008). Interactional differentiation in the mixed-ability group: A situated view of two struggling readers. *Reading Research Quarterly, 43*(3), 228–250.

Pressley, M. (2002). *Reading instruction that works: The case for balanced teaching* (2nd ed.). NY: Guilford.

Pressley, M., Dolezal, S.E., Raphael, L.M., Mohan, L., Roehrig, A.D., & Bogner, K. (2003). *Motivating primary-grade students.* New York, NY: Guilford.

Ranker, J. (2009). Learning nonfiction in an ESL class: The interaction of situated practice and teacher scaffolding in a genre study. *The Reading Teacher, 62*(7), 580–589.

Rasinski, T.V. (1990). Effects of repeated reading and listening-while-reading on reading fluency. *Journal of Educational Research, 83*, 147–150.

Rasinski, T.V., Homan, S., & Biggs, M. (2009). Teaching reading fluency to struggling readers: Method, materials, and evidence. *Reading & Writing Quarterly, 25*(2), 192–204.

Reutzel, D.R. (1999). Organizing literacy instruction: Effective grouping strategies and organizational plans. In L.M. Morrow, L.B. Gambrell, S. Neuman, & M. Pressley (Eds.), *Best practices for literacy instruction* (pp. 271–291). New York, NY: Guilford Press.

Reutzel, D.R., & Cooter, R.B. (2000). *Teaching children to read: Putting the pieces together* (3rd ed.). Columbus, OH: Merrill/Prentice Hall.

Reutzel, D.R., & Fawson, P.C. (2002). *Your classroom library: New ways to give it more teaching power.* New York, NY: Scholastic, Inc.

Reutzel, D.R., & Hollingsworth, P.M. (1993). Effects of fluency training on second graders' reading comprehension. *Journal of Educational Research, 86*(6), 325–332.

Reutzel, D.R., & Wolfersberger, M. (1996). An environmental impact statement: Designing supportive literacy classrooms for young children. *Reading Horizons, 36*(3), 266–282.

Reutzel, D.R., Hollingsworth, P.M., & Eldredge, J.L. (1994). Oral reading instruction: The impact on student reading development. *Reading Research Quarterly, 23*(1), 40–62.

Reutzel, R., Jones, C., Fawson, P., & Smith, J. (2008). Scaffolded silent reading: A complement to Guided Repeated Oral Reading that works! *The Reading Teacher, 62*(3), 196.

Rist, R.C. (1970). Student social class and teacher expectations: The self-fulfilling prophecy in ghetto education. *Harvard Educational Review, 40*, 411–451.

Rosenshine, B.V. (1979). Content, time, and direct instruction. In P.L. Peterson & H.J. Walberg (Eds.), *Research on teaching: Concepts, findings and implications* (pp. 28–56). Berkeley, CA: McCutchan.

Rosenthal, R., & Jacobson, L. (1968). *Pygmalion in the classroom.* New York, NY: Holt, Rinehart, and Winston.

Rupley, W.H. (2009). Introduction to direct/explicit instruction in reading for the struggling reader: Phonemic awareness, phonics, fluency, vocabulary, and comprehension. *Reading & Writing Quarterly, 25*(2), 119–124.

Rupley, W.H., & Blair, T. (1987). Assignment and supervision of reading seatwork: Looking in on 12 primary teachers. *The Reading Teacher, 40*(4), 391–393.

Savage, R., Stuart, M., Hill, V. (2001). The role of scaffolding errors in reading development: Evidence from a longitudinal and a correlational study. *British Journal of Educational Psychology, 71*(1), 1–13.

Schweinhart, L.J., & Weikart, D.P. (1997). The high-scope preschool curriculum comparison study through age 23. *Early Childhood Research Quarterly, 12*, 117–143.

Smagorinsky, P. (1998). Thinking and speech and protocol analysis. *Mind, Culture and Activity, 5*, 157–177.

Smith, F. (1987). *Insult to intelligence.* New York, NY: Arbor House.

Snow, C.E., Burn, M.S., & Griffin, P. (1998). *Preventing reading failure in young children.* Washington, DC: National Academy Press.

Spivak, M. (1973). Archetypal place. *Architectural Forum, 140*, 44–49.

Stahl, S.A. (2004). What do we know about fluency? Findings of the National Reading Panel. In P. McCardle & V. Chhabra (Eds.), *The voice of evidence in reading research* (pp. 187–211). Baltimore, MD: Paul H. Brookes.

Stanovich, K.E. (1986). Matthew effects in reading: Some consequences of Individual differences in the acquisition of literacy. *Reading Research Quarterly, 21*(4), 360–407.

Stanovich, K.E. (2000). *Progress in understanding reading: Scientific foundations and new frontiers.* New York, NY: Guildford Press.

Stanovich, P.J., & Stanovich, K.E. (2003). *Using research and reason in education: How teachers can use scientifically based research to make curricular decisions.* Washington, DC: National Institute for Literacy.

Strickland, D.S., & Morrow, L.M. (1989). *Emerging literacy: Young children learn to read and write.* Newark, DE: International Reading Association.

Stone, C.A. (1998). The metaphor of scaffolding: It's utility for the field of learning disabilities. *Journal of Learning Disabilities, 31*, 344–364.

Swanson, H.L., & Hoskyn, M. (1998). Experimental intervention research on students with learning disabilities: A meta-analysis of treatment outcomes. *Review of Educational Research, 68*(3), 277–321.

Task Force on Education for Economic Growth (1983). *Action for excellence: A comprehensive plan to improve our nation's schools.* Denver, CO: Education Commission of the States.

Taylor, B.M., Pearson, P.D., Clark, K., & Walpole, S. (1999). *Beating the odds in teaching all children to read: Lessons from effective schools and exemplary teachers* (Center for the Improvement of Early Reading Achievement Report No. 2–006). Ann Arbor, MI: University of Michigan School of Education.

Taylor, B.M., Pearson, P.D., Clark, K.F., & Walpole, S. (2000). Effective schools and accomplished teachers: Lessons about primary-grade reading instruction in low-income schools. *Elementary School Journal, 101*, 121–165.

Taylor, B.M., Pearson, P.D., Peterson, D.S., & Rodriguez, M.C. (2005). The CIERA school change framework: An evidence-based approach to professional development and school reading improvement. *Reading Research Quarterly, 40*, 40–69.

Topping, K.J., Samuels, J., & Paul, T. (2008). Independent reading: the relationship of challenge, non-fiction and gender to achievement. *British Educational Research Journal, 34*(4), 505–524.

Treptow, M.A., Burns, M.K., & McComas, J.J. (2007). Reading at the frustration, instructional, and independent levels: Effects on student time on task and comprehension. *School Psychology Review, 36*, 159–166.

Trudel, H. (2007). Making data-driven decisions: Silent reading. *The Reading Teacher, 61*(4), 308–315.

Weinstein, R.S. (1976). Reading group membership in first grade: Teacher behaviors and pupil experience over time. *Journal of Educational Psychology, 68*, 103–116.

Weinstein, R.S. (1977). Modifying student behavior in an open classroom through changes in the physical design. *American Educational Research Journal, 14*, 249–262.

Westat and Abt Associates (2007). *Design of the national assessment of progress under the Individuals with Disabilities Education Improvement Act.* Washington, DC: US Department of Education, Institute of Education Sciences, National Center for Education Evaluation and Regional Assistance.

Westby, C.E. (1999). Assessing and facilitating text comprehension problems. In H.W. Catts & A.G. Kamhi (Eds.), *Language and reading disabilities* (pp. 154–223). Needham Heights, MA: Allyn & Bacon.

Wigfield, A. (1997). Children's motivations for reading and reading engagement. In J.T. Guthrie & A. Wigfield (Eds.), *Reading engagement: Motivating readers through integrated instruction* (pp. 147–33). Newark, DE: International Reading Association.

Wigfield, A., & Guthrie, J.T. (1997). *Reading engagement: Motivating readers through integrated instruction*. Newark, DE: International Reading Association.

Wilkinson, I., Wardrop, J., & Anderson, R.C. (1988). Silent reading reconsidered: Reinterpreting reading instruction and its effects. *American Educational Research Journal*, *25*(1), 127–144.

Worthy, J., & Broaddus, K. (2001). Fluency beyond the primary grades: From group performance to silent, independent reading. *The Reading Teacher*, *55*, 334–343.

22

THE NEW COMMON GROUND

Pulling It All Together

Rona F. Flippo

Did we reach some "real" common ground in the original "Expert Study" and validate it once again in this second edition volume? Yes, I believe we did. Does this common ground provide all the answers to the questions that parents, teachers, and other concerned stakeholders have about reading development and instruction? No, of course it does not. Did we also show some new common ground in our reflections in this book regarding the past 10 years of literacy research? Yes, I believe we did. Will this new common ground provide answers to the concerns that parents, teachers, other stakeholders, and decision-shapers and -makers have about reading development and instruction? Maybe, but maybe not. Will the field of reading education ever have all the answers? Most likely not.

So, what is the common ground and what good is it? What purpose can it serve, and why bother discussing it? What about the reflections concerning the past 10 years of literacy research? What were the findings, and what new common ground do they point to? And finally, where do we go from here? These are the main topics of this summary chapter.

The Common Ground

The common ground may already be obvious to you. At least, it jumps out at me as I reread and reflect on the experts' points of view and the chapters by the other distinguished researchers who have contributed to this current volume. This common ground encompasses so much more than just the lists of experts' agreements displayed in Chapter 1 of this book (also see Flippo, 1998), although they are certainly a part of it. It is so much more than the discussions and research cited throughout this volume that support these experts' agreements. It is bigger than all of these combined findings, and the combined wisdom of all who have participated. And yet, even though it seems so obvious and big, this common ground can be elusive to those who do not know what to look for, or to those who are seeking simple answers.

The real common ground includes the common understandings that *reading is not simple*, and *there are no simple answers or solutions that can be applied to all children and situations*. Instead of simplistic answers, solutions, and one-way-only approaches, the common wisdom of the field continues to point to the need to allow teachers the flexibility to select the methods, approaches, and materials to fit particular children and situations. Reading development and instruction is far too complex and involves far too many variables to try to simplify and prescribe it for all children in all situations (see Flippo, 1999a).

This common wisdom is exemplified when Brian Cambourne says, "Teaching literacy is a lot more complex than I ever imagined"; when Edward Fry says, "There is not any best method of teaching reading"; and when Richard Robinson interprets and restates George Spache's assertion that, based on Spache's lifetime of research and experience in the field of reading, "No single approach to reading was clearly superior to all others." Another thread of this common understanding becomes obvious when Rand Spiro points out, "It all depends."

Yes, we do know that reading development is generally enhanced and hindered by certain contexts and practices, but we also agree that *there are always exceptions*, and the teacher and child, as they work together, are ultimately in the best position to figure out what is helpful (and when) and what is not. Because it does "all depend." The summation of all these understandings, then, is our common ground.

More Threads that Bind

Throughout this volume, reviews of research and discussions from numerous areas and avenues relevant to the experts' agreements are shared. Here are but a few of those: Kathryn Au documents a number of rich examples to show that the experts' agreements are supported by what is known about multicultural education and work with students of diverse backgrounds. Jacquelynn Malloy and Linda Gambrell thoroughly review the research on motivation, provide insights about its relationship to reading achievement, and document many of the experts' agreements that directly coincide with the research on motivation. David Yaden and Joan Tardibuono illustrate and discuss their literacy research with pre-school Latina/o children's writing development, and reveal how their findings complement those of the Expert Study.

Jay Campbell discusses the similarities between the experts' agreements and the perspective of the National Assessment of Educational Progress (NAEP), and indicates that these similarities further reinforce the notion of a common ground of agreement among most reading educators. His chapter also implies that the findings of the NAEP assessment may have been misunderstood by some policy-makers. The NAEP is intended to measure comprehension, not phonics skills: "It would be inappropriate to infer directly from the NAEP reading results that students who scored low on the assessment were necessarily deficient in phonics or phonemic awareness skills."

Timothy Rasinski strongly suggests that the findings from the Expert Study should be shared with parents. Many of the findings, he believes, could be useful to parents and community members to reinforce developing readers. Tim points out that schools of education and reading professionals must get much more involved, and provide parents and the public with the information they want and need.

Cindy Jones, D. Ray Reutzel, and John Smith compare and analyze the many areas where the research findings from the Expert Study (Flippo, 1998, 2001), National Reading Panel (NICHD, 2000), National Literacy Panel (August & Shanahan, 2006), and National Early Literacy Panel (NELP, 2008) converge, report them, and recommend them in their chapter in this volume.

And Richard Vacca (2001), in his first edition chapter of this book, suggested that the agreements that had been uncovered from the Expert Study findings were "a rallying point" that could and should be used to share our common ground publicly.

What Purpose Does All of this Serve?

What good can it do to know there is a common ground among diverse reading researchers, whose agreements on many contexts and practices for teaching reading include an acknowledgment that no answers fit all situations? And that likewise, because of this understanding, there can be no one best way to teach reading to all children?

Knowing that diverse reading researchers *really* do share this common ground could begin to influence the future decisions of policy-makers. All too often in the past two decades we have witnessed policy-makers and other concerned leaders looking for simple solutions regarding reading instruction. Such an awareness of the collaborative wisdom of the reading field, which indicates these simple solutions are neither good nor appropriate for most children's reading development (and in fact, certain agreements even point to harming and making reading more difficult for some children), could help policy-makers redirect their efforts.

If we could convince policy-makers that this search for simple solutions and "the one best method" goes against everything that we (classroom teachers, reading researchers, and other literacy education professionals) know, and against the common ground that we do share, maybe we can stop the destruction we have all been witnessing. Certainly I agree with P. David Pearson when he suggests that if the situation continues "unbridled by saner heads," the real disaster will be victory for one side or the other. David, as well as all the other experts and contributors to this volume, knows that a one-way-only approach to instruction is just not right. As I have indicated elsewhere (Flippo, 1999a), history has shown us when the pendulum swings again—and it will, if we cannot end this quest for "the best way"—there may be other winners and losers, but the saddest outcome is that the children are always among the losers when our policy-makers become so focused on "only one way."

Why is Common Ground Important?

Without an awareness of this common ground, it is far too easy for concerned citizens and politicians to jump on every bandwagon and research finding that comes forward. It is far too easy to look for simple solutions to very complex problems. It is far too easy for many to throw out the research and collaborative knowledge of decades of reading research and reinvent the wheel periodically, searching in vain for the non-existent one best approach. Missing from these misguided searches is awareness that it is the teacher, not the method, who makes the difference; see Duffy and Hoffman (1999) for their take on these "flawed searches for a perfect method."

What about the Past 10 Years Of Literacy Research?

"The Past 10 Years: In Retrospect," the follow-up study, in which all of the chapter authors in this volume have participated, has uncovered very interesting and enlightening results. Although each chapter in this volume addresses the questions posed, it is useful here to summarize the responses, synthesize them, and display them in order to discuss, search for, and find the newest common ground.

Table 22.1 is divided into four columns in order to identify both the positive and negative responses to the first question, *What are the most important things that you believe literacy research has shown over the past 10 years?* and then to categorize the responses to the second question, *How do you think this should inform the contexts and practices of reading instruction in the classroom?*

As I carefully read, examined, summarized, and analyzed these responses, I was not surprised to find how passionate each of the experts from the original study and the other participating researchers (all of them chapter authors in this volume) are about what they have been observing and seeing from the research, how truly alarmed (and even angry) many of them are, and how hopeful others are who believe they see some glimmers of research on "the right stuff." Frankly, none of this would be surprising to anyone who realizes what the last two decades have wrought for the field of reading and other literacy research. I was likewise unsurprised to discover the extent to which I found agreements in many areas, and to take note that researchers from diverse paradigms were again showing agreements—and in additional new areas as well.

TABLE 22.1 The Past 10 years: In Retrospect Response Summary Chart

Researcher	Question 1A *What are the most important things that you believe literacy research has shown over the last 10 years? (Positive)*	Question 1B *What are the most important things that you believe literacy research has shown over the last 10 years? (Negative)*	Question 2A *How do you think this should inform the contexts and practices of reading instruction in the classroom? (Responses and implications as related to the positive research reported)*	Question 2B *How do you think this should inform the contexts and practices of reading instruction in the classroom? (Responses and implications as related to the negative research reported)*
Richard Anderson	• The most important positive finding of the past decade is the persuasive evidence about the importance of stimulating classroom talk (Zhang & Anderson, 2010).	• The most important negative finding is evidence about the dumbing down of instruction because of high-stakes testing of low-level skills.	• Language-rich discussions promote language development, and lead to deeper reading, a better understanding of narrative structure, and accelerate receptive and expressive language development.	• Because high-stakes testing focuses on low-level skills, it is imperative that teachers frequently seek and find opportunities to use and provide extended meaningful communication and discussion in the classroom.
Brian Cambourne		• Despite more than 100 years of research and theory building, our field is *still riven* by theoretical squabbles (emphasis intended). • The current research and practice indicates a lack of an operational definition of what is effective literate behavior and what is effective literacy learning.		• Teacher education institutions and in-service programs should provide significant opportunities for teachers to develop their own critical awareness of how effective reading and effective learning are demonstrated in the classroom. • Classroom teachers must be able to understand and operationalize: What is effective reading? What is effective learning? And build these understandings into the contexts and practices for literacy instruction in their classrooms.

Edward Fry	• NAEP scores have changed very little over the past five decades, we know that there is no magic bullet. • There are many ways to teach reading successfully. • The teacher makes the difference, not the method.	• Focus on hiring good teachers and then allow them to teach reading using the practices that fit best in their particular contexts.
Yetta Goodman	• Research strongly supports the importance of knowledgeable and experienced teachers in children's learning literacy. • Use of integrated practices have been successful in the teaching of reading and writing. • Early literacy research has supported the constructivist nature of literacy learning. • It has become clear that research alone does not drive what goes on in classrooms. • Reading researchers have been excluded from the movement to improve test scores and establish mandated curriculum in reading. • Instead, classroom reading instruction is influenced by what communities believe (not reading researchers) and power relationships in politics and business; disregarding the conclusions of more than a century of reading research.	• Teachers should be encouraged to use integrated practices in the teaching of reading and writing. • Knowledgeable, experienced teachers who use integrated practices and contexts in their classrooms can better assist children with reading and writing development. • Young children could benefit from consideration of more constructivist practices in the classroom. • Ethnically, racially, linguistically, and culturally diverse youngsters, who are not part of the mainstream, are capable learners and what they know must be valued. • Teachers are increasingly told to apply dysfunctional reading practices to their classroom instruction. • Professional literacy organizations are reluctant to get involved by critiquing and protesting these dysfunctional practices, even though common ground (as displayed in this book) exists.

continued

TABLE 22.1 continued

Researcher	Question 1A *What are the most important things that you believe literacy research has shown over the last 10 years? (Positive)*	Question 1B *What are the most important things that you believe literacy research has shown over the last 10 years? (Negative)*	Question 2A *How do you think this should inform the contexts and practices of reading instruction in the classroom? (Responses and implications as related to the positive research reported)*	Question 2B *How do you think this should inform the contexts and practices of reading instruction in the classroom? (Responses and implications as related to the negative research reported)*
Jane Hansen	• The positive trend toward more and more on-line literacy could engage students in terms of both reading and writing, and this should call more attention to the strong connections between reading and writing (Leu, 2002; Hull & Katz, 2006). • A belief in engagement and intention is increasingly evident in the research. • Reading/writing is a unitary endeavor (literacy).	• The gap between reading and writing has actually widened in the past 10 years. Although the term "literacy" is being used more often, and a close look shows literacy in many cases is focusing mainly on reading. • Our high-stakes testing of students has led to devaluing many students, especially African American and Hispanic students. There is a significant disparity between their test scores and those of their white classmates. Plus, diverse students are often segregated into classes/groups/situations with lower achievement-level students.	• More opportunities for online reading/writing could increase students' engagement. • Teachers should be engaged, intentional, know their students as people, value their students' total selves, and search for ways to create contexts, practices, and environments in which their students can become engaged, intentional, know each other as people, and value their total selves. • Keep evaluation in the context of classrooms in which the students know they are valued; classrooms where evaluation energizes them (Fu & Lamme, 2002; Gee, 2004).	• Standardized tests beget standardized curriculum.

	• Rather than seeing the value of diverse groups of readers working together to learn from, teach to, and work with each other, much of the teaching materials script the explanations and interactions between teachers and students. • Some schools, in addition to the ever-present standardized reading program, have now adopted canned writing programs.	• Online literacy may lead to proficiency.
Jerome Harste	The critical literacy curriculum described by Lewison, Lealand, & Harste (2008) suggests four dimensions of social practice that are important tools for use in planning curricular engagements: • Disrupting the commonplace; • Interrogating multiple viewpoints;	• The range of experiential, cultural, and linguistic resources that students bring into the classroom should be the center of the curriculum that can touch their lives and meet their needs. The methods used in the critical classroom are negotiated between what the kids want to learn and the teachers' goals

continued

TABLE 22.1 continued

Researcher	Question 1A *What are the most important things that you believe literacy research has shown over the last 10 years? (Positive)*	Question 1B *What are the most important things that you believe literacy research has shown over the last 10 years? (Negative)*	Question 2A *How do you think this should inform the contexts and practices of reading instruction in the classroom? (Responses and implications as related to the positive research reported)*	Question 2B *How do you think this should inform the contexts and practices of reading instruction in the classroom? (Responses and implications as related to the negative research reported)*
Jerome Harste *(continued)*	• Focusing on sociopolitical issues; and • Taking action and promoting social justice (p. 7). "Critical literacy begins with awareness, ends in social action, and, in between, supports us envisioning a different world" (Lewison et al., 2008, p. 127).		• Teachers should construct curriculum around the big ideas that matter to children. • Teachers are encouraged to be reflective and intentional—seeking to reflect on their own work and world, and guiding children to do the same. • The lessons must address students' learning needs, but also allow students to act independently and make their own choices. • Using strategy lessons, learners explore how language operates.	

- The teacher selects different strategy lessons across the year, focusing in each instance on the strategies used by successful readers.
- Teachers can encourage student investigations, taking a "problem-posing" rather than a "problem-solving" stance to curriculum.
- Practices that involve engagement in grand conversations, the sharing and exploring of meaning, and opportunities to critique what we read and write, develops students' social responsibility and awareness.

- Teachers need to be skilled and avid readers.
- Students need to want to learn to read.
- When needed, teachers should provide ample encouragement to help learners develop a will to read.

- Phonics and other ill-conceived instruction should not be forced on learners.

Wayne Otto

- Literacy research does not seem to have had much of an impact on how reading is actually being taught in actual classrooms.
- Politicians and profit-seekers have taken control of the context of school and the content of schooling (e.g., dumbing down our schools, giving students false reports of their progress, disrupting communities, and undermining public education).

continued

TABLE 22.1 continued

Researcher	Question 1A *What are the most important things that you believe literacy research has shown over the last 10 years? (Positive)*	Question 1B *What are the most important things that you believe literacy research has shown over the last 10 years? (Negative)*	Question 2A *How do you think this should inform the contexts and practices of reading instruction in the classroom? (Responses and implications as related to the positive research reported)*	Question 2B *How do you think this should inform the contexts and practices of reading instruction in the classroom? (Responses and implications as related to the negative research reported)*
Scott Paris	• The *Cambridge Primary Review* (2009) makes it clear that teachers, not policy-makers, need to be in control of instruction. • The Review provides a circumspect view of the key issues; it depolarizes the arguments; and it refocuses attention on the needs and rights of children.	• A pattern of increased national and international testing has become obvious. These tests have revealed negative findings. The *Cambridge Primary Review* (2009) suggests that this means of government control of literacy education was implemented by stealth in the 1990s.	• The *Cambridge Primary Review* (2009) empowers local schools and teachers to design pedagogies and curricula that serve the students in their communities. • The Review warns of the dangers of mandated pedagogy that unduly narrows the curriculum, and it describes how literacy teaching must be embedded in broader contexts of children's educational needs.	• Although national policy-makers have the authority to design and prescribe national curricula and assessments, they must be cautious in order to accommodate the needs of diverse students and the talents of individual teachers.

- Instead of policy prescriptions, this Review admonishes policy-makers to pay attention to the research, to the local community contexts, to a broader curricular agenda, and to the development of teacher competence required to meet the needs of an increasingly diverse population of students.

- Literacy Learning Progressions (2009) provides detailed benchmarks for what students should be able to do with reading and writing in the curriculum at the end of each year of primary education.

- Literacy Learning Progressions (2009) is intended to be a tool for professional development so teachers can share similar expectations and aspirations for their students. It is not a pedagogical recipe; it is an effort to establish common ground among teachers for what students should be able to do within the curriculum.

continued

TABLE 22.1 continued

Researcher	Question 1A *What are the most important things that you believe literacy research has shown over the last 10 years? (Positive)*	Question 1B *What are the most important things that you believe literacy research has shown over the last 10 years? (Negative)*	Question 2A *How do you think this should inform the contexts and practices of reading instruction in the classroom? (Responses and implications as related to the positive research reported)*	Question 2B *How do you think this should inform the contexts and practices of reading instruction in the classroom? (Responses and implications as related to the negative research reported)*
P. David Pearson	• Integrated curriculum, using reading and writing and language, to support inquiry in the disciplines, promotes both disciplinary learning and literacy acquisition. • Pearson, Moje, and Greenleaf (2010) provide evidence that reading and writing (and, with a somewhat smaller evidence base, oral discourse) promote both the acquisition of knowledge and inquiry in science while also improving literacy learning.	• Strategy instruction, especially in the ways in which it has been put into practice in modern curriculum (e.g., basals and kits), stands in need of reform. • Strategy instruction may not be as effective as conventional discussions that, in one way or another, focus on knowledge acquisition (McKeown, Beck, & Blake, 2009; Wilkinson & Son, 2011).	• Learning (knowledge acquisition) should be part of the reading equation from the outset of kindergarten and first grade. Kids should always be reading content that is worth knowing, content that promotes the acquisition of knowledge, insight, human understanding, and joy. And they should be writing about things that matter, about those very understandings, insights and moments of joy.	• Basal readers (and other forms of prepackaged instruction) narrow disciplines and genres.

- Strategy instruction may breed an excessive reliance on abstract, content-free, metacognitive introspection about strategy use (Pearson & Fielding, 1991).

- It's better to think of literature (not language arts but literature) as a discipline on a par with the subject areas of schooling. Then the process parts of the language arts (reading, writing, and language) are released from the sole grasp of literature and are available for all the disciplines.

- Kids must get instant feedback demonstrating to them that strategies are useful—that pulling out just the right tool to help you over a hurdle at just the right moment makes you a smarter, more effective, and more strategic reader.

continued

TABLE 22.1 continued

Researcher	Question 1A *What are the most important things that you believe literacy research has shown over the last 10 years? (Positive)*	Question 1B *What are the most important things that you believe literacy research has shown over the last 10 years? (Negative)*	Question 2A *How do you think this should inform the contexts and practices of reading instruction in the classroom? (Responses and implications as related to the positive research reported)*	Question 2B *How do you think this should inform the contexts and practices of reading instruction in the classroom? (Responses and implications as related to the negative research reported)*
George Spache	• The emphasis on cultural diversity has reinforced the importance of considering and working with individuals from many different cultures and backgrounds.	• There is far less autonomy of the public school curriculum than there should be. • The federal and state governments have become too involved and dominant. • The use of inappropriate, government prescribed tests, procedures, and materials have resulted in inappropriate pedagogical decisions about students' reading instruction. • Teachers' choices and decisions have been ignored and/or drastically altered, fundamentally changing the heart and soul of literacy instruction.	• Classroom contexts and practices should be appropriate to individual learners, and especially to learners of diverse cultures and backgrounds. • The classroom and the teacher are the center of instruction.	• All schools and teachers should be free to develop and implement their own unique curricula assessment and instruction efforts in the classroom. • The endless pressure applied to classroom teachers to mold their literacy assessment and teaching to government mandates, publishers' contrived goals and objectives, as well as the public's unrealistic expectations for the current literacy curriculum, should not influence the contexts and practices of reading instruction. • Inappropriate use of test results in making pedagogical decisions about student learning. • Teachers' choices and decisions are ignored or drastically reduced to meet prescribed test criteria.

	• Teaching time has been shortened in favor of test preparation to meet the demands of "No Child Left Behind" legislation and state mandated testing.	• Ill-structured prepackaged prescriptions for how to read and how to teach reading are inadequate or worse.
Rand Spiro	Trends in reading and writing make Cognitive Flexibility Theory (CFT) more relevant than ever. These trends derive from the rapid spread of learning technologies and the advent of the Web as a pervasive learning environment (Lenhart et al., 2008), and include the following: • The reading paths readers take across hyperlinked, multimedia texts are increasingly personal and idiosyncratic. • As readers criss-cross the Web, reading becomes increasingly intertextual. • Reading is increasingly multimodal.	• Practiced use of new technologies can help manage the increase in cognitive load that comes with greater task complexity. • Reading comprehension instruction should attempt to inculcate the mindset and associated skills identified with CFT and principled pluralism, as well as the more specialized reconceptualization of reading to learn for synthesis of online materials (DeSchryver & Spiro, 2008; Spiro & DeSchryver, 2008). • The new technologies allow the reader to be much more in "the driver's seat," seeking multiple, worthwhile, and relevant content to suit her/his varied purposes.

continued

TABLE 22.1 continued

Researcher	Question 1A *What are the most important things that you believe literacy research has shown over the last 10 years? (Positive)*	Question 1B *What are the most important things that you believe literacy research has shown over the last 10 years? (Negative)*	Question 2A *How do you think this should inform the contexts and practices of reading instruction in the classroom? (Responses and implications as related to the positive research reported)*	Question 2B *How do you think this should inform the contexts and practices of reading instruction in the classroom? (Responses and implications as related to the negative research reported)*
Rand Spiro *(continued)*	• Everyday reading experiences are more and more decisively shaped by readers' procedural and strategic knowledge, as well as by their metacognitive and self-regulatory control. • Reading is increasingly interwoven with writing. • Reading is increasingly social and interactive. New research frameworks (Spiro, 2006; DeSchryver & Spiro, 2008; Spiro & DeSchryver, 2008) are pointing to new approaches, ones in which new kinds of reading environments have been shown to be able to support advanced		• Teachers should try to capitalize on the affordances of reading comprehension and reading to learn on the Web, as they consider comprehension development opportunities for students.	

	comprehension outcomes beyond those possible from single texts, deep learning at a rapid rate, and kinds of synthesis of diverse content.		
Kathryn Au	• A vision of classrooms where students of diverse cultural and linguistic backgrounds are successfully learning to read and write. • Whole-school change that can make this vision a reality for diverse learners a reality in more than a handful of classrooms. • A cognitive engagement framework is suggested (Taylor, Pearson, Peterson, & Rodriguez, 2003, 2005) where teachers strive to provide students with a motivating and meaningful environment for literacy and other learning—where students have ample opportunity to engage in reasoning with text.	Teachers should be supported in their own professional development, and given the time and flexibility to • Have high expectations for their students' literacy learning. • Develop constructivist approaches for teaching and learning in their classrooms with opportunities to share what they have learned with other teachers. • Take ownership of literacy improvement efforts by involving them in creating all elements of their classroom programs, including benchmarks, literacy assessments, and instruction. • Provide, at all grades, ample instruction on reading comprehension and reasoning with text. • Focus instruction on comprehension.	• Pressure to increase scores, especially in low-income areas, leads to reliance on packaged programs.

continued

TABLE 22.1 continued

Researcher	Question 1A *What are the most important things that you believe literacy research has shown over the last 10 years? (Positive)*	Question 1B *What are the most important things that you believe literacy research has shown over the last 10 years? (Negative)*	Question 2A *How do you think this should inform the contexts and practices of reading instruction in the classroom? (Responses and implications as related to the positive research reported)*	Question 2B *How do you think this should inform the contexts and practices of reading instruction in the classroom? (Responses and implications as related to the negative research reported)*
Jacquelynn Malloy Linda B. Gambrell	• We know a great deal about the construct of motivation and how to create classroom contexts that support and nurture reading motivation. • Although an extensive theory and research base with respect to *achievement motivation* has developed, the theory and research on *reading motivation* is still developing, but continues to progress. • There is movement toward developing a better understanding of the situational elements that contribute to reading motivation (Malloy & Gambrell, 2008).		• Incorporating community-centered learning activities of relevant content for authentic purposes shows promise for developing classrooms where reading growth and motivation can flourish. • Research supports classroom environments that are book-rich and provide opportunities for self-selection (Edmunds & Bauserman, 2006), as well as the time to read and allow students to talk about books.	

| David Yaden Joan Tardibuono | • Repeated confirmation of earlier research (Teale & Sulzby, 1986; Yaden & Templeton, 1986) that engagement in early writing, emergent reading, and multiple experiences with printed materials during the preschool years is predictive of acquiring conventional reading and spelling ability early in elementary school.

• Findings from the National Early Literacy Panel (NELP, 2008) identified several early literacy behaviors, which were consistent predictors of learning how to read and spell, including name writing, invented spelling, knowledge of print conventions, concepts of word, and oral language proficiency. | • Expressions of literacy growth will reflect many influences at various times in different degrees in response to particular topics or circumstances that instruction introduces. Influences can include parents, caregivers, and immediate family, as well as neighbors, teachers, and social status (Bronfenbrenner, 2005).

• Young children begin to form notions and understandings about the symbols of written language as they encounter them, and show these understandings in talk, written expressions, or art. These may look nothing like what adults consider to be literacy. Teachers must be flexible in evaluating these unconventional literacy expressions, and insightful as to their possible origins given the environment in which the child is developing. |

continued

TABLE 22.1 continued

Researcher	Question 1A *What are the most important things that you believe literacy research has shown over the last 10 years? (Positive)*	Question 1B *What are the most important things that you believe literacy research has shown over the last 10 years? (Negative)*	Question 2A *How do you think this should inform the contexts and practices of reading instruction in the classroom? (Responses and implications as related to the positive research reported)*	Question 2B *How do you think this should inform the contexts and practices of reading instruction in the classroom? (Responses and implications as related to the negative research reported)*
David Yaden Joan Tardibuono *(continued)*	• The finding that *no one skill alone enhances early literacy ability, but instead it is a broad set of experiences in which children are given regular opportunities to explore and experiment with written language, across multiple contexts.* • The findings of Rowe and Nietzel (2010) that children's "personal interest orientations were related to ways they participated in emergent writing activities" highlight the importance of		• Conventional literacy is predicted by a wide range of experiences a child has, not just direct instruction in one or two skills. • Literacy instruction is shaped, transformed, and given meaning by personality itself. Thus, the content of any literacy instruction should be broadly focused, rather than narrow, and it should seek to tap into some familiar experience of the learner such that what is to be learned benefits from the strength of personal motivation (Rowe & Nietzel, 2010).	

personality development for both engagement in early literacy behavior and the types of engagements preferred.

- Studies by Rowe and Nietzel (2010) and others, have challenged the traditional field of early literacy to become less parochial and exhibit more interdisciplinary by studying literacy growth within the broader field of early childhood development; and identifying key precursors of literacy instead of looking only at reading and writing behavior just prior to kindergarten, when important developmental milestones have already passed.

continued

TABLE 22.1 continued

Researcher	Question 1A *What are the most important things that you believe literacy research has shown over the last 10 years? (Positive)*	Question 1B *What are the most important things that you believe literacy research has shown over the last 10 years? (Negative)*	Question 2A *How do you think this should inform the contexts and practices of reading instruction in the classroom? (Responses and implications as related to the positive research reported)*	Question 2B *How do you think this should inform the contexts and practices of reading instruction in the classroom? (Responses and implications as related to the negative research reported)*
Timothy Rasinski	Literacy research has provided two important insights into parental involvement: • First, research continues to confirm the importance of parental involvement in their children's literacy development. • Second, research has shown that reading fluency is critical to children's literacy development (Rasinski & Stevenson, 2005).		• Schools, school administrators, and teachers must make a concerted long-term commitment to developing and implementing systemic parental involvement programs for the literacy education of their children. • Parents and families must be involved as integral parts of the critical elements of reading instruction.	

| Nancy Padak Timothy Rasinski | • The report of the NRP (2000) called needed attention to fluency and vocabulary as critical aspects of effective reading.
• There has been an increasing number of meta-analyses providing practical guidance for teachers and curriculum leaders. Because few professionals have the time to read and synthesize all the literacy research our field produces, researchers who apply scientific principles to synthesize research results provide guidelines that can be applied to practice. | • Nothing in teaching children to read is "teacher-proof" or easy, even though some publishers and test-makers assert to the contrary. | • Classroom teachers have been alerted that fluency and vocabulary should be considered in their classroom instruction.
• Schools and districts can find much to guide their literacy improvement plans in recent research and meta-analyses. These include:
　○ The power of instructional activities that focus on similarities and differences.
　○ Instructional activities along with parents' reading aloud is more powerful than simply parental read-alouds.
　○ Contexts and practices that can really help struggling readers such as time to read, access to books, focus on fluency, focus on comprehension should be encouraged.
• Classroom teachers should have opportunities to have meta-analyses of pertinent research accessible to them so that they can be aware of the findings and make use of them, if appropriate, within their classrooms. | • Teachers should be cautioned that the suggested "easy-fixes" and/or teaching directly from the teachers' guides will not necessarily work or be beneficial for all students. |

continued

TABLE 22.1 continued

Researcher	Question 1A *What are the most important things that you believe literacy research has shown over the last 10 years? (Positive)*	Question 1B *What are the most important things that you believe literacy research has shown over the last 10 years? (Negative)*	Question 2A *How do you think this should inform the contexts and practices of reading instruction in the classroom? (Responses and implications as related to the positive research reported)*	Question 2B *How do you think this should inform the contexts and practices of reading instruction in the classroom? (Responses and implications as related to the negative research reported)*
Maryann Mraz Richard Vacca	• State and national literacy organizations have called for more substantive inclusion of professional educators in the policy-making process. Literacy professionals can contribute their voices to these efforts.	• The educational challenges of our time are broader than teacher accountability and test scores. The solutions must be broader as well. • Holding teachers accountable and "raising test scores" must be balanced by policy discussions and more appropriate policy decisions.	• Professional associations should use every opportunity to encourage their members and use their resources to share relevant research and information that contributes to the knowledge base for literacy development in the classroom. • Professional teachers should seize opportunities to use contexts and practices that enhance literacy learning in their classrooms, and share their successes with influential policy-makers.	• The voices of literacy professionals must be part of the policy conversations and the policy decisions that drive instructional practices in our schools. • No one is more directly affected by educational policy decisions than students in classrooms and the teachers who teach them.

| Jay Campbell | • In 2009, a new NAEP reading assessment was administered that had been developed based on a new framework. The NAEP reading assessment frameworks are developed through a national consensus process, and represent widely held understandings about the nature of reading and how it should be assessed.
• The new framework calls for an expansion of the types of texts to be represented on the assessment, and more clearly delineates those types at each grade.
• The new framework places more emphasis on the cognition of reading, describing three types of cognitive targets to be assessed. | • Results of the 2009 NAEP, for fourth grade, indicated that, for the first time in the three assessment cycles since 2005, there was no significant gain in reading achievement.
• The lack of progress since 2007 among fourth graders was pretty much across the board, spanning the five reported racial/ethnic groups and the performance distribution (National Center for Education Statistics, 2009). | • More opportunities to read from and discuss varied genres may need to be included in classroom reading and instruction.
• More emphasis may need to be placed on the cognition of reading and "meaning vocabulary" in classroom practice and instruction.
• More opportunities given to students to actually read more in school, and read more books of their own choosing in the classroom could produce higher reading achievement.
• More opportunities and encouragement to read for fun in and out of school could produce higher reading achievement. |

continued

TABLE 22.1 continued

Researcher	Question 1A *What are the most important things that you believe literacy research has shown over the last 10 years? (Positive)*	Question 1B *What are the most important things that you believe literacy research has shown over the last 10 years? (Negative)*	Question 2A *How do you think this should inform the contexts and practices of reading instruction in the classroom? (Responses and implications as related to the positive research reported)*	Question 2B *How do you think this should inform the contexts and practices of reading instruction in the classroom? (Responses and implications as related to the negative research reported)*
Jay Campbell *(continued)*	• The new framework calls for a more focused measurement of vocabulary, defining the construct as "meaning vocabulary," in order to emphasize the relationship between word meaning and text comprehension. • Use of authentic stimulus reading materials continues to be a requirement of the 2009 NAEP. • Self-reported data indicate that students who read more each day had higher achievement on the 2009 NAEP. • Self-reported data indicate that students who were allowed more classroom time reading books of			

their own choosing demonstrated higher achievement on the 2009 NAEP.

- Self-reported data also indicate that students who spend more time reading for fun demonstrated higher achievement on the 2009 NAEP.

Jack Cassidy
Corinne Valadez

- Comprehension is again seen as crucial for reading success.
- Vocabulary is now considered important to reading success.
- Publishers and staff developers are now including more of a focus on comprehension and vocabulary.
- Policy-makers have begun to direct more attention toward struggling/striving readers in Grades 4 and beyond. Although early intervention is still receiving positive attention, funding is now also directed to the needs of older students as well.

- Comprehension and vocabulary development should become more of a focus of instruction in our classrooms.
- Older readers, Grades 4 and up, and struggling readers of all ages, should receive more instructional attention and support, with more appropriate materials.

continued

TABLE 22.1 continued

Researcher	Question 1A *What are the most important things that you believe literacy research has shown over the last 10 years? (Positive)*	Question 1B *What are the most important things that you believe literacy research has shown over the last 10 years? (Negative)*	Question 2A *How do you think this should inform the contexts and practices of reading instruction in the classroom? (Responses and implications as related to the positive research reported)*	Question 2B *How do you think this should inform the contexts and practices of reading instruction in the classroom? (Responses and implications as related to the negative research reported)*
Cindy Jones D. Ray Reutzel John Smith	• There has been a concerted effort to establish and validate "common ground" through evidence-based practices in addition to expert opinion. • Reports offered by the National Reading Panel (2000), the National Literacy Panel on Language-Minority Children and Youth (August & Shanahan, 2006), and the National Early Literacy Panel (NELP, 2008) present compelling and persuasive evidence for making educational decisions.		• Reading instruction should be built on converging standards of evidence from research-based and expert-supported recommendations. • Figure 21.4 (in this volume) presents a list of instructional recommendations for providing effective reading instruction for children, and for accelerating the progress of struggling readers. These include: increasing the volume of reading in school and out of school; establishing strong home–school partnerships; and providing students with	

- A comparative analysis of these (above) reports and the "Expert Study" findings revealed a substantial consensus about those practices and contexts likely to facilitate learning to read.

- Taken together, the Expert Study (Flippo,1998, 2001) and the three reading research reports (August & Shanahan, 2006; National Reading Panel, 2000; & NELP, 2008) offer a more inclusive set of research-based and expert-supported recommendations for providing effective reading instruction for all children, and for accelerating the progress of struggling readers. In doing so, the science of education is moving incrementally forward in providing effective reading instruction, contexts, and practices to help increasing numbers of struggling readers succeed.

opportunity to select their independent reading materials from among appropriately challenging and interesting texts.

Finding Areas of New Common Ground

Before indicating and describing the areas of new common ground, it is important that readers understand that these new data are based on only one round,
with two open-ended questions, and without any opportunities for each of the
participating researchers involved to review and respond further. Therefore,
unlike the original Expert Study (as described in Chapter 1 of this volume)
where I used a Delphi technique (Linstone & Turoff, 1975) and completed four
full rounds of reviews with multiple opportunities for each of the expert
researcher/participants to provide feedback, revise judgments, reflect, critique,
show agreement, show disagreement, and/or edit, these data were not filtered
and then re-filtered more and again in order to finally reach the point of the
expert informants' full agreement. Instead, rather than that, all I am offering
readers here is a compilation of the descriptive areas (of new common ground)
that were derived from the responses to the open-ended questions, and considered common ground when at least two or more of the researchers responded
with like information.

In Table 22.2 you will find each of the areas and the researchers who identified them as the "most important things that they believe research has shown over
the past 10 years (whether positive or negative)," and "how this should inform
the contexts and practices of reading instruction in the classroom." For the
purpose of this new follow-up study, *common ground* is being defined as *agreement
between a minimum of two or more independent researchers*. Clearly, out of the total
pool of 20 chapter authors/researchers, two agreements indicates less significant
common ground than, for instance, eight or nine agreements; however, because
these were responses to open-ended questions, and because the respondents are all
distinguished expert researchers in the fields of literacy and education, I believe
that even two agreements (from researchers with their diverse perspectives) are
worth noting and certainly well worth considering. I also believe that were I to
follow up with additional rounds, again using a Delphi technique, independently
requesting their agreements, I would likely find more support for each of the areas
of new common ground as revealed in Table 22.2.

Lastly, in order to work with the current large number of open-ended and
diverse responses, many of them indicating several responses to each of the
questions (as you can see in Table 22.1), it became necessary to sort the
information each of the researchers offered into various descriptive cluster areas.
Often, some of the information offered from one chapter contained multiple
aspects and fit into more than one descriptive cluster. When that was the case, I
included it under each of the clusters that it fit. For instance, when a researcher
indicated that "policy-makers were negatively interfering with schools," that
this was "affecting teachers' autonomy,"and that the "over-use of high-stakes
testing" was an example of the abuse, I included the responses under three areas
of agreement. Seventeen areas of new common ground (clusters), albeit over-

lapping, have therefore been identified by this follow-up study. These are delineated in Table 22.2, and in the sections that follow they are described based on the responses of the researchers.

While others might group them differently, the evidence (the researchers' actual responses) still serves to provide us with insight to new areas of common ground (as seen through the eyes of literacy and education experts, each icons in the field) that reflect the past 10 years of literacy research, in retrospect, and how these inform the contexts and practices of reading instruction in the classroom.

The New Common Ground Revealed

Need for Teacher Autonomy

This area showed the most indication of common ground. Researchers from nine separate chapters, and representative of diverse paradigms, indicated the critical need for teachers to be afforded the autonomy to make decisions regarding the contexts and practices of reading, and other literacy instruction in their own classrooms, without excessive outside interference. These researchers emphasized that the development of teacher autonomy begins in teacher education programs: teacher education institutions and in-service programs must help new teachers become effective educators, not only by developing awareness of how effective reading and learning should be demonstrated in the classroom, but also by teaching these educators how to identify and employ the instructional practices and assessment options that best fit their individual teaching contexts.

Additionally, researchers suggested that teachers need to be reflective and intentional at all times. They must work hard to develop an understanding of what good reading is and integrate this understanding into the classroom, but they also must be sure to regularly reflect upon and re-evaluate this understanding, as it may vary depending upon individual student needs and contexts. Ultimately, researchers agreed that teachers must be empowered and supported by school administrators, parents, community members, and policy-makers, as they work to design, develop, and implement the best curricula and assessment methods to serve their individual students.

High-stakes Testing has Negatively Affected Classroom Instruction

Many of the researchers (from seven chapters in all, a large number of respondents) have indicated that the high-stakes testing we have been experiencing has been very negative, and the results have negatively informed and affected the contexts and practices of instruction in classrooms.

TABLE 22.2 Areas of New Common Ground

Areas of New Common Ground	Researchers in Agreement
Need for teacher autonomy	Cambourne
	Fry
	Goodman
	Harste
	Paris
	Spache
	Au
	Padak & Rasinski
	Mraz & Vacca
High-stakes testing has negatively affected classroom instruction	Anderson
	Fry
	Hansen
	Paris
	Spache
	Au
	Mraz & Vacca
More time should be spent on comprehension of reading, and vocabulary development	Anderson
	Otto
	Spiro, Morsink, & Forsyth
	Au
	Padak & Rasinski
	Campbell
	Cassidy & Valadez

Knowledgeable and experienced educators are essential	Cambourne
	Fry
	Goodman
	Otto
	Paris
	Au
	Mraz & Vacca
Limitations of prescribed, pre-packaged programs and/or instruction	Hansen
	Pearson
	Paris
	Spache
	Spiro, Morsink, & Forsyth
	Au
	Padak & Rasinski
There are many ways to teach reading (and reading should be taught in many ways)	Cambourne
	Fry
	Spache
	Spiro, Morsink, & Forsyth
	Yaden & Tardibuono
	Mraz & Vacca
Policy-makers' negative interference in schools	Anderson
	Goodman
	Otto
	Paris
	Spache
	Mraz & Vacca

continued

TABLE 22.2 continued

Areas of New Common Ground	Researchers in Agreement
Use of integrated practices promotes reading and writing development	Goodman Hansen Pearson Spiro, Morsink, & Forsyth Au Yaden & Tardibuono
Consideration and respect for diverse cultural and linguistic learners	Goodman Hansen Harste Paris Spache Au
Use of authentic and worthwhile content is important	Pearson Spiro, Morsink, & Forsyth Au Malloy & Gambrell Campbell Jones, Reutzel, & Smith
Importance of stimulating classroom talk and student-driven discussion	Anderson Harste Pearson Malloy & Gambrell

More opportunities and time to read	Malloy & Gambrell Padak & Rasinski Campbell Jones, Reutzel, & Smith
Professionals and professional associations must do more	Goodman Padak & Rasinski Mraz & Vacca
Research alone does not drive or affect instruction	Goodman Otto Jones, Reutzel, & Smith
Engagement in early reading and experiences with printed materials	Goodman Yaden & Tardibuono Jones, Reutzel, & Smith
Establish strong home–school partnerships	Rasinski Padak & Rasinski Jones, Reutzel, & Smith
New technologies hold promise	Hansen Spiro, Morsink, & Forsyth

Some have pointed to the dumbing down of instruction due to the tests. Others have mentioned the focus on low-level skills, the devaluing of diverse students (especially African American and Hispanic students), the surfacing of "canned" reading and writing programs, the fact that teaching time has been lost in favor of test-prep time, and that many of these tests are inappropriate. Holding teachers accountable for raising test scores is equally inappropriate. Instead, all schools and teachers should be free to develop and implement their own unique curricula assessment and instruction efforts in the classroom.

More Time Should be Spent on Comprehension of Reading, and Vocabulary Development

Based on responses from seven researchers (again, a substantial number from my perspective), comprehension, other cognitive foci, and vocabulary are important to reading success, and time must be spent in school to develop and enrich these areas. The new NAEP reading assessment framework (2009), in fact, places more emphasis on the cognition of reading, and calls for a more focused measurement of "meaning vocabulary" in order to emphasize the relationship between word meaning and text comprehension. Several of the authors also suggested that a shift in emphasis to comprehension and vocabulary development is important because the current focus on phonics, and other isolated and low-level reading skills, has not improved reading achievement for many students, particularly across racial/ethnic groups. Teachers must seek and find opportunities to use and provide extended meaningful communication and discussion in the classroom to promote language development, vocabulary growth, and comprehension. Authors from one chapter also suggest that teachers capitalize on the affordances of reading comprehension and reading to learn on the Web, as they consider comprehension development opportunities for students.

Knowledgeable and Experienced Educators are Essential

Researchers from seven of the chapters (a large number of respondents) indicated the need for teachers and others working with children to be both knowledgeable and experienced. Several researchers suggested that it is important to recruit and train future educators who are themselves skilled and avid readers and writers. Additionally, schools should focus on hiring knowledgeable and effective teachers, encourage the continued development of teacher competence through professional development opportunities, and then let these highly effective educators use their acquired skills to improve classroom instruction. Highly effective educators are able to design instruction, use appropriate assessments, select appropriate materials, develop appropriate contexts, and use practices for individual and groups of students based on students' needs, strengths, strategies, and motivations. Ultimately, knowledgeable, experienced and passionate teachers are better equipped with the skills, practice, and patience required to support student reading and writing development.

Limitations of Pre-prescribed, Pre-packaged Programs and/or Instruction

Researchers from seven chapters (a substantial number) showed agreement here, with indications that it was not in students' best interest to use government pre-prescribed, pre-packaged or "canned" materials, rather than materials more appropriate to the children's needs. Unfortunately, pressure to increase test scores, particularly in low-income areas, has led to increased reliance on pre-packaged and standardized curricula and programs. Researchers bemoan this fact, as they feel that standardized curriculum, basal readers, and other forms of pre-packaged instruction drastically alter and narrow disciplines and genres. More often than not these easy fixes are detrimental, as opposed to being beneficial, to many students' literacy development.

There are Many Ways to Teach Reading (and Reading Should be Taught in Many Ways)

Researchers from six of the chapters (again, a fairly large number of respondents) emphasized that there are many different ways to teach reading that can, and should, be used in the classroom. Because NAEP test results have changed very little over the past 10 years, and an emphasis on phonics and more isolated reading skills has not improved reading achievement for most students, especially those representative of diverse racial/ethnic groups, there are obviously many ways to effectively, as well as ineffectively, teach reading. Researchers suggest that teachers, whose choices and decisions regarding literacy instruction are so often ignored, are in fact the best indicators of student literacy improvement. Thus, instead of being ignored, teachers' voices and opinions must be respected and valued. They must be allowed to select the instructional practices that work best in their own classrooms and contexts in order to most effectively reach all learners, including and especially those from diverse cultural, linguistic, and racial/ethnic backgrounds.

Policy-makers' Negative Interference in Schools

Some have blamed politicians and government for the focus on phonics and other ill-conceived mandated instruction being forced on learners and their teachers, narrowing the curriculum rather than enhancing it, and focusing on low-level skills rather than focusing on stimulation of cognition and development of deeper reading and meaningful discussion. Researchers from six chapters (a substantial number of respondents) have indicated that policy-makers and our governments have interfered to the extreme, largely excluding teachers from conversations regarding literacy curriculum. As a result, there is far too little teacher autonomy in public schools, federal and state governments have become too involved and dominant in classrooms, and the use of government prescribed tests has resulted in numerous inappropriate decisions regarding student literacy instruction. As such, researchers have stressed that teachers (and to some extent reading researchers), not policy-makers, need to be in control of designing and implementing effective reading assessment and instructional practices in the classroom. They also explained that literacy teaching should be imbedded in the broader contexts of children's educational needs.

Use of Integrated Practices Promotes Reading and Writing Development

Researchers from six chapters (a substantial number) stress this point, explaining that, because there is such a strong connection between reading and writing, the use of integrated instructional practices in the classroom has proven to be successful in promoting both reading and writing development. Several researchers discussed the idea that, as the world is becoming increasingly digital, online literacy could be used to support an integrated curriculum, by engaging students in terms of both reading and writing. Additionally, one researcher pointed out that using integrated curricula to support inquiry across disciplines results in both disciplinary learning and literacy acquisition.

Consideration and Respect for Diverse Cultural and Linguistic Learners

Again, researchers from six chapters identified this area. They explained that in recent years an increasing amount of attention has been given to diverse learners, as evidenced by research involving whole-school change. Whole-school change is required to make classrooms where students of diverse cultural and linguistic backgrounds successfully learn to read and write together a reality. Unfortunately, rather than seeing the value of diverse groups of readers and writers working together to learn from and teach each other, many pre-prescribed instructional plans standardize the interactions that occur between teachers and students. Teachers, then, need to find ways to use the vast range of experiential, cultural, and linguistic resources that students bring into the classroom to develop literacy skills while also allowing students to explore social issues that affect them, or others things that interest them, through more opportunities for real reading and writing. Ethnically, racially, linguistically, and culturally diverse youngsters who are not part of the mainstream are capable learners, and what they know *must* be valued. Policy-makers must be cautious in order to accommodate the needs of diverse students and the talents of individual teachers.

Use of Authentic and Worthwhile Content is Important

Researchers from six chapters identified this area. They stressed that children should always be reading and writing about content that is worth knowing, and that promotes the acquisition of knowledge, insight, important ideas, human understanding, and joy. Learning should be part of the reading equation from the beginning of kindergarten and first grade. Likewise, children should be writing about things that matter to them about their understandings, insights, and joy. Additionally, students must be regularly afforded the opportunity to select their own independent reading choices, from among appropriate and challenging texts, so that their reading materials are authentic and worthwhile to them. Literacy and other learning are enhanced when students are provided with meaningful text and are motivated to engage with the text. The new technologies allow the reader to seek multiple, worthwhile, relevant content to suit her/his varied purposes. Ultimately, incorporating a variety of content and content activities for authentic purposes, and allowing for a degree of student choice, develops classrooms where literacy growth and other learning will flourish.

Importance of Stimulating Classroom Talk and Student-driven Discussion

Researchers from four chapters indicated the importance of creating a stimulating classroom environment where student-driven talk and discussion are in the forefront of daily classroom activity. More specifically, they suggested that there is persuasive evidence for teachers to create a classroom that emphasizes language-rich discussion in order to promote language development, deeper reading, better understanding of text structure, and acceleration of both receptive and expressive language development. Reading, writing, and oral discourse promote acquisition of knowledge in content areas, and improve literacy learning. Students' talk about books has been seen as promoting motivation to read. Additionally, one researcher suggested that involvement in grand conversations, the sharing and exploring of meaning, and opportunities to critique what they read and write, also promote social responsibility and awareness.

More Opportunities and Time to Read

More opportunities and time to read from and discuss varied genres in school, more opportunities and encouragement to read for fun, and more opportunities to spend time reading in and out of school are called for by researchers in four of the chapters. Additionally, more opportunities given to students to read more books of their own choosing, in the classroom, could also produce higher reading achievement, increase motivation to read, and help struggling readers. An analysis of the more recent NAEP data substantiates the need to focus on these real reading opportunities in classrooms as well as outside of school.

Professionals and Professional Associations Need to do More

Several researchers (from three chapters) indicated that professionals and their professional associations must do more. The professional associations have been reluctant to get involved by critiquing and protesting dysfunctional reading practices in the classroom, but they must do so. Professional associations in the field of literacy should use every opportunity to encourage their members to share relevant research, the associations' own voices must be more of a part of the policy conversations, and their members must get more involved and contribute their voices as well.

Research Alone Does Not Drive or Affect Instruction

In spite of all the research done in our field, researchers from three chapters indicated that it does not seem to have had much of an impact on how reading is actually being taught in classrooms across the country. Instead of being guided by the conclusions of more than a century of literacy research, classroom reading instruction is more often influenced by what communities believe, the power relationships that exist in politics and business, and government mandates and goals.

Engagement in Early Reading and Experiences with Printed Materials

Researchers from three chapters pointed out the importance of early engagement with print and reading materials. Although there has been quite a bit of attention to early literacy development over the past years, the most recent research findings support the importance of early reading experiences, emergent reading, early/multiple experiences with printed materials, and personal interests. Most importantly, these findings have indicated that it is not one skill alone (such as phonological awareness) that enhances early literacy, but instead a broad set of experiences in which children are given regular opportunities to explore, experiment with, and talk about written language across multiple contexts. Young children can benefit from contexts and practices in the classroom that support and enrich these broad literacy experiences.

Establish Strong Home–School Partnerships

Researchers from three chapters indicated the importance of integrating home and school ties. Schools, school administrators, and teachers must make a concerted long-term commitment to developing and implementing systematic parental involvement programs for the literacy education of their children. Parents and families must be involved as integral parts of reading instruction, because research continues to confirm the importance of parental involvement in children's literacy development and, in particular, in accelerating the progress of struggling readers.

New Technologies Hold Promise

Researchers (representative of two chapters) have stressed that increased use of the new technologies has helped and could continue to help engage students in terms of both reading and writing. These new technology tools give learners more control, putting them much more in "the driver's seat." They explain that practiced use of the new technologies can help to manage the increase in cognitive load that comes with greater task complexity, as well as support advanced comprehension outcomes. Additionally, one researcher believes that new technologies have positively increased attention to writing, and the synergy between reading and writing. This should increase opportunities for continued attention to students' writing development as well as their reading development.

Words of Wisdom from the Researchers

Throughout my reviews, and thinking about the new common ground I summarized and analyzed for this new volume as well as the original common ground that we revisited, I also kept going back to many of the chapters in this volume to "really listen" to the voices of the authors. Many of them resonated, but there were some in particular that I wanted to point out and share with readers of this new edition. Read and "really listen" to what they are saying:

BRIAN CAMBOURNE: "Effective literacy classrooms are very complex settings."

RAND SPIRO: "Yes, I still agree with our Expert Study findings, but more so."
   "It still all depends! But even more so!"

P. DAVID PEARSON: "In a sense, strategies are just like phonic rules. They are only a means to an end. It's when a phonic rule or a strategy routine becomes an end unto itself that bad things happen." "We need to keep our eye on the prize of knowledge acquisition … as the natural consequence and by-product of reading." "We'd be better off to think of reading, writing, and language as tools for learning that we can readily apply to disciplinary learning." "Is this too much of a revolution to hope for? I hope not, for the alternatives are too devastating to contemplate. And, if we could really make these things happen, we would be blazing a trail back to the radical middle that I championed in the last edition of this book, and that is a destination toward which I am still trying to guide myself and others."

RICHARD ANDERSON: "The fact is that, like it or not, we are living in an era where we are driven by high-stakes standardized tests. Moreover, we are holding teachers responsible for their children's learning using some Mickey Mouse, simplistic measures; however, children's literacy development and literacy learning are not simple. Rather, they are complex and not easy to measure even if we used the finest instruments and assessments available."

ED FRY: "A good teacher can make most of the various methods work well with most students. A bad teacher can't make any of it work. Rather than the continual focus and arguments regarding methods and approaches, focus instead on hiring good teachers, and then allow them to teach reading using the practices that fit best in the particular contexts. Let the teachers make the decisions regarding how they will teach reading!"

YETTA GOODMAN: "As 'experts, reading researchers,' as we are identified in this book, we must come to understand the limitations of research alone, and work respectfully with teacher researchers/practitioners in this complex enterprise of coming to understand the teaching and learning of literacy in schools."

SPIRO, MORSINK, AND FORSYTH: "...Prepackaged prescriptions for how to read and how to teach reading, how to think and how to problem-solve are inadequate or worse."

MRAZ AND VACCA: "Perhaps if there is a glimmer of hope in this new, and yet somehow familiar, era of literacy education reform it is that there is growing acknowledgement by some policy-makers and some journalists that school reform alone cannot improve student achievement. The tired, but ever present, political mantras of 'hold teachers accountable' and 'raise test scores' must be balanced by policy discussions and policy decisions which reflect that, all too often, the problems for which educators are held 'accountable' lie [outside their influence]. The educational challenges of our time are broader than teacher accountability and test scores. The solutions must be broader as well."

Why Should We Continue to Reflect on this Common Ground?

We should continue to think about and reflect on the common understandings and concerns of the field in order to provide the necessary expertise and leadership for future policy decisions, and for future conversations and discussions with new as well as experienced teachers and other researchers. The field of reading, within the broader field of literacy, just like other fields of expertise, does have a common ground. If we do not remember to reflect on it and nurture its continued development over time, we will continue to be at the mercy of those who lack this expertise and wish to make changes none of us would agree to, individually or collectively. We have seen it happen continually over the past two decades, and, like all things documented in history, it can happen again and again.

A new teacher, responding to the survey for school professionals that appeared in my book *What Do the Experts Say?* (Flippo, 1999b), shared the following:

> I think the idea of establishing a common ground among reading teachers and researchers is an incredibly practical idea, particularly for beginning

teachers like me who seek a foundation grounded in research from which to build and create our own hypotheses about how children become able readers.

Personal communication

Responses from other school professionals have been similar—all have seen the value of common ground, particularly in the continued highly politicized environment. Teachers as well as parents and, of course, the children themselves, are all important to our common ground understandings. As Yetta Goodman suggests, we must have high regard for their roles and their work.

Lest we forget, as some of the experts have reminded us, we must all "continue to search for gaps where our knowledge needs to be deepened and extended" (Linda Fielding speaking for Richard Anderson). We must continue our inquiry. Even though we have learned a great deal, David Pearson tells us that "we can do better." Our agreements will mean very little, says Yetta Goodman, without "professional elementary and secondary teachers who understand what they do in classrooms and why." And Robert Rude, in his point of view chapter on Wayne Otto, urges, "May we all change ... and continue to do so ... so our students become the benefactors of our wisdom and change."

I suggest that continued consideration of and reflection on our common understandings can help us identify *really* important areas of needed research, do better, and continue to learn and grow. I concur also with Jay Campbell, who indicates that our common ground includes very specific contexts and practices, activities, and uses of materials that have direct implication for classroom practice and policy setting. I believe strongly that these common understandings must not be brushed off or ignored. As literacy professionals and others concerned with educational opportunities, development, and outcomes, we would be negligent if we did not continue to share the common ground revealed by the distinguished contributors to this volume with the general public, politicians, parents, and communities with which we interact. Failing this, I fear we will continue to see more evidence of inattention to what we know are important areas in the development and teaching of literacy, and more and more inappropriate interpretations like those that have promoted the current brutal and insensitive testing and curriculum decisions and practices.

What Can and Did Happen? A Caveat from the Past Two Decades Of History

As I looked back at the first edition of this book, I reread Richard Vacca's description (2001), of his amazement and also obvious delight when in the 1996 election year the then incumbent US President (Bill Clinton) made "reading" the centerpiece of his education policy and reform proposals. Yes, it was significant that in 1996, for the first time in US history, reading education was actually part of a presidential platform and presidential interest. Yet only 4 years later, as the 2000 election campaign reflected, not only was reading education a part of George W. Bush's platform for president, but he went much further, letting it be known how he thought reading should be taught—with an emphasis on phonics! Then, not long after, we received the No Child Left Behind Act of 2001 (NCLB, 2002), and very quickly thereafter, we as a field clearly began to be left behind! (Note, in this new edition Yetta Goodman points out that *currently* "reading researchers are even locked out of the movement to improve test scores and establish mandated curriculum in reading.")

We should all be truly astounded: these are instances of what can and did happen, and how *very* quickly it did when *we failed* to make known the common-ground understandings of the field of reading. Yetta Goodman points this out very clearly in her chapter in this new volume when she urges: "We must speak more strongly as experts to highlight our common ground and ask why these are not part of the conversation about reading and writing instruction in the schools." She indicates that she is disheartened that the common-ground research findings we reported in the first edition have had less influence on classroom practice than they did 10 years before, and laments that we have instead actually seen many of the agreements about how to make reading *difficult* for students "visible in many classrooms legitimatized by federal, state and local mandates." Yetta stresses that "we must work harder than ever to collaborate through professional organizations to support the research that makes clear that knowledgeable teachers in collaboration with their students are most successful in developing readers and writers."

Support from the Associations

As you have seen, several researchers in this volume have called for more involvement and more of a voice from the profession and the professional associations. It is clear that we and they have not done enough! Many readers of this volume are members of multiple literacy associations. We must call on these associations, in earnest, to get more involved! Our singular voices alone have not been enough. Tell the associations to do more, to critique the contexts and practices that we know aren't good for most children, to further critique the new areas of common ground raised here, and to gather the research that shows the harm already done to children. Finally, we must ask them and assist them in organizing their memberships, working together with all the other literacy associations to get our *collective* voices heard, widely and loudly. It is more than time for grand conversations and grand actions on the part of everyone who *really* cares and *really* understands the issues, problems, and harm that has been done and must be stopped.

The Emerging Theme

As I look at the responses from the researchers, as summarized in this chapter and depicted in its tables, a theme across all of it has emerged for me. This theme is very telling and it resonates, and it is supported not only here but in the research and publications of others as well (e.g., Nichols & Berliner, 2007; Valli, Croninger, Chambliss, Graeber, & Buese, 2008; Hoffman & Goodman, 2009). The theme is evident: *Teachers must have the autonomy to make instructional and assessment decisions in their own classrooms with their own students, without outside mandates and interference, and without the pressures, limitations, and injustices that result from high-stakes testing and pre-subscribed literacy curricula.*

Where Do We Go From Here? An Encouraging Word

I hope that where we go from here is back to our communities, colleagues, constituents, and the parents, classrooms, and students with whom many of us work; I hope, too, that we continue to share and reflect on the agreements, the threads of wisdom from the common ground in the field of reading, and the areas of new common ground shared in this volume. Asking questions, and discussing and sharing ideas, will help each of us continue to refine and shape our own common understandings—common understandings that will help all of us provide better literacy development environments and opportunities for all children with their diverse and various needs and motivations.

Thus, as you can see, in spite of everything that has happened in the current political environment, I still remain an optimist. The knowledge I have gained from the Expert Study, and as editor of this new volume and the first volume of this book, has further reinforced my belief that the field of reading education does share a common denominator of agreements based on expertise, solid research, professional experiences, and classroom practice. We owe it to our children to keep these agreements and the common-ground areas revealed here in the forefront of decisions, to continue to reflect on them and refine them as we learn more, to demand that our professional associations get more involved, and to *always* keep teachers, parents, the public, and policy-makers fully informed, not forgetting that the well-being and literacy lives of children should be our uppermost concern.

References

August, D., & Shanahan, T. (Eds.). (2006). *Developing Literacy in Second-Language Learners: A Report of the National Literacy Panel on Language-Minority Children and Youth.* Mahwah, NJ: Lawrence Erlbaum Associates.

Brofenbrenner, U. (2005). (Ed.). *Making human beings human: Bioecological perspectives on human development.* Thousand Oaks, CA: Sage.

Cambridge Primary Review (2009). University of Cambridge, Faculty of Education.

DeSchryver, M., & Spiro, R. (2008). New forms of deep learning on the Web: Meeting the challenge of cognitive load in conditions of unfettered exploration. In R. Zheng (Ed.), *Cognitive effects of multimedia learning*. Hershey, PA: IGI Global.

Duffy, G.G., & Hoffman, J.V. (1999). In pursuit of an illusion: The flawed search for a perfect method. *The Reading Teacher, 53*, 10–16.

Edmunds, K.M., & Bauserman, K.L. (2006). What teachers can learn about reading motivation through conversations with children. *The Reading Teacher, 59* (5), 414–424.

Flippo, R.F. (1998). Points of agreement: A display of professional unity in our field. *The Reading Teacher, 52*, 30–40.

Flippo, R.F. (1999a). Redefining the Reading Wars: The war against reading researchers. *Educational Leadership, 57*, 38–41.

Flippo, R.F. (1999b). *What do the experts say? Helping children learn to read*. Portsmouth, NH: Heinemann.

Flippo, R.F. (Ed.) (2001). *Reading researchers in search of common ground*. Newark, DE: International Reading Association.

Fu, D., & Lamme, L. (2002). Assessment through conversation. *Language Arts, 79* (3), 241–250.

Gee, J.P. (2004). *Situated language and learning: A critique of traditional schooling*. New York, NY: Routledge.

Hoffman, J.V., & Goodman, Y. (Eds.). (2009). *Changing literacies for changing times: An historical perspective on the future or reading research, public policy, and classroom practices*. New York, NY: Taylor & Francis/Routledge.

Hull, G.A., & Katz, M. (2006). Crafting an agentive self: Case studies of digital storytelling. *Research in the Teaching of English, 41* (1), 43–81.

Lenhart, A., Madden, M., Rankin-Macgill, A., & Smith, A. (2008). *Teens and social media: The use of social media gains greater foothold in teen life as they embrace the conversational nature of interactive online media*. Washington, DC: Pew Internet & American Life Project.

Leu, D. (2002). Internet workshop: Making time for literacy. *The Reading Teacher, 55*, 466–472.

Lewison, M., Lealand, C., & Harste, J.C. (2008). *Creating critical classrooms: K-8 reading and writing with an edge*. New York, NY: Lawrence Erlbaum Associates.

Linstone, H.A., & Turoff, M. (Eds.). (1975). *The Delphi method: Techniques and applications*. Reading, MA: Addison-Wesley.

Ministry of Education New Zealand (2009). *Literacy learning progressions: Meeting the reading and writing demands of the curriculum*. Ministry of Education, New Zealand.

Malloy, J.A., & Gambrell, L.B. (2008). New insights on motivation in the literacy classroom. In C.C. Block & S.R. Paris (Eds.), *Comprehension instruction* (2nd ed.). New York, NY: Guilford.

McKeown, M.G., Beck, I.L., & Blake, R.G.K. (2009). Rethinking reading comprehension instruction: A comparison of reading strategies and content approaches. *Reading Research Quarterly, 44* (3), 218–253.

National Center for Education Statistics (2009). *The Nation's Report Card: Reading 2009* (NCES 2010–458), Washington, DC: Author.

National Early Literacy Panel (NELP) (2008). *Developing early literacy: Report of the National Early Literacy Panel*. Washington, DC: National Institute for Literacy.

National Institute of Child Health and Human Development (NICHD) (2000). *Report of the National Reading Panel. Teaching children to read: An evidence-based assessment of the scientific research literature on reading and its implications for reading instruction: Reports of the subgroups* (NIH Publication No. 00–4754). Washington, DC: US Government Printing Office.

National Reading Panel (2000). *Report of the National Reading Panel: Teaching children to read*. Washington, DC: National Institute of Child Health and Human Development.

Nichols, S.L., & Berliner, D.C. (2007). *Collateral damage: How high-stakes testing corrupts America's schools*. Cambridge, MA: Harvard Educational Press.

No Child Left Behind Act of 2001 (2002). Public Law No. 107–110, paragraph 115 Stat. 1425.

Pearson P.D., & Fielding, L. (1991). Comprehension instruction. In R. Barr, M.L. Kamil, P. Mosenthal, & P.D. Pearson (Eds.), *Handbook of reading research* (Vol. 2, pp. 815–860). New York, NY: Longman.

Pearson, P.D., Moje, E., & Greenleaf, C. (2010). Science and literacy: Each in the service of the other. *Science, 328*, 459–463.

Rasinski, T., & Stevenson, B. (2005). The effects of Fast Start Reading, a fluency based home involvement reading program, on the reading achievement of beginning readers. *Reading Psychology, 26*, 109–125.

Rowe, D.W., & Nietzel, C. (2010). Interest and agency in 2- and 3-year-olds' participation in emergent writing. *Reading Research Quarterly, 28*, 304–333.

Spiro, R.J. (2006). The "New Gutenberg Revolution": Radical new learning, thinking, teaching, and training with technology … bringing the future near. *Educational Technology, 46* (6), 3–5.

Spiro, R.J., & DeSchryver, M. (2008). Constructivism: When it's the wrong idea and when it's the only idea. In T. Duffy & S. Tobais (Eds.), *Constructivist instruction: Success or failure?* Mahwah, NJ: Lawrence Erlbaum Associates.

Taylor, B., Pearson, P., Peterson, D., & Rodriguez, M. (2003). Reading growth in high-poverty classrooms: The influence of teacher practices that encourage cognitive engagement in literacy learning. *Elementry School Journal, 104*, 3–28.

Taylor, B., Pearson, P., Peterson, D., & Rodriguez, M. (2005). The CIERA School Change Framework: An evidence-based approach to professional development and school reading improvement. *Reading Research Quarterly, 40*(1), 40–69.

Teale, W., & Sulzby, E. (1986). *Emergent literacy: Writing and reading*. Norwood, NJ: Ablex Publishing Corporation.

Vacca, R.T. (2001). A focus on the media, policy-driven literacy practices, and the work of reading professionals. In R.F. Flippo (Ed.), *Reading researchers in search of common ground* (pp. 167–177). Newark, DE: International Reading Association.

Valli, L., Croninger, R.G., Chambliss, M.J., Graeber, A.O., & Buese, D. (2008). *Test driven: High-stakes accountability in elementary schools*. New York, NY: Teachers College Press.

Wilkinson, I.A.G., & Son, E.H. (2011). A dialogical turn in research on learning and teaching to comprehend. In M.L. Kamil, P.D. Pearson, E.B. Moje, & P.P. Afflerbach (Eds.). *Handbook of reading research*, Vol. IV (pp. 359–387). New York, NY: Routledge.

Yaden, D. Jr, & Templeton, S. (Eds.). (1986). *Metalinguistic awareness and beginning literacy: Conceptualizing what it means to read and write*. Portsmouth, NH: Heinemann.

Zhang, J., & Anderson, R.C. (2010). *Language-rich discussions for English Language Learners*. Paper presented at the Annual Meeting of the American Educational Research Association, Denver, CO.

ABOUT THE CONTRIBUTORS

The Editor

Rona F. Flippo, Professor of Education at University of Massachusetts Boston, USA, is the researcher and author of the Expert Study reported in this volume as well as in the first edition of this book, *Reading Researchers in Search of Common Ground* (2001), and author of several related publications, including *What Do the Experts Say? Helping Children Learn to Read* (1999). Her Expert Study has been the subject of an educational television series, broadcast internationally, featuring Rona and many of the contributors to this volume. Rona is also known for her many other publications on reading assessment, reading education, reading tests, and study and test-taking strategies for students at all levels, as well as teacher licensure testing issues. Her strong interest in policy and the politics affecting education have led her toward research and writing for a broad audience, including the general public.

The Experts

Richard C. Anderson, Professor of Education and Psychology and Director of the Center for the Study of Reading at the University of Illinois, Champaign, USA, is first author of the US national report and best-selling book *Becoming a Nation of Readers* (1985). He was Chair of the National Academy of Education-National Institute of Education Commission on Reading 1983–1984, served as President of the American Educational Research Association in 1983, and was elected to the Reading Hall of Fame in 1991.

Brian Cambourne, Principal Fellow and Associate Professor in the Faculty of Education, University of Wollongong, New South Wales, Australia, authored the internationally recognized Conditions for Learning model to explain how literacy learning occurs. He was featured in *The Reading Teacher* Distinguished Educator Series in November 1995, was elected to the Reading Hall of Fame in 1998, and has received numerous national and international honors for his work in the field of literacy education.

Edward Fry, former Professor Emeritus at Rutgers University, New Brunswick, New Jersey, USA, is author of the Fry Readability Graph, used worldwide by publishers, test developers, and educators; he is also known for his Instant Word List. He was President of the National Reading Conference 1974–1976, and was elected to the Reading Hall of Fame in 1993.

Yetta M. Goodman, Regents Professor Emerita, University of Arizona, Tucson, USA, is author of the *Reading Miscue Inventory*. Her research on early literacy led to the concept of "kidwatching" and related publications including *Critical Issues in Early Literacy Development* (2007). She is a past president of the National Council of Teachers of English, and a past board member of the International Reading Association. She was featured in *The Reading Teacher* Distinguished Educator Series in May 1996, and was elected to the Reading Hall of Fame in 1994, serving as its President in 2005.

Jane Hansen, Professor at the Curry School of Education, University of Virginia, Charlottesville, USA, was co-originator of the Author's Chair, an activity in which children share their writing, their peers' writing, and literature, for supportive response. She was President of the National Reading Conference 1994–1995, an elected member of the Elementary Section of the National Council of Teachers of English, and was featured in *The Reading Teacher* Distinguished Educator Series in November 1996. Currently, she leads a continuous Writing Across the Curriculum research project.

Jerome C. Harste, Emeritus Professor in the Department of Language Education at Indiana University, Bloomington, USA, is author of several books on whole language. He was President of the National Reading Conference 1986–1987, and the National Council of Teachers of English 1999–2000, and on the International Reading Association's Board of Directors 1989–1991. He was featured in *The Reading Teacher* Distinguished Educator Series in 1994, and was elected to the Reading Hall of Fame in 1997.

Wayne R. Otto, Professor Emeritus in the Department of Curriculum and Instruction at the University of Wisconsin-Madison, USA, was the principal investigator for the Wisconsin Design for Reading Skill Development— a plan used throughout the United States for managing classroom reading instruction with a focus on specific skill development. He served on the

Boards of Directors of the National Reading Conference 1975–1977 and the American Reading Forum 1980–1984, and was elected to the Reading Hall of Fame in 1992.

Scott G. Paris, Vice President of Research at Educational Testing Service, Princeton, New Jersey, USA, was formerly Professor at Nanyang Technological University, Singapore, and Head of the Centre for Research in Pedagogy and Practice at the National Institute of Education, Singapore. There he conducted research on reading comprehension and assessment while working with educational leaders and policy-makers in Singapore. He was the 2000–2001 Chair of the International Reading Association's Issues in Literacy Assessment Committee.

P. David Pearson, Professor in the Graduate School of Education at the University of California, Berkeley, USA, pursues research on assessment, instruction, and curriculum reform in literacy. He was first editor of the *Handbook of Reading Research* in 1984, and coeditor of subsequent volumes. He codirected the original "Standards Project for English Language Arts" 1992–1994, was President of the National Reading Conference 1985–1986, and on the International Reading Association's Board of Directors 1984–1988. In 1990 he was elected to the Reading Hall of Fame. Currently, he is working with colleagues to build and validate a K–8 integrated science and literacy curriculum.

George Spache, former Professor Emeritus at the University of Florida, Gainesville, USA, authored the Diagnostic Reading Scales, a widely used reading test originally published in 1963. His research on vision and reading led to his development of the Binocular Reading Test. He served as President of the International Reading Association 1958–1959, and President of the National Reading Conference 1962–1964. He was on the American Reading Forum Board of Directors from its founding in 1980 through 1984, and was elected to the Reading Hall of Fame in 1974.

Rand J. Spiro, Professor of Educational Psychology and Educational Technology at Michigan State University, East Lansing, USA, is the originator of Cognitive Flexibility Theory. His books include (with coeditors) *Schooling and the Acquisition of Knowledge*; *Theoretical Issues in Reading Comprehension*; *Cognition, Education and Multimedia*; and *Hypertext and Cognition*. He was a founding member of the Center for the Study of Reading at the University of Illinois at Urbana.

Other Contributors

Kathryn H. Au, Chief Executive Officer of SchoolRise, Honolulu, Hawaii, USA, is known for her research on multicultural issues and literacy achievement. She conducts research on how schools can improve the literacy achievement of students of diverse cultural and linguistic backgrounds. She was President of the International Reading Association 2009–2010 and of the National Reading Conference 1996–1997, as well as Vice President of the American Educational Research Association 1992–1994. She was elected to the Reading Hall of Fame in 1999.

Jay R. Campbell, Executive Director of the National Assessment of Educational Progress (NAEP) at Educational Testing Service, Princeton, New Jersey, USA, is an educational psychologist with expertise in large-scale educational assessment. In the early 1990s, he was the coordinator of the NAEP reading assessment and author of several NAEP reading reports during a period in which the so-called "Reading Wars" reached a crescendo.

Jack Cassidy, Director of the Center for Educational Development Evaluation and Research at Texas A&M University–Corpus Christi, USA, is Associate Dean for Graduate Studies, College of Education, and Professor of Curriculum and Instruction. He is known for his "What's Hot, What's Not in Literacy" studies published in *Reading Today*, and professional journals. He was President of the International Reading Association 1982–1983 and College Reading Association (1999–2000; now Association of Literacy Educators and Researchers), recipient of CRA's A.B. Herr Award for outstanding contributions to reading, and was elected to the Reading Hall of Fame in 2010.

Diane DeFord, Professor and Swearingen Chair of Literacy Education at the University of South Carolina, Columbia, USA, was one of Jerome Harste's graduate students. She had the opportunity to work with him during both her master's and doctoral programs. She has studied teacher's beliefs about literacy and assessment of literacy. She also writes books for children.

Linda G. Fielding, Associate Professor of Education at the University of Iowa, Iowa City, USA, was one of Richard Anderson's doctoral students and his research assistant when Anderson was doing much of his research and reporting for *Becoming a Nation of Readers*. Linda also conducted research with Anderson related to children's voluntary reading; her own research has focused on literacy instruction for struggling readers and writers in regular classrooms.

Benjamin Forsyth, Assistant Professor of Educational Psychology and Foundations, University of Northern Iowa, USA, was one of Rand Spiro's graduate students. Benjamin's work has focused on understanding the kinds of habits of mind that are needed to successfully perform in complex domains, as well as understanding how these affect students' abilities to adapt to new situations.

Linda B. Gambrell, Distinguished Professor of Education at Clemson University, South Carolina, USA, is known for her studies related to motivation and reading comprehension. Linda has served as President of the International

Reading Association 2007–2008, National Reading Conference (1998–1999; now Literacy Research Association), and College Reading Association (1981–1982; now Association of Literacy Educators and Researchers).

Cindy D. Jones, Assistant Professor of Literacy at Utah State University, Logan, USA, researches classroom literacy instruction. She has worked with struggling readers in elementary and secondary classrooms. Cindy recently received the Jerry Johns Promising Researcher Award from the Association of Literacy Educators and Researchers.

Jacquelynn A. Malloy, Assistant Professor of Elementary Education and Literacy at George Mason University, Fairfax, Virginia, USA, is a teacher-educator and researcher focusing on literacy motivation and the contribution of discussion to reading comprehension and engagement. She is also interested in evaluating student engagement when involved in authentic and open tasks, and the teaching of online reading comprehension skills in the late elementary grades.

Paul Morsink, Doctoral student at Michigan State University, East Lansing, USA, is one of Rand Spiro's graduate students. Paul has taught high school and college English and composition for 13 years, and is currently doing research on reading comprehension in digital environments.

Maryann Mraz, Associate Professor in the Reading and Elementary Education Department, University of North Carolina at Charlotte, USA, earned her PhD from Kent State University under the guidance of Richard and Jo Anne Vacca. Maryann is the author of numerous articles, chapters, and instructional materials on literacy education, including Vacca, Vacca, & Mraz, *Content Area Reading: Literacy and Learning across the Curriculum* (10th ed.). She is a board member of the Association of Literacy Educators and Researchers.

Nancy Padak, Distinguished Professor, College and Graduate School of Education, Health, and Human Services, Kent State University, Ohio, USA, directs the Reading and Writing Center and teaches literacy education. She is the Principal Investigator for the Ohio Literacy Resource Center. She has served in a variety of leadership roles in professional organizations, including Presidency of College Reading Association (now Association of Literacy Educators and Researchers) and Coeditor of the International Reading Association's *The Reading Teacher*, and the *Journal of Literacy Research*.

Timothy V. Rasinski, Professor of Education at Kent State University, Ohio, USA, is known for his interest in and work with parents and families of school-aged children. He was Coeditor of the International Reading Association's *The Reading Teacher* 1992–1999, and served as President of the College Reading Association (1997–1998; now Association of Literacy Educators and Researchers). He was elected to the Reading Hall of Fame in 2010.

D. Ray Reutzel, Emma Eccles Jones Endowed Chair Professor of Education, Utah State University, Logan, USA, is known for his interest and work in fluency, comprehension, classroom environments, and teacher knowledge. He was Coeditor of the International Reading Association's *The Reading Teacher* 2003–2007, served as President of the College Reading Association (2007–2008; now Association for Literacy Educators and Researchers), and was on the Board of Directors of the International Reading Association from 2007–2010. He is past recipient of the John C. Manning Public School Service Award from the International Reading Association.

Richard D. Robinson, Professor of Education at the University of Missouri–Columbia, USA, is known for his studies of the history of reading and as a commentator regarding the reading debates of recent years. He has studied and admired the works of George Spache, and has authored publications on content area reading, and issues and trends in literacy education.

Robert T. Rude, Professor of Elementary Education at Rhode Island College, Providence, USA, was one of Wayne Otto's doctoral students during and immediately following the time when Wayne and his colleagues created the Wisconsin Design for Reading Skill Development. Subsequently, Robert's own research has focused on teacher training and directing Rhode Island College's literacy clinic.

John A. Smith, Professor and Chair of the Department of Curriculum and Instruction at the University of Texas at Arlington, USA, has focused his research and grant writing on raising the achievement of struggling readers and also integrating literacy instruction with content area learning. He is the elected President of the Association of Literacy Educators and Researchers from 2012–2013.

Joan M. Tardibuono, Adjunct Professor of Multicultural Education, Reading Education and Supervision of Student Teaching, Department of Teacher Education, California State University, Long Beach, USA, is a bilingual educator and researcher specializing in children's first- and second-language acquisition in diverse urban communities. She pursues her interest in early literacy and bilingual language development through observation of her preschool-age daughter, Erin.

Richard T. Vacca, Professor Emeritus from Kent State University, Ohio, USA, was President of the International Reading Association 1996–1997, while the so-called Reading Wars were receiving constant media attention. He was elected to the Reading Hall of Fame in 2010, and is known for his expertise and books on content area reading for middle and high school students. Currently, he serves on the Board of Directors of the Professor Garfield Foundation dedicated to providing a world-class, free-use educational website for students and teachers.

Corinne Valadez, Assistant Professor of Curriculum and Instruction at Texas A&M University–Corpus Christi, USA, is known for her interest and publications in multicultural literacy. She has also coauthored *What's Hot, What's Not* articles with Jack Cassidy, and served on the International Reading Association's 2010 Standards Committee.

David B. Yaden, Professor of Literacy Studies, Department of Teaching, Learning, and Socio-Cultural Studies, University of Arizona, Tuscon, USA, and Director of the Center for Policy and Research on Children's Early Education and Development, is also Co-Principal Investigator of the First Things First External Evaluation, a tri-university consortium charged with determining the effect of statewide early childhood strategies to improve the health and school readiness of young children.

INDEX

Note: locators in **bold** type indicate figures or illustrations, those in *italics* indicate tables.